A CONCISE HISTORY OF ENGLISH LITERATURE

A CONCISE HISTORY OF ENGLISH LITERATURE

Padmaja Ashok

Orient BlackSwan

A CONCISE HISTORY OF ENGLISH LITERATURE

ORIENT BLACKSWAN PRIVATE LIMITED

Registered Office
3-6-752 Himayatnagar, Hyderabad 500 029, Telangana, India
Email: centraloffice@orientblackswan.com

Other Offices
Bengaluru, Chennai, Guwahati, Hyderabad,
Kolkata, Mumbai, New Delhi, Noida, Patna

First published 2026

ISBN 978-93-5442-724-4

Typeset in Minion Pro 11/13.2 *by*
LiteBook Prepress Services, Chennai 600 069

Printed at
SS Colour Impressions Pvt Ltd, Chennai 600 106

Published by
Orient Blackswan Private Limited
3-6-752 Himayatnagar, Hyderabad 500 029, Telangana, India
Email: info@orientblackswan.com

Contents

Preface

A Concise History of English Literature is a comprehensive book that traces the origin and growth of English Literature right from the oral tradition of the Anglo-Saxon period to the twentieth century.

The book is divided into seven chapters. Each chapter is further divided into three well-defined parts: background to the time period, a literary survey of the period and finally a section in which each important author belonging to the age in question is discussed individually. The study of each author is again divided into four parts: a list of works by the author, life of the author, description of the author's works, and their important features. When students are introduced to an author in this way, they gain a deeper understanding of the writer and are able to appreciate and enjoy the author's works prescribed in their course of study.

It is, however, to be noted that this is in no way an exhaustive study. There are several writers who have not been included and those included have been chosen for their significant contribution to the development of literature down the ages.

The book also has a comprehensive glossary that gives definitions of any literary form or critical term that is mentioned in the course of discussing an author. Neither the student nor the teacher needs to consult different books to understand the various technical terms/forms or concepts that are mentioned. The book also has a list of all the poets laureate as well as all the Nobel laureates of the United Kingdom and ends with a detailed timeline.

From the earliest works like *Beowulf* to the works of contemporary writers, this book has delved into the progression of creative thought through the ages. In tracing the intricate threads of literary history, we are sure to gain a deeper appreciation for the power of words to shape our thoughts. This book, therefore, is not just a chronicle but serves as proof of the enduring legacy of English literature.

Anglo-Saxon Age

450–1066

The history of English literature is intricately interwoven with the history of its land. To trace its origins, one has to go back to the early history of the British Isles which consists of several invasions, each of which influenced the people and the place. Some of the significant ones were those carried out by the Celts, Romans, Anglo-Saxons and Normans. Each in their own unique manner left an indelible mark on English language and culture.

The most important among the early conquerors were the **Celts**, a people from southern Europe who slowly migrated west. Between 800 and 600 BCE, two groups of Celts invaded the British Isles. One group called the **Brythons** (now spelt 'Britons') settled on the largest island, Britain. The other group, known as the **Gaels**, settled in Ireland. The language spoken by both these groups were related but had nothing in common with the Germanic ones later associated with the Angles and Saxons.

Research has shown that the literature of the British Isles began with the **Celtic Druids** (a class of priests who presided over religious rituals that included sacrifice and prayer). These Druids also carried out the duty of memorising and reciting long, heroic poems that preserved ancient myths about Celtic leaders such as Old King Cole of the nursery rhyme. These priests performed the important task of passing on tribal history and stories to an audience that could not read.

The next to invade Britain were the powerful **Romans**. The Romans established camps all over the land and these soon developed into towns. The Roman rule over Britain lasted for more than three hundred years. Their most important contribution to Britain was the introduction of Christianity in the fourth century.

The **Anglo-Saxon** invaders came to Britain in the latter part of fifth century CE and their arrival marked the end of the Roman period. The Anglo-Saxons played a significant role in the shaping of English culture and literature. In fact, it was the Anglo-Saxons who gave England its name and language.

With the coming of the Anglo-Saxons, Christianity declined till it was revived in 597 CE, when the Roman cleric Saint Augustine arrived in England and converted King Ethelbert of Kent to Christianity. The new religion had a deep effect on Anglo-Saxon civilisation. The most important effect was the establishment of schools and the introduction of written literature. Monasteries were established to impart education and also to preserve manuscripts written in Latin, which were copied by scribes.

During the 800s, the **Norse** (people of Norway) and the **Danes** (people of Denmark) attacked England and easily conquered the Anglo-Saxon kingdoms. These conquerors were a seafaring people known as the **Vikings**. Alfred the Great, the Anglo-Saxon king of Wessex, resisted the Viking attacks. As long as he continued to rule, the Danes could not extend their **Danelaw** (the area of Great Britain in which the laws of the Danes held predominance over those of the Anglo-Saxons) to Wessex. After King Alfred died in 899, Wessex became weak and, gradually, the Anglo-Saxons were crushed. The last great Saxon king was Edward the Confessor who ruled till 1066. He was succeeded by his brother-in-law, Harold Godwinson.

❧

The period from 450–1066, known as the Anglo-Saxon period, is also referred to as the **Old English period**. Although the time span covered is very large, the quality and quantity of literature produced is quite scanty. Nevertheless, Anglo-Saxon literature has its own value and significance. It dealt mainly with historical, moral or religious subjects. At first the history was legendary and largely blended with mythical creations. It was mostly in verse, of unknown authorship and fragmentary.

Some of the earliest poets who belonged to the Anglo-Saxon period were the unknown poet who wrote *Beowulf*, Caedmon, and Cynewulf. ***Beowulf*** is to England what Homer's *Illiad* and *Odyssey* are to Ancient Greece. It is the greatest work of English national literature. Like most early epics, *Beowulf* belongs to the domain of oral art. It was handed down from one wandering minstrel to another. Minstrels were bards who narrated stories that were familiar to audiences; these stories were usually sung to the accompaniment of the harp. These early narratives serve as a literary record of the formative stage of English civilisation. The only manuscript of *Beowulf* dates back to the year 1000 and is now preserved in the British Museum. Slightly burnt, it somehow survived Henry VIII's destruction of the monasteries.

It is believed that either Caedmon or the poets who imitated his style, wrote about the Christian myths of Creation and the Fall of Man, the Exodus and the story of Daniel. Cynewulf, the other poet who belonged to this period, wrote works like *Dream of the Rood*, an autobiographical piece; *Christ*, dealing with the themes of Incarnation, Hell, Ascension and the Last Judgment; *Elene*, which recounts the discovery of the Cross by Constantine's mother; and *Juliana*, a story of Christian martyrdom.

Anglo-Saxon poetry is distinguished for its love for adventure, fighting and the sea. A unique feature of this poetry is its use of **alliteration**. In fact, Anglo-Saxon poetry is often called alliterative poetry. Another feature of this poetry is the usage of ready-made descriptive words known as **kennings**. The kenning is a specialised metaphor made of compound words that refer to a person, thing or place. This was a feature unique to old Germanic languages. Examples of kennings are compound words formed by combining two common nouns such as using 'sky-candle' for the sun; 'battle-dew' for blood; and 'whale-road' for the sea. Later kennings became more complex, joining adjectives with nouns. A ship was referred to as a 'foamy-throated sea-stallion' and later as 'foamy-throated stallion of the whale-road'. The early bards used these kennings as they made these poems easier to remember.

These works of the Anglo-Saxon period belonged to the oral tradition and were composed in the vernacular language of the people—a Germanic tongue which is now classified as Old English. But the important instructional texts in the monasteries were written in Latin. Latin continued to be the language of the educated people for a very long time.

King Alfred, apart from defending his country from invaders, gave England what no other king ever gave his country—a history of the nation written in the national tongue. This was *The Saxon Chronicle.* It was written by several writers but Alfred was the moving spirit behind it. The book contains the history of the nation from 60 BCE to 891 CE. The book went on after his death down to 1154, the date of King Stephen's death, and stopped after that.

Middle Ages

1066–1485

1066 is a significant year in the history of England. It was the year when William the Conqueror from Normandy defeated King Harold of England. With the **Norman Conquest**, one could say that England entered the Middle Ages which would continue till the beginning of the Tudor period (1485–1603). During this period, the English language changed from its Anglo-Saxon form to one called **Middle English**. The change from Old English to Middle English was gradual but it could be traced back to one important event—the Norman invasion of 1066.

England witnessed the introduction of the feudal system under the Normans. **Feudalism** was a military and political system in which God was the supreme lord of the land; he was at the top of the feudal pyramid. The king came next and it was believed that he held land by 'divine right'. He could appoint barons as his immediate vassals who would in turn appoint vassals of their own. This would go on all the way down to the landless knights and the serfs. Each vassal owed economic and military allegiance to his overlord. The feudal system permeated the life, art and literature of the period. The institution of knighthood, its related code of behaviour and chivalry became a part of the social fabric. Men above the serf class were expected to be skilled warriors and were sent away from their homes in order to be trained. Once they completed their training, they were 'dubbed', that is, they were tapped on their shoulders with a sword and were thereafter known as knights and bestowed with the title 'sir'.

Women played a subservient role in the feudal system. They had no political rights in a system that was predominantly military. A woman's standing in society depended on the position of her husband or father. In the eleventh and twelfth centuries, with the growing popularity of chivalry, women became more important in the socio-political order. **Chivalry** was a system of ideals which had a strict code of conduct. It involved an oath of loyalty to one's overlord, following the rules of warfare such as not attacking an unarmed man and the adulation of a particular lady. It was believed that revering and protecting a woman would enhance a knight's honour and dignity. This was known as **courtly love** and was seen as an important aspect of chivalry. We can see this being reflected in the tales of King Arthur when Sir Lancelot and Queen Guinevere are drawn together by chivalry and courtly love. Chivalry and courtly love gave rise to the form of literature known as the **romance**, which will be discussed in the section dealing with the literary survey of the period.

The Normans, as the conquerors, looked down upon the Anglo-Saxons for several years. As a result, there was a great divide between the two peoples. Evidence of Norman superiority is pointed out by Sir Walter Scott in his nineteenth-century novel *Ivanhoe*. In the field, he wrote, a domestic animal is often referred to by its Saxon name—swine, sheep or ox. When the same animal appears on the dinner table, however, it takes a French name—pork, mutton or beef. In other words, the raising of farm animals was considered a Saxon activity, whereas the more elegant pursuit of dining befitted the Normans. As the years passed, however, the two races intermingled and blended into one. At first, the Normans spoke French, but later the Norman French blended with the Germanic tongue of the Anglo-Saxons and became English.

The **Crusades** played a significant part in the Middle Ages. These were a series of religious wars that were waged in the eleventh, twelfth and thirteenth centuries by Christian Europe against the followers of Muhammad for the possession of Jerusalem and the Holy Land. They began in 1096 and continued till the fourteenth century. Although the Europeans did not succeed in gaining Jerusalem, they benefitted greatly from their contact with the Middle East. In *The Canterbury Tales*, we meet the knight who had fought in the Crusades. *The Canterbury Tales* offers a greater spectrum of life than that portrayed in *Beowulf*, thus reflecting the increasing cultural exchange of the period.

The kings who ruled England when Chaucer and Langland wrote their immortal works were Edward II (1307–27), Edward III (1327–77) and Richard II (1377–99). Historians refer to this period as the **Middle Ages**. From both the historical as well as the literary points of view, this age is a very important and interesting one. Historically, it has the unique honour of being the age of transition before the Renaissance swept through Europe, bringing about changes in every aspect of human enterprise. From the point of view of literature, it saw the birth of the first great English writer—Geoffrey Chaucer.

It was an age that witnessed several upheavals. Slowly, people were beginning to tire of medieval thinking and ideas. They began to question the practices of the church, although it would take almost a hundred and fifty years for the Reformation movement to take place. **John Wyclif**, the first Englishman to raise his voice against the Catholic Church, was one of the most important contemporaries of Chaucer. He firmly believed that the clergy stood between man and God. He preached that the Bible was the core of spiritual life. His views were adopted by a number of people known as the **Lollards** (a derogatory term to describe their ignorance since they knew only English and not Latin, the more respected language). Between Wyclif and the Lollards, an English translation of the Latin Vulgate Bible was completed in the 1390s. However, both the medieval church and the crown stifled all attempts by Wyclif and the Lollards to correct the Catholic Church of its shortcomings.

❧

Three centuries after the Norman Conquest, English was once more the language of the nation. The Normans realised that they had to adopt the language of the majority. In 1350, English was used in schools and in 1362, Edward III enacted a law stating that both French and Latin must give place to English in the courts of law. The works of **Geoffrey Chaucer** and **William Langland** contributed richly to this growth of English language and poetry. In 1362 when this law was passed, Chaucer was in his twenty-second year and Langland, Gower and Wyclif were middle-aged men who were just beginning their literary careers. During this period, end-rhymes that were introduced from France began to gain popularity over the Anglo-Saxon alliterative verse, and took a permanent place in the history of English poetry.

In the Middle Ages, Europeans had a great fondness for a harp-like instrument called the lyre. Poets often visited palaces and courts and recited poetry to the accompaniment of the lyre. It was from this custom that English **lyric** poetry developed. A well-known lyric of this period is 'The Owl and the Nightingale'. Lyric poetry of this period may be classified into two main categories—secular and religious.

Another popular form of poetry of this period was the **ballad**. The word 'ballad' is derived from an Old French word meaning 'dancing song'. A ballad is a song that tells a dramatic story in verse and is one of the oldest forms of poetry. Ballads began thousands of years ago among people who could not read or write. It is clear from the metre and structure of the ballad that they were originally composed to be sung to music. When the writer is unknown, the ballad is called a **folk ballad** or **popular** or **traditional ballad**. When the author is known, it is called as a **literary ballad**. The most important features of the ballad are simplicity and repetition which are characteristic of oral poetry. Ballads were passed down orally from one generation to another by ordinary uneducated people. Perhaps the narrative portion of the ballad was sung by an individual and the refrain was sung by the audience. Ballads, as we know them, probably took their form in the fifteenth century. There is no proper record of the exact origin of the ballad. They were collected by Sir Thomas Percy, Sir Walter Scott and a few others from the people who still sang them. It was only after 1765, with the publication of Thomas Percy's *Reliques of Ancient English Poetry*, that ballads came to be recognised as a fascinating part of Britain's literary history.

The themes of the ballads were usually tragic and often violent. They spoke of failure in love and war or betrayal by a friend. Later several ballads were composed about the legendary hero **Robin Hood**. The story of a ballad was usually told through dialogue. They began very abruptly with a climactic episode. Stock epithets such as 'blood-red wine', 'yellow hair' or 'merry men' were used. Refrains (repetitions) were another feature of the ballad. The ballads were strictly impersonal in nature. These poems made use of the ballad metre—quatrains of four and three stressed syllables alternatively with the rhyme scheme *abcb.*

Another literary genre that was very popular in the medieval age was the **romance** or **chivalric romance**. These typically narrated stories of knights in shining armour setting off on some quest, experiencing several adventures and rescuing damsels in distress from fire-breathing dragons, wizards and giants. Originally, romances were written in Romance languages like Old French, Spanish, Italian and Romanian but were later written in English.

Religion was an important influence upon literature. This could be discerned in the two forms of drama that were popular during that period—**mystery** and **miracle** plays.

Medieval Drama

Medieval drama flourished from 900s onwards, when the priests enacted brief playlets as part of the church service. This was done for the sake of the masses who could not otherwise understand the Latin services. Thus, the origins of drama are closely linked with the church.

Miracle Plays and Mysteries

Early medieval plays were written by the priests—first in Latin and later in the native language. These plays were known as mysteries or miracles. In England, any religious play was called a miracle, but there is a distinction between the two. Mysteries are stories taken from the Old and New Testaments while miracles are plays based on the lives of saints.

In the Middle Ages, the clergy celebrated the holy days like Christmas and Easter by enacting scenes from the life of Christ. Gradually, these performances were taken over by secular groups like the trade guilds. The guilds enacted the plays on a wagon or on a scaffold in an open space and the audience usually stood around and watched. The actors belonged to the trade guilds. Short plays were grouped together to form a cycle. A cycle represented the entire story from the Creation of Man to the Day of Judgment. These cycles were usually performed in the summer. Settings were not used in miracle plays but importance was given to stage properties. For example, a monstrous head with movable jaws was used to represent Hell.

Four cycles of such plays that are available today are the *York*, *Chester*, *Townley* and *Coventry* cycles.

Moralities

Slowly, the miracle and mystery plays were replaced by the moralities and interludes. In the mystery and the miracle, the serious and the comic coexisted. Now they were separated. The morality concentrated on the serious, while the interlude presented the lighter side of life. Another distinct feature of these plays was the development of characterisation. The morality was didactic in tone and the general theme was the struggle between good and evil for the possession of the human soul. The characters were allegorical in nature—such as Virtue, Vice, Knowledge, Ignorance, Grace or the Seven Deadly Sins. These plays were performed by professionals and travelling actors.

Everyman is one of the most famous morality plays; it was written and enacted between 1509 and 1519. This tells the story of Everyman who is deserted by all his friends—Goods, Knowledge, Strength and Beauty, among others—when he is summoned by Death. Only Good Deeds agrees to go with him.

Moralities began during the reign of Henry VI and were popular until the beginning of Elizabeth's reign. One of the earliest moralities was *The Castle of Perseverance*. The moralities developed gradually to replace the allegorical characters with human characters with distinct characteristics. With the passage of time, comic scenes were included in them in order to relieve the monotony of these plays.

Interludes

These flourished in about the middle of the sixteenth century and were mostly performed at court or in the mansions of the nobles. The interludes aimed at amusing the audience. They had regular characters instead of allegorical figures. These were usually common folk, such as citizens and friars. Sometimes they were performed by villagers, as seen in the 'Pyramus and Thisbe' episode in *A Midsummer Night's Dream*. There was abundant coarse and farcical humour in the interludes. For the first time in English drama, there were set scenes.

John Heywood was a well-known writer of interludes during the reign of Henry VIII. He was a Catholic and a friend of Sir Thomas More. He wrote in the medieval tradition in the spirit of the **fabliaux**—a short, satirical or comic tale in verse, characterised by bawdiness. His originality lay in the fact that he wished to provide pure amusement. His interludes had comic dialogues, modelled sometimes on the French. *The Four P's* written in doggerel (ill-constructed and rough verse) is one of the best known of all interludes. It is about the Palmer, the Pardoner, the Poticary and the Peddler. His *Johan Johan* is another famous interlude which is witty and amusing.

The interludes were a great improvement over the morality play and marked an important stage in the growth of English drama.

Medieval Prose

Until the mid-fourteenth century, English prose was scanty and poor. Verse was the medium for romances and stories. Religious and scholarly work was written in Latin. It was Chaucer who showed, through his prose work *Treatise on Astrolabe* that ideas could be expressed with equal clarity in English as in Latin. Men like John Wyclif wrote in prose and furthered this idea.

Geoffrey Chaucer (1340?–1400)

The Book of the Duchess (1369?)
Anilida and Arcite (1370s)
The House of Fame (1379?)
The Parliament of Foules (1380?)
The Legend of Good Women (1387?–94)
Troilus and Criseyde (1385)
The Canterbury Tales (1386?–1400)

Life

The exact date of Chaucer's birth is not known. It is believed that he was born in London sometime between 1340 and 1343. He spent his formative years in London and was deeply influenced by the busy life of the city. He was the son of a vintner (wine merchant), John Chaucer, and enjoyed a prosperous, middle-class family background. From his childhood, he was familiar with the thriving life of London, the merchants, the wine trade, the busy life of the port and shipping activities. With the help of his father, Chaucer became a page of the third son of King Edward III. From the position of a page, he gradually rose to become a personal attendant of the king. In 1386, he lost all his offices after his patron Duke John of Gaunt was overthrown by his nephew, the young king Richard II, who succeeded his grandfather, Edward III. When Duke Henry of Bolingbroke, son of John of Gaunt, deposed the king and assumed the throne as Henry IV, Chaucer's prosperity was restored. However, he lived for less than a year after that as he died suddenly in 1400.

During his career, he was sent to France and Italy on diplomatic missions where he may have visited Petrarch and Boccaccio whose writings he had already read. These journeys influenced his writings a great deal. Apart from his association with kings and the court, he had several friends in the army, and in France and Italy. He read several books written in Latin, French, Italian and English. He was a great observer of men, manners and nature and this quality is amply reflected in his works.

After he died in 1400, he was buried in Westminster Abbey. In fact, Chaucer was the first poet to be buried in the Poets' Corner there.

Works

Chaucer's place in the history of English literature is very important, as he was the first great poet and is popularly known as the father of English poetry. Although he wrote in the fourteenth century, his thoughts and ideas are very novel even today. This is due to the humour and humanity with which he handled his subjects. *The Canterbury Tales* opens before us a vast spectrum of human beings from different backgrounds who are breathing and alive even today. Chaucer's genius remained unmatched for almost the next two hundred years.

Chaucer was the best chronicler of his times. He wrote in detail about the people and habits of his age. His poetry reflects the life of the Middle Ages and reveals the wide range of experience of the great poet. He is best known for his immortal work, *The Canterbury Tales*, a collection of stories told by a group of pilgrims.

Chaucer's work may be divided into three broad stages—the French, the Italian and the English. It is the last stage that saw his most original work.

FRENCH PERIOD

Chaucer was one of the most learned men of his age and he had travelled a lot. He had visited France on diplomatic missions and had read a considerable amount of French literature which left a deep impression on him. He read the famous *Roman de la Rose* and translated it into the English as *The Romaunt of the Rose*, a fragmentary poem of about eight thousand lines. He modelled his work *The Book of the Duchess* on the French dream-vision form of poetry. Chaucer wrote this graceful elegy on the death of the wife of John of Gaunt. These early works were closely modelled upon the French originals and therefore not considered to be representative of Chaucer's style.

ITALIAN PERIOD

Chaucer visited Italy during the early years of the Renaissance. It is believed that he met Petrarch and Boccaccio there. He was deeply inspired by the glory of Italian literature and there was a marked growth in Chaucer's style. Technically, he was much more skilled than the Italian writers and there was greater originality in his work. His *Anelida and Arcite*, *The Parlement of Foules*, *Troilus and Criseyde*, 'The Clerk's Tale' about the story of Griselda (which was taken from Boccaccio's *Decameron*), *The House of Fame* and

The Legend of Good Women (inspired by Dante) are some of the works written under the Italian influence.

The Parlement of Foules, an allegory, is about the gathering of birds on St Valentine's Day to choose their mates. Chaucer's humour can be seen in this work, where the birds make their speeches and delay their choice by arguments and counter-arguments. We see Chaucer as a keen observer of his contemporaries whom he found to be both lovable and ridiculous.

Troilus and Criseyde, based on a love story by Boccaccio, is a medieval romance with a philosophical message. The poem is set in ancient Troy and describes the tragic love story of Prince Troilus and Criseyde. *Troilus and Criseyde* is considered the first English novel (in verse). Although he had taken the story from the Italian Boccaccio, Chaucer made it his own through his poetic style. He made use of the flexible, seven-line stanza called the **rhyme royal**. This verse form was well-suited for both narration and philosophical comment.

The House of Fame is an unfinished account of a dreamer's visit to the castle of fame. He is guided by an eagle which is one of the first comic characters in English literature. Chaucer presents a surreal journey to a grand palace in the sky where fame is personified as a lady sitting on a throne, accompanied by the wind god Aeolus who holds two trumpets—Fame and Slander.

In *The Legend of Good Women*, Chaucer looks at the true and good women of the past and pays a rich tribute to them. Ironically, his list of good women includes Cleopatra, who can hardly fulfil the role of a virtuous woman, but Chaucer playfully requests the reader not to 'let our heads ache' over Cleopatra's morality. Some of the other well-known, but less controversial women who appear in the poem are Dido, Medea and Lucretia. Chaucer originally planned to write about nineteen virtuous women in this work, but ended up completing only eight, with the ninth one just begun. This work is the first known poem in English, to use the heroic couplet, which Chaucer used with great skill and ease.

ENGLISH PERIOD

This period contains his most well-known work—*The Canterbury Tales*. It was during 1388 that Chaucer had gone on a pilgrimage to Canterbury. This inspired him to write *The Canterbury Tales*. The basic idea for the tales was taken from Boccaccio but its treatment is entirely original. *The Canterbury Tales* ranks among the masterpieces of world literature. It is a collection of stories told by a group of pilgrims on a journey to the shrine of Thomas Becket in Canterbury. Chaucer describes this group as being made up of people from different walks of life, assembling and departing from London. They set off on the pilgrimage from the Tabard Inn in Southwark, London, in the month of April. At the suggestion of the host of the Tabard, who is also part of the group, the pilgrims agree to tell two stories each, one while going to the shrine and another while returning. Chaucer, however, did not complete the book as there are only about twenty-four tales out of which four are incomplete.

Chaucer introduced these pilgrims one by one in 'The Prologue'. The knight, the parson and the plowman represent the three classes of medieval society—the aristocracy, clergy and the working class. The rest of the pilgrims were drawn from the middle class and represent people from different walks of life such as the clerk of Oxenford, who is a scholar and a learned man, the Doctor, the Miller and the Wife of Bath. Chaucer portrays these characters in great detail, telling us about their dress, mannerisms, speech and appearance. In his description of these characters, Chaucer combines irony, humour and quiet appreciation. He even gives a lot of importance to the kind of horse each of the pilgrims rides.

The Canterbury Tales is written in poetic form except for the 'Tale of Melibeus' and 'The Parson's Tale' which are in prose. Chaucer uses the heroic couplet or the rhymed couplet in this work.

Features

- Chaucer wrote in a language known as Middle English, the kind of English that was in use between the years 1100 to about 1485. After the Norman Conquest in 1066, many of the upper class in England learned Norman French and gradually, the inclusion of French words in English became fashionable. The fusion of thousands of French words with the English language took place during this period. Scholars refer to the French-influenced English of this period as Middle English. The opening lines of *The Canterbury Tales* are a good illustaration of Middle English: 'Whan that Aprill with his shoures soote, / The droghte of March hath perced to the roote.'
- Chaucer's contribution to the English verse form is tremendous. He moved away from the irregular and alliterative style of the Old English period. It was he who first imported the decasyllabic line from France to England. Chaucer used this line in both stanzaic form as well as in couplets. In the stanzaic form it was known as the **rhyme royal**. Chaucer used this verse form in his poem *Troilus and Criseyde. The Canterbury Tales* was written in heroic couplets.
- He was known for his satire and irony. In his poetry, we notice a gentle satirical note directed against the aristocratic tradition called 'courtly love'. He often satirised their lofty ideals, elaborate etiquette and literary style. *The Parlement of Foules* reflects this very clearly, where the birds make their speeches and delay their choice by arguments and counter-arguments.
- He was severe in his criticism of the corruption in the medieval church. In *The Canterbury Tales,* his criticism of the rampant evils of the church is evident in his portrayals of the friar, monk, pardoner and summoner. He, however, consciously avoided any reference to the dark and painful events of his time like the plagues and famines.
- At a time when humour was unknown to literature, Chaucer reveals a great variety of humour in all his works.

The shades of humour vary from the kindly and patronising to the farcical and coarse. The main feature of Chaucer's humour is his sense of kindly tolerance towards the foibles and weaknesses of his fellow human beings. His humour is refreshing and well-intended. Sometimes, as in his treatment of the medieval beast-epic material in 'The Nun's Priest's Tale' or 'The Fox and the Cock', his humour takes on the form of boisterous farce. But mostly it is of the finer intellectual sort which touches with perfect sureness all the incongruities of his time. No foible is too small for Chaucer's keen observation.

- It is as a story teller that Chaucer excels. He has a great variety of narrative forms—elaborate allegories, love stories, romances—both religious and secular, tales of chivalrous exploits and humorous farces.
- In Chaucer's works, one can discern some of the flaws of his time such as a fondness for long speeches, digressions and tedious explanations. When one overlooks these weaknesses, he emerges as a great poet.
- His great love of nature is evident in his work, especially in 'The Prologue' and 'The Knight's Tale'. He uses nature to highlight the emotions.
- Chaucer was clearly influenced by the spirit of the Renaissance which focused on humanism. This helped to steer him away from the religious towards the secular. He was a great lover of life and enjoyed writing about human quirks.

John Gower (1330?–1408)

Speculum Meditantis (French) | *Vox Clamantis* (Latin)
Confessio Amantis (English, 1390?) | *Traite* (1397?)

Life

Gower was born in Kent and belonged to a fairly well-to-do family. He was very learned and wealthy, possessing lands in various parts of England. He was a refined and highly moral man.

The Peasants' Revolt, that took place during his lifetime, horrified him as he was not only an upholder of law and order but also a landlord whose sympathies were with the aristocrats.

Gower and Chaucer were friends who admired each other's works. Chaucer, who was a few years younger than Gower, dedicated his *Troilus and Criseyde* to the 'moral Gower'. Gower, in turn, praised Chaucer in his *Confessio Amantis*. Professional rivalry, however, soon caused a rift between the two poets. It is believed that Gower lost his eyesight in 1400 and died a few years later. He was buried at St Mary Overie's, now known as St Saviour's in Southwark.

Works

John Gower used Latin and French and wrote in English only towards the end of his career under the influence of Chaucer. His first work, *Speculum Meditantis* ('mirror of meditation') is a moral poem of about thirty thousand lines. Written in French, it is in the form of a Morality poem in which the poet criticises the immorality of his age. The work offers a fascinating picture of contemporary society. It depicts a noteworthy parade of vices and virtues and the Devil is shown as marrying the seven daughters of Sin.

His next work, *Vox Clamantis,* in Latin deals with Wat Tyler's Rebellion. In it, Gower criticises the peasants for their wild and unruly behaviour. It is a long work which runs into seven books.

His last work *Confessio Amantis*, running into more than forty thousand rhymed octosyllabic lines, was written at the request of Richard II. At the time of writing this work, Gower was a supporter of Richard II. Later, when there was a shift in his political leanings, he substituted the name of Henry IV for Richard II in the poem. The poem consists of tales that illustrate the evils that are a result of the seven deadly sins.

Features

- Gower was a good story teller and for several years, his poems were as popular as Chaucer's *The Canterbury Tales.*

As he was a voracious reader, he knew many strange stories from different sources.

- His works are noted for their strong moral flavour. His stories always convey a moral or lesson to the readers. As a result, his verse suffers from didacticism.

William Langland (1332?–1400)

The Vision Concerning Piers the Plowman (1362?–98?)	*Richard the Redeless*

Life

Not much is known about Langland, also known as Langley. He was born in Shropshire and might have had his education at Malvern. He was probably a member of the clergy and was poor for most of his lifetime. He did not have the charming manner of his contemporary, Chaucer. Langland focused more on the sufferings and miseries of his time, unlike Chaucer who painted the brighter side of medieval life. It is believed that Langland died about the same time as Chaucer in 1400.

Works

The full title of his work is *The Vision of William Concerning Piers the Plowman.* It is also known as *The Book of Piers the Plowman.* This poem exists in three manuscript versions known as the A-Text, B-Text and C-Text. Of these the first version was probably written in 1362. The A-Text, which has about twenty-five hundred lines, is the shortest. The B-Text, contains more than seventy-two hundred lines and was probably written in 1377, while the C-Text, which is the longest, has more than seventy-three hundred lines. This poem describes a series of visions that the poet sees in a dream. These visions deal with allegorical beings like 'Do-well' and 'Do-best' or abstractions like Wit, Study and Faith. He also portrays the men and women of his times such as knights, monks, peasants, preachers and cooks. These people are shown as being in search of Truth and Good.

The main focus of the poem is to expose the shortcomings of the church and to reveal the difficulties faced by the common folk. Unlike Chaucer, Langland portrays the terrible lives of the poor people.

Richard the Redeless (meaning devoid of counsel) is an alliterative poem critiquing the reign of Richard the II. The authorship of this poem is attributed to Langland, based on the poems's style and historical period.

Features

- Langland goes back to the Old English rhymeless measure, which relies heavily upon alliteration. The lines are mostly of uniform length, with a pause in the middle. There are two alliterations in the first-half and one in the second. In spite of this Old English metre, Langland uses a lot of French words.
- He lashes out against the people who do not earn an honest living. The drunkard, the dishonest merchant and the hypocritical preachers come in for severe criticism in his work. Langland's zeal to reform the evils of the church and better the living conditions of the poor is evident.
- We get a very clear picture of medieval life in his work. For example, we get to know how the tradesmen's apprentices stood at the shop doors calling out to passers-by in order to attract them. Langland also refers to many contemporary events that had taken place. He throws light on the manners and customs of the people. For example, we come to learn about the practice of rich people buying up great quantities of provisions and selling them at a profit to the poor.
- There is a sincerity and dignity in his work. As an artist, he was not equal to Chaucer. His portraits of negative characters are better than that of the good ones. But his power of observation was very sharp.
- He was one of the important religious poets of his time. He undertook the difficult task of drawing people's attention to the shortcomings of the church. *The Vision of Piers the Plowman* was popular during his lifetime. Langland is remembered today as a visionary, an advocate for the

purification of the church and a critic of the corrupt practices of his day.

John Wyclif (1324–84)

John Wyclif, often referred to as the first Protestant and the enemy of the pope, wrote in prose. When there was a struggle between the king and the pope, Wyclif was drawn into it. He attacked papal supremacy and since he wanted to gain public support for his cause, began writing in English; he had written only in Latin till 1380. He also popularised his ideas through priests known as 'poor priests'. They were later known as **Lollards**. The Lollards were poor, but educated, men. They travelled from one parish to another, criticising the friars. The movement of Wyclif and the Lollards was checked and suffered a serious setback due to the Peasants' Revolt of 1381.

Wyclif's literary importance lies in the fact that he completed the first translation of the Bible into the English language. Although faulty, it is an important milestone in the history of translations of the Bible, including the famous Authorised Version of 1611.

English prose in the fifteenth century was still formless and insignificant. Latin still continued to enjoy a more privileged position among the learned.

William Caxton (1422–91)

An important name during the second half of the fifteenth century is William Caxton. He was the first English printer and faced the difficulties of trying to give form and shape to the English language which was still evolving. For a long time, the development of reading in English depended not on the writers of the language, but on printers. The greater part of Caxton's work took the form of prose translation. He employed the spoken language, but avoided terms that were too rustic. He made use of several French words and spent several years translating French literature and printing it. He admired French prose and wished to bring the same clarity to English prose. He thus played an important role in the development of English prose. He kept alive the romances that were popular during the medieval times.

Among the important prose versions of the old romances published by Caxton was **Sir Thomas Malory**'s *Morte d'Arthur*. Malory tells the tale of Arthur's triumphant reign, his unfaithful wife Guinevere, who takes Lancelot for her lover, and the glory of Galahad. It is England's first book in poetic prose and is narrated in the simple style of a fairy tale. It kept alive the medieval concept of chivalry.

Caxton was a great admirer of Chaucer and printed *The Canterbury Tales* and *Troilus and Criseyde*.

Tudor Age

1485–1603

A new era began in England in 1485 when the Tudor dynasty commenced. Henry IV of the House of Lancaster had ascended the throne after the unpopular ruler Richard II was forced to abdicate in 1399. His descendants Henry V and Henry VI ruled till 1461, after which the throne was occupied by Edward IV, Edward V and Richard III of the House of York. In 1455, during the reign of Henry VI, the Duke of York, a descendant of Edward III, claimed the throne leading to the famous Wars of the Roses (named after the white rose emblem of the House of York and the red rose emblem of the House of Lancaster.)The Wars of the Roses came to an end with the coronation of Henry Tudor (a descendant of the House of Lancaster), who later married Elizabeth of the House of York, thus marking the onset of Tudor England.

During the Tudor period, England passed from the medieval to the early modern times. During the Tudor period, England passed from the medieval to the early modern times. It was a remarkable period when English life and thought were stirred by the Renaissance and the Reformation. The five Tudor rulers gave to England a much longed for peace after the tumultuous Wars of the Roses. They were Henry VII, his son Henry VIII and the three children of Henry VIII—Edward VI, Mary and Elizabeth I. England witnessed tremendous changes during the reign of the Tudors. They were responsible for laying the foundation of the British kingdom and strengthening the monarchy. This period is important from both the historical as well as the literary points of view as it was the time when English literature began to grow and flourish.

The two great movements—the **Renaissance** and the **Reformation**—which were sweeping across Europe at that time, gradually reached the shores of England. These movements brought in their wake tremendous changes that irrevocably altered the mindscape of the country.

In order to have a good understanding of this period, it has been divided into two sub-chapters—the early Tudor period (1485–1558) and the Elizabethan Age (1558–1603).

EARLY TUDOR PERIOD (1485–1558)

Henry VII (1485–1509)
Henry VIII (1509–47)
Edward VI (1547–53)
Mary (1553–58)

As mentioned earlier, two great movements were taking place in Europe during the early Tudor period. One was the **Reformation** or the breakup of the Roman Catholic Church and the other was the **Renaissance**. The Renaissance was a great movement that swept through Europe from the 1400s and 1500s to the 1600s. The term 'renaissance' itself is a French word originating from the Latin *'rinascere'*, meaning 'rebirth' and it represents a renewed interest in the classical writings of ancient Greece and Rome. In the Middle Ages, people forgot Greek, and the Latin that they were familiar with was of a debased variety. This renewed interest in the classics saw the revival of Greek and a reformed Latin. The new energy was conducive for the creation of beautiful works of art.

The effects of the Renaissance were not seen in England until the final two decades of the fifteenth century. By then, ideas popularised by the Renaissance had already been spreading across Europe for more than a century. Since the Renaissance had begun in Italy, most of the prominent Renaissance figures were Italian. Among the most well-known of them were Dante Alighieri (1265–1321), author of *The Divine Comedy;* Francesco Petrarca (1304–74), popularly known as Petrarch, who wrote poetry in a new fourteen-line form called the sonnet; Leonardo da Vinci (1452–1519) and Michelangelo (1475–1564), who were painters and sculptors.

The insatiable thirst for knowledge resulted in a great burst of exploration. All over Europe adventurous men set out across the wide oceans in search of wealth and knowledge. Brave seafarers like Christopher Columbus, Vasco da Gamma and Magellan, aided by the development of the compass and the advances in astronomy, ventured far and wide. England, too, joined the race and soon became known as the 'Queen of the Seas'. Some of the well-known British mariners were Sir Francis Drake, Sir John Hawkins and Sir Walter Raleigh.

The most important feature of the Renaissance was **humanism**, which emerged from the study of ancient Greek and Roman literature. Petrarch, the great Italian lyric poet who perfected the sonnet and the ode, which later influenced the English poets, is often called the father of humanism He unearthed the writings of the ancient Latin writers Cicero and Livy. Latin literature remained unknown in Europe after the decline of the Roman Empire. The humanists were interested in the ancient classics not only for their literary style but also for their wisdom in interpreting life. The humanist's approach to life was in sharp contrast to that of the medieval scholar. According to medieval thinking, life on earth was something to be ashamed of and despised. They viewed man as a sinful creature who should devote his entire life in trying to attain heaven after death. The humanists rejected this view completely and celebrated the human body and life on this earth. According to them, life was to be enjoyed.

Humanistic literature is realistic, critical and often humorous. For example, Chaucer in his *Canterbury Tales* and Boccaccio in his *Decameron* narrated humorous stories that reveal a deep understanding of human nature. Thomas More, another humanist, was highly critical of the society of his times. He was far ahead of his contemporaries, when he advocated education for women in his book *Utopia*. All these humanists examined life in a frank and honest way.

Humanism reflected itself in art and sculpture too. Although religion continued to be the dominant theme, Renaissance painters and sculptors gave up the stiff and artificial style of medieval art and created realistic and richly detailed pieces. Humanists such as Da Vinci, Donatello and Michelangelo created masterpieces that presented men and women as majestic and admirable creatures.

Humanism took a long time to really have an impact on the poetry and prose of England. This was because the national language was still in a formative stage. Prose especially lacked a strong tradition and the best humanists, such as Sir Thomas More, still wrote in Latin. In the field of poetry, too, after Chaucer, there was a great vacuum until Spenser began to write in 1579.

As far as painting and sculpture were concerned, England had no tradition of her own. Hans Holbein the Younger, a German artist, who was invited to England by Erasmus, was known for his lifelike portraits during the early Tudor period. But England lagged behind as she had no tradition to claim as her own. By the time the Renaissance could really sweep through England, the **Reformation** (the religious movement that lead to Protestantism) too, was making its presence felt. The plastic arts did not find a favourable climate to flourish in as Puritanism, which was an offshoot of the Reformation, was spreading its influence in England. The Puritans discouraged art and other forms of artistic expressions, as they felt that they were a distraction to religious life.

Up to the fifteenth century, English literature was almost totally imported from France. Even Chaucer wrote under a strong French influence, but with one major difference—French literature was aristocratic in nature, whereas English literature was more conscious of the masses. Poetry, consisting of popular ballads, and theatre that was accessible to all classes of people are evidence of this quality of English humanism.

ଔଈଔ

Early Tudor Drama

With the Renaissance spreading across the continent, there was a revival of the classics, especially the plays of Seneca (the

Latin dramatist who lived between 3 BCE and 65 CE). The English dramatists tried to imitate classical drama, especially its five-act structure and set scenes.

Tragedy

Gorboduc (1561), the first English tragedy, was written by Thomas Sackville and Thomas Norton. This play was performed before Queen Elizabeth I; it was later called *Ferrex and Porrex.* It was divided into five acts and each act ended in a chorus, like its classical Senecan model. It differed from the classical style in its use of blank verse, which was used for the first time in English drama, and in its subject matter, which was taken from the legendary chronicles of Britain.

Comedy

Ralph Roister Doister (1552?) is considered to be the first full length English comedy. It was written by Nicholas Udall. Udall was the headmaster of Westminster School, where it was a custom to perform Latin plays on special occasions. Udall's play, written in five acts, followed the classical rules of Latin comic plays. The idea of substituting an English play for a comedy by Plautus or Terence (who were famous Latin playwrights) might have occurred to Udall. Although *Ralph Roister Doister* was based on the plays of Plautus, it has a distinct native flavour. The characterisation is commendable; it is another milestone in the history of English drama.

Gammer Gurton's Needle (1575) is another important play that was modelled on Latin comedy, but whose treatment was native. It is the second English comedy that was popular during the sixteenth century. It contained one of the interludes of John Heywood. The play gives us a good account of typical village life in Tudor England.

Both the plays follow the classical model in that they are divided into five acts with each act introducing a new character. The unities of time and place are followed as the action takes place in a single day and on the same street. However, there is stiffness and a lack of literary grace in these early plays.

Early Tudor Prose

The 'New Learning', humanism, that swept the shores of England, did much for the development of prose. The presence of the Dutch scholar and teacher Erasmus inspired the Englishmen of his age. The two English scholars William Grocyn and Thomas Linacre, who visited Italy, brought back with them the classical ideas of Florence. John Colet and Sir Thomas More were two of the men who were inspired by them.

Early Tudor Poetry

After Chaucer, poetry declined in England for the next century and a half. With the impact of the Renaissance upon England, there was a revival of the ancient classics. During the reign of Henry VIII two English poets, the Earl of Surrey and Sir Thomas Wyatt, travelled to Italy and were impressed with the sonnets of Petrarch. It was through them, that the sonnet became a popular literary form during much of the Elizabethan age.

Sir Thomas More (1477?–1535)

Life of Pico of Mirandola (1510)
History of Richard III (in Latin, 1515?)
Utopia (1516)
A Dialogue Concerning Heresies (1528–29)
A Dialogue of Comfort against Tribulation (1534)

Life

He was the son of John More, a justice of the King's Bench. He studied at Oxford, where he came into contact with the 'New Learning' that was being spread by Grocyn, Linacre and Colet. He also became a close friend of Erasmus while at Oxford.

Cardinal Wolsey introduced him to Henry VIII. More held many important posts in the English government which even took him abroad. It was on a visit to Antwerp that he wrote his great work entitled *Utopia*. He was the typical Renaissance man—a writer, scholar, statesman and diplomat. He was one of the important humanists of his times.

After Wolsey fell out of the king's favour, More was asked to become Lord Chancellor. At that time Henry VIII was engaged in a bitter fight with the pope. When More disapproved of Henry VIII's defiance of the pope, he was imprisoned in the Tower of London. Henry VIII asked More to change his views and accept his Act of Supremacy which declared that the king was the supreme head of the church. When More refused to do so, he was beheaded on 6 July 1535.

Works

More was trained as a classical scholar; therefore, his first language for writing was Latin. His most important work *Utopia*, was written in Latin.

An example of a work in English is his *Life of Pico*, considered to be the first book in classical English prose. It is, however, not an original work, but a translation of the biography of Pico by his nephew.

Most of his religious works were in English and were often controversial in nature. The most important of these are *Dialogue against Lutheranism and Tyndale* and *Dialogue of Comfort against Tribulations*. The first of these presents a series of conversations between More and a messenger; it reflects More's responses to the Reformation. He was a devoted Catholic who did not approve of the Reformation Movement. His dialogues are a blend of piety and good humour and reveal More both as a saint and a humorist.

Utopia is his most famous work. The word 'utopia' means 'no place'. The book is an account of an ideal society where every citizen has equality and justice. It denounces luxury and idleness. It is often referred to as 'the first monument of modern socialism' and is of special interest for the social reformer. Written in Latin and published in 1516, it is also known as *Utopia, or the Discourse of Raphael Hythloday of the Best State of a Commonwealth*. Ralph Robinson translated it into English in 1551.

It consists of two parts. In the first, there is a vivid description of the terrible evils that England was suffering from due to war—lawlessness, the wholesale and foolish application of the death penalty, the exploitation of the peasants, the greed of the rich and the corruption in the church. In the second part, in contrast to all this, the character, Raphael Hythloday describes the customs of Utopia, a remote island in the New World. This account of a society that is almost perfect touches upon every aspect of life such as religion, administration, crime and punishment, education, law and justice, work and leisure and politics. In his attempt to portray an ideal society, More inadvertently satirises his own society. Therefore, one may consider *Utopia* to be the first political satire to be written by an Englishman.

In it, More highlights the injustice of inflicting cruel punishments, like hanging, even for petty thefts. He gives an outline of an ideal government in which people are required to take an oath that they would choose only the most suitable person for office. The people of Utopia are expected to work only for six hours a day and the rest of the day was to be spent 'for the improvement of their minds'. They hated wars and looked down upon 'the glory gained by war'. Utopians built no prisons. Criminals were taught to do useful work and were not tortured or executed. More also condemned many evils of his day such as religious intolerance and the enclosures in the countryside. In his Utopia, 'no man is poor, none in necessity, and though no man has anything, yet they are all rich; for what can make a man so rich as to lead a serene and cheerful life…?'

However, there were some serious drawbacks in More's ideal land. It was a very dull place where both men and women wore the same clothes. Incurably sick people were killed off and it was compulsory for everyone to attend lectures before having their breakfast.

Utopia was far ahead of its times and, in it, one can see how the spirit of the Renaissance affected the thinking of Thomas More. In its rejection of war and advocacy of taxing only the rich, More's fair-mindedness and sensitivity are revealed. He was a true humanist and a child of the Renaissance.

He wrote his *Dialogue of Comfort against Tribulation* when he was imprisoned in the Tower of London. This is in the form of a conversation between two Hungarian gentlemen who are awaiting the attack of an invading Turkish army. It is More's most personal and honest work in which serious thought and humorous anecdotes exist together. This reflects More's own approach to his impending death and shows that he still retained his sense of humour.

Features

- More's work was known for its scholarship. He was a very learned man who had travelled widely and he used his experience in his writings.
- He was a humanist who wrote to better the condition of the people. His works are full of philosophical discussions and he emphasised the importance of education and reason.
- His *Utopia* is one of the earliest satires which critiques contemporary society.
- His writings reveal him to be a devout Catholic. He defended the Catholic Church against the reforms of Martin Luther.

Bible

During the Middle Ages, the only Bible that was commonly used was the Latin Vulgate text. Wyclif undertook the translation of the Bible into English as he felt that the vast majority of people who could not read Latin must be able to read it. Unfortunately, Wyclif was identified as part of the Lollards who had antagonised the church. Therefore, the licensed production of the English Bible was delayed for another hundred-and-fifty years. In 1516, Erasmus produced his great edition of the Greek New Testament at Cambridge.

William Tyndale (1494–1536)

William Tyndale undertook the task of translating the Bible into English in 1525. It was he who gave the Bible its modern form. An important feature of Tyndale's translation is that he relied more on the original Hebrew and Greek versions rather than on the Latin one. Thomas More severely criticised Tyndale's translations for not including certain Catholic terms like 'grace', 'confession' and 'penance'. Tyndale also substituted words like 'church' and 'priest' with the words 'congregation' and 'elder'. Tyndale's translation is known for its rhythmic grace and verbal charm and it later had an important impact upon the Authorised Versions of the Bible.

Sir Thomas Wyatt (1503–42)

Wyatt was a humanist who visited the continent on diplomatic missions. He brought back to England, the new poetic patterns used by Dante and Petrarch. Wyatt exhibited a great skill in using the amazing diversity of metrical experiments. He introduced the strict counting of syllables through his poems in which he used the terza rima and ottava rima. His most important contribution was to the **sonnet** form. The sonnet is a lyrical poem of fixed form—fourteen lines of iambic pentameter rhymed and organised according to several intricate rhyme schemes. He wrote thirty-two sonnets in the Petrarchan style. Typically, a Petrarchan sonnet was divided into two parts—the octave (eight lines) and the sestet (six lines) with a pause called caesura in between. The rhyme scheme for the octave is *abbaabba* and that of the sestet is *cddcee* or variations of these rhymes.

Wyatt is also remembered for his short lyrical pieces, of which some fifty or sixty still survive. The mood of his poems is nearly always that of a brave-hearted but forsaken lover. The rumour that he had been Anne Boleyn's lover before she married Henry VIII, adds a new dimension to the poems. Through these poems, Wyatt demonstrated for the first time that great poetry could be written without the backing of any narrative or allegory and that the poet could achieve greatness by giving vent to his personal feelings.

Henry Howard, Earl of Surrey (1517–47)

Surrey is often compared unfavourably with Wyatt, although his sonnets reveal greater variety and are easier to understand. The chief qualities of Surrey's work are grace and a tenderness of feeling. His poems are pictorial and discursive in nature. His range is greater than that of Wyatt's, extending beyond love poetry to elegy and autobiographical verse. He also translated parts of the *Aeneid* in **blank verse** which was used for the first time in England.

His treatment of the sonnet form is different from that of Wyatt's. Being fond of the compressed form of the epigram, he used it in his sonnets which are epigrammatic. The three quatrains (a stanza of four lines) with alternate rhymes, ending with a closed couplet (*abab cdcd efef gg*), which is popularly known as the Shakespearean form of the sonnet, was invented by Surrey. Compared to Wyatt, the number of sonnets he wrote is fewer. Most of them are based on personal observation and experience. The most famous one is the one on the Lady Geraldine: 'From Tuscan came my lady's worthy race'.

His most preferred verse form was the **poulter's measure**. This verse form was gradually replaced by blank verse, which is considered much superior to poulter's measure. Interestingly, both the best as well as the worst of the poetry of the second-half of the sixteenth century can be seen in Surrey's work.

Wyatt and Surrey's works

The poems of Surrey and Wyatt first appeared in the anthology called *Tottel's Miscellany* in 1557. Their contribution to Tudor poetry is immense. They not only introduced the sonnet form, but also other verse forms and metres to England. Surrey's translation of *Aeneid* was an important event in the history of English literature as it introduced the blank verse, which was later used to their advantage by Marlowe and Shakespeare. Wyatt and Surrey were the forerunners of the exuberant Elizabethan poetry. After them, there was a lull in English poetry up till the time of Sir Philip Sidney.

ELIZABETHAN AGE (1558–1603)

Queen Elizabeth was one of the most successful monarchs to have ruled England. An important change brought about by

Elizabeth was the **Anglican Settlement** which brought to an end the violent oscillation between the extreme Catholicism and extreme Protestantism of her predecessors. Although the Catholics and the Protestants were forced to accept the Anglican Settlement, there was a sect called the **Puritans** who opposed it. The Puritans were English Protestants who had fled England during the reign of Queen Mary. During their exile on the Continent, they came under the strong influence of John Calvin and when they returned to England after Elizabeth ascended the throne, they were disappointed with the compromise made by the Anglican Church. Elizabeth was, however, able to suppress them with the help of John Whitgift, the Archbishop of Canterbury, who hated the Puritans. This aspect of social life was reflected in the literature of the period—for example, the scenes where the Puritanical Malvolio is ragged in Shakespeare's *Twelfth Night*. By the end of Elizabeth's reign, England had three religious groups—the Anglicans who supported Elizabeth, the Catholics who rejected the Act of Supremacy and the Puritans who demanded a stricter form of worship.

Society during the reign of Queen Elizabeth was very energetic and dynamic. It was an age that witnessed young and vigorous people with a zest for life, emerging from the Middle Ages and stepping into the passionate life of the Renaissance. The people were exuberant due to the defeat of the Spanish Armada and patriotism was at an all-time high.

Physical pleasures such as bear-baiting, cockfighting, hunting, dancing around the maypole and gambling were pursued. It was a great age for drama as theatre-going was the rage of the time. People enjoyed dressing in bright colours and loved shows, parades and games. There were several reasons for the vitality of the Elizabethans. The full impact of the Renaissance was felt in England and the intellectuals began to focus on humanism which gave importance to the role of the human being in the world. The break with Rome filled the people with a sense of freedom. Further, the advancements made in the world of science and the geographical discoveries added a touch of boldness and adventure to the already heady population. The circumstances were just right for the great plays of Shakespeare and Marlowe and the poetry of Sidney, Spenser and several others.

ଓଃଐଣ୍ଡ

Elizabethan Drama

Theatre

English drama came into full bloom during the reign of Queen Elizabeth. Playwrights moved away from the religious themes that were favoured by the earlier period and began writing secular plays inspired by the classical models of ancient Greece and Rome. Tragedies and comedies were carefully crafted in blank verse, using rich, poetic language and imagery.

Although the art of drama in England was almost three centuries old, the idea of performing plays in a permanent building was new. Plays were earlier performed in the courtyard of inns or in the houses of noblemen. The first theatre was built by James Burbage in 1576. By the end of the century, eight more theatres were built on the north and south of River Thames. Of these, the most well-known was the Globe. The buildings were externally round or hexagonal and generally had three main parts—the building proper, the stage and the tiring house or backstage. When a flag was flown from its peak, it indicated that there would be a performance on that particular day. The building proper was a wooden structure with three stories surrounding a spacious inner yard open to the sky.

Inside there was a large projecting platform on trestles (a wooden or metal structure with two pairs of legs used for supporting a flat surface) which formed the stage. The floor of this platform contained a trapdoor which everybody pretended led down to hell; through this witches or devils emerged. The ceiling over part of the stage was painted with elaborate suns, moons and stars and contained a trapdoor through which angels, gods and spirits could be lowered on a wire and even made to 'fly' over the other actors' heads.

Towards the rear of the stage there was a two-storeyed structure consisting of a gallery at the upper level and a curtained space below that. The gallery was put to several uses. The upper gallery was used to seat some important spectators and also as a place for the musicians to perform. At times, parts of the play would be performed there. It served as a balcony, a palace tower or the hills. The curtained area below was used mainly for 'discoveries'. For example, in *The Merchant of Venice*, the curtain is drawn to reveal three small caskets in one of which is hidden Portia's picture.

General admission to the theatre cost one penny, which entitled one to be a groundling (a spectator who stood in the yard to watch a performance). If they paid a little more, they could occupy a seat on the galleries. The most expensive seats of all were the chairs set right on the stage on both its sides.

An important feature of the Elizabethan stage was the absence of stage setting and a drop-curtain. The audience was quick to use its imagination and this made up for the lack of movable scenery on the stage. For instance, when a character came on to the stage with a lantern, they knew at once that it was night even though the play was performed in broad daylight. They were very sensitive to the lines being uttered on the stage. For example, the following lines from the opening scene of *Hamlet* recreated, as no stage setting ever successfully could, a perfect sunrise.

> But look, the morn in russet mantle clad,
> Walks o'er the dew of yon high eastward hill.

Similarly, when Shakespeare wished to depict a forest scene, he did not resort to the painted backdrops of modern theatre. Instead, a few bushes and small trees were placed on the stage and the actors created the rest of the scenery by evoking images in the spectators' minds through their dialogues. For example, when Rosalind in *As You Like It* looks around her and exclaims, 'Well, this is the Forest of Arden', the audience is mentally transported to the required place.

The absence of a drop-curtain posed certain problems to the dramatist. Since there was no way he could indicate to his audience that the scene was completed, he had to resort to various methods to convey the same. Usually, a scene written in blank verse would suddenly have a rhyming couplet to indicate the conclusion. The dramatist also had to take pains to vacate the actors from the stage in a natural manner. We notice several scenes in which the characters tell each other where they were planning to go and make plans to meet later. Also, provisions had to be made to clear the stage of 'dead bodies' if any. In *Hamlet*, the stage is strewn with several dead bodies and Horatio appears on the stage to give instructions for them to be carried away for burial.

Yet another interesting feature of Elizabethan theatre was the fact that women were not allowed to act on stage. All the female roles, therefore, had to be played by young boys whose voices had not yet cracked. This was one of the reasons for so many of Shakespeare's plays having women characters disguising themselves as men. For example, Portia, Rosalind, Celia and Viola to name a few.

University Wits

John Lyly (1554–1606)
Thomas Kyd (1558–94)
George Peele (1558–97)
Christopher Marlowe (1564–93)
Robert Greene (1560?–92)
Thomas Nashe (1567–1601)
Thomas Lodge (1558?–1625)

These men were known as the University Wits since they had all been educated at Oxford or Cambridge. The universities were centres for classical studies and the plays of Seneca were very influential there. These were tragedies that were known for their horror and their exaggerated characters. The language was rhetorical and hyperbolic. They dealt with the theme of revenge and had stock characters such as the messenger who reported disasters, the ghost and the nurse. They were divided into five acts. Senecan tragedy had a profound impact upon English drama. The influence of Seneca was especially felt in the universities. From there, it spread to the popular stage when the University Wits began writing their plays.

The University Wits were great scholars and believed that a sound education was necessary for a career as a writer. They came just before Shakespeare and had a great impact upon him. The works of the University Wits have the following salient features:

- The themes of their plays chiefly dealt with the lives of great heroes such as King David and Tamburlaine.
- Since the plays were about heroic figures, the treatment of the subject had to be grand. The plays were full of long, bombastic speeches and violent and emotional scenes that often became loud and unruly.
- The preferred medium of these plays was the blank verse.
- The plays were all tragedies and there was no comic relief in them. Humour was rare in these plays and if there was any, it was crude and unpolished. The only dramatist in this group to attempt comedy was Lyly who is the forerunner of the romantic comedy.

Elizabethan Poetry

1557 is an important year in the history of English poetry, for it was in that year that a printer named Richard Tottel published a collection of poems called *Songs and Sonnets*. This volume, which was popularly called *Tottel's Miscellany*, contained some of the best poems by Sir Thomas Wyatt and Henry Howard, Earl of Surrey. The sonnet form became so popular that by 1595, there were several poets who were writing in this form. The century after *Tottel's Miscellany* was one of the greatest ages of English poetry. C.S. Lewis, in his *English Literature in the Sixteenth Century*, refers to the period beginning from Lyly's *Euphues* (1579) to the death of Queen Elizabeth in 1603 as the golden age of poetry.

The above years, which coincided with the reign of Queen Elizabeth, did indeed mark the golden period in English literature and history. It witnessed the flowering not only of drama but of poetry too. Giants like Shakespeare, Sidney, Spenser and Ben Jonson lived and wrote their masterpieces during that time.

It was the age of romance. Inspired by the prose romances *Euphues* and *Arcadia*, by Lyly and Sidney respectively, poetry, too, used romantic elements such as chivalry and courtly love. Poetry as a literary form flourished as the Elizabethans favoured lyric poetry rather than the narrative type that was popular with their medieval predecessors. The lyrics were published as collections by single authors and sometimes as anthologies which came after *Tottel's Miscellany.* Many of the lyrics were included as songs in the dramas of the time.

The sonnet, which is a part of lyric poetry, was a favourite and poets experimented with this form extensively. The sonnet cycle, which is a series of sonnets that fit loosely together to form a story, was very popular during this period. The first of the great sonnet cycles was *Astrophel and Stella* by Sir Philip Sidney.

The pastoral was the preferred style during the Elizabethan Age. The pastoral describes an imaginary world of simple idealised rural life in which shepherds and shepherdesses fall in love and while away their time blissfully, singing songs and dancing. Spenser's *Shepherd's Calendar*, 'Colin Clouts Come Home Again' and *Astrophel* are all written in the pastoral style.

Elizabethan Prose

Prose took a back seat to poetry and drama in the Elizabethan Age. Latin was still the preferred language of the scholars and English prose had a distinct Latin flavour. Prose writers of this period used long words and ornate sentences which made their work difficult to comprehend. Many of the prose works were influenced by Lyly's euphuism and Sidney's arcadianism, which is to say that they were marked by the characteristics of poetic prose. The prose of this period was decorative rather than simple and clear.

Romances

The publication of Lyly's *Euphues* in 1578 is an important milestone in the history of British prose, as it discovered the presence of the reader of fiction. The fiction-reading public had come into existence, or was at least ready to do so. A large part of the readership was composed of women. Fiction, mainly in the form of romances dealing with fighting and love, became popular. Sidney's *Arcadia,* published after his death, was a very influential book. Thomas Nashe's *The Unfortunate Traveller* (1594) is about a travelling hero. Although it is not a novel, it contains the elements of the novel as a literary genre. Two other romances deserve mention as Shakespeare made plays out of them—Robert Greene's *Pandosto* (1588) which became *The Winter's Tale* and Thomas Lodge's *Rosalynde* (1590) which became *As You Like It.*

Travel Writing

Writing about travel, exploration and discovery was very popular during this period. The spirit of the Renaissance drove men across the seas in search of new lands. Most of the earliest accounts of English discovery and exploration were collected and published by Richard Hakluyt in his *Principal Navigation, Voyages, and Discoveries of the English Nation* (1589–1600) and by Samuel Purchas in *Purchas his Pilgrimes* (1625). Both the books contain fascinating accounts of the experiences of sailors.

Literary Criticism

Literary criticism forms a major branch of Elizabethan prose. Most of the work belonging to this period was based on the ideas of European writers who were in turn inspired by the ancients. As a result, there was a great chasm between the literary criticism and the literature that was produced during that period. The critics did not try to adapt their views to the unique features of contemporary English literature.

One of the main issues that occupied the minds of the learned was the question of morality in literature. Stephen Gosson in his book *The School of Abuse* (1579) attacked all secular literature for propagating lies. It was in reply to this attack that Sidney wrote his *An Apology for Poetry.* In it, he defends the poet and hails him as the first lawgiver and ranks him higher than the philosopher and the historian. At the same time, he finds fault with contemporary writings, including his own, and praises classical literature. When one examines his *Arcadia,* one is able to see the contradiction between his creation and his criticism. This was the case with all the other writers as well. When they wrote as critics, they recommended the rules of the classicists, but did not follow them in their own works. Even Ben Jonson was guilty of this.

John Lyly (1554–1606)

Euphues, The Anatomy of Wit (1579)
Euphues and his England (1580)
Alexander, Campaspe and Diogenes (1584)
Sapho and Phao (1584)
Gallathea (1587)
Endymion (1591)
Midas (1592)
Mother Bombie (1594)
The Woman in the Moon (1597)
Love's Metamorphosis (1601)

Life

He was born in Canterbury and had his education in Oxford. He was involved in politics and became a member of parliament several times. While in Oxford, he wrote his first play *Euphues*, which made him famous.

Works

PROSE

Euphues, Lyly's novel, has two parts—*Euphues, The Anatomy of Wit* and *Euphues and his England. Euphues* is an important part of courtly fiction that was widely read by the women of the sixteenth century. The first part begins in Naples and describes the love and courtship between the heroine Lucilla and the two suitors, Euphues and Philautus. The novel consists of a number of letters written by Euphues, that satirise the fickle nature of women.

In the second book, Euphues and Philautus come to England. There is a very flattering description of England in this book. *Euphues* is a book with a very slim storyline, but it is full of advice. Its importance lies in the fact that it has given to the English language the new word 'euphuism'. This comes from the affected and artificial style in which the two parts of the novel have been written. Lyly uses a lot of odd conceits and very long and complex sentences. This style of writing prose which came to be known as 'euphuism' had a great impact upon the Elizabethan prose writers. They tried to use decorative language in their work in order to make it as artistic as poetry. In Lyly's work, sentences are arranged in antithetically balanced clauses and parallelisms. There is extensive use of alliteration and wordplay. The comparisons and similes involving mythology and natural history and the use of proverbs make reading difficult.

DRAMA

His important plays include *Alexander and Campaspe*, *Sapho and Phao*, *Endymion* and *Midas*. They dealt with idealised love and reflected the typical attitude of the Elizabethan courtier. The emphasis was on style, song and witty dialogue. These plays would later influence Shakespeare's romantic comedies.

Features

- His plays were written in prose intermingled with verse. They were mythological and were almost like masques.
- His plays are all comedies and follow the classical structure. His plots, however, are romantic and violate the unities of time and place.
- His characters not only speak in a gentlemanly way, but also behave in a tender and magnanimous manner. In this, his works could be seen as moral comedies.

George Peele (1556–96)

The Arraignment of Paris (1584)
The Honour of the Garter (1593)
The Fall of Troy (1589)
The Battle of Alacazar (1594)
Farewell to Norris and Drake (1589)
The Old Wives' Tale (1595)
The Hunting of Cupid (1591)
The Love of King David and Fair Bathsheba (1599)
Edward I (1593)

Life

He was born in 1556 and educated at Christ's Hospital between 1565–70. Later he studied at Broadgate Hall, now renamed Pembroke College, Oxford.

After completing his education, he went to London and joined Marlowe, Greene and Nash. Together, they tried to eke out a living through their plays. Peele was also an actor and a member of Lord Admiral's Company.

Works

His play *The Arraignment of Paris* is in the form of a pastoral or masque. It was a tribute to Queen Elizabeth and had some melodious passages. His work was predominantly courtly and patriotic. *Edward I* is a long chronicle play and is one of the first plays about English history. *The Old Wives' Tale* satirised popular contemporary drama that combined elements of fantasy and folklore. *David and Bathsheba* is a spiritual drama which contains several beautiful lines of blank verse.

Features

- Peele's writing has a poetic and lyrical quality which makes his plays elegant.
- He skilfully combined different genres such as the pastoral, the comic, the tragic and fantasy. His play *The Old Wives' Tale* is a good example of a blend of folklore and fantasy.
- He crafted well-defined characters that underwent transformations.
- His works occasionally addressed issues of his time.
- His work was predominantly courtly and patriotic.

Robert Greene (1558?–92)

Prose
Mamillia (1580?)
Pandosto (1588)
Menaphon (1589)
Drama
Alphonsus, King of Aragon (1587?)
Friar Bacon and Friar Bungay (1589)
Orlando Furioso (1591)
The Scottish History of James the Fourth (1592)

Life

Born in Norwich, he studied at Cambridge and later at Oxford. He wrote his first work *Mamillia* while at Cambridge and this made him well-known. He was short-tempered and jealous and therefore quarrelled easily with his friends. He is remembered chiefly today for his pamphlet *Groat's Worth of Wit* in which he attacked Shakespeare and referred to him as an 'upstart crow'.

He married the daughter of a rich man, spent all her money and left her and his child after a year. He died after a few more years of riotous living in a poor shoemaker's house, owing him money.

Works

He began his literary career as a storyteller and prose writer. *Mamillia,* his first prose work, contains a number of adventurous and romantic stories and became an instant success. This work reveals his quiet wit and powerful imagination. His next work *Pandosto* was the inspiration for Shakespeare's *The Winter's Tale.*

Inspired by Marlowe's *Tamburlaine,* Greene wrote *Alphonsus, King of Aragon. Friar Bacon and Friar Bungay* is his best drama and gives a good representation of Elizabethan life. *Orlando Furioso* is a dramatisation of a part of Aristo's famous romance of the same name. The play is a strange blend of adventure and comedy where Greene portrays scenes that depict Orlando's insanity as comic. It is written in skilful iambic pentameter lines that alters to prose for the scenes depicting Orlando's insanity. The play contains traces of satire, too, when Orlando's insanity is attributed to the fact that he is a poet. Greene's historical play *The Scottish History of James the Fourth* narrates the story of James IV who is married to the daughter of the king of England, but is in love with another woman. Greene portrays these two women very effectively.

Features

- Greene was a versatile playwright who wrote comedies, tragedies, romances and historical plays.
- He combined prose and poetry in his plays, adding depth and variety to his work.
- Greene was skilled at creating memorable and distinct characters who exhibited noticeable traits and quirks.
- He used humour and satire to entertain and comment on social norms and practices.
- Greene had a great eye for romance and this feature made him one of the important forerunners of Shakespeare.
- His plays, which reflect his deep insight into the human character, contributed to the development of drama. He had the skill of presenting a story in a lively manner.

Thomas Lodge (1558–1625) and Thomas Nashe (1567–1601)

The dramatic work of Lodge and Nashe is not rated very high. Thomas Nashe is remembered for his prose work, *The Unfortunate Traveller* which is important in the develwopment of the novel. Lodge's romance *Rosalynde: Euphues' Golden Legacie* was the inspiration for Shakespeare's *As You Like It.*

Thomas Kyd (1558–94)

The Spanish Tragedy (1592) *Cornelia* (1594)

Life

Very little is known about the life of Thomas Kyd. He was born in London and was educated at Merchant Taylor's School. He knew French, Italian, Spanish and Latin and did a lot of translations. He was imprisoned for some of his writings which were considered to be blasphemous.

Works

Kyd is one of the most well-known of the University Wits. He is famous for the 'blood and thunder' style that was popular in pre-Shakespearean drama. He is best remembered for his *The Spanish Tragedy* which closely adheres to the style of the Senecan revenge tragedy. (Seneca was a dramatist of Ancient Rome who wrote revenge tragedies.) It has a plot that involves murder and sudden death and is a forerunner of the great tragedies of Shakespeare. It is the story of a nobleman's revenge for his murdered son. Kyd made use of classical elements such as a ghost, a lot of bloodshed and violence, a chorus, a lofty poetic style and the division of the play into five acts. This play was a remarkable improvement from earlier drama and occupies an important place in the development of English drama. It was this play that influenced Shakespeare when he wrote his *Hamlet*.

The only other play that is attributed to Kyd is *Cornelia* which is a translation from French.

Features

- He popularised the Senecan revenge tradition in contemporary drama through his play *The Spanish Tragedy.*
- He used blank verse in *The Spanish Tragedy* and helped to establish this poetic form as the norm for English tragedy. Kyd created a new style by fusing classical tragedy with the crude popular drama of his day.
- Kyd was one of the pioneers of characterisation in drama. His characters often display a variety of emotions reflecting their inner turmoil. His characters are shown grappling with moral dilemmas and questions of integrity.
- His plays contain soliloquies, a narrative device that would be used often by Shakespeare.

Christopher Marlowe (1564–93)

Drama

Tamburlaine the Great (two parts, 1587)
The Tragical History of the Life and Death of Doctor Faustus (1588?)
The Jew of Malta (1589)
Edward II (1593?)
The Massacre of Paris (1593)
The Tragedy of Dido (written with Nashe, 1593)

Poetry

Hero and Leander (1598)

Life

He was born in Canterbury to a shoemaker. After spending his childhood at Canterbury, he went to Cambridge and got his degree in 1583. After leaving the university, he went to London and began his literary career. During the six years that he spent in London, he wrote his poem *Hero and Leander* and his plays.

Even while Marlowe was busy with writing, he became involved in political and religious controversies. He befriended all kinds of infamous people and he fell into disrepute. Before he could be arrested, he got involved in a drunken brawl in a tavern and was stabbed to death. He was just twenty-nine and, in his death, the world lost a great dramatist who might have eclipsed even Shakespeare.

Works

Tamburlaine the Great, written in two parts, was his first play. Marlowe endows his hero with the spirit of the Renaissance, by making him a superhero whose quest for power is limitless. It is the story of a Scythian shepherd-robber who becomes an awe-inspiring conqueror called Tamburlaine. His ambition makes him cruel to all those who come in his way. He wins the crown of Persia and Turkey and marries the princess of Egypt, Zenocrate. The second part of the play continues the story of his magnificent conquests. When Zenocrate dies, Tamburlaine is shattered and later dies of a mysterious illness.

Doctor Faustus is about an ambitious young German scholar. His thirst for knowledge is so great that he turns to magic after going through all the other branches of learning. In a conflict between the good and evil angels over Faustus, the evil angel emerges successful. Faustus, through his magical powers, summons the evil devil Mephistopheles, who agrees to serve him for twenty-four years in exchange for Faustus's soul. Faustus spends the next twenty-four years, travelling throughout the world and enjoying himself thoroughly. At the end of the stipulated period, his conscience urges him to repent for his sins, but he is prevented from doing so by Mephistopheles. Faustus is now filled with terror at the prospect of being taken away to Lucifer. As the clock strikes the doomed hour, he cries out in anguish, but is carried away by the devils.

The Jew of Malta is about a greedy merchant called Barabas who hates Christians. His entire wealth is confiscated when he refuses to obey the decree of the governor of Malta. His house is converted into a Christian convent, but Barabas, who has buried a part of his wealth in its foundation, persuades his daughter to fetch it. He then takes revenge by killing the governor's son. He later tries to kill the governor and the other Christians. When his daughter, disgusted at her father's cruelty, goes back to the convent, Barabas kills everyone there including his daughter. The rest of the play is about his subsequent cruelty and deceits, till he perishes in a trap that he sets for the Turks.

Edward II is about the downfall of King Edward II due to his excessive fondness for Gaveston. There is a quarrel between the king and the nobles and Gaveston is executed. The queen too turns against the king and joins Mortimer, the king's enemy. Together, they drive the king out of the country. Mortimer becomes a tyrant and imprisons the king. Edward is tortured and killed in a cruel manner—in one of the most powerful scenes in English drama. The play ends when the young prince, who later takes the title Edward III, avenges his father's death by beheading Mortimer and imprisoning Isabella, the queen.

The last two plays of Marlowe are inferior pieces, and fragmentary.

His poem *Hero and Leander* narrates the tragic love story of the title characters. It has a lyrical beauty and freshness that exceeds a similar poem by Shakespeare, *Venus and Adonis*. The famous and oft-quoted line, 'Whoever loved that loved not at first sight', is from this poem by Marlowe.

Features

- Marlowe was responsible for taking drama from crude medievalism to poetic romanticism. He was the founder of the romantic tragedy that would be perfected later by Shakespeare. In his plays, the didactic purpose that was prominent in the old tragedies is absent. He transformed drama from a mere vehicle for moral lessons into a rich aesthetic experience.
- He raised the subject matter of tragedy by choosing heroes of great stature. Tamburlaine is a conqueror, Faustus is a highly learned scholar, Barabas is an extremely wealthy man and Edward II is a king. They were all, with the exception of Edward II, typical Renaissance men—eager to learn more and achieve greater heights.
- He created lifelike characters unlike the wooden characters of earlier drama. His heroes are all superhumans caught between conflicting emotions. His characters may appear exaggerated and unnatural but they are full of life. It was at

this time that the English had defeated the Spanish Armada and were giddy with the joy of victory. It was also the period of 'the Great Voyages of Discovery'. These heroes, therefore, were seen as representatives of the spirit of the age.

- He improved and perfected the blank verse so that it became the most popular metre for English drama. The blank verse of the classical school was hard and rigid. Marlowe developed it into a flexible poetic form for tragedy. In his hands, it became a medium for expressing varying emotions.
- Earlier English plays were formless in which a series of scenes were just strung together. In Marlowe's plays, there is a unity in the structure, which gives them coherence and clarity, especially his *Edward II*. The five-act structure of drama was perfected by Marlowe.
- His plays are highly poetic. They are full of rich similes and descriptions and he has given us several immortal lines such as the following from *Doctor Faustus*:

  Was this the face that launched a thousand ships
  And burnt the topless towers of Ilium?

  And the lines from *Edward II*

  But what are kings, when regiment is gone,
  But perfect shadows in a sunshine day?
- He made use of imagery from the classics, astronomy and geography which made Ben Jonson coin the phrase, 'Marlowe's mighty line' in reference to his writing style.
- All his plays revolved around a great hero. The rest of the characters paled before him. Marlowe did not bother much with his women characters.
- His plays were intensely tragic and unrelieved by any comic scenes. If at all there were comic scenes, as in *Doctor Faustus*, they were only a low type of buffoonery.

William Shakespeare (1564–1616)

Historical Plays
Richard III
Henry VI (early 1590s, in three parts)
Richard II (1595)
Henry IV (1597)
Henry V (1598)

Comedies
Love's Labour's Lost (1591)
Two Gentlemen of Verona (1591)
The Comedy of Errors (1592)
The Merchant of Venice (1594)
A Midsummer Night's Dream (1594–95)
The Taming of the Shrew (1595)
The Merry Wives of Windsor (1598)
Much Ado about Nothing (1599)
As You Like It (1600)
Twelfth Night (1600)

Tragedies
Romeo and Juliet (1592)
Julius Caesar (1601)
Hamlet (1602)
Othello (1604)
King Lear (1605)
Macbeth (1606)
Antony and Cleopatra (1608)

Poetry
Venus and Adonis (1593)
Sonnets (1594?)

Life

Shakespeare is the greatest dramatist of England, but very little is known about his life. He was born at Stratford-on-Avon and had a little formal education at the local grammar school till he was twelve or thirteen years old. When he was eighteen, he entered into a hasty marriage with Anne Hathaway and had three children. Soon, he left for London and very little is known about his early struggle there.

At that time, London was sparkling with the plays of the University Wits. The theatre was the centre of attraction and was truly national. There was a constant demand for new plays and stories, for the Elizabethan audience's thirst for entertainment could not be easily satisfied. Into this scene, Shakespeare arrived with nothing but his natural genius. He had not studied at Oxford or Cambridge and had no profound knowledge of the classical languages. He did not boast of possessing any theory of drama or poetry. His only desire was to capture the interest of the audience.

It is believed that he began his career at the theatre as a stable-boy and as an actor. From these humble beginnings, he rose to become the greatest playwright of all time. This was because he had a talent that was flexible and which could easily be adapted to different styles and genres. He also had an instinctive knowledge of what the audience desired and he wrote for them. For example, soon after England defeated the Spanish Armada, Shakespeare realised that patriotism was the predominant emotion. He quickly read *The Chronicles* and produced his historical plays that were so popular.

He was quick to learn from the University Wits who were writing plays at that time. He was inspired by Lyly's witty dialogues, Kyd and Marlowe's tragedies, and Greene's lively style. Soon he became the most popular dramatist and there was a constant demand for his plays. He performed frequently before Queen Elizabeth who enjoyed his plays greatly.

At about that time, people began to be concerned about dramatic laws and theories. After the publication of Sidney's *Defence of Poesie* in 1595, the learned section of the public was concerned about the classical rules of drama such as the three unities and dramatic decorum. Ben Jonson, who followed the classical rules, began to write his plays which were very different from those of Shakespeare's. Shakespeare was aware of all this, but he dismissed it and continued to write for popular enjoyment. Critics soon divided the playwrights into two classes—those who wrote free drama and the classicists. Shakespeare was the master of free drama and Ben Jonson, of classical drama.

At the young age of fifty-two, Shakespeare's health began to fail and he died in 1616. He was buried in Stratford Church.

Works

DRAMA

Since Shakespeare's plays were not published until seven years after his death, we do not know the chronological order of their composition. The only way in which his plays could be classified and studied is by dividing them into four periods. As we examine the various plays, we can easily see the growth and development of the great dramatist.

The first period of Shakespeare's literary career was between 1590 and 1594 when Shakespeare rose rapidly in the realm of

British drama. During this period, he wrote historical plays, a revenge tragedy and several light comedies. Some of the features of his early works include an inclination to follow closely the sources of his plays and to give more importance to plot and incident over character. Even his language tended to be more flowery in his early plays. But one can discern the versatility of the playwright even at this early stage.

The historical plays include the three parts of *Henry VI*, *Richard III*, and *King John*. The three parts of *Henry VI* give us a dramatic account of the Wars of the Roses. Shakespeare combined his poetic talent with his gift of storytelling. *Richard III* is a play that depicts the evil character of Richard who murdered his brother and his two young nephews in order to gain the crown for himself. This play is based on Holinshed's *Chronicles*. The influence of the cruel conqueror of Marlowe's *Tamburlaine* can be seen in *Richard III*.

Shakespeare was quick to recognise the popularity of tragedy among the audience when the plays of Kyd and Marlowe triumphed. He gave to the world of drama his own revenge tragedy, *Titus Andronicus*. This is a coarse and ill-constructed melodrama that obviously belonged to the early experimental period of Shakespeare's career.

Shakespeare next realised that he had a great potential for comedy. Inspired by Lyly's witty dialogues, Shakespeare produced his *Love's Labour's Lost*, which appealed to the cultured and learned. Simultaneously, he adapted a play by Plautus to provoke loud laughter from the less learned audiences. This was his *The Comedy of Errors*. *The Two Gentlemen of Verona* was his first romantic comedy inspired by Greene's work. *The Taming of the Shrew* also belongs to the early period. In these plays, we see the verse-medium gradually blossoming into the beautiful and graceful blank verse for which Shakespeare is so famous.

The second period of his works was between 1595 and 1600. By the time Shakespeare wrote his *A Midsummer Night's Dream*, *The Merchant of Venice*, *Much Ado About Nothing*, *As You Like It*, *The Merry Wives of Windsor* and *Twelfth Night*, the influence of Lyly and Greene had become dim. He had mastered the art of plot construction. Instead of a number of episodes being loosely strung together, we have a well-unified plot. This was a period of rapid growth and development, when Shakespeare displays a marked increase in his understanding of human nature and behaviour. We have immortal characters such as Puck, Viola, Jaques and Malvolio in these plays. These plays are some of his best romantic comedies, a type of comedy developed by Elizabethan dramatists and perfected by Shakespeare. It narrates a love story in which the heroine is both beautiful and virtuous and who sometimes disguises herself as a man. This love is crossed by several difficulties and hardships but finally ends happily. It is easy to see that all the above-mentioned plays of Shakespeare fit beautifully into this pattern.

His later historical plays such as *Richard II*, the two parts of *Henry IV*, and *Henry V* reveal a critical genius who did not owe anybody anything. These are among the most powerful creations in the genre of historical drama and are memorable for the immortal characters Falstaff, Prince Hal and Richard II. These plays are partly based on Holinshed's *Chronicles* and partly on the plays by lesser-known dramatists.

Romeo and Juliet is a romantic tragedy based on a poem by Arthur Brooke. It is a lyrical and beautiful tragedy that is both youthful and intense. We do not find the gloom of his later tragedies in this play. Juliet's nurse and Mercutio are two of the liveliest and comic characters in Shakespeare's works.

Julius Caesar is the first of his three Roman plays. The main idea for the play was taken from North's translation of *Lives* by the ancient Greek biographer Plutarch, but the greatness of the play is entirely due to the creative genius of Shakespeare. The magnificent language, the grand scenes and memorable characters have all contributed to the evergreen popularity of the play.

The third period of Shakespeare's works was between 1601 and 1608. This was the period of his great tragedies. There is a seriousness in his work that reveals an intense mind. Even the two comedies that are believed to belong to this period, *All's Well That Ends Well* and *Measure for Measure,* are more depressing than amusing. The cause for this gloom is unknown, but his four major tragedies, *Hamlet, Othello, King Lear* and *Macbeth*, mark the full maturity of his genius. The plays of this period show his great fluency with words and the blank verse too is at its best.

The two comedies, *All's Well That Ends Well* and *Measure for Measure* have little of the gaiety and romance of his earlier romantic comedies. Shakespeare seems more intent on focusing, in an ironic and cynical manner, on the imperfections of his contemporaries.

With *Coriolanus* and *Antony and Cleopatra,* the Roman trilogy is complete. Both these plays are once again partly based on Plutarch's *Lives.* Although the gloomy mood persists, we witness, especially in *Antony and Cleopatra,* the magnificence of Shakespeare's versification and diction. The final scenes, in which Antony and Cleopatra meet their destruction, are some of the most powerful scenes to be ever written in the history of drama. In *Coriolanus*, Shakespeare puts before the audience, the eternal conflict between personal popularity and political success, public interest and private life.

His four great tragedies belong to this period. *Hamlet*, the most discussed play of Shakespeare, has complex characters and a complicated plot. The inner conflicts of Hamlet's troubled mind are revealed in the eloquent soliloquies like the one which begins 'To be or not to be…'.

Othello is a great tragedy based on the shortcomings and follies that are common to the ordinary human being. Of the four great tragedies, *Othello* is the simplest and the most direct. In Iago, we meet the typical evil-minded villain who, unable to bear the success and happiness of his friends, plans their destruction.

King Lear, partly based on the *Chronicles* and partly on Sidney's *Arcadia*, is a powerful tragedy. In this play, Shakespeare's tragic view of humanity is revealed when the characters realise their mistakes only when it becomes too late to prevent their destruction. *Macbeth* is a tragedy in which Shakespeare explores man's troubled conscience when faced with evil deeds. It is the shortest of Shakespeare's plays. In it, the supernatural element plays an important part. Ambition and a blind belief in the supernatural drive Macbeth and his wife, Lady Macbeth, to their doom.

George Sampson, in his *The Concise Cambridge History of English Literature*, calls *Troilus and Cressida* 'a history without dignity, a comedy without laughter and tragedy without tears, but we are bound to admit that it is a masterpiece of its kind'. As a tragedy, it is neither noble nor stirring. In stature, it falls much lower than Shakespeare's great tragedies.

To the last, fourth period (1609–13), belongs a history play *Henry VIII*, the romance *Pericles* and the three comedies, *Cymbeline, The Winter's Tale* and *The Tempest*. His last history play *Henry VIII* is loosely constructed. It narrates the eventful history of Queen Elizabeth's father, Henry VIII, and England's break with the Roman Catholic Church. Scholars often debate over the authorship of *Pericles* as it has many odd patches. In it, we see a strange mixture of Shakespeare's earlier and later styles of writing. The three comedies are ranked very high for their poetic diction. These plays, however, are improbable and removed from reality, perhaps to suit the changing trends in theatrical fashions. *The Tempest* is clearly his swansong, where Shakespeare seems to be bidding farewell to his audience. In the symbolic breaking of the staff and the burial of the book by Prospero, we see Shakespeare's own leave-taking after a busy career as a dramatist.

POETRY

Venus and Adonis is famous for its voluptuous imagery and its wit. Published three years after the first three books of *The Fareie Queene*, it is a typical love poem of that period. Based on Ovid's *Metamorphoses* (a collection of stories in verse), it narrates the tragic love story of the goddess Venus and the mortal Adonis.

The Rape of Lucrece, again inspired by Ovid's *Metamorphoses*, is about Lucretia, the virtuous wife of a Roman nobleman. This poem is written in seven-line stanzas with the rhyme scheme *ababbcc*, known as rhyme royal. As a poem, it is inferior to *Venus and Adonis*. Both these works were dedicated to the Earl of Southampton, Shakespeare's patron.

In the Elizabethan age, it was very fashionable to write **sonnets** and sonnet sequences. Shakespeare wrote 154 sonnets that have a form of their own, known as the English or the Shakespearean sonnet. The Shakespearean sonnet has three quatrains and a final rhyming couplet. The rhyme scheme is *abab cdcd efef gg*. The sonnet was at the height of its popularity at that time, with poets like Drayton, Spenser and Sidney writing several sonnets. Shakespeare's sonnets reveal a greater maturity of mind when compared to his earlier poetical works, *Venus and Adonis* and *The Rape of Lucrece*. Scholars have been trying to learn about Shakespeare's life through these sonnets. However, they have not arrived at any conclusion regarding his personal life. It is not clear whether they are a reflection of his personal experiences or just the poetical imagination of an artist. The various studies only indicate that the first 126 sonnets were addressed to a young nobleman and that the next twenty-six were addressed to a dark-haired woman known as the 'dark lady'. The authorship of the last two sonnets seems doubtful as they seem unrelated to the rest of the sonnets.

These poetical works of Shakespeare are some of the finest lyrical pieces to be written during his time. In these poems, we note Shakespeare's deep understanding of human emotions and his genius in transforming them into lyrical expressions.

Features

- Shakespeare was a versatile genius who excelled in a wide range of genres like tragedy, comedy, romance, historical drama and poetry.
- His command over language is unparalleled and the English language is indebted to him for several words. He used nouns as verbs for dramatic effect as for example, in *Richard II* we have Mowbray saying '…you have enjailed my tongue…'. According to the Oxford Dictionary, more than two thousand words were coined by Shakespeare. Apart from expanding English vocabulary, he has also contributed several idioms and phrases that are in common use today. For example, 'good riddance', 'breaking the ice', 'dead as a door nail', and 'hob-nob', to mention just a few.
- He created immortal characters who have served as prototypes for centuries to come: Romeo and Juliet as the eternal lovers, Iago as the greatest villain and Hamlet and

King Lear as two of the most tragic heroes drama has ever produced.

- Shakespeare was a master in understanding human nature and presenting different facets of it on the stage. In his plays, we see love, jealousy, ambition, betrayal and power.
- His soliloquies are another interesting feature of his plays. These soliloquies offer insights into the minds of complex characters.
- Shakespeare's plays are known for their use of dramatic irony, in which the audience is in knowledge of something that the characters are ignorant of. *Othello*, especially, abounds in dramatic irony when Othello addresses the evil Iago as 'honest Iago'.
- Shakespeare's plays reflect the society of his time. For example, the unpopularity of the Puritans at that time is seen in the play *Twelfth Night*, in which the Puritanical Malvolio is ragged by the fun-loving Sir Toby and his friends.
- His plays are timeless as the themes are still pertinent in the twenty-first century. Audiences belonging to different backgrounds are still able to identify with the characters and the themes.

Ben Jonson (1572?–1637)

Comedy
Every Man in His Humour (1598)
Every Man Out of His Humour (1599)
Cynthia's Revels (1600)
The Poetaster (1601)
Volpone or The Fox (1605)
Epicoene or The Silent Woman (1609)
The Alchemist (1610)
Bartholomew Fair (1614)
The Devil is an Ass (1616)
Staple of News (1625)
The New Inn (1629)
Eastward Ho (with Chapman and Marston, 1604)

Masque
The Satyr (1603)
The Pirates (1603)
Blackness (1605)
Oberon, The Fairy Prince (1611)
The Masque of Beauty (1608)
The Masque of Queens (1609)

Historical Tragedy
Sejanus (1603)
Catiline (1611)

Life

He was born at Westminster, one month after the death of his father. He studied in Westminster School, after which he became an apprentice in his stepfather's trade of bricklaying. Unsatisfied with this trade, Jonson enlisted as a private soldier. He returned to London when he was about twenty years old and got married. It was at this stage, that he took to acting and writing plays. Though he was unsuccessful initially, he later became popular for his masques during the reign of James I. Jonson was made poet to the king and he was a well-known figure in the literary world. He presided over the literary men of his day at his favourite haunt, the Mermaid Tavern.

He died in 1637 and was buried in Westminster Abbey. Over the bas-relief placed on the wall to mark his grave are written the words, 'O Rare Ben Jonson'.

Works

Jonson, through his plays, raised the status of drama and made it a part of serious literature. He was a classical scholar who had read a lot of Greek and Latin and was impatient with the errors committed by the dramatists of his age, including Shakespeare. Yet for all his scholarship, his plays leave us cold. This is because, in him, intellect and emotion did not fuse together into a passionate whole as it did in Shakespeare. His art was shadowed by his enormous intellect.

Ben Jonson wrote tragedies, comedies, masques and farces. In all his writings, he revealed himself as a classicist. He was against the prevalent style of writing of his time and believed that only the discipline of the classics could control the romantic exuberance of Elizabethan literature. For him, literature's primary duty was to instruct the people. He was against the themes and conventions of contemporary drama. He considered himself as a reformer of the stage and aimed at raising it both artistically and morally. Therefore, there is a didactic strain in all his writings.

Since Jonson admired the classics, he did not mix up the various genres. His work can therefore be neatly divided into comedies, tragedies and masques.

EARLY COMEDIES

Jonson set off to write his comedies in the satirical, realistic tradition of classical drama. It was his wish to reform the drama of his times. According to Jonson, the function of comedy was to reform human foibles by ridiculing them on the stage. He was interested in creating characters and in this, his contribution to drama is very important because he introduced the **Comedy of Humours**. This is a type of drama that portrayed individuals as being dominated by one distinguishing character. It was based upon the ancient physiological theory of the four humours which were considered to be the four primary fluids that the body was made up of—blood, phlegm, yellow bile and black bile. An imbalance of these was believed to produce four kinds of dispositions—sanguine, phlegmatic, choleric and melancholic. Jonson's plays are filled with characters that have one such predominant humour which makes them peculiar and eccentric.

Jonson's early comedies include *Every Man in His Humour*, *Every Man out of His Humour*, *Cynthia's Revels* and *The Poetasters*. These reveal his great skill as a dramatist. In them, his plot construction, humour and wit are at their sparkling best.

Every Man in His Humour is an Italian comedy set in Florence. It presents a battle of wits between a father and son. Jonson makes use of the stage to critically analyse contemporary British society. This play is remembered for its unforgettable characters: Bobadill, Knowall and Wellbred. The play was received very well by the public, as they could recognise the insincerities of their time being reflected in it.

Every Man Out of His Humour is again a satiric comedy in which ten to twelve characters' follies are exhibited in the first four acts. In the final act, each character is kicked 'out of his humour' to be a more normal person. The play is contrived and the dramatist's moral aim is too obvious.

Cynthia's Revels is a tribute to Queen Elizabeth. In it, Jonson projects himself in the character of Criticus, who is always right and who is highly extolled by the Queen. People laughed at Jonson's self-importance and for a while there was a war of the theatres in which John Marston satirised Jonson. Jonson retaliated through his next play *The Poetaster.* This play is set in Rome during the reign of Augustus. It is about the great poets of that age and their patrons. Jonson identifies himself with the great poet Horace and satirises Marston as the poetaster. Soon Dekker, another contemporary dramatist, replied to this with his play *Satiromastix, or The Untrussing of the Humorous Poet.* Dekker's play was very popular and Jonson decided to withdraw from this stage war and began writing his tragedies.

HISTORICAL TRAGEDIES

His two important historical tragedies are *Sejanus* and *Catiline.* Here Jonson followed the rules of classical drama strictly, making his plays rigid and dull. In attempting to follow the three unities of time, place and action, and in trying to avoid the mingling of the tragic and the comic, Jonson was able to create only pedantic plays. They were full of information and revealed his learning and scholarship, but, artistically, they were not successful.

MIDDLE COMEDIES

In this category, we may place *Volpone or The Fox*, *Epicoene, or The Silent Woman*, *The Alchemist* and *Bartholomew Fair.* These represent his best works. The dialogues are realistic and natural, the plots are well executed and the satire is more maturely handled.

Volpone, which is supposed to be set in Venice, is entirely English in treatment. Jonson makes use of the beast fable here, to bring out his characters' unique personalities. The chief villain is the fox (Volpone) who is assisted by the fly (Mosca). The other characters are all birds of prey—crow, vulture and raven. The play brings out the most contemptible qualities of human beings in a satirical and cynical manner.

The Silent Woman is a light comedy, almost farcical at times. It is about an old man, Morose, who cannot tolerate noise. His nephew plays a trick on him by making him marry a boy dressed up as a woman who is supposed to be very silent. After the wedding, Morose discovers that his 'wife' is not only very noisy, but also a boy.

The Alchemist is another comedy that deals with trickery. This play is set in London during the plague of 1610. In it, Jonson presents knaves, a law clerk, a merchant, a pleasure-loving knight, puritan preachers and a rich young man and his sister. *The Alchemist* and *Volpone* are in blank verse, while *The Silent Woman* is in prose.

Bartholomew Fair gives us yet another view of London—this time of the lower classes at Smithfield. The vices and characters are, however, the same here too, although they are more in number. Structurally, it is inferior to the earlier comedies, but the satire and wit are powerful and brilliant.

LATER COMEDIES

There is a gradual decline in his later comedies, *The Devil is an Ass*, *The Staple of News* and *The New Inn*. These have a romantic charm, but lack the constructive skill and wit of his earlier plays. Dryden called these plays 'mere dialogues'.

MASQUES

Jonson became interested in writing masques from 1610. Some of his famous masques are *The Masque of Beauty*, *The Masque of Queens* and *Oberon, the Fairy Prince*. These are full of folklore, classical imagery, colourful interludes and passages of exquisite imagination. Jonson made the form of the masque popular during the Jacobean times.

Features

- Unlike Marlowe and Shakespeare, Jonson turned to the classics for inspiration. He strongly believed in following the classical rules and style.
- Jonson was a reformer for whom the aim of drama was to instruct and teach. He could not tolerate vices like hypocrisy and insincerity and he attacked these violently through his satirical comedies.
- Ben Jonson was a very versatile writer. He could write tragedies, comedies, masques and farces. The scope of his genius was very wide. He could write in both blank verse and prose.

- Jonson's plays are well-known for their unique characters. He gave to English drama a new form of comedy based on the theory of humours. His insistence on the humours clashed with his attempt to be realistic, as the 'humorous' characters ended up being caricatures. His plays are full of 'types' such as the jealous husband, the cunning rich man or the anxious father.

Edmund Spenser (1552–99)

The Shepherd's Calendar (1579)
The Faerie Queene (Books I–III, 1590)
Complaints (1591)
Astrophel (1595)
'Colin Clout's Come Home Again' (1595)
Amoretti and *Epithalamion* (1595)
Prothalamion (1596)
The Faerie Queene (Books IV–VI, 1596)
Four Hymns (1596)

Life

Spenser was born in London to a journeyman cloth-maker. He had his schooling at Merchant Taylor's School and later went to Cambridge where he took his MA. While at Cambridge, he received a sound education in the classics and also developed strong anti-Catholic feelings. These proved to be strong influences which were later reflected in his poetry. He spent several years in government service in Ireland. Whenever he visited London, he spent his time with a group of extremely gifted writers including Walter Raleigh and Philip Sidney. They met regularly at the Mermaid Tavern, which was the centre of wit and literary grace.

In 1594, he married Elizabeth Boyle. Although he held many positions and was given a lot of land, it is generally believed that he died in poverty at the age of 47. He is buried in the Poet's Corner of Westminster Abbey.

Works

Spenser's place in the English poetic tradition is indisputable. He was the first modern poet to fully explore the poetic resources of the English language and took English poetry to new heights. He inspired later poets like Milton and Keats in different ways.

To Milton, he was England's first epic poet and Keats was inspiredby the high romance in his poetry.

Spenser combined in his poetry the diverse elements that were current in the Tudor period. It was a period of great change and transition. England was in the throes of two great movements that were transforming Western civilisation—the Renaissance and the Reformation. Latin, Italian and French were still considered superior to English. There was a clash of various ideologies, such as classical, medieval, humanist, Puritan, Protestant and Catholic. The urgent need of the hour was for a poet who could synthesise all these and at the same time, form a vital link to the last great British poet, Chaucer. Spenser was seen by his contemporaries as the 'New Poet' who could accomplish this mighty task. His poetry marks a culmination of all these ideas and a new beginning in English poetry.

The Shepherd's Calendar was his first major poem. It is a pastoral poem (a form popular during the Renaissance), and consists of twelve pastoral eclogues which are short poems about country life written as dialogues between shepherds. This work was inspired by classical poets like Virgil and Theocritus and is remarkable for its style. At a time when poets wrote ragged and crude rhymes, Spenser's poem came as an artistic surprise. He wrote with admirable ease although he experimented with rhyme and metre. There are as many as five different forms of stanzas in heroic or ten-syllabled lines. Technically, it was far ahead of its times and dealt with several older metres in a fresh and original manner. The twelve eclogues, representing the twelve months of the year, give an artistic unity to the poems. This was one of Spenser's achievements, as he was the first poet to link eclogues to form a harmonious whole. For the first time, an English poet seemed to triumph over his European rivals. The publication of this poem brought fame to Spenser.

The Faerie Queene was his masterpiece and though he worked at it for twenty years, he left it incomplete at his death. It is an allegory containing personifications of abstract ideas like faith, pride and hypocrisy. Spenser was deeply influenced by Chaucer and the two Italian poets, Ariosto and Tasso. The poem sets out, as he says in a letter to Sir Walter Raleigh, 'to fashion a gentleman … in virtuous and gentle discipline'. It is a long and complicated allegory planned in twelve books of which only six were completed. The main characters of each of the six books represents a certain virtue such as holiness, temperance, chastity, friendship, justice and courtesy. Many of the adventures begin at the court of Gloriana, the Faerie Queene (an idealised version of Elizabeth I). Twelve of her knights, who represent the different virtues, set out on their adventures. Apart from the moral allegory, there is also a political allegory depicting the conflict between Queen Elizabeth and Mary, Queen of Scots.

The narrative is descriptive and full of colour and beauty. Spenser makes use of archaic words and alliteration and revives the medieval age of chivalry in a romantic light. He makes use of a special stanza form which is now popularly known as the **Spenserian stanza**. This is a stanza of nine lines in which the first eight lines are written in pentameter (lines of ten syllables paired in five feet) and the ninth line is in hexameter (twelve syllables in six feet). The long line is known as the alexandrine because some of the early French poems on Alexander the Great were written in hexameters. The rhyme scheme is *ababbcbcc*. This form gives a musical effect to the whole poem.

Although he began his *Faerie Queene* in August 1580, he could not make much progress on it as he was appointed as secretary to the new governor of Ireland. His official life in Ireland kept him busy and affected his poetic output for nearly ten years. It was, therefore, only in 1589 that he completed the first three books of the poem and then the next three in 1596.

In the meanwhile, he wrote several minor poems which appeared in a volume entitled *Complaints: Containing Sundry Small Poems of the World's Vanity*. This volume reflects the growth of Spenser's style from his earliest beginnings to full maturity. The first poem in the book, 'The Ruins of Time', is an elegiac poem addressed to the Countess of Pembroke condoling her on the loss of several of her relatives, particularly her uncles who were the earls of Leicester and Warwick and her brother Sidney. It is written in slow-moving rhyme royal. The most important poem in *Complaints* is 'Mother Hubbard's Tale'. It is his only work written in heroic couplets. It is a satirical poem containing four tales of an evil fox and an ape. The satire works on four levels—agricultural, clerical, social and imperial. The third part gives us a detailed view of the typical Renaissance gentleman, which is an unlabelled character sketch of Sir Philip Sidney.

The next poem worthy of mentioning is 'Colin Clout's Come Home Again'. It is a pastoral poem in which Colin Clout, the shepherd (representing Spenser), meets the Shepherd of the Ocean (Sir Walter Raleigh) who takes him to the court of Cynthia (Queen Elizabeth). He is impressed by courtly life and pays rich compliments to the queen, her courtly poets and the ladies-in-waiting. This sense of joy is short-lived when he discovers the base jealousies and intrigues of the court. A disillusioned Colin escapes and returns to the simplicity of a shepherd's life. Spenser sustains the pastoral style in the poem admirably. The poem is also equally important as a poetic autobiography.

'Astrophel', printed in the same volume as 'Colin Clout's Come Home Again' is an elegy written to mourn the death of Philip Sidney. In this, Sidney is portrayed as a shepherd of Arcadia, wounded by a boar.

The next major work of Spenser is *Amoretti*, a sonnet sequence culminating in the 'Epithalamion' addressed to Elizabeth Boyle. These sonnets tell the story of the poet's wooing of a mistress, who at first spurns him but later accepts him. This is the only work where Spenser does not resort to allegory. Earlier in his career, Spenser had ignored the sonnet form. It was Sidney who first wrote a sonnet sequence *Astrophel and Stella* in 1591, long after Wyatt and Surrey introduced the sonnet to England. Inspired by Sidney, Spenser wrote his *Amoretti*. He altered the Petrarchan form of the sonnet to suit his own individual style. Spenser's sonnets are divided into three quatrains linked artistically by rhyme and ending in a rhyming couplet. (*abab bcbc cdcd ee*) They differ from Shakespeare's sonnets in both form and sentiment. Shakespeare's sonnets, too, contain three quatrains and a rhyming couplet, but there is no interlinking rhyme between the quatrains (*abab cdcd efef gg*). In content, there is a gloom pervading Shakespeare's sonnets as he talks about his mistress deceiving him with his friend. Spenser's sonnets, on the other hand, highlight the purity of love and trace the ups and downs of a lover's fortunes until his wedding day. The eighty-nine sonnets of *Amoretti* reveal the remarkable craftsmanship of Spenser.

The *Epithalamion*, which is the culminating poem of the sonnets, has no equal and is definitely one of Spenser's highest achievements. It is a lyrical poem in twenty-three stanzas that describes the wedding day of Spenser and Elizabeth Boyle. The splendid use of the refrain and the correct blending of English folklore, pagan mythology and Christian symbols reveal the original poetic genius of Spenser. The 'Epithalamion' reflects 'New Poetry' in all its lyrical complexity, hitherto unseen in English.

The *Prothalamion*, a wedding poem written to celebrate the double wedding of Lady Elizabeth and Lady Catherine, daughters of the Earl of Worcester, is equally brilliant in imagery and harmony. The haunting refrain, 'Sweet Thames, run softly, till I end my song' lends a special flavour to the poem.

In 1596, Spenser published his *Four Hymns*. The first two in honour of Love and Beauty, were written when he was young. The latter two, in honour of Heavenly Love and Heavenly Beauty, were written much later. These hymns were written in rhyme royal, which was most suitable to abstract themes. They have been a favourite subject of study for those interested in examining the influence of Plato on Spenser. There was a renewal of interest in Plato during the Renaissance and Spenser was exposed to a great deal of it during his days at Cambridge. According to the Platonic doctrine, one progressed from a specific embodiment of beauty to a contemplation of the idea of beauty for its own sake. This elevated approach to beauty was considered to be divine and a religious activity. In Spenser's time, writers blended medieval courtly love with Platonism and Christianity. Spenser had his own unique approach to it, which can be seen in *Four Hymns*.

Features

- Spenser was known as 'the poet's poet'. Poets in England during the early sixteenth century were busy trying to experiment with a great variety of lyric measures in order to restore to English poetry, the combination of flexibility and regularity which was present in Chaucer, but lost during the rapid shift in language from Middle English to Modern English. They were essentially craftsmen trying to hammer out a disciplined poetic style. It was at this time that Spenser's *The Shepherd's Calendar* with its wide variety of rhymes made a formal entry as 'the New Poetry'. There are five different forms of stanzas in heroic, or ten-syllabled, lines. The right tone is struck and there is an exact balance between diction and verse form. The style is most suitable to the subject matter and everything that is incongruous is avoided.

- In emphasising the importance of decorum, Spenser not only revealed the primary critical preoccupation of his age, but also exhibited his awareness of the urgent need of English poetry of that period. Decorum was, sadly, lacking in the majority of the early Tudor poets who chiefly used the poulter's measure. Spenser's work put an end to all this and served as a shining example for generations of poets.
- Spenser introduced a special stanza form in *The Faerie Queene* known as the Spenserian stanza. His alteration of the Petrarchan sonnet is well-known and the Spenserian sonnet became a model for several English poets.
- His *Faerie Queene*, although incomplete, proved to the world that an elaborate form like the epic could be written in the English language.

Sir Philip Sidney (1554–86)

Heroic prose romance
Arcadia (1590)
Sonnet sequence
Astrophel and Stella (1591)
Literary criticism
An Apologie for Poetrie (1595)

Life

Philip Sidney was born in 1554 in Kent. His father was Sir Henry Sidney who was the Lord Governor of Ireland. After studying in the famous Shrewsbury School, Sidney went to Christ Church, Oxford. He left Oxford without taking a degree. Through his uncle Robert Dudley, the Earl of Leicester, who was Queen Elizabeth's favourite, Sidney entered the court. He went on a three-year tour of the continent and absorbed a great deal of history. When he returned to England, he was an accomplished writer.

While visiting the Earl of Essex at Chartley Castle, Sidney fell in love with the Earl's twelve-year-old daughter, Penelope. Although this did not culminate in marriage, it inspired him to write a series of sonnets addressed to her. These became famous as *Astrophel and Stella*.

In 1586, while on an assignment in the Netherlands, he was wounded and died of injuries just before his thirty-second birthday.

Works

All his writing was done between the years 1578 and 1582. Although he became the most admired of all English writers during the hundred years after his death, none of his works were published during his lifetime.

Arcadia is a prose romance including poems and pastoral eclogues. It is a story of love and chivalry set in the ideal Arcadia. In this work, Sidney combined the pastoral and the chivalrous. The importance of *Arcadia* lies in its style and marks a well-defined stage in the history of the novel. Up to the time Sidney wrote *Arcadia*, writers imitated Lyly and his euphuism. Sidney invented a new style called 'arcadianism' in which romance was given a pastoral flavouring. Sidney made language most ornamental and sugary in this work. His images and metaphors were bold and original. He endowed life and feeling to inanimate objects. For example, cool wine seemed 'to laugh for joy' as it neared a lady's lips. It is the most poetic prose imaginable. It contains long sentences, with a lot of digressions. Sidney's *Arcadia* influenced a whole century of poets including Shakespeare and the Metaphysical poets.

He wrote *An Apologie for Poetrie* in 1580, but it was published only after his death as *The Defense of Poesie*. This is the first important work in the genre of literary criticism in English literature. In it, he defines poetry and classifies it into different categories such as pastoral, lyric, heroic, among others. After Horace and Longinus, there was no significant contribution to literary criticism until Sidney. Sidney's *Apologie* appeared at a very crucial period—the Elizabethan Age—when literature was manifesting itself in different genres: drama, poetry, prose and prose romance. There were several attacks on poets and their craft during that age. Sidney, in his work, defends them against such charges and gives to the art of poetry a dignity. Sidney defended poets from being called liars by pointing out that they never pretended to be giving factual information in the first place. 'The poet nothing affirmeth', he argued. He demonstrated the superiority of poetry over philosophy and history in the teaching of virtue. According to Sidney, the poet was the first lawgiver. The historian's influence was limited as he was chained to truth and the philosopher was obliged to be obscure and abstract. It was the poet who painted the ideal picture of the world. 'Nature never set forth the earth in so rich tapestry as diverse poets have done ... Her world is brazen, the poets only deliver golden.' While discussing English poetry, Sidney lamented that no noteworthy poetry was written after Chaucer. But he expressed confidence that significant literary work in every genre, including drama, could be written in the English language.

Astrophel and Stella is the first famous sonnet sequence in English. It contains 108 sonnets and eleven songs and is an important milestone in English Renaissance poetry. It narrates the tragic love of Astrophel ('the lover of a star' in Greek) for Stella ('star' in Latin). It is a very personal poem depicting Sidney's love for Penelope Devereux. In these sonnets, Sidney made use of the Petrarchan model which had been neglected in England since Surrey's time. The sonnets contain several metaphors and images and display a striking range of tone. Sidney was interested in experimenting with classical metres in England.

Features

- Writers of prose before Sidney were mostly imitators of Lyly and his euphuism. After Sidney's *Arcadia*, 'arcadianism' replaced euphuism for a while. Arcadianism is a mingling of the pastoral and the chivalrous. Sidney combines the fantasies of both these genres to narrate stories that are soaked in romance. In his prose, Sidney lends life and feeling to inanimate objects. This was later known as 'pathetic fallacy' by modern critics.

- Sidney's style was most ornamental. He made use of fine metaphors and exhibited the English language at its best. Shakespeare was influenced by Sidney's flowery style. There are some flaws in his style, however. Some of his sentences are long and clumsy. At times, his grammar is questionable. But one may excuse him when one remembers that the English language was still evolving in the sixteenth century.
- After Surrey and Wyatt, there was a lull in sonnetry. Sidney's *Astrophel and Stella* helped to revive it again. He made the sonnet sequence popular. After Sidney's *Astrophel and Stella*, there was a spurt of sonnet writing between the years 1591 to 1597. During that period about twenty sonnet collections appeared. Most of these were love sonnets. Sidney's sonnets were written in the strict Petrarchan form but displayed a wide range of tone, metaphor and imagery which had a great influence on his contemporaries. Other sonneteers who produced brilliant poems were Spenser and Shakespeare.
- Sidney's *An Apologie for Poetrie* is the first text in English to discuss the art of literature. The *Apologie* is an important milestone in the history of English literary criticism as it represents the popular critical principals of the Renaissance thinkers. In it, Sidney highlighted the weaknesses of contemporary writers and encouraged them to take their writing more seriously. He focused more attention on the deeper philosophical issues of literature rather than on its technical and external matters. His contribution to English literary criticism is significant.

Francis Bacon (1561–1626)

Essays (1597, 1613, 1625)
Advancement of Learning (1605)
Novum Organum (1620)
History of the Reign of King Henry VII (1622)
The New Atlantis (1626)

Life

Francis Bacon was born in London in 1561. His father was Sir Nicholas Bacon, Lord Keeper of the Great Seal. His mother, Anne Cooke, was deeply religious and possessed great knowledge of the classics. Bacon was influenced by his mother from a very early age.

He had his early education at home and then at Trinity College, Cambridge, and later studied law in London. He quickly rose in his career and became Lord Keeper of the Great Seal and Lord Chancellor of England. He was a great success as a lawyer, parliamentarian and politician. He became very wealthy and lived in a very grand and extravagant style. He was accused of taking bribes, found guilty and ordered to give up all offices of state. He spent the rest of his life in his country cstate where he concentrated on his writing and scientific experiments. One wintry day, Bacon got out of his carriage carrying a dead chicken to freeze it in the snow in order to test the preservative powers of the cold. This fact, which is common knowledge now, was unknown then. Bacon became ill due to the exposure to the cold and died in 1626.

Works

His works include philosophical and scientific writings such as the *Novum Organum* which will not be discussed here as it is in Latin. His important works in English are the *Essays, Advancement of Learning, History of the Reign of King Henry VII* and *New Atlantis.*

Bacon is chiefly remembered for his aphoristic essays. Bacon was the first Englishman to make use of the word 'essay' to describe a brief discourse in prose. He got this word from Montaigne, the French essayist. The root meaning of the word 'essay' is 'trial' or 'attempt'. Bacon's collection of essays grew over the years; by 1597, he had written ten; by 1613, thirty-nine and by 1625, fifty-eight.

While the French writer, Montaigne, is mainly concerned with his individual opinions in his essays, Bacon is concerned with the type of reader he is addressing. Bacon's essays are noted for their style and for their striking observations about life. They contain his personal reflections upon the men, manners and morals of his time. His pithy and witty advices reveal him as one of the finest prose stylists of English literature. Some of his famous aphorisms are: 'Reading maketh a full man, conference a ready man, and writing an exact man'; 'Knowledge is power'; and 'The world's a bubble and the life of man less than a span.'

Advancement of Learning is a philosophical treatise, which unlike most of Bacon's works, appeared in English, not Latin. It consists of two books. In the first book, he glorifies the dignity and benefit of learning. It states and answers the arguments that were presented against learning. In the second volume, he makes a detailed classification of all kinds of knowledge, pointing out the deficiencies of each branch. He is critical of learning which is based on the three branches of study—history, poetry and philosophy. He traces their relationship to the faculties of memory, imagination and reason. Instead, he advocates an education based on the scientific method of observation, skepticism and testability. This work was translated by Bacon into Latin in 1623.

Bacon wrote *History of the Reign of King Henry VII* in praise of the first Tudor sovereign and primarily to please King James I. Stylistically, it is a remarkable work where the narrative flows in an orderly manner.

New Atlantis is a treatise of political philosophy in the form of a fable. *New Atlantis* is essentially a utopia, in which Bacon outlines an 'ideal state'. It is an account of a visit to an imaginary island of Bensalem in the Pacific and a description of the social conditions prevailing there. In *New Atlantis*, Bacon continues the utopian tradition begun by Thomas More, although his views differ from those of More's. Whereas More gave importance to the social, Bacon focused on the intellectual improvement of the community. More advocated for the simplicity of life, whereas Bacon favoured external splendour. The main theme of *New Atlantis* is the pursuit of knowledge. Bacon was the first philosopher to suggest the improvement of society through science. Many of the scientific possibilities suggested by Bacon which appeared impossible at that time have become realities today. For example, 'Some Degrees of Flying in the Ayre...Ships and Boats for going under water....' In fact, his recommendation for a college of scientific research in *New Atlantis* led to the founding of the Royal Society.

Features

- Bacon disliked vain abstractions. He advocated the method of induction. That is, to collect facts and from there to arrive at a principle. The main feature of Bacon's philosophical position lay in the emphasis of the critical analysis of one's experience. When one recalls the superstitious nature of Bacon's contemporaries, one is able to understand how valuable Bacon's ideas are.
- Bacon was one of the first prose writers of his country. His essays are considered as classics that are studied by schoolchildren even today. They contain several maxims packed with practical wisdom. His name is almost synonymous with the aphoristic essay.

Seventeenth Century

1603–1714

After the death of Queen Elizabeth in 1603, the Tudor dynasty came to an end. It was followed by the Stuart dynasty consisting of James I, Charles I, Charles II, James II, William and Mary and Queen Anne. In this chapter, we will look at the important events of the seventeenth century under two headings—

- Early Stuarts, the Commonwealth and Protectorate (1603–60)
- Restoration (1660–1714)

EARLY STUARTS, THE COMMONWEALTH AND PROTECTORATE (1603–60)

James I (1603–25)
Charles I (1625–49)
The Commonwealth and Protectorate (1649–60)

After more than a hundred years of stable rule under the Tudors, a strong sense of patriotism and loyalty to the crown was developed in the English people. However, just forty years after Queen Elizabeth died, the English shocked the world by beheading their king and abolishing monarchy. When we study the history of early-seventeenth-century England, we are astounded by the fact that the Golden Age of Elizabeth, with its triumphant defeat of the Spanish Armada, should be so closely followed by a bloody civil war.

The political and religious grievances that eventually led to the English Civil War existed even during Elizabeth's reign. But

Elizabeth, with her brilliant diplomacy, had kept all grievances under control. Her Anglican Settlement, which took a middle course between Catholicism and Protestantism, left both the groups dissatisfied. Although the Puritans disapproved of her flamboyant court, they were prevented from showing their antagonism too openly. All this changed when James I ascended the throne.

The Catholics, the Protestants as well as the Puritans were disgruntled with James I as each sect expected some changes in their favour. The Roman Catholics had great expectations from him as he was the son of Mary, Queen of Scots, who was Catholic. The Protestants expected James to continue the Anglican Settlement of Elizabeth while the Puritans expected him to favour them as he was brought up in the Presbyterian Kirk (Church) of Scotland.

The hopes of all the sects were dashed when James initially swung towards the Catholics by revoking the fines against them. The resultant influx of Catholic clergy who had earlier fled from England, made him quickly reintroduce the fine. The Catholics showed their ire by plotting to blow up both Houses of Parliament in the infamous Gunpowder Plot.

The Puritans were disgruntled when James rejected the Millenary Petition signed by a thousand clergymen. This dissatisfaction led to the Puritans leaving England and setting sail to America, the New World, in search of religious freedom.

On the political side too, James was not popular as he firmly believed in the **Divine Right of Kings** (the belief that kings were directly appointed by God and thus not answerable to anyone but God). This led to a clash of opinions between him and the English Parliament.

When James I died in 1625, his son Charles I inherited all these problems along with the throne.

A civil war finally broke out in 1642 in which the nobles, the gentry and the king were on one side, known as the Royalists or the Cavaliers. The townsmen and yeomen who fought for the Parliament, were known as the Roundheads and were led by Oliver Cromwell. In 1645, Cromwell defeated the Cavaliers. The defeated king sought the help of the Scots to restore him to the throne. A second civil war followed in 1648, but was soon put down by the Parliamentary army. Charles I was tried and found guilty and executed on 1 January 1649. With the execution of Charles I, the Stuart line came to an abrupt end.

After the fall of monarchy, a new form of government called the Commonwealth led by Oliver Cromwell came into force. Calling himself the Lord Protector, he ruled as a dictator until his death in 1658. This period is therefore known as the Protectorate. During that time, all forms of entertainment were banned and the theatres were closed for eleven long years. Acts were passed against swearing, duelling, gambling, horse racing, cockfighting and bear-baiting. The Sabbath was strictly enforced. The army made surprise visits to houses and checked the kitchens for traces of any food which was forbidden during the Sabbath. All this made the English people hate the Protectorate. After Cromwell died, his son Richard succeeded him but he was unequal to the task of ruling a nation that was in a state of unrest. Charles II was invited to return to England and monarchy was reintroduced. Although Puritanism came to an end with the restoration of monarchy, its political aspects lived on in the politics of the Whig Party in England. In fact, the origin of political parties in England may be traced back to the Civil War. The supporters of the king, known as the Royalists, later came to be known as the Tories. The Tories are popularly known as the Conservatives today. The supporters of the Parliament, known as the Roundheads because of their closely-cropped haircuts, were later known as the Whigs and are known as the Liberals today.

❧❧

Jacobean Drama

Jacobean drama is the name given to the plays written during the reign of James I (in Latin, James is known as Jacobus). At the beginning of the seventeenth century, there was a new approach to life that came into being. James I, who ascended the throne in

1603, lacked the humanism of his predecessor, Elizabeth. With his firm belief in the theory of divine right, he was arrogant and prone to flattery. As a result, the theatre which was a meeting place for all classes in the Elizabethan Age slowly began to appeal only to the courtly classes. This meant that the audience now consisted of more learned people when compared to the earlier age.

The subject matter of the plays also underwent a change, reflecting the changing attitude and society of the seventeenth century. People had tired of the tales of intrigue that were sourced from Italian short stories and the patriotic themes drawn from Holinshed and, later, Plutarch. In the new era, there was a demand for foreign ideas of increased potency. Dramatists began to lean towards the declamatory themes and exaggerated sentiments of Spanish drama, the new plots of intrigue, crime and licentiousness of Italy and a revival of the revenge tragedy.

In fact, Jacobean tragedy is often considered to be synonymous with the **revenge tragedy**. Shakespeare's *Hamlet*, Middleton's *The Revenger's Tragedy*, Middleton and Rowley's *The Changeling* and Webster's *The White Devil* and *The Duchess of Malfi* are obsessed with revenge and reflect the political and sexual corruption that was rampant at the time. Dramatists used a brilliant, highly sophisticated and satirical language in their works. One witnessed bloodthirsty scenes, graveyards, ghosts and every kind of sensational horror in these plays. The dramatists seemed to compete with each other in presenting gorier methods of murder and torture. By the end of the play, the stage was strewn with several dead bodies. One could trace the origin of the Jacobean revenge tragedy to Seneca's tragedies which were popular during the Elizabethan Age.

Shakespeare's greatest tragedies and tragicomedies belong to this period. Ben Jonson continued to write in the early Jacobean Age. Some of the other prominent dramatists of this period were George Chapman, John Heywood, Thomas Dekker, Thomas Middleton, John Marston, John Webster, John Fletcher, Philip Massinger, Francis Beaumont and John Ford.

Jacobean Poetry

The poetry of the reigns of Elizabeth and James I is separated only for the sake of chronological convenience. Many poets such as Shakespeare, Drayton and Chapman, who had written when Elizabeth was alive, continued to do so in the reign of James I. There are, however, certain developments in poetry that caused a subtle change in the style and content. At the height of Elizabeth's reign, when people were charged up with ideas of growth, colonial expansion and patriotism, literature too reflected this exuberance. Poets like Sidney, Spenser and Shakespeare were excited with the newness of the developing poetic forms, such as the sonnet, and were flushed with the freshness of English vocabulary. There was little room for morality and religion except for the attempt made by Spenser in his *Faerie Queene.*

In the seventeenth century, poetry became much more serious in tone—more religious, didactic and intellectual. Three main groups of poets emerged during this period:

- Ben Jonson and the Cavalier Poets
- The Followers of Spenser
- Donne and the Metaphysical Poets

Ben Jonson and The Cavalier Poets

'Cavalier' is the name given to the supporters of Charles I in the civil war that took place in the mid-seventeenth century. It is derived from the Italian word for horseman or knight and therefore has overtones of courtly gallantry. Though not considered to be a major school of poetry, several Cavalier poems are still very popular today. Cavalier poetry more than any of the other arts, reflects the life and culture of upper-class English society. During the reign of Charles I, people belonging to the upper class were learned and theologically-oriented. The Cavaliers wrote in a higher, more elegant and artificial style than the Metaphysicals. Their poetry was eminently English and, at the same time, had strong classical leanings. They can be seen as the forerunners of the neoclassical poets of Queen Anne's age.

The tone adopted by the Cavalier poets was colloquial and cultivated. Thomas Carew, Richard Lovelace, Sir John Suckling, Robert Herrick, Edmund Waller and John Denham are some of the important Cavalier poets. Although they did not belong to any formal group, they were all followers of Ben Jonson. A majority of the Cavalier poets liked to call themselves the 'Sons of Ben' and were popularly known as the 'Tribe of Ben'. Jonson's influence on the Cavaliers was great. We can discern it in their urbanity of tone, control of emotion and overall carefulness of art. Ignoring the sonnet form, like Jonson, they preferred to write short and precise lines. Their poetry is known for an idiomatic diction and a courtly style. On the whole, they composed witty and polished lyrics of gallantry.

Ben Jonson, their ideal, though more well-known as a dramatist, had to his credit a considerable body of poetry. Satire and harshness were the hallmarks of his poetry. He had classical leanings and imitated the Greek poets. Unlike Spenser, he was not influenced by the British writers of the Middle Ages. Instead, he turned to the Greek and Latin classical writers. He admired the Latin love of form and morality. Ben Jonson could be considered the forerunner of the neoclassical style which would become predominant later in the seventeenth century.

Followers of Spenser

The preferred style of this school of poets was either the pastoral or the allegorical. They also favoured writing in the sonnet form. Among the followers of Spenser are George Wither, William Browne, Phineas Fletcher, Francis Quarles and William Drummond. There is a love for natural scenery in the works of these poets. They favoured poetic forms such as the lyric, the sonnet and the romance and they enjoyed writing in an artificial style. These poets had great veneration for the ancients and admired Ariosto, Tasso and other foreign religious writers. The influence of Spenser, however, began to gradually wane by the time Charles I ascended the throne.

Donne and the Metaphysical School

While the followers of Jonson embraced the classical and didactic style of writing and the Spenserians preferred the pastoral and the allegorical, Donne violently rejected conventional poetical forms. He wrote in a style that was opposed to the idealised concept of love that was popular with the Elizabethan poets. Donne and his followers, George Herbert, Henry Vaughan, Richard Crashaw, Andrew Marvell and Abraham Cowley are known as the 'Metaphysicals'—a name given to them by Dr Samuel Johnson in 1779 in his book *Lives of the Most Eminent English Poets* while discussing the life of Abraham Cowley. The name was taken by Johnson from Dryden's *Discourse on Satire* in which he said that Donne's poetry 'affects the metaphysics'. The word 'metaphysical' is derived from the Latin word *metaphysica*, a combination of two words 'meta' and 'physica'. The word 'meta' means 'beyond' or 'after' and 'physica' literally means 'work', but in this context may refer to anything having a concrete shape. According to R.S. Hillyer, 'Poetry, which deals with correlation between the real world and the after-world, concrete and abstract, soul and being, as well as reality and perception using philosophical methodology is called Metaphysical Poetry.' Donne is the chief exponent and pioneer of Metaphysical poetry. The features of metaphysical poetry are:

- There is a sharp rejection of the romantic and idealised view of sexual love which was popular during the Elizabethan Age. The Metaphysical poets revolted against chivalric love and artificial verses. When Donne began to write, Spenser was at the height of his fame. In spite of that, Donne revolted against the Petrarchan, pastoral and allegorical style that was favoured by Spenser.
- The Metaphysicals employed the rough give-and-take of everyday speech in their poems instead of the high poetical style of Spenser and the other Elizabethan poets. For example, 'For God's sake hold your tongue, and let me love…', 'Death be not proud, though some have called thee / Mighty and dreadful, for thou art not so'.

- The poems had a dramatic or rhetorical form or involved a heated debate with a coy mistress or an intruding friend.
- Wit is another important aspect of Metaphysical poetry. Passion, sentiment and sensuality were all given a lower status than wit. The ingenious use of paradox, puns and startling comparisons abound in this type of poetry. Metaphysical poetry is characterised by an unusual degree of intellectualism. Even in love poetry, the images and figures of speech are drawn from subjects such as law, medicine, astronomy and old legends.
- Yet another unique feature of Metaphysical poetry is the use of 'conceits' (an extended fanciful metaphor that makes a surprising or unexpected comparison). Dr Johnson in his *The Life of Cowley*, describes a conceit as a metaphor in which 'the most heterogeneous ideas are yoked by violence together'. Metaphysical poems often had shocking conceits in which very dissimilar objects were compared. In Donne's most famous conceit, he draws a parallel between his and his beloved's souls and the two legs of a geometric compass.
- Another interesting feature of Metaphysical poetry is the 'unification of sensibility'. It was T.S. Eliot who first coined the term 'unified sensibility'. According to him, unified sensibility is the fusion of thoughts and feelings. Usually, poets emphasised either intellect and reason or feelings and emotion. The separation of intellect and emotion is known as the dissociation of sensibility. For instance, in neoclassical literature emphasis was laid on intellect and emotion was pushed to the background. Metaphysical poets did not dissociate feeling from reason and tried their best to fuse the two elements.

Jacobean Prose

There were two main branches of English prose at the beginning of the seventeenth century—the religious and the secular. The Anglican Settlement of Queen Elizabeth had stirred a hornet's nest. Both the Catholics as well as the Puritans were not very happy with it and several pamphlets were published denouncing Anglicanism. It was at that time that **Richard Hooker** (1554?–1600) published his masterly work *Of the Laws of Ecclesiastical Politye*, in defence of the Anglicans. Apart from its important place in the contemporary religious controversy, it is considered to be a masterpiece of English prose. In it, Hooker praises Elizabeth for her via media approach to the religious question that was troubling England. His book is a brilliant example of a massive structure with a careful arrangement of ideas and lofty prose style. The style is highly Latinised, both in structure as well as vocabulary.

The most outstanding example of religious prose of the period is the *Authorised Version of the Bible* that was published in 1611. Fifty-four scholars were appointed by James I to work on the translation of the Bible. There were, of course, several translations of the Bible already, but the king and others disapproved of the interpretative comments printed in them. It was decided that the new translation would follow the most authoritative Hebrew and Greek texts available. The translators tried to keep the language as clear as possible while retaining the phraseology of the past. They rejected words that had become too archaic. The fifty-four clergymen worked in small groups, each translating a section of the scripture. A committee of bishops was appointed to provide the final review. This Bible was published seven years after it was commissioned.

The English Bible has been the most influential book in the world. Poets, novelists and dramatists have all been influenced by it. It is the most quoted text and for over 350 years, writers have imitated it and paraphrased it. Milton and Bunyan based most of their important works completely on it.

The Bible is responsible for shaping the English language as well. Phrases and words like 'loving kindness', 'tender mercy' and 'long suffering' are taken from it. Expressions such as 'casting pearls before swine' and 'waiting until the eleventh hour' originated from this source. When we refer to 'the wisdom of Solomon' and 'the patience of Job' we are quoting the Bible.

Even when the Bible was first published in 1611, its language was not modern. The English used in it was very similar to that used by William Tyndale more than seventy years earlier; in this period the English language had undergone much change. For example, in 1611 people were addressing each other as 'you', but the Bible kept the archaic 'thou' and 'thine'. The language, which sounds remote, lends it dignity and grandeur. The King James Bible stands with Shakespeare as an exemplar of the English language.

Parallel to religious prose, there grew a secular prose. Francis Bacon's work, for example, is far from theology and Christian morality. To him goes the credit of introducing the essay form to England. In his essays, he is preoccupied with the art of succeeding in life. His essays are full of pithy aphorisms that impart practical wisdom. Bacon's *Essays* is the first true English prose-classic.

One of the most popular essay-like forms of the seventeenth century was the **character**, a literary type modelled and named after the 'characters' of the Greek psychologist Theophrastus. A character is a short, usually witty sketch of a distinctive type of person. This form became popular in the early-seventeenth century when Theophrastus was translated, first into Latin in 1592, and then into English in 1616. Characters described an individual as having some moral characteristics which were responsible for their subsequent actions. Bishop Hall's *Characters of Virtues and Vices* (1608) is the first English book of characters. Sir Thomas Overbury's *Characters* (1614) is a collection written by him and some of his friends. Samuel Butler (1612–80), author of *Hudibras* also wrote characters.

There were several writers who were interested in scientific subjects. Some of them were Robert Burton, Sir Thomas Browne and Izaak Walton. Robert Burton was an eccentric humanist who combined the contemporary scientific interest with the pedantry of a long-established humanist methodology. His *The Anatomy of Melancholy* (1621) is modern in its scientific thrust, but medieval in its form. He makes a vast and systematic attempt to examine the subject of melancholy. In the first part, he gives us the definition, the causes, symptoms and nature of melancholy. In the second part, he discusses its cures and in the third, he offers special studies of the melancholies of religion and love.

George Chapman (1559–1634)

Comedies
The Blind Beggar of Alexandria (1596)
An Humorous Day's Mirth (1599)
All Fools (1605)
Monsieur D'Olive (1606)
Eastward Hoe! (with Jonson and Marston, 1605)
The Gentleman Usher (1606)
Monsieur D'Olive (1606)
May Day (1611)
The Widow's Tears (1612)

Translations
Seven books of the *Iliad* (1598)
Twelve books of the *Iliad* (1608)
The Whole Works of Homer, Prince of Poets (1616)
The Georgics of Hesiod (1618)

Tragedies
Bussy D'Ambois (1607)
The Conspiracy of Charles, Duke of Byron (1608)
The Tragedy of Byron (1608)
The Revenge of Bussy D'Ambois (1613)
Caesar and Pompey (1631)
The Tragedy of Chabot (1639)

Masque
The Memorable Masque (1613)

Poetry
Ovid's Banquet of Sense (1595)
Completed Christopher Marlowe's *Hero and Leander* (1598)
The Shadow of Night (1594)

Life

Chapman was born in Hertfordshire in 1559 and was educated at both Oxford and Cambridge. He joined a theatrical company and toured Germany. His learning was extensive and by 1598, he had written *The Shadow of Night* and other poems and established his name as a writer. Although he had written several tragedies and comedies, most of them are lost. He is chiefly remembered today for his translation of Homer, especially after Keats wrote his famous sonnet, 'On First Looking into Chapman's Homer'. He died in 1634, the same year as his friend John Marston.

Works

Chapman's fame as a dramatist, rests on *Bussy D' Ambois* and *The Revenge of Bussy D' Ambois,* its sequel. They are set in the court of Henry III of France. Unlike his contemporaries, he represented Frenchmen in his plays without caricaturing them.

His comedies were better than his tragedies. *All Fools*, *Monsieur D'Olive* and *The Gentleman Usher* are his best comedies. There is no attempt at moralising in his comedies and his style is less forced. The comedies display a pleasant romanticism. *All Fools* is modelled on Terence and is about different types of fathers—indulgent and strict.

Features

- Although his poetry did not have much of an impact on the subsequent development of English poetry, it influenced T.S. Eliot who admired his work.
- It is as a translator that he excelled. He translated the twelve books of the *Iliad* and the *Odyssey* and the *Georgics* of Hesiod.
- In his translation of the *Iliad*, he used iambic heptameter and in the *Odyssey*, the iambic pentameter. The Greek original was in dactylic hexameter, also known as the heroic hexameter. His translation of Homer is recognised by critics to be one of the very best in the English language.

John Marston (1575–1634)

Poetry
The Scourge of Villainy (1598)
Drama
Antonio and Mellida (1602)
Antonio's Revenge (1603)
The Malcontent (1604)
The Dutch Courtesan (1604)
Eastward Hoe (with Jonson and Chapman, 1605)
The Metamorphosis of Pygmalion's Image (1598)
Parisitaster or The Fawn (1606)
Sophonisba (1606)
What You Will (1607)
The Insatiate Countess (1613)

Life

He was believed to have been born in Coventry and was educated at Brasenose College, Oxford. His father was an English lawyer and his mother was Italian. Although he began his legal career at the Middle Temple, he had already made his mark in the world of letters with his *Pygmalion's Image* and *The Scourge of Villainy*. He next started writing plays which he continued for about eight years. Then he took orders and was given the living of Christchurch.

Works

The most cynical of the Elizabethans, he published a number of satires in 1598 which were distasteful to the public. *The Scourge of Villainy* and *The Metamorphosis of Pygmalion's Image* were burned by the order of Archbishop Whitgift in 1599. When he next turned his attention to drama, he revealed the influence of the revenge tradition of Seneca whom he admired. His comedy *The Malcontent* occupies a significant place in the history of English drama and anticipated *Hamlet*, *Measure for Measure* and even *The Tempest.* It is however an ill-constructed comedy about a cynical man who attacks all his acquaintances. His other comedies are less gloomy.

Features

- He specialised in the revenge tradition of Seneca, which was popular during his time.
- The language used in his plays was coarse and violent. This made him known as 'a ruffian in his style'.
- Marston satirised society in his comedies.
- Modern critics find his works insincere. Occasionally, his works reveal his brilliance but there is no consistency in his works. There are patches of striking pathos and lyrical irony. Marston seems to have made railing against society in an ironical manner, fashionable.
- His tragedies are full of violence and the language used is coarse when compared to that of his contemporaries.

Thomas Dekker (1572?–1632?)

The Shoemaker's Holiday (1599)
Old Fortunatus (1600)
Patient Grissil (with Chettle and Haughton, 1603)
Match Me in London (1604)
The Witch of Edmonton (with Ford and Rowley, 1621)
The Virgin Martyr (with Massinger, 1622)
The Sun's Darling(1624)
Match Me in London (1631)

With Webster

Westward Hoe (1606)
Northward Hoe (1607)

With Middleton

The Honest Whore (Part I, 1604)
The Roaring Girl (1611)

Pamphlets

The Wonderful Year (1603)

Life

Little is known about Dekker's life. He lived in London and led a hand-to-mouth existence. It is believed that the plots of his comedies and tragedies were inspired by his own life. He began writing for the stage from 1594. Unfortunately, he was obliged to write in collaboration with mediocre playwrights like Henry Chettle, William Haughton and John Day. But he also collaborated with some of the best playwrights of his age such as Jonson, Middleton, Drayton and Webster. Only eight of the nine plays written solely by him have been preserved. Of these, only four deserve mention. He was imprisoned several times during his lifetime and died in 1632.

Works

He succeeded Greene and Nashe as a prose writer. However, he did not write novels, but social studies and pictures of London life. *The Wonderful Year* is about the year in which Queen Elizabeth died and James I succeeded to the throne. It was also the year in which one of the great plagues occurred.

The Honest Whore is Dekker's best-known work. The idea of a 'fallen' woman being called honest could only occur to Dekker. The two parts of the play are set against the backdrop of Bridewell and Bedlam. *The Shoemaker's Holiday* brings alive the city of London in all its vivaciousness and joy. We see a London of honest tradesmen and workers rather than crafty courtiers.

Features

- Dekker's plays and his pamphlets were known for their detailed and realistic descriptions of everyday life in London.
- London was the theme of most of his plays. Unlike his contemporaries who were either satirical or bent on highlighting only the vices of society, Dekker focused sympathetically on the underdogs.
- He was known for his sense of humour and wit and his plays were full of clever wordplay, puns and comic situations.

- Although Dekker is no match for an intellect like Jonson, he had what many of his contemporaries lacked—charm. He belonged to the romantic school of Shakespeare and revealed a great ability to adapt to the styles of the new drama.

Thomas Middleton (1570–1627)

Blurt Master-Constable (1602)
Michaelmas Term (1607)
Your Five Gallants (1606)
A Trick to Catch the Old One (1608)
A Mad World, My Masters (1608)
A Chaste Maid in Cheapside (1612)
No Wit, No Help Like a Woman's (1612)
The Mayor of Quinborough (1615–20?)
Women Beware Women (1622)
The Witch (1623)
A Game at Chess (1625)

With Dekker

The Roaring Girl (1611)

With Rowley

A Fair Quarrel (1617)
The Old Law (1623)
Anything for a Quiet Life (1624?)
The Changeling (1624)
The Spanish Gipsy (1625)

Life

He was born in London in 1570. Hardly anything is known about him, except that he was as attached to London as Dekker and Heywood. It is believed that he held the post of City Chronologer and that he wrote speeches for special public occasions.

Works

He began his literary career by writing a series of satirical comedies. *A Trick to Catch the Old One* and *A Mad World, My Masters* are among the best of his comedies. His *A Game at Chess* is a political satire which created a riot.

By about 1612, this writer of comedies turned his attention to tragedy. In collaboration with William Rowley, he wrote some remarkable plays like *A Fair Quarrel, The Changeling* and *The Spanish Gipsy.* They were realistic plays and very different from the melodramas of the time. Of these, *The Changeling* is a masterpiece that could be compared to a Shakespearean tragedy.

In it, tragic force and passion are brought out very effectively through the use of a verse that is disjointed and full of movement.

Features

- Middleton was a very versatile writer who wrote in many forms such as comedies, pageants and masques. His comedies are light, sometimes bordering on the farcical and paint a picture of the common life of London.
- He was a close observer of his times and was adept at presenting critical pictures of the same.
- Middleton had a unique dramatic style. The prose that he used in his comedies was simple, natural and idiomatic, which easily slipped into verse. Jacobean dramatists made extensive use of blank verse, strictly adhering to the iambic pentameter which characterised Jacobean drama. Middleton adopted a more flexible style of writing and often deviated from the strict iambic pentameter pattern. This style of writing came as a welcome change.
- Middleton did not care to convey any didactic messages through his plays. His characters were mostly types of vagabonds and thieves.

Thomas Heywood (1574?–1641?)

Drama

The Four Prentices of London with the Conquest of Jerusalem (1592?)
King Edward IV (in two parts, 1599)
The Troubles of Queen Elizabeth (in two parts, 1605 and 1606)
A Woman Killed with Kindness (1603)
The Fair Maid of the Exchange (1607)
The Golden Age (1611)
The Silver Age (1613)
The Brazen Age (1613)
The Iron Age (in two parts, 1632)
The Fair Maid of the West (1631)
The Hierarchy of the Blessed Angels (1635)
England's Elizabeth (1631)
The Royal King and Loyal Subject (1602)
The English Traveller (1633)
A Wise Woman of Hogsdon (1638)
Fortune by Land and Sea (with Rowley, 1655)
The Late Lancashire Witches (with Richard Brome, 1634)

Non-Dramatic Works

Troia Britannica (1609)

An Apology for Actors (1612)
Gunaikeion (1624)

Masque
Love's Mistress (1636)

Life

He belonged to Lincolnshire and was a student at Cambridge. He wrote for Henslowe's Admiral's Men (a company of actors for which most of the dramatists of the period, except Shakespeare, wrote) and later became a prominent dramatist who wrote for the popular theatres of the day. He claimed to have had a hand in writing 220 plays and was one of the most prolific writers of the day. Most of his plays, however, are lost today.

Works

Although Heywood is not rated as a very great dramatist, he is certainly a very versatile one. He wrote with equal ease in various genres that included chronicle plays, comedy of manners and romantic drama.

The earliest play that made him famous is *A Woman Killed with Kindness*. It is the story of an unfaithful wife who, overcome by the extreme goodness of her wronged but forgiving husband, droops and expires with shame and remorse. The play is set against the background of the contemporary English countryside.

The Four Prentices of London with the Conquest of Jerusalem, *King Edward IV* and *Queen Elizabeth* are his chronicle plays. Heywood combined in these chronicle, history and popular romance. Between 1611 and 1613, he wrote a series of plays, *The Golden Age*, *The Silver Age*, *The Brazen Age* and *The Iron Age* in which he dramatises classical mythology. In *The English Traveller*, he again went back to his favourite theme of forgiveness.

Features

- Heywood was successful with the chronicle, history, the romantic drama and the comedy of manners.
- He also wrote at least one masterpiece in the genre of domestic drama.
- His plot construction was weak and his verse remains, for the most part, mediocre.

John Webster (1580?–1624?)

The White Devil (1612)
The Duchess of Malfi (1612–13)
The Devil's Law Case (tragicomedy, 1623)

With Dekker
Westward Hoe (1606?)
Northward Hoe (1607?)

With Rowley
A Cure for a Cuckold (1625)

With Ford
A Late Murder of the Son upon the Mother (1624)

With Middleton
Anything for a Quiet Life (1624)

With Fletcher
The Faire Maide of the Inn (1625)

Life

Very little is known about the life of John Webster. It is believed that he was the son of a prosperous coach-maker in London. He was made a freeman of the Merchant Taylors' Company in 1603, but he had started writing plays by 1601.

Works

His literary output could be divided into three periods—the first, that of collaboration (1602–07); the second, that of the two great tragedies (1610–14); and the third, that of the tragicomedy (1620 onwards). During the first period, he served as a sort of apprentice-collaborator with Dekker, Middleton, Marston and Heywood.

The highlight of his career was the middle period when he wrote his two great tragedies, *The White Devil* and *The Duchess of Malfi*. Both are revenge tragedies containing scenes of horror. Webster's contribution to this genre is significant. He belongs to the long succession of writers beginning with Kyd who was inspired by Seneca.

When one studies the course of the motive of revenge in drama, one notices several interesting facts. Gradually, the presence of the ghost in revenge drama is dispensed with. Earlier, it was the hero who went in search of revenge in order to right a wrong. Slowly, the character of the avenging 'hero' becomes no better than a villain who just uses revenge as an excuse for his own evil deeds. In some cases, there is forgiveness and repentance at the end, for example, in Shakespeare's *The Tempest*.

Webster gives yet another twist to the revenge tradition. In his *The White Devil*, our sympathies are no longer with the avengers, but with their victim. In this play, revenge is depicted as a passion born out of wounded pride. Webster takes this even further in *The Duchess of Malfi*, where the victim is the heroine. The avengers are seen paying for their sins in the last act. The old concept of revenge as a sacred duty, as it was depicted in *The Spanish Tragedy* and *Hamlet*, is completely transformed.

It is through these two tragedies that Webster lives today. Vittoria and the Duchess—the two protagonists of *The White Devil* and *The Duchess of Malfi* respectively, are among the greatest creations of Jacobean drama. Webster reveals himself as a true poet in these plays. His sombre images are the highlight of his poetic style.

Features

- He added new dimensions to the genre of the revenge tragedy by presenting a gruesome vision of humanity in his plays.
- Through his work, he raised melodrama to the level of true poetry.
- In his characterisation, he was second only to Shakespeare.

John Fletcher (1579–1625) and Francis Beaumont (1584–1616)

Fletcher
The Faithful Shepherdess (1610)
Wit Without Money (1639)
Valentinian (1610–14)
The Loyal Subject (1618)
The Mad Lover (1616)
The Woman's Prize (1604–17)
The Chances (1617)
Monsieur Thomas (1619)
The Humourous Lieutenant (1619)
Woman Pleased (1620)
The Wild Goose Chase (1621)
The Pilgrim (1621)
The Island Princess (1621)
A Wife for a Month (1624)
Rule a Wife and Have a Wife (1624)

Beaumont
Salmacis and Hermaphroditus (1602)
The Woman Hater (1605)
The Knight of the Burning Pestle (1607?)

Beaumont and Fletcher
Four Plays in One (1608)
Philaster (1609)
The Scornful Lady (1610)
The Maid's Tragedy (1610–11)
A King and No King (1611)
The Coxcomb (1612)
Cupid's Revenge (1612)
The Captain (1612–13)
The Knight of Malta (1619)
The Honest Man's Fortune (1647)
Other works with Massinger, Rowley and Middleton

Lives

Fletcher was born in Sussex and was educated at Corpus Christi College, Cambridge. Little is known about his early life. He was the son of a clergyman who later became bishop of London. He lost his father when he was just seventeen. Fletcher wrote plays both to satisfy his creative urge and to earn his livelihood. His pastoral drama *The Faithful Shepherdess*, though a failure on stage, is an excellent example of the genre and Milton, by taking it as the model for his *Comus*, paid a huge tribute to it.

Beaumont was born in Leicestershire and was the son of a judge of the Court of Common Pleas. He studied in Pembroke College, Oxford. He left college without a degree when his father died in 1598. With the idea of following in his father's footsteps, he joined the Inner Temple. However, literature seemed to have a stronger attraction for him than law and it is believed that he wrote the Ovidian poem, *Salamacis and Hermaphroditus* at this time. His earliest known play *The Woman Hater* is a Jonsonian comedy of humours. *The Knight of the Burning Pestle*, too, is attributed to Beaumont alone. After that, he began his famous collaboration with Fletcher and other well-known dramatists. Beaumont died when he was just 28 and was buried at Westminster Abbey.

Works

When Fletcher was about twenty-eight years old, he began to write in collaboration with Beaumont. Together, Beaumont and Fletcher wrote several comedies, tragedies and tragicomedies. There are twelve tragedies and twenty tragicomedies written by them. Critics are of the opinion that Fletcher was mainly the inventive or creative partner while Beaumont was the critical and correcting partner. Both of them turned to Shakespeare rather than Ben Jonson for inspiration. They, therefore, belong to the romantic and not the classical school of British drama.

The Maid's Tragedy and *Philaster* are among the best of the plays written by them. *Philaster* is a tragicomedy inspired by Shakespeare. *The Maid's Tragedy* contains the unforgettable character Evadne, the king's mistress, who is portrayed as a fierce and shameless woman who ends up killing her seducer in bed. Other memorable plays by the two dramatists include *The Scornful Lady*, *A King and No King* and *The Coxcomb*.

Features

- They took the institution of collaboration to new heights. Although several dramatists wrote in collaboration, this pair was exceptional. Of course, dramatists like Shakespeare and Jonson seldom collaborated with other playwrights.
- Their plays abound in creating 'types'—the perfect hero who is wronged, the lustful tyrant, the patient wife or maid, the faithful friend, the wicked woman and the irresponsible fop.
- They redefined tragicomedy by infusing it with colour and music.
- The popularity of their plays throughout the seventeenth century had a definite impact upon the development of the neoclassical drama of the eighteenth century.
- Beaumont and Fletcher are remembered for their skill in dramatic construction, their natural dialogues and poetical passages. The most remarkable feature of their plays is the number of lyrics that lie scattered throughout.
- Their plays reflect the changing fashion in the art of drama. During the reign of James I, the audience was more interested in entertainment that was light, which did not make any demands on the intellect. This could be one of the reasons for the popularity of court masques. There was a general lowering of moral standards. These changes were reflected in the plays of Beumont and Fletcher. In fact, their

plays have been critiqued for being immoral and for using indecent language.

- The early-seventeenth century witnessed the growing popularity of the tragicomedy. Even Shakespeare, quick to feel the pulse of his audience, abandoned tragedy and wrote tragicomedies like *Cymbeline* and *The Winter's Tale.* Tragicomedy was given a new meaning by Beaumont and Fletcher. Earlier, plots that seemed doomed to end in disaster were given happy endings; *The Merchant of Venice* and *Much Ado About Nothing* by Shakespeare, *The Old Law* by Middleton and *The Gentleman Usher* by Chapman, are a few popular examples of this. Beaumont and Fletcher resorted to romance, unusual settings and a world that was filled with beauty, colour, music and sparkling language. They avoided both the logical sequence of cause-and-effect of the tragedies of Marlowe and Shakespeare as well as the inescapable realism of Jonson's comedies. While Marston, Chapman and Jonson resorted to satire, Beaumont and Fletcher took to extravagant romance. It was Fletcher who was more 'modern' of the two and was keen to give the audience what they wanted. He altered the blank verse by adding more syllables in order to give it a conversational fluency. This was, however, seen by the critics as a weakening of the blank verse.

Thomas Carew (1595?–1640)

'A Rapture'	'Ask Me No More'
'To Saxham'	*Poems* (1640)

Life

Carew (pronounced Carey) belonged to 'the Tribe of Ben'. He was the third of eleven children and was born in West Wickham in Kent. He was educated at Oxford, but left without a degree. After an unsuccessful stint at the Middle Temple and being dismissed from his position as secretary to Sir Dudley Carleton, he won the favour of Charles I and was appointed to his court. He was very popular in the court and was a renowned wit of his day. He was a close friend of John Suckling, Ben Jonson and Edward Hyde.

Works

A collection of his lyrics published as *Poems* in 1640, after his death, contains several songs, pastorals, elegies and poetic dialogues. Many of the songs and love poems are addressed to an unidentified 'Celia'. The longest poem of the collection, 'A Rapture', is 166 lines long and is sensuous in nature. In it, he invites Celia to throw honour to the winds and enjoy the various forbidden pleasures of the flesh. 'An Elegy Upon the Death of the Deane of Pauls, Dr John Donne' is a notable poem in this collection. Another poem, 'To Saxham', celebrates life in the countryside. A number of his poems deal with the craft of poetry. For example, his elegy on John Donne is an excellent piece of literary criticism which analyses the metaphysical qualities of Donne. Similarly, his poem on Ben Jonson examines the style and content of the author.

Features

- His themes belong mostly to the city and the court and not the countryside or the parsonage.
- His style and versification are highly refined and polished.
- All his poetry is amorous in nature, where he is revealed as trying to persuade his lady-love to comply with his wishes.

Richard Lovelace (1618–58)

Lucasta (1649) — 'To Althea, from Prison'
Lucasta: Posthume Poems (1659) — 'To Lucasta, Going to the Warres'

Life

He was educated at Charterhouse School and Gloucester Hall, Oxford. He belonged to a wealthy family in Kent. He was imprisoned twice during the Civil War for being a supporter of Charles I. After the execution of Charles I, he was freed but lived a wretched life and died in poverty.

Works

His most famous poems are the ones addressed to Lucasta and Althea. These are also considered to be the best examples of Cavalier poetry.

As a poet, he had several interests. His rural background inspired him to write an interesting group of poems—'The Ant', 'The Snail', 'The Toad and The Spider', 'The Falcon' and 'The Grasshopper'. In these poems, Lovelace combines keen observation with superstition. Their mildly moralising tone and literary allusions are characteristic of the poetry of this period.

In his love poems, he was fresh and exuberant without being vulgar like Suckling. He was one of Donne's most ardent imitators and we discover several conceits in his poems. Though he was not considered to be a great poet, some of his most memorable lines are very familiar to us:

Stone walls do not a prison make,
Nor iron bars a cage;
Minds innocent and quiet take
That for a hermitage.
If I have freedom in my love,
And in my soul am free,
Angels alone that soar above
Enjoy such liberty.

Poems like these have given Lovelace a permanent place in the history of English poetry.

Features

- His poems are the best reflection of the Cavalier attitude to life and war. On reading his poems, we get a very clear picture of the code of chivalry and the public values of the seventeenth-century country gentleman. Although he was an inconsistent poet and sometimes careless and amateurish, he had a fine sensibility.
- A poet of varied interests, he wrote about love, nature and contemporary life.
- Artistically, he was not rated very highly as he is considered to have had a stilted and artificial style.

- He was never a 'Son of Ben' and did not follow the style of Ben Jonson.

Robert Herrick (1591–1674)

Hesperides (1648) *Noble Numbers* (appendix to *Hesperides*)

Life

Robert Herrick was the seventh child of a wealthy goldsmith who had died under mysterious circumstances when Robert was a baby. There is no clear record of his education. He was apprenticed to his uncle, a goldsmith who was also the MP for Leicester. He left his apprenticeship and joined St John's College, Cambridge. After completing his BA and MA, he was ordained a priest. He was involved with the literary circle of his time, particularly the group around Jonson. By 1625, Herrick had made a name for himself as a poet. When he was given the living of Dean Prior, a remote village in the South Devonshire countryside, he had to leave London. By 1647, he was ejected from his living by the Puritans and he once again returned to London.

In 1660, after the Restoration, he was reinstated at Dean Prior where he remained for the rest of his life. He died in 1674, the same year as Milton.

Works

He was a 'Son of Ben' and rejected metaphysical wit. Although Herrick is listed as a Cavalier poet, in his songs he evoked the style of Spenser and Shakespeare. His lyrics reveal his command over metre and rhyme. Herrick's poetry reflects the spirited, objective and perfectly ordered poetry of the Latin poets. He was able to connect the country life, love, rural superstitions, flowers and pets of his own day with that of Emperor Augustus's time. Such themes are used in his poems 'To Robin Redbreast', 'His Winding-Sheet' and 'His Last Request to Julia'. He loved nature and children and was also deeply interested in mystical rites, games, festivals and ceremonies.

His collection *Hesperides*, which is the classical Greek name for a mythological garden at the western edge of the world, contains about twelve hundred secular poems and the appendix of religious poems called *Noble Numbers*. Published at a politically turbulent time in London, Herrick's poems were ignored by his contemporaries. Interest in them revived only in the nineteenth century. Most of his poems are very short, but there are a few which are over a hundred lines long. There is no order in the anthology which contains both his coarsest epigrams and his most inspired poems. One of his most well-known poems is 'Corinna's Going a-Maying', written in five fourteen-line stanzas. It is almost as rich a poem as any by Spenser and is considered one of the best lyrics on May Day.

Features

- He followed the classical style of Ben Jonson. In his poems, we can discern the moral attitude of and a taste for the Latin poets.
- Herrick was known for his light and airy style of writing poetry. He wished to focus on folk customs and festivals like May Day and the harvest festivals, especially because the Puritans were trying to suppress them.
- He dedicated his talents to religion once he entered the church.

John Suckling (1609–42)

Poetry
Fragmenta Aurea (1646)
Drama
Aglaura (1638)
The Goblins (1646)
Brennoralt (1646)

Life

Suckling hailed from an old Norfolk family and was educated at Trinity College, Cambridge. He travelled widely and was knighted in 1630. He lived in great splendour at court and was the leader of the Royalist Party during the Civil War. As the parliament rebelled against the king and gained control of the government,

Suckling joined a conspiracy to free a Royalist leader from the Tower of London. The plot was exposed and he was forced to flee to France, where he is believed to have committed suicide in 1641.

Works

Compared to Carew, Suckling was far less serious as a poet. His chief works are included in *Fragmenta Aurea*. It contains several poems, letters and plays. Two of his well-known works, 'Ballad upon a Wedding' and 'A Session of the Poets', are included in this volume. 'A Session of the Poets', in which various poets of the day such as Jonson, Carew and D'Avenaut vie with each other for 'the poetic laurel', is an interesting document of contemporary opinion on these writers.

Aglaura and *The Goblins* are two of his plays and reflect Suckling's professional admiration for Shakespeare. *Brennoralt* is a tragedy that throws light on the author himself. The plays are important today chiefly for the songs that they contain. One of his best-known poems, 'Why so pale and wan, fond lover?' is a song from *Aglaura*.

Features

- Suckling's fame rested on his lyrics. He is considered one of the most elegant and brilliant of the Cavalier poets.
- His poetry did not reflect any influence of Ben Jonson. He was a poet of improvisation, who wrote spontaneously and did not care to fine-tune his poems.

John Donne (1572–1631)

Poetry
Satires (1590s)
Elegies (1590s)
Holy Sonnets (1610–11?)
Songs and Sonnets (?)
The Progress of the Soul (1601)
Holy Sonnets (after 1610)

Prose
Pseudo-Martyr (1610)
Ignatius His Conclave (1611)
Biathanatos (1611)
Death's Duell (1630)
Essays in Divinity (1640)
LXXX Sermons (1640)
Fifty Sermons (1649)
XXVI Sermons (1660)

Life

Donne was born into a devout Catholic family. His father was warden of the Ironmonger's Company in London and his mother was the daughter of the dramatist, John Heywood. He attended both Oxford and Cambridge and joined Lincoln's Inn as a law student. In 1598, he became secretary to Sir Thomas Egerton, Lord Keeper of the Great Seal, but was dismissed from service because he secretly married the Lord Keeper's niece. For the next fifteen years, he had to undergo very difficult times financially. He renounced his Catholic faith and was ordained as an Anglican deacon in 1615. He became divinity reader at Lincoln's Inn, where many of his sermons were preached. In 1621, he was made dean of St Paul's by King James I. From 1621 until his death, Donne became famous as the greatest of England's preachers. He had written several formal satires in verse in the early 1590s. His various well-known poems like 'A Valediction Forbidding Mourning', 'Ecstasy', and 'Canonisation' were written at various, unknown times in the early years of his life. Although he wrote during the Elizabethan Age, most of his works were published only after his death in 1633.

Works

He began writing at a very young age and had written many of his best poems before he was twenty-five. As a young poet, he reacted against Spenser's school of poetry as he considered the mythological, pastoral and allegorical to be artificial and insincere. He disliked the highly regular metres and the chivalrous conventions of Ben Jonson, equally. Instead of high poetic style, he preferred to shock his readers with the directness of the spoken language. He rejected the gods and goddesses of mythology and believed in the subtle, understated style of writing.

Donne began writing poetry around 1593. To the 1590s, belong most of the *Satires, Elegies* and *Songs and Sonnets.* We can find some of his most famous poems like 'A Valediction Forbidding Mourning', 'The Canonization' and 'The Good-Morrow' in his early poetical output.

His *Holy Sonnets* and other divine poems belong to the last period of his life, after the death of his wife. His poetry may be studied under three headings—love poetry; occasional poems and verse letters; and religious poems. The first contains his best-known poems such as 'The Sun Rising', 'The Dream', 'The Good-Morrow', 'The Flea', 'Ecstasy', 'The Canonization' and 'A Valediction of Weeping'. These poems range from the passionate to the cynical and the flippant. There is, however, a constant introspection and analysis in all his love poems. They are, above all, profoundly sensuous.

Donne gave paramount importance to wit which sometimes resulted in hyperbole. His poetry relied a lot on intellect and in order to understand them, the reader too needed to be equally well-read and intelligent. His poems are, at times, burdened with allusions to philosophical doctrines and contemporary science. In his early secular poems, we find irony and a certain drive for creating elaborate conceits. Through the conceits, Donne was able to bring all his varied interests very effectively into his poetry. Donne did not consider any activity as being unpoetical. This was the quality that T.S. Eliot would later praise, saying that Donne had 'a mechanism of sensibility which could devour any kind of experience'.

The next group of poems, the occasional poems, is the least important when compared to the earlier secular/love poems and the later religious poems. *Satires* belongs to this period. In 'The Progress of the Soul', he attacked Queen Elizabeth bitterly.

Religious poems form the bulk of his remaining works. Of these, *The Holy Sonnets* reveal his noteworthy skills. In 'A Hymn to God the Father', his assured faith is fully made evident. In his religious poems and hymns, he treats God as a conqueror or a ravisher. We find wit and emotional intensity in these poems too—only the themes are different. His attempts at longer poems such as 'The Anatomy of the World' and 'Of the Progress of the Soul', also called 'The First Anniversary', are not too successful as Donne's wit is best suited to shorter flights of fancy.

As a poet, he was admired up to the Restoration, but was neglected in the eighteenth century. It was in the early-twentieth century that Donne once again gained literary favour after T.S. Eliot revived a taste for metaphysical verse.

Features

- Donne's poetry is known for its use of metaphysical conceits. He was a master at creating comparisons between seemingly unrelated objects or ideas. For example, in his poem 'The Flea', he uses the image of the flea that has bitten both him and his lady-love. He argues that since their blood is already mingled, there is no need for her to resist his advances:

  Mark but this flea, and mark in this,
  How little that which thou deniest me is:
  It sucked me first, and now sucks thee,
  And in this flea our bloods mingled be.
- Donne's writings are characterised by their intellectual complexity. His poems and especially his sermons explore profound philosophical and theological questions and present different concepts and ideas. In his prose piece, 'Meditation XVII', he says, 'No man is an island, entire of itself; every man is a piece of the continent, a part of the main.'
- There is a lot of wit and wordplay in his poems. Donne is known for his use of puns, clever twists of phrases, playful language and far-fetched images. For instance, while bidding goodbye to his mistress prior to setting off to sea, he begs her, in 'A Valediction of Weeping':

  Let not the wind
  Example find
  To do more harm than it purposeth:
  Since thou and I sigh one another's breath,
  Whoe'er sighs most is cruellest, and hastes the other's death.
- Donne's poems are personal and emotional in nature. The themes of his poems are drawn from his own personal experiences. Apart from these, the contemplation of death and mortality is another favourite theme of his poems.

Richard Crashaw (1612–49)

Steps to the Temple (1646) *Delights of the Muse* (?)

Life

Crashaw was orphaned by the age of nine. He was educated at Charterhouse and Pembroke Hall, Cambridge. He converted to Roman Catholicism in 1645 and fled to Paris. He travelled to Italy and died in Loreto.

Works

His first collection of poems *Delights of the Muses* was published after his death. Of this collection, 'Music's Duel' is the most famous poem. It is a translation of a poem by a Jesuit about a competition between a lute-player and a nightingale in which the nightingale fails and dies. 'Wishes, to his Supposed Mistress' is another brilliant poem written in a unique rhythm. It enlists all the gifts which he would wish his lady-love to possess.

Crashaw's sacred poetry collection *Steps to the Temple* contains the best of the poet, the translation of Marini's poem on the Massacre of the Innocents. 'The Weeper' makes use of every conceit that was ever inspired by a weeping mistress and he transposes the poem to a religious level. His best-known poems are those addressed to St Theresa— 'Hymn' and 'The Flaming Heart'. Both poems celebrate the bliss of martyrdom.

Features

- His poems are full of conceits. In fact, critics feel that they are extravagant.
- Compared to George Herbert, whom he admired greatly, Crashaw was less intellectual.
- In his lyrical flights, he was equalled only by Shelley.
- The strangeness and obscurity of his poetry is similar to the work of the symbolists of the twentieth century.
- His poems are rich in music and imagery.

Henry Vaughan (1621–95)

Poems with the Tenth Satire of Juvenal Englished (1646)
Silex Scintillans (1650)
The Swan of Usk (1651)
Solitary Devotions (1652)
Flores Solitudinis (1654)

Life

Henry Vaughan was the son of a Welsh gentleman, Thomas Vaughan. He had a twin brother who was a magician. Very little is known about his education and early life. His early poetry was secular and included fashionable love verses. It is believed that some profound spiritual experience after the death of his younger brother William, or the defeat of the Royalists in the Civil War could have brought about a change in his attitude. Vaughan began writing a lot of religious verse after that period. Although there is no record of a medical degree, Vaughan began practising medicine by the 1640s and continued until his death in 1695.

Works

His writing clearly reveals that he was a follower of both Donne and George Herbert. He was a mystic at heart like Crashaw. He had a great love for music and nature. In fact, he worshipped God, not in the Church but out in the open.

He began his poetic career writing secular poems. His first collection *Poems* contains poems like 'Les Amours' and 'To Amoret: The Sigh'. In these poems, we can make out the influence that Donne had on Vaughan. He published another volume of secular poetry called *The Swan of Usk* or *Olor Iscanus* in 1651. It was around that time that some great crisis in Vaughan's life took place, which made him strongly religious.

In the collections of religious poems—*Silex Scintillans, Solitary Devotions* and *Flores Solitudinius*—the influence of George Herbert is clearly visible. 'The World' and 'The Retreat', two of his best poems reveal his remarkable mysticism. Compared to Herbert, Vaughan is capable of sustained writing and greater fluency, but he lacks Herbert's sense of timing. Vaughan tends to write beyond the climax and his images too are not sharply focused. It was from the poem 'The Retreat' in which Vaughan associates childhood with 'whiteness', the symbol of purity, through phrases like 'dear, harmless age', and 'an age of mysteries', that William Wordsworth found his inspiration for 'Intimations of Immortality'. Both the poems focus on the loss of childhood innocence and a longing for a purer past. We see evidence of Donne's metaphysical wit in this poem by Vaughan. Other well-known poems of Vaughan are 'The Waterfall', 'Cock-crowing' and 'The Night'.

Features

- His contribution to mystic poetry was significant. He influenced later poets like Wordsworth.
- His poetry had a musical quality and his choice of epithets was excellent.
- His poems were often obscure and the versification was not very skilful.

Abraham Cowley (1618–67)

Poetry
Poetical Blossoms (1633)
Poems (1656)
The Mistress (1647)
Verses Lately Written upon Several Occasions (1663)

Pastoral Drama
Loves Riddle (1638)

Satire
The Puritan and The Papist (1643)

Epic
The Civil War (?)

Prose
A Discourse by Way of Vision Concerning the Government of Oliver Cromwell (1661)
A Proposition for the Advancement of Learning (1661)
The Visions and Prophecies Concerning England (1661)

Drama
The Guardian (1650)
Cutter of Coleman's Street (1663)

Life

Cowley was the posthumous son of a London stationer and studied at Westminster School and Trinity College, Cambridge. He was a precocious child who wrote *Pyramus and Thisbe*, a verse romance, by the age of ten and another called *Constanta and Philetus* two years later. When the English Civil War broke out, he left Cambridge and joined Oxford. He was a Royalist and displayed his support by writing a satire, *The Puritan and the Papist*, and a political epic, *The Civil War*. When the Royalists were defeated, he left for Paris where he stayed till 1654. He was suspected of being a Royalist spy and imprisoned briefly. When monarchy was restored in 1660, he expected to be rewarded richly, but was disappointed. He died in 1667 and was buried at Westminster Abbey.

Works

During his lifetime he was considered to be the greatest poet of the period, surpassing Robert Herrick and even John Milton. Milton, himself, ranked Cowley along with Shakespeare and Spenser as the three great English poets. With the passage of time, his reputation has reduced considerably. Today, he is considered an important link between the Renaissance and modern times. He is also considered to be the last of the Metaphysicals and the forerunner of the English classicists. His poetry abounds with conceits, hyperboles and antitheses.

One of his earliest collections of poems, *The Mistress*, was reprinted in 1656 as part of a fourfold collection of poems: *Miscellanies*, *The Mistress*, *Pindarique Odes* and *Davideis*. His best poems are the lyrics in *Miscellanies*. 'The Chronicle' is one of his most anthologised poems. It is a ballad which narrates, in jest, the tale of all the women who captured his heart.

Cowley wished to imitate Pindar and wrote several irregular verses fashioned after the Pindaric ode. He imitated the Pindaric matter and style, but did not conform to the regular verses of Pindar. He introduced the irregular ode, allowing each stanza to find its own pattern of varying line lengths, numbers of lines and rhyme schemes. The regular Pindaric ode on the other hand contained strophes and antistrophes in one type of stanzas and epodes in another.

Cowley next attempted to write an epic. His *Davideis* is an epic based on the biblical history of King David. He planned to write twelve cantos, but completed only four. In going back to Homer and Virgil for inspiration in this attempt, he anticipated Milton.

This work abounds in **antitheses** (contrasts or oppositions in meaning written in parallel grammatical structures; for example, 'Willing to wound, and yet afraid to strike') and **epigrams** (originally inscriptions on monuments; now referring to any witty sayings or short poems that contain a sharp turn of thought). He wrote in rhyming decasyllabic couplets, thus anticipating Pope's *The Rape of the Lock*.

Cowley gave a lot of importance to wit but rejected puns and artificial similes. His poem 'Against Hope' is the best example of his wit; in it he made abundant use of ingenious imageries.

After 1656, he turned his attention to prose. Today, he is remembered more for his prose than his verse. Cowley's *Essays*, especially 'Of Myself', is often read.

Features

- His work combined the qualities of both Donne's Metaphysical school and Ben Jonson's classicism.
- He was the forerunner of the neoclassical style of Dryden and Pope.
- He gave to English poetry the irregular ode that would be highly popular with Romantic poets like Wordsworth.
- He had no ear for music. As a result, even his best verses are considered to be dry and lacking melody.

Andrew Marvell (1621–78)

'Horatian Ode upon Cromwell's Return from Ireland'	'The Nymph Complaining'
	'The Garden'
Satires: A Collection of Poems on Affairs of State (1679)	'To His Coy Mistress'
	'Bermudas'

Life

Marvell was the son of a Yorkshire parson and was educated at Hull Grammar School and at Trinity College, Cambridge. During the four years of the Civil War (1642–46), he visited the Continent. Between 1650 and 1652, he was the tutor of the twelve-year-old Mary Fairfax, daughter of the Parliamentarian Lord Thomas Fairfax. It was while he resided there that Marvell wrote some of his best poems. In 1653, upon Milton's advice, he became his assistant in the office of the Latin Secretary to Cromwell's Council. In 1659, he entered Parliament. After the Restoration, Marvell supported the opposition, but his tact and sense of fair play kept him out of trouble in spite of writing satires like 'The Last Instructions to a Painter'.

Works

He wrote about nature, but did not approve of the pastoral convention that was followed by Spenser. We can discern the Romantics' exalted love for nature in his poems. Poems like 'The Garden' foreshadow the sensuousness of Keats and the meditative mood of Wordsworth.

His love poems, though not numerous, are remarkable for their grace, irony and wit. 'To His Coy Mistress' is among his most well-known poems, which recalls the passion of Donne. It is one of the best examples of Metaphysical poetry, where Marvell combines paradox and exaggeration to produce a comic effect. The lines 'The grave's a fine and private place, / But none, I think, do there embrace', from the poem is proof of this. His 'The Definition of Love' is another example of a typical Metaphysical poem where he resembles Donne even more.

Patriotism was another important factor of his poems. His 'Horatian Ode Upon Cromwell's Return from Ireland', 'First Anniversary of the Government under His Highness the Lord Protector' and 'Poem upon the Death of his Late Highness the Lord Protector' reveal Marvell's character. While expressing sympathy for the king, he admires Cromwell for being a better ruler. As an impartial viewer, he appreciates the virtues of both men. His deep patriotism may be discerned in his *Satires: A Collection of Poems on Affairs of State* which were published in 1689, after his death.

His poetry may be divided into two major portions—prior to the Restoration and after the Restoration. The earlier poems were mostly lyrical and reveal an admiration for nature. His poems after the Restoration are satirical attacks on the vices and tyranny of the church and the state.

Features

- It was Marvell's style of satire and use of the heroic couplet that Dryden adopted.
- He combined, in a unique manner, the virtues of both the Puritan and the Cavalier schools of thought.
- While he retained the complexity of Shakespeare's language, his poetry also reflects the deterioration and coarseness that was brought about by the Restoration.
- His best work reflects the tradition of both Jonson and Donne.
- Along with Milton, Marvell is an important Puritanical poet. Although he was a Puritan, there was no trace of the harshness or gloom that is usually associated with Puritanism in his poetry. In fact, religion had no impact upon his verse. He was filled with the joy and mirth of life and was a great lover of nature. His deep respect for the Bible and his piety did not prevent him from enjoying the pleasures of life.

John Milton (1608–74)

Poetry

'On the Death of a Fair Infant' (1628)
'At a Vacation Exercise' (1628)
'On the Morning of Christ's Nativity' (1629)
'On Arriving at the Age of Twenty Three' (1631)
L'Allegro (1631)
Il Penseroso (1631)
"Lycidas" (1637)
Poems (1645)
Paradise Lost (1667)
Paradise Regained (1671)
Samson Agonistes (1671)`
Pro Populo Anglicano Defensio (1651)

Masque

Comus (1634)

Pamphlets and Prose

Of Reformation in England and the Causes that Hitherto have Hindered it (1641)
The Reason of Church Government (1642)
The Doctrine and Discipline of Divorce (1643)
Areopagitica (1644)
Tractate of Education (1644)
Tetrachordon (1645)
Tenure of Kings and Magistrates (1648)
Eikonoklastes (1649)
Defensio Secunda (1654)

On the Late Massacre in Piedmont (1655)
Treatise of Civil Power in Ecclesiastical Causes (1659)
The Ready and Easy Way to Establish a Free Commonwealth (1660)

Life

John Milton was born in Bread Street, Cheapside, London, on 9 December 1608. He was educated at St Paul's School and at Christ's College, Cambridge, where he was nicknamed 'the Lady of Christ's'. He began writing poetry while he was at Cambridge. Apart from some Latin elegies and epigrams, Milton wrote some English poems too. 'On the Death of a Fair Infant' was written to commemorate the death of his niece. 'On the Morning of Christ's Nativity' and the companion poems, 'L'Allegro' and 'Il Penseroso', were also written while at college. These early poems reveal Milton's literary genius.

On leaving Cambridge, he took up residence with his father at Horton which was seventeen miles from London. Here, he spent the next six years studying Greek and Latin classics, mathematics, music and science. However, he seemed dissatisfied with himself, as is revealed in the sonnet 'On His Having Arrived at the Age of Twenty-Three'. But during the six years he spent at Horton (1632–38), Milton wrote some of his best poems and the masque *Comus*. In 1637, his mother died and in the same year Edward King, whom he had known at Cambridge, too passed away. Milton wrote the famous elegy 'Lycidas' to commemorate Edward King's death.

In 1638, Milton went to Europe. He visited Paris, Rome, Naples, Genoa, Pisa and Florence. He spent a considerable amount of time in Italy absorbing the spirit of the Renaissance. After spending fifteen to sixteen months in Europe, Milton was brought back to England by the news of the Civil War. For the next twenty years, he wrote only prose except for a few sonnets. Of these, the most famous one is 'On His Blindness'. During those twenty years, Milton worked on behalf of the English Parliament and the Commonwealth and he wrote mostly to support the Puritan cause.

In 1641, Milton married Mary Powell. This was not a happy marriage as the difference between their ages and ideologies was vast. Soon after the marriage, Mary Powell went back to her father's house and returned to Milton only three or four years later when under duress. After delivering three daughters, she died in 1652. In 1656, Milton married again, but his second wife died the very next year. He married for the third time in 1663, when he was blind and fifty-five years old. His third wife, Elizabeth Minshull was just twenty-five at the time of their marriage; she lived for fifty-three years more after Milton's death.

In 1649, Milton became the Latin Secretary and had an official post in the government. As he was blind, he needed an assistant. It was then that Andrew Marvell stepped in to help Milton. Milton continued in this post till the Restoration in 1660, when he was arrested. He was, however, released soon. After 1660, he retired from public life and wrote his immortal works—*Paradise Lost*, *Paradise Regained* and *Samson Agonistes*.

After several months of ill health, Milton died on 8 November 1674 and was buried in St Giles Church, Cripplegate.

Works

As a poet, Milton stands alone in his century and cannot be grouped with any of his contemporaries. In him, we witness a fusion of the two great movements that were sweeping across Europe for more than a century—the Renaissance and the Reformation. As a classical scholar, his works were soaked in the pagan beauty of Greek and Latin literature. At the same time, as a Puritan he believed in Christianity and the Bible. Paganism and Christianity, nature and religion—these antithetical elements, instead of destroying each other, fused beautifully in his soul to give to the world immortal works of poetry.

His works could be divided into three parts—early poems or minor poems, prose writings and major poems.

EARLY/MINOR POEMS

The poems that he wrote while at Cambridge and at Horton are often referred to as Milton's 'minor poems', despite their poetic excellence. When he was twenty, he wrote his first masterpiece, the ode 'On the Morning of Christ's Nativity'. The poem, which celebrates the end of paganism, hardly bears any resemblance to any contemporary work. The ode reveals Milton's exquisite choice of words, imagination and classical leanings.

The twin poems 'L'Allegro' and 'Il Penseroso' written in the pastoral vein, are among the most beautiful poems to be written in the English language. These twin poems hold a mirror up to the poet's emotions—first, when he is in a joyous mood and then when he is in a melancholy mood. He paints two contrasting pictures in these poems. In one, he extols the joys of nature, the spring, the morning, the men and women at work and their simple lives. In the other, he describes the pleasures of solitude, the sunset, the nightingale's song and the night. Through a series of vivid images, Milton evokes the spirit of Mirth and Melancholy.

Comus and *Lycidas* were written by Milton during his stay at Horton. *Comus* is a masque in which Milton upholds virtue and morality. It is the story of a sister who is separated from her two brothers and is tempted by a magician, Comus, to join his carefree troupe. The girl, who is morally very strong, resists the temptation. *Comus* gave Milton an early opportunity to dramatise an idea that he firmly believed in—that human beings have the free will to choose between good and evil. *Comus* surpasses all other Renaissance masques by the sheer beauty of its language and the profundity of its thought.

'Lycidas', the last of his 'minor poems', is an elegy written to mourn the death of Edward King. It is a pastoral elegy, as it imitates the classical elegies which used the imagery of shepherds and the flock. Milton combines and fuses both pagan and Christian views of death in a way that was characteristic of the Christian humanists. It again reveals Milton's genius as a poet as the versification and style are flawless. 'Lycidas' is the best example of a pastoral elegy. **A pastoral elegy** represents both the mourner and the one he mourns as shepherds (the Greek word for shepherd is pastor). This form of poetry was first practised by the Greek poet Theocritus and imitated by Virgil. During the Renaissance, it was revived in Europe. There are certain conventions that are followed by the pastoral elegy.

- The speaker begins with an invocation to the muse(s).
- All nature joins in mourning the shepherd's demise.
- The mourner blames the guardian angels and nymphs for neglecting their charge.
- There is a procession of appropriate mourners.
- There is a description of the flowers that are brought to deck the hearse.
- At the end, there is a note of consolation.

Milton's 'minor poems' also include several sonnets such as 'O Nightingale' and the one written on his twenty-third birthday. Before he turned thirty, Milton's literary achievements were enough to rank him with Spenser and Wordsworth. The Horton period of Milton's life came to an end in April 1630, when he began his European travels.

PROSE

The twenty years between 1640 and 1660 are often referred to as Milton's 'lost years'. Those were the years given to politics and pamphlet warfare by him. Milton wrote extensively in support of the Parliamentary party, because of which he was identified as a Puritan. To label Milton thus is to limit the merits of the person. Milton did share some of the ideals and attitudes of the Puritans, such as their extreme dislike of kings and bishops. However, he differed greatly from them in advocating divorce and in defending the freedom of the press.

His pamphlets could be studied under three headings:

- Episcopacy Controversy: Bishop Joseph Hall had issued a strong argument supporting Archbishop Laud, who was a favourite of King Charles I and was hated by the Puritans. In answer to Hall, five Puritan ministers issued a pamphlet under the portmanteau name, 'Smectymnuus'—a word created by arranging the initials of their names. Milton joined this controversy by supporting the Puritan ministers as his private tutor in London, Thomas Young, was one of them. His first controversial pamphlet was titled *Of Reformation Touching Church Discipline in England and the Causes that Hitherto have Hindered it.*

- Divorce Controversy: Between 1642 and 1643, irked by his first wife's desertion, he wrote his pamphlets advocating divorce: *The Doctrine and Discipline of Divorce* and *Tetrachordon*. In the midst of all these pamphlets, he published his earlier poetical works as *Poems of Mr John Milton*.
- Monarchy Controversy: When the Long Parliament passed a printed ordinance called the **Licensing Act** requiring all publications to be licensed by a board of trustees, Milton refused to follow its dictates and the matter was brought before the Parliament. Milton wrote his famous *Areopagitica* addressed to the Parliament, in which he defended the right to freedom of speech and freedom of the press. In it, his prose style reached its zenith.

In 1649 when Charles I was executed, he wrote *Tenure of Kings and Magistrates*. He was commissioned to write *Eikonoklastes* in order to turn public opinion from sympathising with the martyred king. But even Milton could not undo the pitfalls of killing a king. In 1652, Milton lost his eyesight. During this period, he wrote some of his best sonnets like the ones commemorating Cromwell's rise to power, 'To the Lord General Cromwell' and 'To Sir Henry Vane the Younger' and 'On His Blindness'.

MAJOR POEMS

With the Restoration of monarchy, Milton fell on difficult days. His life was in danger and he went into hiding. He was a ruined man, poor and neglected. Yet, it was from these ashes that he rose. Milton had always wanted to write something that 'posterity would not willingly let die'. He had studied Homer, Virgil and the Greek dramatists, Aeschylus, Sophocles and Euripides. He wanted to write something to equal them. After much thought, he chose the Bible and set out on his lofty mission 'to justify the ways of God to man'.

It is believed that he had begun work on ***Paradise Lost*** as early as 1641. When he was forced to retire in 1660, he finally had the time to complete it. He finished writing it by 1665 and it was published in 1667. Milton received ten pounds for it and his widow sold the copyright for an additional eight pounds.

Taking just a few verses from the Book of Genesis, Milton developed a magnificent epic of 10,565 lines in twelve books. He used the conventions and devices of the classical epic to make the poem a work of art. His vast learning and experience gave the poem a profoundness that is breathtaking. The epic features of *Paradise Lost* are:

- The hero of an epic is superhuman or of cosmic importance. In the *Iliad,* it is the Greek warrior, Achilles; in the *Ramayana*, it is Rama, who is an incarnation of Vishnu. In *Paradise Lost,* Adam, the first man to be created by God, is the hero.
- The setting of the epic poem is usually very grand and vast. The sweeping battlefields of the Trojan War in the *Iliad,* the entire Indian subcontinent, including Sri Lanka, in the *Ramayana* are the settings of the two great ancient epics. In *Paradise Lost,* the action takes place across heaven, earth, hell and the cosmos.
- There is great action involved in an epic. In the *Iliad,* we witness the brave feats of Achilles in the Trojan War. In the *Ramayana*, we are given an account of the terrible war between Rama and Ravana. In *Paradise Lost,* there is a great war in heaven between God and Satan.
- An epic always describes a long and arduous journey. In the *Odyssey,* Odysseus wanders all over the world before returning home. In the *Ramayana*, Rama undertakes a long journey from north India to Sri Lanka in search of his wife. *Paradise Lost* depicts Satan's journey through Chaos to the newly-created Earth.
- It is common practice for gods and goddesses to participate in the action of epics. The Greek epics have the Olympian gods fighting alongside the Greek heroes. Rama, himself, is an incarnation of Vishnu in the Indian epic. In *Paradise Lost,* Milton brings in God, Christ and the angels.
- The language used in an epic is elevated and majestic, befitting the action that is being depicted. It is narrated in a ceremonial style using a formal language. In *Paradise Lost*,

Milton uses Latinate diction, stylised syntax and a sonorous metre.

- Epic similes and epithets are other formal devices used to enhance the grandeur of style. *Paradise Lost* is full of magnificent epic similes, which refers to a long digression in the narrative in which the poet makes a lengthy comparison.
- A vast expanse of time is covered in an epic. The time covered in the *Iliad* and the *Odyssey* is ten years. In the *Ramayana,* it is the entire lifetime of Rama and in *Paradise Lost,* the time covered is eternity, stretching from the events leading to the creation of Earth to the Second Coming.
- The epic begins with a proposition (a statement of its theme) and an invocation (a prayer to the muse or the guiding spirit). Milton began *Paradise Lost* with the following lines:

  Of man's first disobedience, and the fruit
  Of that forbidden tree, whose mortal taste
  Brought death into this world, and all our woe,
  With loss of Eden, till one greater man
  Restore us, and regain the blissful seat,
  Sing heav'nly Muse
- The narrative starts in medias res (in the middle of things). *Paradise Lost* opens in Hell, where the fallen angels try to gather forces and plan their revenge. It is only in Books V to VII that we learn about the actual beginning of the story when Raphael relates to Adam about the war in heaven and the events leading to Satan's visit to Eden.
- There are catalogues of characters as in Milton's description of the procession of fallen angels in Book I.
- Another epic convention is epic games. In *Paradise Lost* Book I, the fallen angels indulge in a number of games to while away time till Satan returns after exploring Earth.

Paradise Regained is the complement of and reply to *Paradise Lost*. It deals with the temptation of Christ in the wilderness. According to Milton's interpretation of the scriptures, Paradise was lost due to the weakness of Adam and Eve and was regained by Christ's resistance to temptation. In *Paradise Regained*, Satan is depicted as a smooth-talking cunning creature. Milton describes the thoughts and mental struggle of Christ in a very human manner. There is a striking autobiographical note in *Paradise Regained*. Satan's offering of Greece, her literature, philosophy and learning, to Christ is very close to Milton's own fascination for classical literature. In Christ's rejection of the offer, Milton reveals that even the poetry of Greece pales before the Bible. *Paradise Regained* was written in four books and was published in 1671.

Samson Agonistes is a tragedy published along with *Paradise Regained* in the same volume. It is a closet drama modelled on Greek tragedy and strictly adheres to its principles. The three unities of time, place and action are observed. The whole action takes place in one day and in one place. The action revolves around the vanquished and betrayed Samson who is in prison. He is visited by friends and is finally taken away to provide entertainment for the Philistines, when he destroys the entire assembly, including himself, by pulling down the pillars. The play bears a close resemblance to Milton's own life at the time of writing it—he was blind and a survivor of the lost Republican cause amidst the alien Royalists. In his last poem, Milton gave vent to his frustration at losing a political battle and also his contempt for women.

Features

- He enhanced all the poetical forms that he attempted—the sonnet, the elegy, the ode and the epic.
- His contribution to the classical dramatic forms was significant—*Comus* is considered the best masque in the English language and in *Samson Agonistes*, he revives the classical Greek tragedy.
- He gave a new lease to blank verse by using it so grandly in his epics.

John Bunyan (1628–88)

Some Gospel Truths Opened (1656)
A Vindication (1657)
The Holy City or *The New Jerusalem* (1665)

Grace Abounding to the Chief of Sinners (1666)
The Confession of my Faith and a Reason of my Practice (1672)
The Pilgrim's Progress (1678)
The Life and Death of Mr Badman (1680)
The Holy War (1682)

Life

Bunyan was born near Bedford and was a tinker, like his father. He had little formal education. He was drafted into the Parliamentary army when he was sixteen and served there for the next two years. In 1649, he got married and his wife introduced him to two religious works—Dent's *Plain Man's Pathway to Heaven* and Bayly's *Practice of Piety.* These books along with the Bible, the *Book of Common Prayer* and Foxe's *Book of Martyrs* were his staple reading matter and led him to think seriously about religion. He joined a nonconformist church in Bedford and began to preach. He was arrested for preaching without a licence and was jailed for the next twelve years. He wrote several religious books while in jail. After he was released from prison in 1672, he became a pastor, but was again imprisoned in 1675. It was then that he began writing *The Pilgrim's Progress,* which was at one time considered to be the most popular book in England after the Bible. The poetry of Milton and the prose of Bunyan are the finest and most characteristic literary outcome of English Puritanism.

His fame as a preacher spread far and wide and he was familiarly called 'Bishop Bunyan'. He died in a friend's house in London due to a chill caught while on a long ride through a rainstorm.

Works

He was over thirty when the Cromwellian Republic came to an end. It was, therefore, in a hostile climate that Bunyan went on to write *The Pilgrim's Progress*, the most popular book to express the faith of Puritanism. His work, though strictly belonging to the Restoration period, has nothing in common with Restoration literature.

Bunyan was a gifted storyteller and though one cannot call him the founder of the modern novel, he was definitely one of its pioneers. Between 1656, the date of his first book, and 1688, the date of his last, Bunyan wrote nearly sixty books. Of these, only four are considered significant today—*Grace Abounding*, *The Pilgrim's Progress*, *The Life and Death of Mr Badman* and *The Holy War*.

In *Grace Abounding*, Bunyan narrated the story of his own spiritual journey, beginning with his humble birth, his wicked childhood and youth, his exploits in the army, and his gradual awakening to religion, thanks to his wife. The book also recounts his experiences in prison and the final call to the ministry. The prose is lucid and simple and the tone is one of utmost sincerity.

The Pilgrim's Progress is an allegory in the form of a dream. In the dream, the author sees Christian, with a burden on his back, reading a book. Christian learns that the city in which he and his family are living will be burned to ashes soon. He consults Evangelist, who advises him to leave the City of Destruction. Unable to persuade his family to come with him, Christian sets off by himself. He travels through the Slough of Despond, the Interpreter's House, the House Beautiful, the Valley of the Shadow of Death, Vanity Fair, Doubting Castle, the Delectable Mountains, the Country of Beulah and finally reaches the Celestial City. He meets several allegorical characters such as Mr Worldly Wiseman, Faithful, Hopeful, Giant Despair and many others, on his journey to the Celestial City. In the second part of *The Pilgrim's Progress*, Bunyan relates the story of Christian's wife, Christina undertaking the same journey.

The work is remarkable for the vivid portraiture of the characters, the numerous incidents, the touches of pathos, humour and sublimity and the naturalness of the narrative in simple English. In an objective manner, Bunyan describes the spiritual progress of every Christian soul. His prose combines, at once, the flavour of popular speech with the dignity of the Authorised Version of the Bible. This style appealed to the learned as well as the unlearned.

The Life and Death of Mr Badman is a very different type of book. It is a realistic novel which focuses on the worldly life of the later Stuart period. The protagonist is one who does not shake off his evils and dies a sinner. The story is interesting and it is valuable as far as the history of the English novel is concerned.

Another important allegory that Bunyan wrote is *The Holy War*. He went back to his days in the army for inspiration. It is an allegory of the progress of the Christian soul as well as the history of the English church. In *The Holy War*, the city of Mansoul is captured by Diabolus. The builder of the city sends some people, including his own son Emmanuel, to recover it. After a severe battle Emmanuel succeeds, but there is a downfall after the re-establishment of the king. Diabolus recaptures the city but is not able to take its citadel. Finally, he is defeated by Emmanuel. Compared to *The Pilgrim's Progress*, *The Holy War* neither has good characterisation nor a realistic representation of humanity.

Features

- Bunyan's *The Pilgrim's Progress* is almost a synonym for the form of the allegory. He gave allegory a new lease of life by introducing vivid characters. *The Pilgrim's Progress* is also the most perfect representation of the Evangelical faith.
- As a story, *The Pilgrim's Progress* ranks on a level with *Robinson Crusoe* and *Gulliver's Travels*. Bunyan's contribution to the development of fiction is significant.
- To English prose, he gave a style that was both simple and picturesque.

RESTORATION (1660–1702)

Charles II (1660–85)
James II (1685–88)
William III and Mary II (1689–1702)

The term 'Restoration' refers not only to the restoration of monarchy, but also to the restoration of the Church of England and the old social hierarchy and customs. Politically, it restored the king, the parliament and its law in place of military dictatorship; ecclesiastically, it restored the Bishop (during the

Commonwealth, the Puritans had favoured a Presbyterian church government where the congregation was governed by a council of elders, rather than by bishops), the Book of Common Prayer and the Anglican church in place of Puritanism; socially, it restored the nobles and the gentry to their hereditary positions as the acknowledged leaders of local and national life. These changes had a great impact upon the literature of the period which cannot be understood or appreciated without a proper understanding of the times to which they belong. The writers who lived during that age were acutely conscious of the changing tastes of their readers and audiences and wrote to please them. The religious conflicts that ended in the Civil War, were firmly put aside and people looked forward to a period of peace and prosperity.

When Charles II was recalled from France, the people, who were disillusioned with the Protectorate, looked forward to an end to the conflict between the Puritans and Anglicans and the one between the Crown and the Parliament. However, soon after the Restoration two disasters dampened the spirit of the people considerably. One was the **Plague of London** in 1665 and the other was the **Fire of London** in 1666. These calamities changed the landscape of London and altered the lives of the people. The plague killed seventy thousand people and the Great Fire destroyed over half of the city's houses and buildings. These events were accurately captured in the diaries of two contemporary writers, Samuel Pepys and John Evelyn.

After Charles II died in 1685, his brother James II ascended the throne. The people were dissatisfied with James II as he was a Catholic. They, however, tolerated him since they did not want to cause a disruption once again. They hoped that he would be succeeded by his Protestant daughter, Mary. Their hopes, however, were dashed when James had a son and it became evident that Catholicism would become the predominant religion. Therefore, they demanded the abdication of James and invited Mary's husband, William III of Orange, to invade England. Once William landed on English soil, James abdicated his throne and fled to France. This is known as the **Glorious**

Revolution or the **Bloodless Revolution.** William and Mary ruled till 1702.

ↂↂↂↂ

Restoration Drama

The Puritan government had closed the theatres in September 1642 and though there were surreptitious performances, English drama had virtually come to a standstill between 1642 and 1660. With the restoration of Charles II to the throne, the theatres were reopened. There was a great change both within the theatre and in the plays that were produced after the Restoration. Restoration drama consisted of two types of plays—comedy of manners and heroic tragedy.

Theatre

The Restoration theatres were very different from their Elizabethan counterparts. During the Elizabethan Age, the stage did not have any scenery, decoration or drop-curtain. As the plays were usually performed during the afternoon, the stage was only half-lit. In Elizabethan and Jacobean theatres, boys whose voices were not yet broken, had played the female roles. All this changed with the Restoration. The Restoration theatre was completely roofed in and the stage was artificially lit with candles. It had footlights and elaborate moving scenery and the female roles were played by women.

Audience

Even the audience was very different from that of the preceding ages. Shakespeare depended a great deal on the imaginative faculties of his audience to make up for the absence of stage settings. With the help of just a line or two, audiences could completely create, with their mind's eye, a scene in far-away Egypt or Venice. The Restoration audience on the other hand, was deficient in imagination and needed artificial props to aid them.

Another important difference lay in the fact that Restoration theatre catered to private audiences as opposed to the public audiences of the Elizabethan and Jacobean theatres. Most of the people who visited the Restoration theatre were wits and gallants hailing from the upper classes of society. The dramatists, keeping their audience in mind, reflected in their plays the amoral life of the courtiers in the 1660s. The fashionable men went to the theatre to show off their fine clothes and carriages and to socialise. The theatre was a place where appointments were made, duels arranged and mistresses picked up. The playhouse thus earned a dubious reputation and was shunned by respectable citizens. The dramatists reacted by ridiculing this middle-class morality. The extreme licentiousness of Restoration drama was not because these times were coarser than the Elizabethan Age, but because the Royalists wished to strike back against Puritan oppression. They looked upon morality with cynicism and ridiculed it.

Comedy of Manners

This type of comedy was the form that was most identified with the Restoration. Comedy of manners was a type of drama that was prevalent even earlier. Shakespeare's *Love's Labour's Lost* and *Much Ado About Nothing* are examples of this genre. It however, reached its point of perfection during the Restoration. As a genre, it had certain unique features:

- It satirised the amoral behaviour of upper-class society. Sometimes it bordered on the vulgar although its aim was to reform through ridicule.
- The characters were often trying to deceive either themselves or others. For example, an old woman trying to appear young, a jealous husband or a flirtatious wife.
- The dramatists made use of wit and repartee (a verbal dual in which there is a quick give and take of short dialogues).
- The plot focused on the love intrigues of young aristocrats and often contained bedroom scenes where a character was concealed behind a curtain.

Excellent writers of this type of comedy were Sir George Etherege, William Wycherley and William Congreve. By the end of the century, comedy of manners declined and was replaced with the sentimental comedy of Oliver Goldsmith. His contemporary, Richard Sheridan, however, revived the wit and humour of the comedy of manners but without its indecency. It was revived once again by Oscar Wilde in the nineteenth century.

Heroic Tragedy

A heroic tragedy is a type of drama that aspired to epic grandeur and dealt with the exploits of great warriors in love and battle. It was immensely popular during the Restoration period and had certain distinct features.

- The theme of a heroic tragedy was the conflict between love and honour.
- The hero was an elevated character and the heroine, a virtuous lady. The characters were not well-rounded and were usually exaggerated.
- The language used in such plays was elevated and elaborate, often bordering on the bombastic. The plays had extremely dramatic situations with scope for pompous speeches.
- Usually, the epigrammatic form of the closed heroic couplet was used.
- These plays were influenced by the French and the Spanish. One can discern the French influence of Corneille whose plays depict the conflict between love and duty.
- Examples of the heroic tragedy include Dryden's *Love Triumphant* and *Conquest of Granada*. Other dramatists who wrote heroic tragedies were Nathaniel Lee and Thomas Otway.

Restoration Prose

There was a marked development in the prose style of the period. The long-winded sentences, overburdened with imagery and containing several parentheses, disappeared. The French style of writing was popular and its influence made itself felt on English prose. This was first seen in the short, clear and crisp sentences of the Restoration. Dryden's prose was clear, precise and full of vigour and proved to be a very strong influence on later writers.

Prose was applied to a variety of new literary uses in the latter half of the seventeenth century. Most important among these were literary criticism, diary-writing, the novel and history. Dryden's criticism is an important milestone in the history of literary criticism. He wrote several essays about drama which laid the foundation for British literary criticism. These essays, along with his translations of classical writers, represent what many literary historians consider the first modern prose in English. Written in a clear and direct style, they are colloquial in tone.

The diaries of John Evelyn and Samuel Pepys took autobiographical writing to a new height and proved to be excellent and accurate chronicles of the period. John Bunyan's *Life and Death of Mr Badman* paved the way for the development of the novel in the second half of the century.

If the prose of Dryden and Samuel Butler displayed an anti-Puritan feeling, it did not however mean that the Puritan tradition in England was dead. A great body of Puritan literature was flourishing in the second-half of the seventeenth century. Arthur Dent's *Plain Man's Pathway to Heaven*, which was first published in 1601, continued to be reprinted and read throughout the century. Richard Bernard's prose allegory *The Isle of Man* also enjoyed a good readership. John Bunyan's books gave a definite direction to the prose of this period. Through its beautiful combination of the Biblical and homily styles, Bunyan's prose appealed both to the learned as well as the unlearned.

The founding of the Royal Society in 1662 also had its impact on English prose. Men like John Locke were interested in reforming prose by making it clear and simple. They advocated a lucid and distinct vocabulary. We, thus, see that all the influences—the French, the Puritan and that of the Royal Society—were in one direction: simplicity and clarity. The changes and development of the late-seventeenth-century prose style played a very important part in making the English novel possible.

Satire

Satire flourished in the second-half of the seventeenth century and the eighteenth century. The Restoration was largely instrumental in encouraging satire. After the fall of Puritanism, there was an open denunciation of the false spiritual authority and hypocrisy of the insincere Puritans. The contemporary rivalry between the Whigs and the Tories over the issue of the successor of Charles II gave tremendous scope for political satires. Classical literature, which was exercising its influence through the translations of Horace and Juvenal into English, favoured satire and made this style of writing fashionable. Besides, satire was in fashion in France and with the Restoration, when the Royalists returned to England from France, they made it popular. Satire continued to be popular in England until the end of the neoclassical period, that is, the mid-eighteenth century.

According to M.H. Abrams, 'satire is the literary art of diminishing a subject by making it ridiculous and evoking toward it attitudes of amusement, contempt, indignation, or scorn'. It may be written in any form—prose, poetry, drama or novel. Satire may be divided into two main categories—formal or direct satire and informal or indirect satire.

Formal satire uses the first person and addresses either the reader or a character within the work itself directly. Formal satire may be further divided into two types—the **Horatian satire** and the **Juvenalian satire.** In the former, the speaker is an urbane, witty and worldly man and in the latter, he is a serious moralist who uses a declamatory voice to point out the vices of society. An example of the Horatian satire is Pope's *Epistle to Dr Arbuthnot.* Dr Johnson's *London* and *The Vanity of Human Wishes* are examples of Juvenalian satire.

Indirect satire is usually a narrative in which the author creates characters who make themselves ridiculous. The objects of the satire are, thus, the characters themselves. One type of indirect satire is known as **Menippean satire** named after the Greek philosopher, the cynic Menippus. The main feature of this type of satire is its use of extended dialogues or debates, in which a group of people, representing various professions, present their points of view in a ludicrous manner typical of their background. Lewis Carroll's two *Alice* books could also be classified as Menippean satires.

John Dryden (1631–1700)

Poetry
Heroique Stanzas (1658)
Astrea Redux (1660)
To His Sacred Majesty (1660)
Annus Mirabilis (1667)
Song for St Cecilia's Day (1687)
Alexander's Feast (1697)
Religio Laici (1682)
The Hind and the Panther (1687)

Comedy
The Wild Gallant (1663)
The Rival Ladies (1664)
Sir Martin Mar-all (1667, with the Duke of Newcastle)
Secret Love (1667)
An Evening's Love (1668)
Marriage a-la-Mode (1672)
The Assignation (1672)
The Spanish Friar (1681)
Love Triumphant (1694)

Adaptations
Adaptation of *The Tempest* (1667)
Adaptation of *Troilus and Cressida* (1679)
The State of Innocence and Fall of Man (1674)—adaptation of *Paradise Lost*

Heroic Tragedy
The Indian Queen (1664)
The Indian Emperor (1665)
Tyrannick Love (1669)
The Conquest of Granada (1670)
Aureng–Zebe (1675)

Tragedies in Blank Verse
All for Love (1678, in blank verse)
Don Sabastian (1689)
Amphitryon (1690)

Literary Criticism
An Essay of Dramatic Poesie (1668)
A Defence of an Essay (1668)
Preface to Fables Ancient and Modern (1700)

Satire
Absalom and Achitophel (1681)
Mac Flecknoe (1682)
The Medal (1682)

Translations
Ovid's *Epistles* (1680)
Virgil (1697)
Fables, Ancient and Modern (1700)

Life

Dryden was the son of a staunch Puritan rector. He had his early education at Westminster School and went to Trinity College, Cambridge for his higher studies. On leaving Cambridge, he was appointed as secretary to the chamberlain of Oliver Cromwell.

He had begun writing poetry when he was in school and continued to do so at the beginning of his literary career. After the accession of Charles II, Dryden changed his political views and became well-received at court. He then turned his attention to drama to earn his livelihood, devoting nearly fifteen years to theatre before he returned once more to poetry—this time as a satiric and didactic poet. He was appointed poet laureate in 1668 and two years later, he was made the royal historiographer. Dryden was frequently seen at Will's Coffee House. He became involved in the contemporary political strife between the Whigs and Tories. He used his poetical skills to produce some of the best satires of all time.

Dryden made use of his literary skills to support the Church of England in *Religio Laici*. After his conversion to Catholicism, however, he wrote *The Hind and the Panther* supporting his new faith. In 1688, after the Glorious Revolution, when William and Mary ascended the throne, Dryden refused to swear allegiance to them. He, therefore, lost his position in court. He spent his last years translating the classics.

Works

Dryden was the most important literary figure of his time. He dominated the world of letters in the last quarter of the seventeenth century. He excelled as a poet, dramatist, literary critic, satirist and translator. T.S. Eliot declared that 'Dryden is the ancestor of nearly all that is best in the poetry of the eighteenth century' and Matthew Arnold observed, 'Here at last we have the true English prose, a prose such as we would all gladly use if only we knew how'. His literary career could be studied under five headings—poetry, drama, literary criticism, satire and translation.

POETRY

Dryden is the last and the greatest of the transitional poets whose works combine the fading echoes of the Renaissance and the renewal of the neoclassical school. He published his first important poem *Heroic Stanzas* to commemorate the death of Oliver Cromwell, five years after he left Cambridge. A year later, when he wrote *Astraea Redux* hailing the return of Charles II to the throne, there is a definite reversal in Dryden's politics. In his next important early work *Annus Mirabilis*, Dryden commemorated the Great Fire of London and England's victory in the war with Holland. These early works reflect the impact that William Davenant and Edmund Waller had upon the formation of Dryden's style. At this stage, Dryden was striving hard to display his skill in using language and imagery which was often characterised by wit and cleverness. Although he was to emerge as the greatest poet of the age, Dryden was still trying to discover his genius. His early poems were panegyric as he was good at writing complimentary verses. This tradition of verse compliment in English goes back to Jonson. Much of the complimentary verses by Dryden were written on special occasions. For instance, 'To My Hounured Friend Sir Robert Howard, on his Excellent Poems', 'To My Hounoured Friend Dr Charleton' and 'To My Dear Friend Mr Congreve, on his Comedy Called *The Double Dealer*'.

It was much later that he discovered that his true wit was in satirical verse. He also discovered the merit of the ancients and, under their influence, his poetry slanted towards the classical.

Towards the end of his career, he was engaged in writing religious poetry. *Religio Laici* reveals Dryden as a master of verse argument. It is a poem of 456 lines in heroic couplets in which Dryden defended the Church of England. He praised the Anglican religion for striking the right balance between the fanaticism of the Catholics and the Dissenters. In 1686, he became a Roman Catholic and wrote *The Hind and the Panther*, defending the Roman Catholic point of view. It is in the form of a beast fable, in which the hind represents the Roman Catholic Church and the panther, the Church of England. He made use of other animals too—the bear to represent the Independents, the wolf, the Presbyterians, the hare, the Quakers and the ape, the Freethinkers.

The strong dance-like rhythms of Restoration poetry attracted Dryden, who followed musicality in his later lyrical poetry. His attempt to imitate the effects of music through language culminated in his *A Song for St Cecilia's Day* and *Alexander's Feast*. Poems in praise of music for St Cecilia's Day were fashionable in the seventeenth century and Dryden was just following this popular custom. His two odes, written in Pindaric fashion, were the best of their kind. Dryden's best Pindaric ode is 'To the Pious Memory of the Accomplished Young Lady, Mrs Anne Killigrew'. In this poem, one can see the fusion of rhetorical splendour and genuine emotion.

DRAMA

Dryden was nearly thirty years old at the time of the Restoration. When the theatres were reopened, he was quick to see the vast potential of the theatre and turned his attention to the writing of plays. The king and several Royalists had fled to France and Spain after their defeat in the Civil War. When they returned to England after the Restoration, they brought back with them a taste for the French school of tragedy and the Spanish school of comedy. Dryden's plays reveal the influence of both. Dryden followed Corneille and Racan by using rhyme and combined it with the popular Elizabethan iambic pentameter to form rhyming couplets. The flamboyant nature and the high-flowing sentiment of his plots were inspired by the Spanish playwrights. Dryden's drama can be studied under the following headings: heroic tragedies, comedies and tragicomedies.

Dryden's most famous **heroic tragedies** were *The Indian Emperor*, *The Conquest of Granada* and *Aureng-Zebe*. In these plays, there is a spirit of romanticism that was characteristic of the English theatre during the Renaissance. But this romanticism was stifled by Dryden due to his obsession with dramatic rules. Dryden's plays were far superior to those of his contemporaries as his use of the rhymed couplet was superb. His heroic tragedies were full of improbable situations and had larger-than-life characters. *The Conquest of Granada* is the most brilliant of his heroic plays and it made Dryden the most popular dramatist of his day. He was greatly impressed by the didactic nature and the rhetorical splendour of the rhymed couplet and helped to popularise it during his time.

Soon the public tired of the artificial nature of the heroic tragedy. The high sentiments and affectations of the genre were ridiculed by the Duke of Buckingham in his play *The Rehearsal* (1671), where Dryden himself was satirised. Although Dryden did not abandon heroic drama immediately, he was quick to understand its limitations. His play *Aureng-Zebe* (1675) registers a transition from the heroic tragedy to a purer tragedy. He even slipped into blank verse in several places. The transition was complete in *All for Love* (1678), which was written entirely in blank verse. In *All for Love*, he turned to history and tried to present characters and events in a more plausible manner. After the Glorious Revolution, Dryden produced two more plays—*Don Sebastian* and *Cleomenes. Don Sabastian* is a romantic play in blank verse and prose. *Cleomenes* was styled along the lines of French classical tragedy, but with unrhymed verse.

During the years that immediately followed the downfall of the Puritans, drama concentrated almost exclusively on attacking their moral hypocrisy. The **comedies** of that period broke away from the romanticism of the late Elizabethan theatre. There was no verse, but only prose in the plays. The dramatists looked to Ben Jonson, who had also satirised society in his plays, and to Moliere for their themes. The sole aim of Restoration comedy was to amuse and many dramatists, including Dryden, resorted to writing this type of drama in order to achieve popularity. *The Wild Gallant*, *An Evening's Love*, *Marriage a la Mode*, *The Assignation* and *The Spanish Friar* are some of his best comedies. But these were not very successful with the audience.

LITERARY CRITICISM

Johnson called Dryden 'the Father of English Criticism'. There was no criticism in English before Dryden. Sidney's *Apology* was more of an ethical and philosophical defence of the genre of poetry. Dryden's contribution to literary criticism is great. *Essay on Heroic Plays*, prefixed to *The Conquest of Granada*, the prefaces to *All for Love* and *Fables* and *An Essay on Dramatic Poesy* are some of his writings in this genre. He began his work as a literary critic as early as 1664 when he wrote a dedication at the beginning of his play *The Rival Ladies*. He continued to write some criticism till the very end of his life in the form of either an essay or a preface. He was a workshop critic as all his criticism was connected to his own writings as a poet and dramatist and was written to defend and vindicate his works. This tradition of workshop criticism was later carried on by Coleridge, Matthew Arnold and T.S. Eliot. Dryden enjoyed a certain advantage which helped him succeed as a critic: he was a creative writer with a sound knowledge of the ancient classics.

An Essay of Dramatic Poesy is the only work of criticism that Dryden published as a separate work. It is in the form of a dialogue or literary discussion between four characters. The ideas that are taken up for debate are—the moderns versus the ancients; the contemporaries versus the Elizabethans; the English versus the French and the use of rhyme versus blank verse in drama. By using the technique of the dialogue form, Dryden was able to give the work an air of objectivity. His purpose was mainly to defend English drama against French drama and to justify the use of rhyme in his tragedy. The work also reveals Dryden's support for the tragicomedy and rejection of the three unities, despite his admiration for Aristotle. This shows that he was not dogmatic in his views on the classical rules of drama. By presenting the different points of view in his *Essay*, he made the classical tradition available to his age. His criticism came at the right time—when there was a transition in literary style. He was instrumental in shaping the neoclassical school of literature and literary criticism. He was the first to write descriptive criticism. Before him, criticism was mostly judicial and legislative.

SATIRES

Dryden was more than fifty when he wrote his great satires—*Absalom and Achitophel*, *The Medal* and *Mac Flecknoe*. By that time, Dryden had discovered where his true genius lay and his poetic expression reached perfection. He was quick to see an opportunity in the current political crisis between the Whigs and the Tories regarding the succession of Charles II. The Whigs, led by the Earl of Shaftsbury and the Duke of Buckingham, supported the Duke of Monmouth, the illegitimate son of Charles II, while the Tories wanted James, the Catholic brother of Charles II. This led to the notorious Popish Plot of Titus Oates and the abortive attempt to place Monmouth on the throne. Using this political situation as the backdrop, Dryden wrote *Absalom and Achitophel* in two parts. Using the Biblical story of the rebellion of Absalom against his father, King David, Dryden represented Monmouth as Absalom and Shaftsbury as the wily counsellor Achitophel plotting against Charles, who is represented as King David. *Absalom and Achitophel* is one of the best satires in the English language. This poem appeared about one week before Shaftsbury was tried for treason but subsequently acquitted. To celebrate the victory of his acquittal, the Whigs struck a medal. This prompted Dryden to write his next satire *The Medal*, in which he denounced Shaftsbury and the middle-class Whigs.

Thomas Shadwell replied to Dryden's *The Medal* with his *Medal for John Bayes* which was a crude piece of writing. Provoked by this, Dryden attacked Shadwell in his *Mac Flecknoe*. In that poem, Dryden portrayed Shadwell with humorous contempt. David Daiches points out that 'it is this combination of geniality with witty contempt that gives the poem its special flavour'. In the poem Flecknoe, who was the epitome of bad poetry, nominates Shadwell as the heir to the throne of dullness. Dryden made excellent use of the heroic couplet to strike out at Shadwell:

> The rest to some faint meaning made pretense,
> But Shadwell never deviated into sense.

This personal satire had all the trappings of a mock-heroic poem which would be an inspiration later for Alexander Pope.

TRANSLATIONS AND ADAPTATIONS

When William and Mary ascended the throne, Dryden found himself out of favour at court as he refused to show allegiance to the new monarchs. He spent his last years studying and translating classical literature. He undertook the translation of Juvenal and Perseus and published it in 1693 with a brilliant preface, 'A Discourse Concerning the Origin and Progress of Satire'. In 1697, his translation of Virgil was published. This work was more of an Englishman's interpretation of the classical story than a strict translation of Virgil. This book was scathingly attacked by Swift in his *Battle of the Books*. Dryden reproduced Chaucer and Boccaccio and published it under the title *Fables, Ancient and Modern*. The preface to *Fables* is one of the best examples of Restoration prose.

Dryden's adaptations of Shakespeare are noteworthy. Shakespeare was considered old-fashioned in form and language and it was appropriate to retell the stories to suit the demands of the new age. *The Tempest* was adapted by Dryden into *The Tempest, or The Enchanted Island* with a few changes like a sister for Caliban and a female Ariel. *All for Love* may not be considered as an adaptation but is a free treatment of the story of Antony and Cleopatra. *Troilus and Cressida, or Truth Found Too Late* was a failure, but the preface that was printed with it, 'Preface Concerning the Grounds of Criticism in Tragedy' in which Dryden offered a reasonable application of Aristotelian theory to English practice, is noteworthy.

Features

- Dryden's influence over the world of letters during his own time and for all times is tremendous.
- As the father of English prose, he gave English language a new respectability.
- As a critic, he succeeded in giving shape to neoclassical literature and criticism. He was the first to write descriptive criticism which focuses on analysing and appreciating a literary work without trying to establish literary theories
- As a poet, he perfected the heroic couplet which was to be used almost exclusively in the next fifty years or so. His satirical and didactic poems are the best in the genre. He was able to present his arguments exquisitely in polished metrical form.
- He made abundant contributions to Restoration drama. Apart from the heroic tragedies and comedies, he helped to revive Shakespeare through his adaptations.
- His translations of Virgil and Ovid were inspiring and were avidly read by his contemporaries.

George Etherege (1635?–91)

Love in a Tub (1664)
She Wou'd, If She Cou'd (1668)
The Man of Mode (1676)
Letter-Book (1928)

Life

Etherege was born in Berkshire and was the eldest of six children. Very little is known about his early life. It is believed that Etherege spent part of his early years in France. After he returned to London, he quickly learnt the ways of the world. *Love in a Tub*, his first play, was a great hit and brought him fame and fortune. He married a wealthy widow and was knighted in 1680. As he was handsome and witty, he was sent on many diplomatic assignments. He died in Paris in 1691.

Works

Etherege could be considered as the first accomplished practitioner of Restoration comedy when he wrote his first play, *Love in a Tub*. It is a partly-serious comedy written both in prose and rhymed couplets. The comic plot dealing with gallants, fools, tricksters and all kinds of ladies, was written in prose. The 'heroic' subplot, written in heroic couplets, depicts the conflict between love and loyalty of the unnaturally high-minded protagonists. Although the two sections were not woven together skilfully, this play was the foundation of the comedy of manners and the heroic tragedy that were so popular in the Restoration period.

His next play *She Wou'd, if She Cou'd* was much more carefully constructed. In it, Etherege mocks the fashionable vices of the day. Although the language is light and witty, his tone is cynical. His last play *The Man of Mode* has some of the most brilliantly witty dialogues of Restoration comedy.

Feature

- He set the tone for Restoration drama with his plays. The dramatists who followed after, adopted the genres of the comedy of manners and heroic tragedy. They also continued to write in the same witty manner.

William Wycherley (1640–1716)

Love in a Wood (1671)
The Gentleman Dancing Master (1672)
The Country Wife (1674)
The Plain Dealer (1676)
Miscellany Poems (1704)

Life

He was educated first in France and then at the Queen's College, Oxford. He enrolled as a student at the Inner Temple. He led a rakish and frivolous life in London. After his first play became a success, he enjoyed the patronage of the Duchess of Cleveland, Charles II's mistress. He married a wealthy widow, the Countess of Drogheda. Towards the end of his life, he became a friend of Alexander Pope, who revised many of his works.

Works

His first play *Love in a Wood* is a comedy of intrigue set in St James's Park. It is a superficial comedy in which one can anticipate the action easily. The characters too are unidimensional and not well-etched. *The Gentleman Dancing Master*, which is about the contemporary craze for foreign customs, is again not very skilfully constructed.

By far, the most interesting of his plays are the last two—*The Country Wife* and *The Plain Dealer*. The two plays reveal Wycherley's dissatisfaction with the amorality of the Restoration period. *The Country Wife* is a polished play that has a lot of witty dialogues. Beneath the wit, one is able to see Wycherley's disgust at the unscrupulous selfishness of the age.

The Plain Dealer, too, conveys the dramatist's sense of outrage at the decadence of human nature and society as a whole. This play was inspired by Moliere's *Le Misanthrope* and is extremely witty.

Features

- The coarseness of his plays reflects the society that it depicts. Wycherley was quick to understand the tastes and demands of his audience and gave them what they enjoyed best—licentiousness.
- Through his plays, we get a very vivid picture of the society of his day—the fashions of the young noblemen and ladies, the suggestive conversations and intrigues.
- His characterisation is not very good as the characters lack complexity.
- Behind his cynicism, one is able to make out his secret idealism and his disapproval of the low moral values of his times.

William Congreve (1670–1729)

Play
The Old Bachelor (1693)
The Double Dealer (1694)
Love for Love (1695)
The Morning Bride (1697)
The Way of the World (1700)

Novel
Incognita (1691)

Life

Congreve was born near Leads and was educated at Trinity College, Dublin. He was a classmate of Jonathan Swift. He studied law for a while at the Middle Temple but gave it up. He began his literary career in 1691 with the publication of a novel, *Incognita*, and later wrote several comedies which won him fame. Congreve held several government posts and was well-acquainted with Swift, Richard Steele and Alexander Pope. He died in 1729 and was buried at Westminster Abbey.

Works

In *The Old Bachelor,* Congreve combined farce, satire and Ben Jonson's comedy of humours. The play has witty dialogues, but the plot construction is weak. His next play, *The Double Dealer* was an improvement on the previous one. Maskwell, the villain, was the inspiration for Richard Sheridan's Joseph Surface in *The School for Scandal* and is the prototype of the melodramatic villain.

Love for Love is the most satirical of Congreve's plays. It exposes the hypocrisy of the age which believed in saying one thing and doing another. It has elements of the Jonsonian comedy of humours and has stock characters such as the bluff sailor, the witty and resourceful servant, the unsophisticated girl from the countryside and the vain beau.

The Way of the World was Congreve's last and best comedy. The plot contains all the ingredients of a comedy of manners—witty lovers, the hopeful wit, intrigue and adultery. The play has brilliant repartee between the hero and heroine—Mirabell and Millamant. The tone of the play, however, is not purely comic as it has undertones of sadness. The dramatist seems aware of the ironies and ambiguities of life. Through his play,

Congreve attempted to expose the excesses and abuses of society. Through the exaggerated portrayal of the social customs of the age, he wished to highlight its superficiality. For example, the contemporary vanity and pretension and the obsession with physical appearances and pursuit of advantageous marriages. He wished to draw the attention of the audience to these issues through ridicule and good-natured laughter.

Features

- Congreve was known for his sharp and witty dialogues. His plays are full of clever wordplay and satirical humour and his dialogues elevated the dignity of Restoration comedy.
- Congreve's prose style was the best of his age. He had the unique knack for using exact words.
- He played a crucial role in the development of Restoration comedy. His creations influenced the work of subsequent dramatists.
- Through his plays, Congreve enhanced the genre of the comedy of manners. He was very skilful in weaving brilliant plots of intrigue and his characterisation was also lively. His thinking was very clear and he wrote in a lucid style with precise turns of phrase.

John Evelyn (1620–1706)

Fumifugium (1661)
Sculptura (1662)
Sylva (1664)
Navigation and Commerce (1674)
Memoirs or *Diary* (1818)
Life of Mrs Godolphin (1847)

Life

Evelyn was born in Surrey and educated at Balliol College, Oxford. He was a great supporter of the Royalists and disliked the Civil War. He lived on the Continent till 1652. In 1660, he became a member of the Royal Society of London. From 1685 to 1687, he was Commissioner of the Privy Seal and treasurer of Greenwich Hospital from 1695 to 1703. He later returned to his birthplace where he died in 1706.

Works

Evelyn wrote on a variety of subjects. In his *Fumifugium,* he gave several suggestions for controlling the smoke in London. He advocated the use of English dresses instead of foreign fashions in *Tyrannus, or, The Mode. Sylva* revived the spirit of planting trees in England.

He is, however, remembered chiefly for his diaries in which he recorded his impressions from 1641 until his death. In his diaries, we get a lot of information on life in the second-half of the seventeenth century, both in England and on the Continent. Evelyn described his travels abroad and shared his concerns about London. Although he did not write every day, historians give him credit for his detailed and precise account of the life of that period. Through his diaries, one is able to form a picture of English life during the reign of Charles II, James II and William III.

Samuel Pepys (1633–1703)

Diary (1660–1669) *Memoirs of the Royal Navy* (1690)

Life

He was the son of a tailor in London. He was educated at St Paul's School and Trinity Hall and Magdalene College, Cambridge. Through the influence of his relative, the Earl of Sandwich, Pepys obtained a minor secretaryship and was later appointed Clerk of the Privy Seal as well as Clerk of the Acts. He had started diary-writing from 1 January 1660 but in 1669, he developed symptoms of blindness and gave it up.

For the next thirty-two years, he did not make another entry. He was made Secretary to the Admiralty in 1673 and Master of Trinity House in 1676. In 1678, he was committed to the Tower of London on charges of being a part of the **Popish Plot**—a fictitious plot created by Titus Oates that alleged that the Jesuits were planning to assassinate Charles II and replace him with his Catholic brother, James II. Pepys was released in 1680 when it was discovered that he was innocent. In 1683, he was sent to Tangier which he documented in an interesting diary. In 1684, he was reappointed Secretary to the Admiralty where he worked sincerely to provide the country with an efficient fleet. His *Memoirs of the Navy* was an outcome of these experiences. After the Glorious Revolution, he was forced to retire to Clapham where he lived till his death.

Works

His diary gives us an accurate and detailed account of the years between 1660 and 1669. The diary was written in a private code which was a combination of shorthand, foreign words and phrases and contractions of his own invention. He recorded the events of his daily life, including a frank disclosure of his various affairs. In it, he shares his interest in music, theatre, painting and collecting books. It also reflects his awareness of the growing scientific spirit of the times. He included in the diary, gossip about the court of Charles II. He never intended for his diary to be read by the public and therefore wrote in a candid style. It was decoded only in 1825.

His diary has proved to be a very important document as it records all the important events of that period. There is a colourful account of the Restoration, the Great Plague of 1665 and the Great Fire of 1666. As a human document, Pepys's diary has great appeal.

Eighteenth Century

1700–1830

The eighteenth century was very eventful in England's history. Beginning with the reign of Queen Anne, it went on to witness the reign of the Hanoverians—George I, II and III.

Queen Anne (1702–14)
House of Hanover
George I (1714–27)
George II (1727–60)
George III (1760–1820)

It was the century in which two bloody revolutions took place, altering forever the history of the world—the American War of Independence and the French Revolution. It was also the century when the Industrial Revolution and the Agrarian Revolution altered the landscape of England irrevocably. A whole new way of life began during the eighteenth century. In this chapter, we will look at the eighteenth century under three headings:

- Age of Swift and Pope (1700–40)
- Age of Johnson (1740–80)
- Pre-Romantics and Romantic Revival (1780–1830)

Social hierarchy was given a lot of importance during Queen Anne's Age. People were very conscious of their place in society; this aspect of society was satirised by Pope in his mock epic *The Rape of the Lock*. Socially, the age was very interesting as a number of new fashions were introduced. The gentlemen and ladies led a life of luxury and leisure. They enjoyed playing cards and gambling. Gentlemen of all classes were addicted to drinking heavily. Smoking tobacco in long and ornamental pipes was considered to be fashionable with the men. Taking snuff was yet another habit of the age and men carried their snuff in ornamental boxes made of silver or amber. Duelling was common among the gentlemen and most disputes were settled with a duel. Outdoor activities like cockfighting, horse-racing and horse-riding, fishing, shooting and snaring birds were very popular. Cricket was a new game that emerged during Queen Anne's time.

Great attention was paid to dressing by both men and women of the nobility. Elaborate wigs were popular with the men and women wore intricate gowns and several petticoats.

Coffee and tea, the two new drinks introduced in England, became popular with both men and women. An important feature of Queen Anne's reign was the establishment of **coffee houses**. There were about five hundred coffee houses in London alone at the time. The coffee houses were centres of social and political discussions; there were distinct coffee houses for different groups of people. For instance, the Whigs visited St James's Coffee House. The poets, critics and their patrons met at Will's Coffee House. The Quakers and the Dissenters frequented coffee houses that exclusively catered to them. In an age when there were no newspapers, coffee houses served the purpose of keeping its patrons well-informed about current affairs.

The social hierarchy that was prevalent during the time of Queen Anne, continued as the century progressed. The bustling city of London was different from other places in England. People from the countryside were wonder-struck at the busy streets, magnificent buildings, street lamps and shops. Apart from being the political capital, it was also the seat of fashion and society. Literature, drama and music flourished in London. The royal court was no longer the centre of fashionable life as it had been during Elizabeth's reign. People of fashion congregated in the houses of the noblemen or at public places like clubs, gambling houses or theatres.

Gambling and drinking which gained popularity at the beginning of the century became rampant as the century progressed and resulted in making society uncouth and brutal. As a result of the industrial and agrarian revolutions, there was a mass migration of the people from the countryside to the cities. This caused the proliferation of slums where people had to live in unsanitary and overcrowded conditions. There was a moral degradation and the poor had no protection against unemployment. They often landed in debtors' prisons. Churchgoing became irregular and thousands of slum dwellers who did not belong to any church were considered to be ignorant heathens.

During the late-eighteenth century and early-nineteenth century, several industrial and agricultural changes took place which had a tremendous impact upon society. The French Revolution cast a long shadow across British consciousness and succeeded in causing a break in the historical continuity of the nation. The sudden demolition of monarchy and the emergence of a new social order posed fresh challenges to the people not only in France and England, but across Europe. There were mixed responses to the social upheaval. While the enthusiasts welcomed the collapse of a tyrannical aristocracy and the emergence of democratic and egalitarian ideals, the sceptics were full of apprehension and anxiety at witnessing the end of a familiar way of life. All this had its impact upon the literature of the age. Several writers who were repelled by the coldness of the Machine Age and the confused reaction to the social upheaval brought on by the French Revolution sought to get away from the harsh realities of contemporary life by escaping to a distant past and tried to recapture the glory of an earlier age.

Attempting a literary survey of a period such as the eighteenth century is a very complex exercise, for it contains several literary giants ranging from Pope and Swift to Jane Austen and the Romantics. The century began with neoclassical literature which was popular till about 1740 and its end witnessed the blossoming of the Romantic Revival. In between, a new genre—the **novel**—took root through the books of Daniel Defoe and Jonathan Swift and flourished in its full form in the works of Richardson and Fielding. Another form that was extremely popular during this time was the **periodical essay**. Both these forms gave to English prose a new dimension and respectability. However, in spite of its great variety, one may discern certain characteristic features in the literature of the eighteenth century that make it stand apart.

A notable feature of the literature of the period was its close connection with politics. The government was anxious to make use of writers to propagate its views and the writers were only too eager to oblige. Writers like Defoe, Steele, Addison, Swift, Burke and Gibbon were very active politically. Johnson often made incursions into the field of politics on matters of current interest and Hume was sent on several diplomatic missions. Even poets such as Gay, Congreve, Thomson and Cowper were involved to some degree in politics. Pope and Goldsmith were the only two poets who were not actively involved in politics.

Another interesting trait of the age was the concept of patronage. The practice of dedicating a work and finding a patron was considered to be almost as important as securing a publisher. This practice was common even among great authors such as Dryden, Thomson, Swift and Young. Attitudes towards patronage, however, were changing. For example, Goldsmith, who was himself poor, dedicated his work to his brother, who was also a poet but poorer than him. Johnson forced people to redefine the meaning of a patron in his famous letter to Lord Chesterfield: 'Is not a patron, my Lord, one who looks with unconcern on a man struggling for life in the water, and when he has reached ground, encumbers him with help?' From then on, authors gradually began to look to their readers alone for patronage.

The influence of France on England was yet another characteristic feature of the eighteenth century. In drama, Corneille, Racine and Moliere made their influence felt. The English, notably Alexander Pope, devoured the satires of Boileau. Fielding and Smollett owed a good deal to the French novelist and playwright, Lesage. On the whole, the French influenced taste and style rather than ideas.

The eighteenth century is often referred to as the Age of Enlightenment and Reason. It was the period that witnessed the advancement of science. Men like Edmund Halley and Sir Isaac Newton did much to explain the 'how' of several natural phenomena such as the appearance of the comet and the law of gravity. These scientific and rational explanations gradually began to erode the religious beliefs of some people. If God did not send comets to warn people, perhaps He did not interfere at all in man's affairs. People began to look upon the universe as an immense piece of clockwork set in motion by a creator who had withdrawn himself from it. This view, part of a complex set of ideas known as **Deism**, made people feel self-satisfied and complacent. Deist ideas appear in the writings of such philosophers as Jean-Jacques Rousseau and Voltaire of France and Immanuel Kant of Germany.

AGE OF SWIFT AND POPE (1700–40)

It was a rich age in literature and is often compared to the glorious period of Augustus in ancient Rome. During the reign of the Roman emperor Augustus, Latin literature reached its height in the hands of literary giants like Virgil, Horace and Ovid. The English writers of this period of the seventeenth century, like Pope, tried to recapture the philosophical and literary ideals of ancient Rome. Reason and common sense dominated the learning of that period and writers attempted to find balance and harmony in their works. People had little time for fancy and wished to be led by reason. Since there was such a strong revival of the classics, it was also known as the Neoclassical Age. Pope's poetry is a brilliant example of the neoclassical style, exhibiting wit, elegance and moderation. He perfected the heroic couplet and made it the staple medium for poetry for the best part of the century.

To use terms such as 'neoclassical' to define a whole period is to be reductive as it destroys the individuality of each writer by trapping him in a cobweb of generalisations. A look at some of the major writers who could be placed in this group will immediately prove the veracity of the above statement. Dryden, who belonged to the previous century, and Pope and Goldsmith, who came in the second-half of the seventeenth century, could be considered neoclassical poets. In the genre of prose, the century has writers like Swift, Addison, Steele and Defoe. We can see at once how unique each of their talents is. However, there are certain salient literary features which will be discussed through the course of this chapter that distinguish them as neoclassical writers.

Neoclassical Poetry

The literature of the new age reflected the triumph of classical ideals. During the Renaissance, when the classics were revived, it was the substance or the theme of the classics that had attracted the writers. In neoclassical literature, it was the classical form that was imitated. Horace's *Ars Poetica* was considered to be the epitome of artistic correctness and the neoclassical writers strove to follow the 'rules' of his art. They believed that it was vital to observe the rules of the various genres such as epic, tragedy, comedy and the pastoral in order to reach artistic perfection. Pope aptly sums this up when he advises writers in his *An Essay on Criticism:*

> Be Homer's works your study and delight,
> Read them by day, and meditate by night.

Although they admired the classical genres of epic and tragedy, they wrote their masterpieces in lesser forms such as the comedy of manners, satire and essays on prose and poetry. But their classical leanings were reflected in their choice of the rigid closed couplet.

Enlisted below are a few features that are unique to neoclassical literature.

- The neoclassicists considered literature to be an art which had to be studied and perfected through hard work and practice. According to them, Homer and Shakespeare had natural genius and were a rarity and did not have to follow rules They believed, in the words of Pope, that their work therefore had 'a grace beyond the reach of art'. The common man however, had to labour to achieve literary fame.
- In neoclassical literature, intellect and wit were given priority over emotion and imagination. Unlike the Romantics, neoclassical writers did not value creativity or originality. Man's rationality and common sense were valued above all other faculties. They believed that the world was a carefully

ordered creation of God with man in the middle of the **Great Chain of Being**. According to the American critic, Arthur O. Lovejoy, in his book *The Great Chain of Being*, the chain represents the ladder-like hierarchy of life on earth extending from the lowest animals up to God. This idea may be traced back to Plato and was popular during the Renaissance. As a rational being, man had to understand that the great truths about the world were well-known and fixed. The writer's duty was merely to express these truths in the appropriate language. 'True wit', according to Pope 'is what oft was thought but ne'er so well expressed.'

- The strong Romantic spirit which manifested itself throughout the Elizabethan period, could not be sustained forever. There was a decline in its exuberance by the beginning of the seventeenth century, when it dwindled into the artificiality and violence of Jacobean drama. The Civil War and rise of Puritanism developed a close link between literature and politics. This became very pronounced in the Neoclassical Age and we see that writers like Dryden, Pope, Addison, Steele and Swift wrote several satires with political overtones.
- There is very little of nature in neoclassical literature which was largely urban and centred around the court and genteel life. The focus was more on men and manners and a poet's task was to instruct and entertain. The ideal of neoclassical humanism was not art for art's sake, but art for man's sake.
- Although man was the subject of much neoclassical literature, these works were highly objective. The poet seldom looked within himself nor gave expression to his own innermost feelings. Neoclassical poetry was always about men in general.

Prose

Prose had already modernised by the end of the seventeenth century when short, lucid sentences replaced the heavy and cumbersome prose of the earlier part of the century. This practice continued in the eighteenth century with the writings of Addison and Goldsmith. We have seen how prose was used by writers such as Dryden, Pepys and Bunyan to produce diverse literary forms such as criticism, diary-writing and the novel. In the eighteenth century, all these forms were developed further—criticism by Bentley and Samuel Johnson; the periodical essay by Defoe, Steele, Addison, Johnson and Goldsmith; history by Hume, Robertson and Gibbon; and philosophical writing by Berkley and Shaftesbury. It was a great age for prose, especially the periodical essay and the novel both of which developed rapidly.

Periodicals

The Oxford Companion to English Literature defines the periodical as 'a term taken to describe any repeating series of [a] literary journal, magazine or review'. The literary periodical flourished in the eighteenth and nineteenth centuries contributing richly to the development of the essay as a genre. *The Gentleman's Journal* published in 1692, was the first of its kind. Daniel Defoe was a journalist and to him goes the credit of inventing the entire craft of the periodical. In 1704, his periodical *The Review* appeared; it continued till 1713. *The Tatler* (1709–11) and *The Spectator* (1711–12), the work of Addison and Steele, made the form of the literary periodical very popular in the eighteenth century. This was followed by Johnson's *The Rambler* and Goldsmith's *The Bee*.

These magazines contained essays on the manners and characters of the contemporary period, tales, gossip, letters and allegories. They served the role of a newspaper, giving the rapidly rising middle class the latest items of news along with a story or an essay. In an age that was slowly turning its back upon the theatre, which had fallen into ill-repute, the periodicals proved to be a great success.

Addison and Steele gave to the prose essay a dignity and form. In the new age, which was deeply interested in politics and philosophy, prose proved to be a more suitable medium than poetry. During the eighteenth century, when the art of critical exposition and journalistic realism played a more important role than creative imagination, the periodical essay proved to be the most suitable vehicle for public expression.

Drama

The influence of the French dramatists continued to dominate during the reign of Queen Anne. The changing social behaviour and manners demanded new subjects in theatre. People were tired of the excesses of Restoration drama. The comedies of Colley Cibber, Steele and Rowe reflect the growing taste for sentimentalism and catered chiefly to middle-class tastes. At the same time, Addison's tragedy, *Cato* (1713), adhered strictly to classical rules and was a great success when it was enacted. A brilliant comedy that was classical in treatment, *The Beggar's Opera* (1728), by Gay was received very well by the public. It was a parody in which the dramatist attacked the facile sentimentalism in some of the contemporary works. Thus, the theatre between 1700 and 1740 accurately captures the divergent aspects of the period.

Daniel Defoe (1660-1731)

Novels
Robinson Crusoe (1719)
Farther Adventures (1719)
Life and Adventures of Mr Duncan Campbell (1720)
Captain Singleton (1720)
Moll Flanders (1722)
A Journal of the Plague Year (1722)
The History of Peter the Great (1722)
Memoirs of a Cavalier (1722)
Colonel Jack (1722)
Roxana (1724)
Memoirs of Captain George Carleton (1728)

Non-Fiction
Tour through the Whole Island of Great Britain (1724–26)
The Complete English Tradesman (1726)
The Complete English Gentleman (1890)

Poetry
The True-Born English Man (1701)
Hymn to the Pillory (1703)

Pamphlets
The Shortest Way with Dissenters (1702)
Giving Alms no Charity (1704)
The Apparition of one Mrs Veal (1706)

Periodical
Mercator (1713)
The Review (1704)

Life

Defoe was born in London to a butcher named James Foe. He changed his name to 'Defoe' in 1695. He went to Morton's Academy for Dissenters with a career in ministry as a goal, but gave it up. He established himself as a hosiery merchant and travelled to France, Spain and other parts of the Continent. He actively supported William III during the Glorious Revolution and was a devoted subject. Defoe wrote his first work *The True-Born Englishman*, a long satire in prosaic verse, in order to defend William III whom many considered a foreigner. In his early writings, he dealt with controversial subjects like politics and religion which landed him in prison for almost four months.

For several years, he earned his living through journalism. He began his own periodical *The Review* and ran it single-handedly from 1704–13. He wrote his famous novels only in his later years when he was almost sixty. He died in his lodgings in Ropemakers' Alley in 1731 and was buried at Bunhill Fields.

Works

Defoe was a prolific writer and it is difficult to tell exactly how many works he produced. It is believed that he wrote nearly 550 works which included poetry, theology, economics, geography and fiction. He was an eloquent representative of the middle class and wished to reform public manners and morals.

His first important work was *The True-Born Englishman* in defence of William III. It is a long satire in verse that is written in a prosaic style. In it, he argued that the English nation was made up of people from diverse origins and that it was unfair to condemn the king for not belonging to England.

His second work *The Shortest Way with the Dissenters* an ironical satire in prose, was misunderstood by both the churchmen and the nonconformists and resulted in Defoe's imprisonment. While in prison, he wrote a mock-Pindaric ode *Hymn to the Pillory.*

He began *The Review*, a political newspaper, in 1704. Adopting a matter-of-fact manner, he wrote about domestic and foreign politics and on ecclesiastical and commercial subjects. In the same year appeared his pamphlet *Giving Alms no Charity* and in 1706, *The Apparition of Mrs Veal,* which was a vivid report of a contemporary ghost story. Between 1708 and 1709, his chief work was *History of the Union*, which was comprehensive and accurate. By 1718, Defoe tired of politics and turned to writing fiction.

As a journalist and pamphleteer, he developed a straightforward prose and works like *Mrs Veal* reveal his skilful use of minute details. He was the most wonderful observer of facts. In short, his lifetime of writing helped him to shape himself into a novelist.

FICTION

He wrote most of his fiction in the next few years (1717–24). On 25 April 1719, appeared the first volume of *Robinson Crusoe* based on the real adventures of Alexander Selkirk, who was stranded for four years on an island. It was in the form of a series of imaginative stories written as memoirs in order to give it an impression of veracity. He embellished the narrative with many romantic incidents taken from the marooned seaman's adventures. Defoe added several incidents to the real story and wrote an extraordinarily convincing account of the shipwrecked Crusoe's survival on the deserted island. The book was an immediate success and revealed Defoe's genius as a storyteller. Several critics recognise this book as the first English novel, although some dismiss it as being a mere collection of incidents.

Encouraged by his success, Defoe followed it with *The Farther Adventures of Robinson Crusoe* in which Crusoe returns to the island with Friday. A year later, he wrote *Serious Reflections during the Life and Surprising Adventures of Robinson Crusoe.* However, it is only the first book that has continued to remain popular.

Defoe's next important work of fiction is *Roxana,* the story of Mlle Beleau who is the beautiful daughter of French Protestant refugee parents. It traces her notorious career passing from one protector to another in England, France and Holland. She becomes very wealthy and is known by the name 'Roxana'.

NON-FICTION

Defoe's *The Complete English Tradesman* and *The Complete English Gentleman* reveal Defoe as a spokesperson of the middle class. Restoration literature had catered exclusively to the tastes of the aristocracy. Defoe, in these books, gives voice to the aspirations of the middle class and their desire to be given a just and recognisable place in social hierarchy. *The Complete English Gentleman* reflects the merchant class's desire to rise up the social ladder through hard work. By educating their sons and grandsons, they hoped that one day they would become indistinguishable from the noble families.

Features

- In his works, we hear the real voice of the middle class for the first time.
- His influence on the evolution of the English novel was enormous. His keen eye for detail and powerful narrative style made him a good storyteller. He was the master of plain prose, who could write lucidly. His journalistic curiosity combined with his great imagination in creating an immortal work like *Robinson Crusoe.*
- His contribution to the growth of the periodical is significant. When Defoe began *The Review* in 1704, the English newspaper was less than fifty years old. When *The Review* was suppressed, he at once began to edit a new trade journal *Mercator.* These were important milestones in the history of the periodical.
- His novels clearly reflect the rapidly growing strength of the middle class. People began to make use of opportunities that were available both at home and abroad and were soon becoming wealthy. Puritans formed a vast majority of the middle class and they glorified hard work and toil. They also believed in the power of education and were avid readers.

Jonathan Swift (1667–1745)

Prose

The Battle of the Books (1704)
A Tale of a Tub (1704)
Bickerstaff Papers (1708–1709)
A Journal to Stella (1710–13)
A Modest Proposal 1729)
Gulliver's Travels (1726)

Poetry

'Baucis and Philemon' (1708)
'Cadenus and Vanessa' (1708?)
'The Grand Question Debated' (1729)
'Verses on the Death of Dr Swift' (1739)

Pamphlets
The Importance of the Guardian Considered (1713)
The Public Spirit of the Whigs (1714)
Drapier's Letters (1724)

Life

Swift was born in Dublin after the death of his father. He was the descendant of a well-known Yorkshire family and was educated at Trinity College, Dublin. He was employed as secretary by Sir William Temple. Even while he was in the employment of Temple, Swift had written a great portion of *The Battle of the Books* and *A Tale of a Tub.* It was in the Temple household that he had met Esther Johnson, whom he mentored and had given the nickname, 'Stella'. On the death of Temple in 1699, he took orders and was appointed to a small living in Ireland. He, however, spent much of his time in London and was actively involved in the political and religious controversies of the day. Here he became acquainted with Addison, Steele, Congreve and Pope.

In 1710, he became an important supporter of the new Tory government and wrote several pamphlets and articles defending it. He became powerful and received great respect. Yet, Queen Anne was slow in recognising his merits. After Queen Anne's death, the Whigs became powerful with the ascent of George I. This ended Swift's political importance. He spent the rest of his life as the dean of St Patrick's. He was bitter as his political efforts had all gone in vain. Although he missed his literary friends and life in London, he took up the cause of the Irish and fought against the abuses of British rule. He wrote the most famous of his books, *Gulliver's Travels*, while serving as dean. With old age, both his physical as well as mental health declined and he died on 19 October 1745, leaving all his money to set up a hospital for the mentally ill.

Works

PROSE

Swift was the most powerful prose writer of the first-half of the eighteenth century. *A Tale of a Tub* was probably written in 1696, but was published only in 1704. It is, on the surface, a story of three brothers fighting over their father's will, but actually it is a satire on the religious beliefs and learning of his time. The three brothers, Peter, Jack and Martin, represent the three main branches of contemporary Christianity—Catholicism, Calvinism and Anglicanism. The book was written from the Anglican point of view with Swift attacking the Catholics and the Calvinists. He traced the entire history of Christianity in an allegorical form. His mocking tone and sharp humour did not spare even Anglicanism. Finally, he ended up antagonising all the religious sects. The work is well-known for its entertaining digressions, one of which is about critics. Attacking the critics of his day, Swift points out how they lacked true knowledge: instead of entering a palace through the main gate, they entered it from the backdoor. Critics pretended to be knowledgeable by merely familiarising themselves with the titles and indexes of books. *A Tale of a Tub* is a brilliant piece of satire, where Swift's wit is at its sparkling best.

The Battle of the Books was written to defend Temple who was involved in a controversy between the 'ancients' and the 'moderns'. It is in the form of an allegory in which the old and new books in a library wage a war. Swift, supporting the ancients, amused himself by ridiculing several of his contemporaries including Dryden. His famous definition of satire appears in this book: 'Satire is a sort of glass wherein beholders do generally discover everybody's face but their own'. The highlight of the work is the fable of the bee and the spider in which the bee represents the ancients and the spider, the moderns. Through this fable, Swift concludes that the moderns produced nothing but dirt and dust while the ancients gave us honey and wax representing sweetness and light. Swift makes use of the images and devices of the epic to create a mock-epic in prose. As a brilliant attack of the pedants, *The Battle of the Books* is an excellent piece of satirical humour.

Swift loved playing pranks and jokes and his *Bickerstaff Papers* is one of his most well-known hoaxes. In this work, a fictional astrologer named Isaac Bickerstaff was used to ridicule John Partridge, a popular astrologer of Swift's time. Swift satirised Partridge's predictions by publishing his own predictions, including a prediction of Partridge's death. He carried it a step further by publishing a notice announcing Partridge's death which the public believed.

He shared with Defoe the honour of being one of the pioneers of the English novel. In his famous novel, *Gulliver's Travels*, he combined satire with a travel narrative. His *Gulliver's Travels* along with Defoe's *Robinson Crusoe* paved the way for the full-fledged novels of Richardson and Fielding. In it, Swift satirises not only the petty nature of human beings, but also the gross exaggerations of travellers recounting their adventures. Swift declared that his intention in writing the novel was 'to vex the world rather than divert it'.

Gulliver's Travels is a novel in four parts in which the protagonist, Lemuel Gulliver finds himself on the island of Lilliput, Brobdingnag, the flying island of Laputa and the country of the Houyhnhnms. The novel was a huge success and was read by both adults as well as children.

PAMPHLETS

In 1708, Swift began writing a series of pamphlets on religious issues. He was a powerful propagandist for the Church of England and Ireland. The first of the series, 'An Argument against abolishing Christianity', is a brilliant attack on the writers who had censured religion. In 'The Sentiments of a Church of England Man with respect to Religion and Government', he issued a warning to both political parties in England. His other religious pamphlets were 'A Project for the advancement of Religion and the Reformation of Manners' (1709) and 'Letter concerning the Sacramental Test' (1708), in which he attacks Defoe. Apart from religious pamphlets, Swift wrote several political pieces including many relating to Ireland.

Of Swift's correspondence, the most important is that with Esther Johnson, popularly known as *A Journal to Stella*. His prose, which is simple and straightforward, is at its best here. It offers the most intimate picture of the author and is, at the same time, an important historical document. It gives us a lot of information about his relationship with the lady during the two and a half years of correspondence. Besides the personal details, the *Journal* throws valuable light on the social life of the day, both in London as well as in Dublin.

POETRY

He began writing Pindaric odes after the fashion of Cowley. These poems were not very good and Dryden on reading them commented, 'Cousin Swift, you will never be a poet'. This enraged Swift so much that he savagely attacked him in *The Battle of the Books*. He, however, gave up writing odes after that and began writing lighter verse, modelled on Butler. One of the best pieces in this category is 'Baucis and Philemon'. Swift soon discovered that he was good at writing the short octosyllabic couplet (rhymed couplets of eight-syllable lines, usually in iambic pentameter). His unique talent in versification was revealed in 'Cadenus and Vanessa' in which he describes, under a classical disguise, his relationship with Esther Vanhomrigh, whom he called 'Vanessa'. Another famous poem by Swift is 'On the Death of Dr Swift', a moving piece which has a mixture of humour and pathos.

Features

- Swift was among the greatest writers of his time. He gave a lot of importance to order and decorum in his views on life, politics and religion. He had no sympathy for the metaphysical and the speculative and attacked them mercilessly in his works. While he had the greatest contempt for mankind, he held great affection for his friends.
- His prose was direct and plain and contained a cadence and rhythm unique to him. He had a clear and precise way of expressing himself. He did not make use of any stylistic tricks or ornamentation. He concealed his inner bitterness with an outward calm.
- His contribution to fiction is significant as his *Gulliver's Travels* is still being read. Some of the words he coined in this book, such as 'Lilliputian' and 'Yahoo', have become a part of the English language.
- His works, however, did not contain any lofty ideals or any prophetic statements. Spirituality is strangely absent in his work.

- Swift was a master satirist who was more interested in ridiculing mankind than in correcting it. In his writing, all the faults and vices of humanity were highlighted but he did not display any hope for the world. He had great scorn for his fellow men and enjoyed exposing their absurdity. As a satirist, he was very harsh and bitter and did not spare anyone who dared cross his path in the literary world. When compared to the satires of Alexander Pope, which gently mocked the foibles of his age without bitterness, one is shocked by Swift's sharp raps on the knuckles. An example of his satire is this quotation from *Gulliver's Travels*—'I cannot but conclude that the Bulk of your Natives, to be the most pernicious Race of little Vermin that Nature ever suffered to crawl upon the surface of the earth'.

Joseph Addison (1672–1719)

Contributions to periodicals	**Play**
The Tatler (1709–11)	*Cato* (1713)
The Spectator (1711–12)	**Poetry**
The Guardian (1713)	'The Campaign'
Freeholder (1715–16)	

Life

He was the son of the dean of Lichfield and was born in the rectory in Wiltshire. Younger by six weeks to Richard Steele, his school friend, Addison was educated at the Charterhouse and Oxford. Through the help of Dryden, he made the acquaintance of influential politicians like Lord Halifax. He was sent to the Continent to learn foreign manners and languages and he visited France, Italy, Switzerland, Austria, Germany and Holland. He wrote a great part of his tragedy *Cato* while travelling abroad.

In 1704, he was commissioned to write a poem on the victory of Blenheim and he obliged by writing 'The Campaign'. He was appointed under-secretary of state and was member of parliament from 1708 till his death. In 1709, he went to Ireland as chief secretary to the lord lieutenant and in the same year, began his literary collaboration with Steele. He contributed richly to Steele's *The Tatler* and *The Spectator.* He enjoyed the friendship of Swift and Pope and when his play *Cato* was enacted, it became a huge hit and was praised by Pope.

He was at the height of fame and wealth when he began the periodical *The Freeholder* in 1716. In the same year, he married the dowager countess of Warwick. An overindulgence in wine and ill health forced him to resign from the high office of secretary of state. He disassociated from Swift when the latter went over to the Tories; he also had a difference of opinion with his other friends, Steele and Pope. He died in 1719 and was buried in Westminster Abbey.

Works

POETRY AND DRAMA

His poem 'The Campaign' which he was asked to write to commemorate the victory of Blenheim, celebrated the valour of British freedom. It pleased the Whig politicians tremendously and bettered his prospects.

His verse tragedy *Cato* (1713) was very well received by the London public. It was the story of Cato, the last of the Roman republicans, who fought to preserve liberty from the usurpation of Caesar. The play was produced at a time of great political activity in England and the theme enabled both the parliamentary parties to identify themselves with it. It was a Roman tragedy combined with the sentimental chivalry of a French romance. The artificial and bombastic style appealed immensely to the taste of the eighteenth-century audience. The play is a neoclassical tragedy that adhered strictly to the three unities and all the other Aristotelian dictates of a tragedy.

PROSE

Addison's travels abroad resulted in the publications *Dialogue upon the usefulness of Ancient Medals* (posthumously published in 1721) and his *Remarks upon Several Parts of Italy* (1705). He was a true humanist who wrote in Latin, but later turned his attention to his own time and country.

Addison's chief claim to fame, however, lies in his contribution to the periodicals—*The Tatler* and *The Spectator*. *The Tatler* was a medley of essays, short stories, drama, criticism and local news. It was due to Addison that the essay as a form took shape and developed. Bacon's essays were a collection of epigrammatic sentences and he also wrote several character sketches or satires. Addison made the essay a popular vehicle for expressing opinions and gave it a dignity by writing with grace. Unlike Steele who had a more colloquial style, Addison wrote in a restrained and polished manner.

Addison used his training as a scholar and his literary talent to criticise the men and manners of his time. He was totally against the excesses of the Restoration and wished to shape public opinion through his essays. Although he allied himself with the Whigs, he expressed himself in a poised and dignified manner. He was equally critical of the cynicism of the Cavaliers and the gloomy austerity of the Puritans. Through his essays he tried to highlight the favourable aspects of each side and attempted to bridge the gap between them. Addison wished to popularise a style of writing that was free from the contemporary style which was affected and extravagant. These features of Addison could be seen in his writings when he began contributing essays to Steele's periodical *The Tatler* which was in production between 1709 and 1711.

Addison joined Steele once again when *The Spectator* was begun a few months later. There were a total of 555 issues of the periodical, which appeared every day. Unlike *The Tatler*, *The Spectator* was more literary and was preoccupied with improving the manners and morals of the middle-class readers. Addison was the one who created the fictitious Mr Spectator with a character and mind of his own. In fact, the portrayal of Mr Spectator bears a close resemblance to Addison himself. Together, Addison and Steele introduced a set of representative English characters—Sir Roger de Coverly, a country gentleman; a lawyer; Will Honeycomb, a fop and wit; a clergyman; and Sir Andrew Freeport, a merchant.

The Spectator reflected the changing times, when the focus of literature was shifting to the middle class. While Jacobean and Restoration literature catered exclusively to the rich and the aristocratic, the periodical essay appealed to middle-class readers.

After *The Spectator* was discontinued in 1712, Addison tried to revive his play *Cato* unsuccessfully. His attempts at prose comedy resulted in *The Drummer*, which was a failure.

Richard Steele (1672–1729)

Tract
The Christian Hero (1701)
Drama
The Funeral (1701)
The Lying lover (1705)
The Tender Husband (1705)
The Conscious Lovers (1722)

Periodicals
The Tatler (1709–11)
The Spectator (1711–12)
The Guardian (1713)
The Englishman (1713–13)
The Theatre (1718–20)

Life

Steele was born in Dublin a few weeks before Addison and was educated with him at the Charterhouse. He next went to Oxford and from there joined the army. In 1706, he was appointed gentleman waiter to Prince George of Denmark. In 1707, Steele was appointed editor to the official organ of the government, *The London Gazette.* He was married twice as his first wife had died soon after their marriage. In 1709, he started *The Tatler*, a periodical dealing with 'gallantry, pleasure and entertainment'. This was succeeded by *The Spectator* and *The Guardian*. Steele was actively involved in the politics of his time. He was a staunch supporter of the Hanoverian succession and was knighted in 1715. His long collaboration with Addison came to an end in 1718 due to political differences. Steele's final years were spent in retirement near Wales and he was buried at St Peter's Church.

Works

The Christian Hero was Steele's first work. It reflected his missionary zeal and was considered as a guide to good conduct for a long while. In it, Steele attempted to encourage educated men to go to the Bible for moral edification.

DRAMA

Steele next turned his attention to the stage and wrote three comedies—*The Funeral*, *The Lying Lover* and *The Tender Husband*. He attempted to continue the style of Restoration comedy, but aimed at advocating virtue and denouncing vice. Due to this desire on the part of Steele to impart a moral lesson, his comedies were not artistically good. Steele soon discovered that comedy was not a suitable medium to correct the morals of society.

PROSE

It was only five years later that Steele discovered his true calling in the coffee houses of London. Coffee houses were places where men of intelligence met and exchanged ideas. These were the men who helped to shape the taste and thought of society. For the first time, men with literary leanings could share and exchange views on literature in an informal manner. It was this aspect of life which brought about a marked change in the writings of the eighteenth century. Up till the Restoration, writers were not exposed to the luxury of sharing their ideas with like-minded people through informal conversation. The coffee house discussions brought about a change in their style of writing which became more colloquial and mirrored the commonplace ideas and trifles of everyday life. This exchange of ideas helped to shape the middle class and taught them to conduct themselves in a cultured manner that was free from pedantry. What could not be achieved by theatres or universities was accomplished with ease by the coffee houses.

Steele began *The Tatler*, a journal that would appeal to the coffee houses. He began it not only for financial gains, but also with the noble intention of improving his fellow countrymen. It appeared thrice a week and contained essays that would appeal to different coffee houses. Borrowing the pseudonym 'Isaac Bickerstaff' from Swift, Steele assumed the role of a commentator on civilised life. *The Tatler* was a huge success as the readers could immediately identify themselves with it. Steele found an able collaborator in Addison who contributed several essays to the periodical.

After discontinuing it in 1711, he immediately began *The Spectator* with the collaboration of Addison. Steele's contribution to *The Spectator* was very different from that of Addison. He tried to suppress his true leanings towards the unconventional and preached regularity of conduct. He advocated decorum and dignity in public behaviour. In some of his essays, he expressed his views on education, on the evils of indulging in elaborate dressing and reading romances. All these ideas resulted in hardening British society which was bitterly satirised later by the Victorian writers. Thus, while Addison helped to shape literary taste, Steele's writings shaped the manners and morals of the day.

After *The Spectator* was stopped in 1712, Swift began several periodicals like *The Guardian* to which Addison contributed five essays. In 1722, Steele produced his last comedy *The Conscious Lovers.* It contains Steele's views on life and the society of his day.

Features of Addison and Steele's Works

- Addison and Steele were the voices of the emerging middle class. At a time when norms of public decency were restored after the excesses of the Restoration, the essays of Addison and Steele helped in consolidating the values and morals of English society.
- They were great satirists who knew how to ridicule without hurting. They were social reformers who were able to find the correct balance between wit and virtue. 'Coverley Papers' (the essays in which Sir Roger de Coverley appears) reveal the moral purpose of the writers.
- Their contribution to the genre of the prose essay is tremendous. They were responsible for developing the essay as a means of education as well as entertainment.

Alexander Pope (1688–1744)

First Period
Pastorals (1709)
An Essay on Criticism (1711)
The Rape of the Lock (1712, revised 1714)
'Ode for Music on St Cecilia's Day'
'Windsor Forest' (1713)
'Elegy to the Memory of an Unfortunate Lady'
'Eloise to Abelard'(1717)

Second Period
Translation of *Iliad* (1720)
Translation of *Odyssey* (1725–26)

Last Period
Duncaid (1728-42)
Imitations of Horace (1733)
An Essay on Man (1733–34)
Moral Essays (1731–35)
An Epistle to Dr Arbuthnot (1735)

Life

Alexander Pope was born in London on 21 May 1688. His father was a Roman Catholic linen-draper and his mother was the daughter of William Turner, who had supported Charles I. Pope belonged to the Catholic religion at a time when Catholicism was frowned upon. As a result, he could not join any school or university and had his education only through priests and private tutors. He spent all his time studying Greek, Latin, Italian and French works. He read classical and modern writers, poetry, criticism, drama and metaphysics.

He was a sickly child and his body was stunted due to a serious illness at the age of twelve. He suffered from constant headaches and was very weak. By the time he was thirty, his condition was so bad that he needed assistance to even get dressed. In spite of all these misfortunes, Pope had a great love for poetry and his talent for writing poetry manifested itself early. In his own words:

As yet a child, nor yet a fool to fame,
I lisped in numbers, for the numbers came.

At the age of sixteen, he wrote *Pastorals* which was published in Jacob Tonson's *Poetical Miscellanies.*

Pope had several friends in the contemporary literary circle such as Wycherley, Addison, Swift, Gay and Arbuthnot. A club called 'The Scriblerus' was formed by Pope and some of his friends, for the purpose of warning off incompetent writers from entering the field of literature. Pope busied himself with the translation of Homer which gave him financial independence. In 1718, he moved to Twickenham with his mother, where he spent the rest of his life. He lived in a modest villa on the banks of the Thames. He enjoyed fame and fortune and had several friends and admirers. In the five acres of grounds attached to his villa, Pope indulged his interest in landscape gardening. It was in Twickenham that he met his friends Swift, Bolingbroke, Congreve and Gay. Finally, on 30 May 1744 Pope breathed his last and he was freed from the pain and physical discomfort that had constantly accompanied him.

Works

One of his earliest works was *Pastoral*, written in the form of four dialogues—one for each season. The style is mostly imitative and artificial, but the versification reveals the Pope's gift for poetry. In the same year, he published 'Windsor Forest', which contains several elegant descriptions of the forest. Again, Pope's genius which slanted more towards the court and city, could not do justice to a poem that depended on nature. In *Windsor-Forest*, Pope combined the description of the countryside with the historical and literary associations of the district. This work reveals the fact that Pope was not strong in the appreciation of nature. His approach is largely conventional and pseudo-classical.

His sacred eclogue *Messiah* was published in the May 1712 issue of *The Spectator*. Pope attempted to put the messianic prophecies of Isiah in the form of a Virgilian eclogue. The use of artificial epithets and style only resulted in lowering the majesty of the eclogue. The work was criticised for its artificial poetic diction.

An Essay on Criticism was Pope's first full-length work on the laws and history of literary taste. In highly polished heroic couplets, Pope spelt out the main critical ideals of his age. In part one, he outlined the general qualities that a critic had to possess—true taste, an understanding of the relation between art and nature, the meaning and interpretation of rules and a reverence for the ancients. In the second part, he outlines the specific laws for the critic—humility, a consideration of the whole work of art in its entirety and an understanding of the author's aim. After listing examples of false critics, he ends by praising good nature in a critic. In the third part, he outlines the ideal character of a critic—integrity, modesty, tact and courage. In the final part, he gives a historical survey of criticism. This work is an important milestone in the history of literary criticism as it gives us an account of the commonly held critical views of the Augustan Age.

In the following year, Pope published his famous mock-epic *The Rape of the Lock,* that catapulted him to fame. A mock-epic is an imitation of the serious epic, following all its conventions and features, but having a trivial subject for its theme. In *The Rape of the Lock,* Pope makes use of the epic form to narrate the story of the theft of a lock of hair from a lady's head. When Lord Peter cut off a lock of Miss Arabella Fermor's hair, a rift was created between the two families. Pope was asked by John Caryll, a mutual friend, to write a poem in order to 'laugh the two families together'. It is a flawless work of art that combines, in the right measure, burlesque, wit, humour and morality. In it, Pope satirises the social customs of the Age of Queen Anne by giving a profound treatment to the trivial. The poet is humorously indulgent in his descriptions of the heroine Belinda's dressing table, the game of ombre, the elaborate preparation of coffee and the final battle. The poem is a brilliant mock-epic in five cantos. It is the most original of all Pope's poems and may be regarded as a chronicle of the fashionable life of the time of Queen Anne's rule.

His attempt at lyric poetry which resulted in the 'Ode for Music on St Cecilia's Day' made him understand that he was not cut out for such writing. With the publication of *The Temple of Fame*, a paraphrase of Chaucer's *The House of Fame*, in 1714, the first stage of Pope's career ended.

He next focused his attention on translating Homer's *Iliad* in six volumes, the first part of which appeared in 1715 and the last in 1720. *The Odyssey* was then translated by him five years later with the assistance of two Cambridge scholars. For his ten years of devotion to Homer, Pope earned several thousand pounds. This gave him financial freedom and he moved to Twickenham.

It was at Twickenham that Pope entered the third stage of his writing career. It was during this period that he wrote his satirical and philosophical poems. *The Dunciad* was written in four books at the suggestion of Swift who gave him much encouragement. It is a work that was inspired by personal hurt and resentment rather than any broader motive. The poem ridicules mediocre writers, prejudiced critics, pedantic scholars and foolish scientists. It was originally designed as an attack against dullness and pedantry—an activity of the Scribelerus Club. The first edition of *The Dunciad* appeared in 1728, but Pope kept working on it, adding the names of many more people whom he disliked. In the first edition, Pope had as hero Lewis Theobald, a scholar who had found fault with his edition of Shakespeare. In the revised edition which appeared in 1743, Pope substituted Colley Cibber as the hero of the Dunces. The poem also does not have the unity of action that *The Rape of the Lock* does. It is a collection of episodes that are loosely strung together. The goddess Dulness is depicted as choosing an heir to the throne of Dulness. Apart from being too personal, the poem suffers from being overburdened with the names of obscure authors who are long forgotten. As a result, in spite of its brilliant passages, it is the most neglected of Pope's works.

An Essay on Man is a philosophical poem in which he shares his ideas on morality, friendship, poetry and good taste. It contains several well-known lines such as 'Hope springs eternal in the human breast'. This work was inspired by Bolingbroke and Shaftsbury. Though it lacks a sustained philosophical progression of ideas, it gives us an impression of contemporary thought.

Pope's *Moral Essays* published between 1731 and 1735, contains four satirical poems in the form of letters. In one of these, he highlights the follies of women and in another, of men. Two of the essays satirise people who misuse wealth. Later, he added a fifth epistle addressed to Addison. This work reveals Pope's skill in satirising characters.

In 1733, on the suggestion of his friend Bolingbroke, he wrote the first of the miscellaneous *Imitations of Horace* entitled 'Satire I', a paraphrase of the first satire of the second book of Horace. This was in the form of a dialogue between the poet and William Fortescue, a lawyer. Being charged with malignity, Pope defends himself by saying that his writing was inspired only by the love of virtue.

In 1735, *An Epistle to Dr Arbuthnot* was published. It is one of Pope's best pieces of irony in which he presented a positive picture of himself as an independent and good-natured man in search of truth. It is at the same time, a pungent attack of his enemies with particular focus on Addison. Pope did not make a complete collection of his satires. It was his first editor Bishop

Warburton who collected the poems written in *Imitation of Horace* and published them using the 'Epistle to Dr Arbuthnot' as the prologue. With this and the publication of *The New Dunciad* in 1742, his literary career came to an end.

Features

- With Pope, the classical spirit in English poetry reached its zenith. His poetry truly represented the age which gave importance to the social behaviour of man rather than nature and which focused on the knowledge of the town instead of romance or pathos.
- Pope made the heroic couplet his own by using it exclusively. He was an incomparable craftsman who perfected it. In his hands, it became an excellent tool for satire.
- Pope's contribution to satirical writing is tremendous. As a satirist, he was very different from Swift. Pope attacked men and not mankind, whereas with Swift, it was just the opposite. Pope's attacks were always against individuals who had crossed his path and seldom against human society as a whole. His satires could be classified under the genre of the formal satire which is written in the first person. This 'I' may address the reader, as is the case in his *Moral Essays* or else characters within the work itself, known as 'adversaries'. The adversaries function as a guide to the satiric speaker's comments as is the case in *An Epistle to Dr Arbuthnot*.
- Pope's three major works, *The Rape of the Lock*, *The Dunciad* and *An Essay on Man*, serve as excellent chronicles of his age. We get a very clear picture of the follies and foibles of his time. His *An Essay on Criticism* gives us valuable information about the merits and demerits of eighteenth-century poetry and the critical views held by the men of that age.
- He made the genre of the mock-epic very popular with his *The Rape of the Lock*.

AGE OF JOHNSON (1740–80)

As we move deeper into the century, there is not much change in the prevalent ideology. Classicism was still very strong, but with the passing away of Alexander Pope in 1744, neoclassical poetry which had reached its zenith had no suitable successor. Johnson's presence, however, ensured the continuation of the classical tradition. The middle class made its presence felt in politics, manners and literature. Gradually, the awakening of emotional tendencies and imagination could be discerned in the minds of writers and readers alike. Seeds of change were slowly taking root, but men like Johnson tried very hard to preserve traditional values that were slowly being undermined by the new outlook of the middle class. He was a classicist who believed in the strict adherence of rules almost as much as he believed in God. The literature of this period reflects the tension between reason and sentiment.

Poetry

The poetry of this period defies strict categorisation. It was basically a period of transition and innovation. Dryden and Pope, though dead, continued to wield their influence over the poets of the mid-eighteenth century. To correct and to teach were regarded as the highest offices of poetry. The restraint in poetical feeling was reflected in both style and form of expression. The heroic couplet continued to be the standard measure for poetry down to, and even past, the time of Goldsmith. Goldsmith may be said to have given the heroic couplet its final touch of grace.

Poets continued to write didactic or satirical verses. Johnson's two satires, *London* (1738) and *The Vanity of Human Wishes* (1749) are good examples of the Juvenalian satire. At the same time, there could be discerned a search for the new order of Romanticism. This could be seen as early as 1730, when Thompson published *The Seasons.*

Transitional Poets

Gradually, the classicism of Dr Johnson and his contemporaries began to wane as passion and the creative power of imagination surged to the foreground. A group of poets who were responsible for bringing about this change in attitude succeeded in forging a bridge between classicism and romanticism. They drew attention to the prevalent social problems and also steered the attention of their works towards nature—which would soon become the mainstay of the English Romantics. Some of the poets who belonged to this period of transition are James Thomson, Oliver Goldsmith, Thomas Gray, William Collins and William Cowper. The works of the transitional poets had the following features:

- The most obvious change was seen in the decline of the heroic couplet that had been popular in the neoclassical age. Attempts at widening the domain of poetry and reviving blank verse were first attempted by James Thomson. Thomson's 'Winter' (1725) was an inspiration to Cowper and Wordsworth. Like Thomson, Thomas Gray too avoided the heroic couplet but did not abandon rhyme.
- Yet another change that could be seen in the middle of the century was the increased use of the Pindaric ode, especially by Gray and Collins. This form proved to be best suited for the transitional age as it was classical yet free from the strict rules of the heroic couplet. This interest in the Pindaric ode paved the way for the popularity of the lyric when Romanticism was revived at the end of the century. Gray's 'The Bard' (1757) and Collins's 'The Passions' (1747) are good examples of this type of poetry.
- Thomson took poetry out of the town and into the country and rediscovered the glory of nature. Gray, too, widened the scope of poetry by employing imagery from nature, although he did not make it his subject. The return to nature was continued by Cowper and Burns and helped in spreading a love for rural poetry. These poets prepared the way for the Romantic Revival that occurred at the end of the century, when Wordsworth and his school of poets

wrote a completely different kind of poetry from that of Dryden and Pope.

- Emotion and imagination were given priority over intellect and wit.
- The new generation of poets made an attempt to break away from the stereotyped conventions of 'poetic diction' of the neoclassical poets.
- 'Sensibility' which was present in a very feeble manner in the literature of the early part of the century, became more pronounced as the century progressed and began to supersede reason. Goldsmith brought in tenderness to poetry without changing its form. Reason still held sway and was upheld by Johnson, but its influence was rapidly diminishing. **Literature of sensibility** was a particular cultural phenomenon of the eighteenth century. It was a moral theory that was developed as a reaction to seventeenth-century stoicism which had upheld reason and an unemotional approach to life as the best virtues. It was a violent reaction to Thomas Hobbes's theory that man was innately selfish. Writers took to extolling the virtues of benevolence and sympathy. The Earl of Shaftsbury's *Characteristics of Men, Manners, Opinions, Times, etc* (1711) provided a philosophical discussion on this shift in taste.

Prose

Cicero, the Roman writer, was the role model for much of mid-eighteenth-century prose. He was admired for his balanced and polished style. Johnson, and later Gibbin, developed a Latinate style that was dignified and rhetoric in nature. Balanced phrases and sonorous antithesis were some of its distinct features. Writers made use of words and grammatical constructions which originated in Latin. Latinate diction tended to be more abstract and included long polysyllabic words.

The periodical essay had enjoyed its heyday with *The Spectator*. A generation later, Samuel Johnson's *The Rambler* (1750–52) appeared. But Johnson's heavy prose style, with his use of long words, did not appeal to readers. Another periodical of the mid-eighteenth century was *The Adventurer* (1752–54) begun by John Hawkesworth, to which Johnson contributed. A successful periodical, *The World* (1753–56), was edited by Edward Moore with contributions from Horace Walpole and Chesterfield. Goldsmith's *The Bee* (1759) and Johnson's *The Idler* (1758–60) followed. The periodicals took on a political flavour during this period. Monthly magazines became fashionable. *The Monthly Review* (1749) and *The Critical Review*, founded by Smollett in 1756 were regarded as the leading magazines of their kind. Goldsmith wrote several articles for the latter. His 'Chinese Letters' enriched *The Public Ledger* (1760), a daily. The first issue of *The Times* appeared in 1788.

Fiction

The mid-eighteenth century witnessed the first great development of the novel. It rapidly became popular and replaced drama, which was losing its respectability especially among the middle class. Although Defoe had written a large number of novels and Swift wrote his *Gulliver's Travels* earlier, they are not counted by critics as novels in their true form as they lack structure. They are episodic and are loosely strung together. Also, they dealt with far-fetched adventures with which the average reader could not identify. After 1740, appeared books that depicted the current reality with which readers could connect immediately.

Samuel Richardson's *Pamela, or Virtue Rewarded* is regarded as the first English novel as it contains a well-developed plot rather than disconnected episodes. This is an **epistolary novel** (a story told entirely through letters), a form that was immensely popular during the eighteenth century. Henry Fielding is another important pioneer of the English novel. His *Tom Jones* (1749) which is a **picaresque novel** (a novel that describes the adventures of a lovable rogue) is told from the point of view of an intrusive, omniscient narrator. Smollett, Laurence Sterne and Goldsmith are other important eighteenth-century novelists.

Histories

It was in the mid-eighteenth century that history was written in English for the first time. Some of the great names here are Hume, Robertson and Gibbon. Gibbon is considered one of the greatest historians of England.

Drama

This period had very poor dramatic output. The Restoration drama that belonged to the previous generation had burnt itself out. It was essentially an age of prose and fiction, with changing trends in the genre of poetry. The only two significant playwrights from this period are Oliver Goldsmith and Richard Sheridan.

There are several reasons for the decline of drama. One of the chief causes was the growing importance of the actor over the play itself. Actors like Burbage, Garrick and Betterton were some of the popular actors of the age and people flocked to the theatres to see them perform. The playwright was thus forced to churn out material that would suit the stars. This state of affairs continued up to the end of the nineteenth century. Another reason for the decline was the fact that the pious Evangelists frowned upon the theatres for being the breeding ground of licentiousness and immorality.

Theatre itself underwent several changes. Greater importance was given to creating the setting and the earlier platform stage gave way to the modern picture-stage. A platform stage was a raised platform at one end of the room and the audience sat at a lower lever to watch the performance. The picture stage or proscenium stage, having an arch or a framed opening was designed to create a sense of enclosure with the actors, props and lighting. Lighting effects were introduced and visual illusions became a must.

Samuel Johnson (1709–84)

Periodicals
The Rambler (1750–1752)
The Idler (1758–1760)

Poetry
London (1738)

The Vanity of Human Wishes (1749)
Biography
Life of Mr Richard Savage (1744)
Drama
Irene (1748)
Translation
A Voyage to Abyssinia by Father Jerome Lobo (1735)
Dictionary
Dictionary of the English Language (1755)
Travel Writing
A Journey to the Western Islands of Scotland (1775)
Literary Criticism
Shakespeare (1765)
Lives of the English Poets (1779–1781)
Novel
Rasselas, The Prince of Abyssinia, A Tale (1759)

Life

Johnson was born in Lichfield. His father was a bookseller and Johnson spent a lot of time going through books while growing up. He went to Lichfield Grammar School and later spent fourteen months at Oxford University, leaving it without a degree. He worked for a while as an undermaster at Market Bosworth. He was not interested in his job and turned his attention to writing. The first of his books, a translation of *A Voyage to Abyssinia* by Father Lobo, was published during this period.

He got married to Mrs Elizabeth Porter, a widow who was older than him. He left his teaching career and moved to London. He began contributing essays and poems to *The Gentleman's Magazine*. His literary career blossomed here with the publication of two satires, a biography, several essays and a drama. He next revived the periodical essay and began *The Rambler* in 1750.

His wife died in 1752, plunging him into an abyss of grief. Receiving a pension of three hundred pounds per annum in 1762 relieved Johnson a great deal. It was during this period that he met his biographer, Boswell. Along with Boswell, he travelled to Scotland and the Hebrides. Johnson breathed his last in Bolt Court and was buried in Westminster Abbey.

Works

Johnson was the greatest force in the literary world of the eighteenth century. He was a poet, critic, journalist and editor and was considered a giant in the world of letters.

His first work was the translation of *A Voyage to Abyssinia* by Father Lobo. The literary interest of this work today lies in its short preface. He began working as a journalist for *The Gentleman's Magazine* and was a **Grub Street writer**. This term referred to impoverished writers who had to write articles for publishers for a pittance, which was also known as 'hack work'. This was an important phase in the condition of the English writer, who was emerging from the indignity of patronage and becoming an independent negotiator with the publisher. His most notable contribution to this journal was the half-fictional 'Parliamentary Debates', which were received by the reading public as being authentic speeches by the politicians of the day.

POETRY

His works in the genre of poetry are satires modelled on Juvenal. They were unlike the typical satires of the day, which were mostly petty and political. Johnson's satires have a strong moral sense and point out human delusions and weaknesses. He made use of the heroic couplet to lend moral weight to his verses. His most famous poem is 'The Vanity of Human Wishes', in which he mocks human aspirations. The poem *London* records his friendship with the poet Richard Savage who was also poor and struggling like Johnson.

BIOGRAPHY

The Life of Mr Richard Savage marks an important stage in the evolution of the biography. In it, Johnson shows the world how to present an authentic version of a subject's life. This work helped to highlight his name as an important prose writer of his age.

DRAMA

In his play *Irene* written in blank verse, Johnson adhered strictly to the rules of French rhetorical tragedy. The story was taken from Knolles's *The General History of the Turks* and is about the fate of Irene, a Greek slave loved by the emperor, Mohomet. It was produced by Garrick, but was not very successful.

ESSAYS

Johnson next turned his attention to the periodical essay and began *The Rambler* in 1750. The title is ironic, since none of the essays ramble. They were written in an ordered and steady manner, reflecting the vitality of Johnson's brilliance. In the almost half-a-century between the appearance of *The Tatler* and *The Rambler*, journalism had undergone a lot of changes. Johnson's essays, unlike those of Addison and Steele, are more prosaic. Addison and Steele wrote in an easy and light style and their essays had an endearing narrative quality about them. Johnson, on the other hand, wrote in a serious and majestic style. He had a Latinate style that was both abstract and witty at the same time. He specially wished to establish a high standard of the English language. His next venture in this direction was *The Idler*. The essays of *The Idler* are more relaxed in manner. In this, he introduced the character Dick Minim.

Through *The Rambler* and *The Idler*, Johnson conveyed his own views and his philosophy of life. He touched on various topics like the behaviour of women in the theatre, the nature of realism in fiction and the benefits of the biography.

DICTIONARY

Earlier dictionaries were only vocabularies that gave the meaning of difficult words. Nathan Bailey had attempted to record all the words in the English language. Johnson, in his dictionary, omitted all the technical terms and only aimed at purifying the language and standardising its pronunciation. His *Dictionary*, was the product of great scholarship and was the basis for several later versions. One of the special features of his *Dictionary* is the inclusion of quotations. His definition of words helped in bringing clarity of meaning. He was extremely sensitive to the subtle shades of meaning and this earned him the highest respect among his contemporaries.

Johnson was concerned with advocating the good usage of English, which he discovered in the works of sixteenth and seventeenth-century writers. He had six assistants and worked for nearly nine years, filling about eighty large notebooks with definitions of more than forty thousand words. Some of these definitions are humorous; for example,

> patron: one who countenances, supports or protects. Commonly a wretch who supports with insolence, and is paid with flattery.

NOVEL

During the period in which he was writing essays for the *Idler*, Johnson lost his mother. At that time, he wrote a serious story—*Rasselas*—which was more of a parable than a novel. It is a moral story set in a fictional version of Abyssinia. The characters are depicted as being on a quest for happiness with the guidance of a sage. The novel ends with the discovery that 'human life is everywhere a state, in which much is to be endured, and little to be enjoyed'. Johnson's narration conveys his disillusionment with life in an unsentimental manner.

His travel with Boswell resulted in his book *A Journey to the Western Islands of Scotland*. In it, he makes observations on the changing social structure and manners of the Scottish people.

LITERARY CRITICISM

Johnson's importance in the history of English literary criticism rests chiefly on the preface to his edition of Shakespeare and on his collection of essays, *Lives of the English Poets*. These established Johnson as one of the best critics in the English language.

'Preface to Shakespeare' reflects Johnson's neoclassicism, transcending the rigid notions of literature and presents the cultural significance of the bard. In it, we discern Johnson's commitment to the Horatian idea that literature should instruct and entertain. He was quick in recognising Shakespeare's greatness in portraying characters that reflected human nature and his abstinence from depicting any important individual or political faction for personal gains. Johnson points out how Shakespeare's plays were a 'mirror of life'. He also defended Shakespeare's lack of regard for the three classical unities.

His book *Lives of the English Poets* was published between 1779 and 1781. It is a collection of prefaces to a ten-volume collection of fifty-two English poets, from Cowley to Gray. No living poets were included in it. Some of the important poets included were Milton, Dryden, Addison and Pope. Writing the prefaces gave Johnson an opportunity to express his views on poetry. He began each section with a brief biography, then provided a survey of the poet's philosophy of life and ended with a criticism of his poems.

The most striking feature of *Lives* is the balance of biography and criticism. Johnson was able to connect the man with his work. His work was at his best only when his own views coincided with those of the poet he was writing about. In spite of wishing to be objective, Johnson succumbed to his prejudices. For example, his dislike of Milton's politics made him judge the poet harshly. His views on Milton's *Lycidas* reveal Johnson's limitations as a critic. His dislike of the pastoral convention coloured his reading of the beautiful poem. In spite of such indiscretion on his part, *Lives of the English Poets* is a remarkable piece of literary criticism.

Features

- His sharp wit and his ability to assess people and politics made him a formidable figure in his time.
- His *Dictionary* was an important milestone in the development of English vocabulary and pronunciation.
- As a critic, he was able to bring a better understanding of the classical rules to a rigid neoclassical public.
- His lofty and sonorous prose style gave a new respectability to English prose, elevating it to new heights.

Samuel Richardson (1689–1761)

Familiar Letters (1741)
Clarissa (1747–48)
Pamela; or Virtue Rewarded (1740)
The History of Sir Charles Grandison (1753–54)

Life

He was born near Derby and as a boy, read widely and was a popular storyteller among his friends. Timid by nature, he spent his time writing letters for young lovers and telling stories to his friends. He was inclined towards Puritanism, which influenced his writing.

In 1706, he was apprenticed to a printer and in 1715, was admitted a freeman of the **Stationers' Company**. This was begun by a royal charter of 1557 according to which one could not print anything for sale without being a member of the Company.

According to the rules of the Company, every member had to enter the name of any book that he desired to print in a register. This register has proved to be a valuable record of all the books that were published. In 1721, Richardson set up his own business and was a much-sought-after printer. He was asked to print the journals of the House of Commons and he also published most of the works of the prominent authors of his day.

Works

Pamela is an **epistolary novel**. It was published in two volumes and was an immediate success The story is presented in the form of a series of letters, written by a good-looking maid to her parents. It is the story of Pamela, a beautiful servant-maid, who attracts the attention of her master Squire Brown. She resists his advances and finally he is able to get her only when he marries her. The sequel to the novel reveals the virtue and patience of the heroine even in the face of her husband's infidelity. The most significant aspect of the novel is its moral tone.

His next novel *Clarissa* is considered to be his best. Here, the heroine hails from a wealthier background. In her effort to escape from an undesirable marriage that her parents were arranging for her, she becomes a victim of the dashing rake Lovelace. She, too, like Pamela, refuses his advances although she is attracted to him. She is finally drugged and raped by him. After that, she loses her sanity and several adventures later, she embraces religion as her refuge. Clarissa's death moved much of Richardson's audience to tears.

This was followed by his last novel *Sir Charles Grandison*. So far, his protagonists had been female characters with male characters being portrayed negatively. In this novel, Richardson decided to present to the world, a model gentleman who was both sensitive and highly principled. The result is a picture of a stiff and priggish man, who is self-centred and artificial. This work has not found enduring appeal as in it, the moralist in Richardson triumphed over the artist.

Features

- Richardson is generally recognised by critics as the founding father of the English novel. He was the first to write a novel dealing with everyday manners and ordinary people in a sentimental way. The French, especially, hailed him as a pathfinder in the field of fiction. Richardson was adept at creating characters and providing readers with psychological insight into their motives and thoughts. His Puritanical background enabled him to balance private morals with public social forces. His influence on the development of the novel is tremendous.
- His epistolary method of presenting the story was suitable to his concern with the inner workings of his characters' minds. It is almost like the soliloquy in a drama, in which the thoughts of the characters are brought out. Its function is not unlike the stream-of-consciousness technique of modern fiction.
- His prose displays the charm of native English simplicity and is coloured by its racy idioms.
- He introduced sentimentality into the English novel.
- He presented to the world the female point of view and thus triggered several women to continue this tradition. Fanny Burney and Jane Austen were inspired by his work.
- On the negative side, he was too didactic in nature and his novels were far too long.
- His constant analysis of characters' feelings and motives becomes too tedious. This, combined with a slow-moving plot, make his novels a little cumbersome to read.
- There is hardly any humour in his fiction. The sentimental treatment of the story and the shadow of sin that troubles the conscience of the characters give the novels a sombre quality.

Henry Fielding (1707–54)

Drama

Love in Several Masques (1728)

The Author's Farce and the Pleasures of the Town (1730)

Tom Thumb later *The Tragedy of Tragedies* (1730)
The Covent-Garden Tragedy (1732)
The Mock Doctor (1733)
Don Quixote in England (1734)
The Historical Register for the Year 1736 (1737)
The Miser (1733)
The Intriguing Chambermaid (1734)

Novel

Joseph Andrews (1742)
A Journey from this World to the Next (1743)
Jonathan Wilde the Great (1743)
Tom Jones, A Foundling (1749)
Amelia (1751)

Life

Fielding was the son of a lieutenant and studied at Eton. After a futile attempt to elope, he settled in London. He began his career as a dramatist and wrote several satires and burlesques before he discovered his talent as a novelist. His satires became too harsh and he was arrested under the Licensing Act of 1737. After this, he turned his attention to essay writing and some of his best articles appeared in *The Champion.*

His career as a novelist began with his parody of Richardson's *Pamela*. It was quite by accident that Fielding discovered his ability to write fiction. At the same time, he devoted himself to law and journalism. He was made a magistrate and he served the community with sincerity. Throughout his life, he was interested in bringing about social and legal reforms both as a writer and as a magistrate. He suffered from ill health and was advised to go to Lisbon to recuperate. It was while in Lisbon that he died.

Works

DRAMA

He began his literary career with drama. His first play *Love in Several Masques* was written in the manner of the Restoration comedy. He soon turned to farce and the burlesque. In *The Author's Farce and the Pleasures of the Town,* he makes fun of the contemporary taste for opera and pantomime and in *The Tragedy of Tragedies*, he satirises the heroic tragedies of the Restoration. He followed these up with several more comedies and farces.

As a dramatist writing comedies, Fielding had certain drawbacks. He lacked a deep understanding of human emotions.

He was only good at depicting the external features of life. For this, the burlesque and farce were more suitable. His satires *Pasquin* and *The Historical Register for 1736* went too far in poking fun of Walpole's government. This caused the introduction of the Licensing Act in 1737 after which his dramatic career came to an abrupt end.

NOVEL

The name of Fielding marks another important milestone in the development of the English novel. He is remembered for popularising the picaresque tradition in the novel.

Fielding was disgusted with the excessive virtue of *Pamela* and decided to write a parody of it. This resulted in *Shamela*, which is the story of Pamela's brother Joseph Andrews being tempted by his mistress. In this work, Fielding portrayed the innocent heroine of Richardson's novel as a wicked temptress. As he wrote about the various adventures of Joseph Andrews, he realised that it could be a full-fledged novel. This resulted in the famous book *The Adventures of Joseph Andrews*. The novel is clearly inspired by Cervantes as Fielding himself has stated in his title page. In this book, Fielding expounds a moral code of his own. For him, virtue was something that was innate and he did not place much importance on public esteem. He was inspired by Swift's use of the mock-heroic and made use of it to expose the gap between what people really were and what they pretended to be. The picaresque tradition offered him ample scope to expose his characters to different situations, such as adventures by wayside inns, and enabled him to portray the variety of English life. Fielding referred to this work as 'a comic epic poem in prose' in the preface to the novel. This novel, although a major innovation in form and style, is less popular than *Pamela*.

In 1743, Fielding published three volumes of *Miscellanies*. In the first volume, there were a few poems which were soon forgotten. The second volume contained the novel *A Journey from this World to the Next*. In the third volume, we have the brilliant work *The Life of Mr Jonathan Wilde*, a story based on the life of a notorious thief. Jonathan Wilde poses as a 'great man' among thieves and cheats. Fielding uses this character to satirise the 'great man' in politics, Sir Robert Walpole. It reflects the author's contempt for the men who build their success on the ruins of simple and good people. Fielding's contempt for hypocrisy finds its best expression in this novel.

Fielding developed the comic epic in his next novel *Tom Jones*. It is the first long novel to be written in English that has artistic unity. The hero, unlike Joseph Andrews, is far from perfect. He has his faults but is lovable in spite of them. It is the story of a foundling who ultimately discovers his true identity. Like its predecessor, *Tom Jones* too is a picaresque novel and offers much scope for variety. It consists of eighteen books and what is interesting about the novel is that Fielding introduces each book with an address to the reader. In these introductions, he discusses the craft of fiction. The novel proves to be not only a description of eighteenth-century England but also a discourse on novel-writing. It is a remarkable work as it discusses great truths and morals in an interesting way.

His last novel *Amelia* is considered by critics as being inferior to the other two. In it, Fielding tried to take a middle path between the comic and the tragic. He paints the picture of Amelia Booth as a virtuous middle-class wife and in the course of the narration, draws our attention to several social abuses. At the time of writing this novel, Fielding was a magistrate and his preoccupation with his duties is clearly reflected here. Apart from that, he was getting older and as a result had mellowed down a great deal.

Features

- He made the picaresque novel popular in England. His *Tom Jones* occupies an important position in the history of English fiction.
- His novels helped arrest the increasing sentimentality that was popularised by Richardson.
- He had a strong moral sense and believed in the inner goodness of human beings rather than in external trappings. He did not agree with the view that in order to be good one should lead a life of abstinence. He believed in enjoying life.

Tobias George Smollett (1721–71)

Fiction
The Adventures of Roderick Random (1748)
The Adventures of Peregrine Pickle (1751)
The Adventures of Ferdinand Count Fathom (1753)
The Life and Adventures of Sir Lancelot Greaves (1762)
The Expedition of Humphery Clinker (1771)

History
A Complete History of England (1757–58)

Drama
The Regicide (1739)

Poetry
'The Tears of Scotland' (1746)
Advice (1746)
Reproof (1747)

Travel Writing
Travels through France and Italy (1766)

Life

Smollett was born in Scotland and went to Glasgow University. He was apprenticed to a surgeon and went to London at the age of eighteen, in order to earn his living. He tried his hand at drama, but his play was not a success. He joined the navy as a surgeon and sailed to the West Indies. He met Anne Lassells in Jamaica and married her. After returning to London, he set up a medical practice.

He wrote a few poems and satires during that period. He then decided to try his hand at something more challenging and wrote the novel *Roderick Random*. With this began his career as a novelist. Like Fielding, Smollett too was asked to go abroad for his health. After the death of his only daughter, he and his wife set off for France and Italy. His travels abroad resulted in a book *Travels through France and Italy*. Finally, he succumbed to death in 1771 soon after his last novel was published.

Works

DRAMA

The Regicide was a drama based on the life of James I. He brought it with him when he went to London, but no one was interested in producing it.

POETRY

Smollett's first work to be published was the poem 'The Tears of Scotland'. It is a passionate attack of the British suppression of the Jacobites at Culloden. The next two poems *Advice* and *Reproof* satirised life in London. But his poetry, too, like his tragedy was not a success.

FICTION

Smollett ranks third after Richardson and Fielding in the history of the English novel. In his work, he introduced the sea as the background for the first time. He skilfully combined the roughness of naval life with an element of sentimentality. He, too, like Fielding preferred the picaresque form of the novel.

While Fielding was inspired by Cervantes's work, Smollett acknowledged Le Sage as his model. Smollett breathed new life into the picaresque tradition by creating interesting characters and placing them in backgrounds hitherto unexplored in the world of fiction. In *Roderick Random,* Smollett used many incidents from his own life. It is the story of a young Scot who is abandoned. Like Smollett, he too goes to London in search of a livelihood. Then follows a series of adventures and incidents, in which the author reveals the coarseness of daily life. The plot is episodic with incidents following one another rapidly. There is a lot of violence and bloodshed which makes the reader recoil in disgust.

His next novel *Peregrine Pickle* is very lengthy and tedious. It is narrated in the third person, unlike the previous book which was in the first person. The adventures are described in a less savage way, but the novel suffers from a lack of smooth development of plot. *The Adventures of Ferdinand, Count Fathom* is the story of a scoundrel and his adventures. There is little humour to relieve the savagery that is portrayed in it.

Translating *Don Quixote* inspired Smollett to write *The Adventures of Lancelot Greaves*. In it, Smollett depicts a knight-errant in armour visiting contemporary England. The irony is inferior when compared to that of Cervantes.

His best novel was his last one—*Humphery Clinker.* This, too, is a picaresque novel in which the characters are travelling. The novel is narrated through letters which reflect the nature of their writers. It describes the adventures of a Welsh family on a tour of Great Briton and Smollett takes us with them through Bath, London, Scotland, Edinburgh and the Scottish Highlands.

Features

- While Fielding excelled in the novel of character, Smollett's talent slanted towards the novel of incident. He continued to write in the tradition of the picaresque novel.
- His work is remarkable for the variety of incidents and characters. He had an easy and, at times, even a poetic style of writing. His style of writing is characterised by vivid descriptions and a colourful portrayal of characters.
- Smollett's novels are known for their satire and social commentary. He used his works to criticise various aspects of society, including the medical profession. Through them, we get an insight into the everyday life of his times.

Laurence Sterne (1713–68)

The Life and Times of Tristram Shandy (1759–67)
A Sentimental Journey through France and Italy (1766)

Life

Sterne was born in Ireland and was the son of an army officer. His early exposure to life in the barracks gave him first-hand knowledge of military life. He went to a school in Yorkshire and later went to Jesus College, Cambridge. Here, he was deeply influenced by John Locke. Sterne entered the church and obtained the living of a Yorkshire parish. He got married to Elizabeth Lumley and after several stillbirths, one daughter was born to them. He became a justice of the peace and enjoyed a good reputation. After a while, he handed over his parish to the care of a curate and began to write his novel *Tristram Shandy*.

When he went to London in 1760, he was already a recognised author. Sterne continued writing further volumes of *Tristram Shandy* which were highly popular. He had contracted tuberculosis when he was quite young, and his health began to deteriorate gradually. He left for France along with his wife and daughter with the hope of improving his health. His tours to France and later to Italy gave him enough matter to write his travelogue. His condition became worse and he died in London.

Works

Sterne transformed the novel by expanding its scope and loosening its structure. His entry into the world of letters marks a new stage in the history of the novel. The new element of sentiment or sensibility was becoming prominent in the genre and Sterne was its master. Hitherto, the novel was little more than a mirror of contemporary men and manners. Sterne rejected the old forms such as the novel of manners, the picaresque novel and even the usual narrative style.

Tristram Shandy was published in nine volumes and revolutionised the concept of the novel. It was the most original novel and had no predecessors. The reader has to wait till almost half the novel is over before the title character is born and he plays no part in the rest of the novel. The novel is revealed through episodes, conversations and digressions. It is full of incomplete sentences, dashes, blank pages and peculiar syntax. The chapters vary in size ranging from several pages to a single, short sentence. In spite of all these technical innovations, the characterisation of Uncle Toby, Corporal Trim and Doctor Slop are very well etched.

Sterne blends sentimentality with humour in a pleasing manner and narrates the story in a lively and very witty style. The novel is not chronologically arranged. Sterne was influenced by Locke who believed that our minds were a blank slate at birth and our ideas were formed through the experiences that we received through our senses; these ideas did not come to us in any proper order. This is the underlying concept for the unique structure of *Tristram Shandy* which reflects the disorder of human life. In this, he anticipates the stream-of-consciousness technique that was to become famous in the twentieth century.

His *A Sentimental Journey through France and Italy* is an unconventional travel book in which he speaks about his various love affairs. He focuses on the unusual incidents and the variety of people whom he meets during his travels.

Features

- Sterne was responsible for taking the novel to new heights. He employed unconventional techniques like digressions and non-linear narration. His technical innovations were far ahead of his times and anticipated the stream-of-consciousness novels of Virginia Woolf and James Joyce.
- Sterne was known for his sharp wit and his satirical portraiture of contemporary society and beliefs.
- He was adept at creating complex characters in a lifelike manner.
- Another unique feature of his works is Sterne's direct interaction with his readers, inviting them to participate in the narrative process, in a technique known as 'metafiction'.
- His combination of the sentimental with the comic had a special appeal for people.

Oliver Goldsmith (1728–74)

Periodicals
The Bee
The Busy Body
The Monthly Review
The Critical Review

Prose
Citizen of the World (1762)
Essays (1765)

Novel
The Vicar of Wakefield (1766)

Drama
The Good-Natur'd Man (1767)
She Stoops to Conquer (1773)

Poetry
'The Traveller; or a Prospect of Society' (1764)
'The Deserted Village' (1770)
'Retaliation' (1774)
'The Haunch of Venison' (1776)

Life

Oliver Goldsmith was born in Ireland but there is very little information about his early life. He was educated at Trinity

College, Dublin, and later studied medicine at Edinburgh for a few years. He travelled for a while in the Continent and reached London in 1756 as a penniless man. He supported himself by working as a reviewer and hack writer for *The Monthly Review* and several other periodicals.

Goldsmith met Dr Johnson who invited him to join the famous literary club founded by him. In spite of this, Goldsmith continued to struggle and had to do a lot of hack work in order to support himself. It was his poem 'The Traveller' that launched him into the literary world. His comedies were received well. He never married and his relationship with one Mary Horneck remains a mystery.

There are some interesting anecdotes about Goldsmith in Boswell's *Life of Johnson*, which represent him as a tender-hearted man who was given to dressing extravagantly. When he died, Johnson wrote the following epitaph for him: 'Oliver Goldsmith: A Poet, Naturalist, and Historian, who left scarcely any style of writing untouched, and touched nothing that he did not adorn...'

Works

PROSE

Goldsmith began his literary career by writing essays and critical tracts for various periodicals. He wrote on a wide variety of topics in his prose, ranging from the imaginary letters of a Chinaman about English society (*The Citizen of the World*) to essays in poetic prose such as his immortal 'A City Night-Piece'. In *The Citizen of the World*, Goldsmith portrayed a foreign traveller writing home about the strange customs that he had encountered in England. This format, which was popular at the time, was conducive to Goldsmith as he was able to expose the shortcomings of the society in which he lived. In this book, a Chinese traveller Lien Chi shares his views of British society in an ironical manner. Goldsmith also published a collection entitled *Essays*, which contained some of the best essays that had appeared in *The Bee* and other periodicals.

POETRY

Goldsmith did not write many poems, but the few he wrote are remarkable for their lyrical beauty and sincerity of emotion.

'The Traveller', his first poem, is about his wanderings through Europe. Written in heroic couplets, it is about four hundred lines long. There are many beautiful passages about the places he had visited. 'The Deserted Village', his most famous poem, is about his genuine sorrow at the destruction of the English countryside. The poem captures the changing landscape of England when the Industrial and Agrarian Revolutions were making rapid strides. We can hear his pain in the lines, 'Sweet smiling village, loveliest of the lawn, / Thy sports are fled, and all thy charms withdrawn; / Amidst thy bowers the tyrant's hand is seen, / And desolation saddens all thy green'. His other poems include the ballad called 'The Hermit' and the witty 'Elegy Written on a Mad Dog'.

NOVEL

The Vicar of Wakefield was the only novel written by Goldsmith. It narrates the story of the Primrose family's misfortunes and troubles. In it, Goldsmith contrasts the idyllic simplicity of the Primroses with the rogues and cheats of life. This work can be seen as a **sentimental novel** which highlights the hardships encountered by a virtuous character in an evil world. Some critics consider it to be a satire of the sentimental novel as it is only with the help of the character William Thornhill that the family is finally rescued and not because of the goodness of the vicar Dr Primrose.

DRAMA

Goldsmith is remembered for his two lively comedies which he wrote in prose. These plays were in sharp contrast with the sentimental and tearful comedies that were flooding the London stage. Goldsmith's plays can, thus, be seen as anti-sentimental dramas whose only aim was to make people laugh. *She Stoops to Conquer* ranks among the best comedies to be written in English. It is the story of a shy young man who mistakes a country mansion for an inn, treats the master of the house as the innkeeper and his daughter as a maid. The play is remembered for the amusing character Tony Lumpkin who plays a prank on the hero. Goldsmith styled the play on the format of the Restoration comedy but avoided its grossness. *The Good-Natur'd Man,* however, was not as successful as *She Stoops to Conquer.*

Features

- Goldsmith was a very versatile writer who wrote prose, poetry and drama.
- His essays are based on a variety of subjects and he displays a conversational style. His writing reveals his deep empathy for people and their struggles. In his well-known 'A City Night-Piece', he questions contemporary society in a voice filled with agony: 'Poor houseless creatures! The world will give you reproaches, but will not give you relief.'
- Goldsmith was a critic of the rapid changes that were being caused by industrialisation. 'The Deserted Village' portrays his sorrow at the depopulation of rural areas.
- His works are equally known for their wit and humour. His play *She Stoops to Conquer* is full of comic situations and satiric dialogues that poke fun at the social conventions of the day.

Richard Brinsley Sheridan (1751–1816)

The Rivals (1774)
St Patrick's Day or *The Scheming Lieutenant* (1775)
The Duenna (1775)
A Trip to Scarborough (1776)
The School for Scandal (1777)
The Critic or *A Tragedy Rehearsed* (1779)

Life

Sheridan was born in Dublin, Ireland, in the year 1751. He grew up in the world of theatre and drama as his mother was a playwright and his father was an actors' manager till the family moved to London. Sheridan attended a grammar school in Dublin and, later, he was trained in fencing and horse-riding.

At the age of twenty-one, he eloped and married Elizabeth Ann Linley. The couple lived in London where he began writing his plays. Sheridan's plays were a success; he wrote and produced an opera *The Duenna* which was performed seventy-five times. He became a partner in the Drury Lane Theatre and later, its sole owner.

He was hailed as one of the greatest dramatists of his time with the success of plays like *The Rivals* and *The School for Scandal.* His plays were all performed in his own theatre until it was destroyed by a fire in 1809. One can experience a sample of his ready wit, when he quipped, 'A man may surely be allowed to take a glass of wine by his own fireside', when he was questioned as to why he was drinking a glass of wine while watching his theatre burn down.

He entered parliament and made some memorable speeches that were admired by Edmund Burke and William Pitt. He held important posts like the receiver-general of the duchy of Cornwall and the treasurer of the navy. When he lost both positions in the re-election to Parliament, he was financially ruined and his creditors closed in on him. He became very sick and died in poverty. He was buried at the Poets' Corner of Westminster Abbey.

Works

His first play *The Rivals* has all the features of the comedy of manners, but has a fresh approach. He wrote in a style known as 'artificial comedy', which is a type of comedy that focused on the superficiality and affected nature of contemporary society—a style that appealed to his audience. The play depicts the authority of an older generation in confrontation with the strategies of a smarter, younger generation. Sheridan displays an extraordinary linguistic variety which includes the innovative oaths of Bob Acres—'Odds blushes and blooms', 'Odds triggers and flints'; the Irishisms of Sir Lucas O'Trigger; and the interesting misapplications of the immortal Mrs Malaprop—'Sure, if I reprehend anything in this world it is the use of my oracular tongue, and a nice derangement of epitaphs!' and 'He's the very pineapple of politeness!' It is from this last character that the word 'malapropism' was derived.

His next few plays, *St Patrick's Day*, *The Duenna* and *A Trip to Scarborough* enjoyed success on the stage, though they are not read much today. His *A School for Scandal* is undoubtedly his best play. The play exhibits Sheridan's mastery of language and complex plotting. It is basically a moral fable which contrasts the two brothers—Joseph Surface, a sentimental and pompous villain, and Charles, a virtuous and generous libertine. There is a lot of intrigue and a marvellous exposure of affectation and petty hypocrisy. It contains stock characters that have genuine lives of their own. The dialogues are full of sparkling wit and repartee.

His last play *The Critic* pales in comparison to the earlier plays. It portrays the petty wars of the theatres and the scheming critics who supported sentimental drama. It was topical and had a greater appeal for the contemporary audience than it does for us today.

Features

- Sheridan's plays are well-known for their intrigue. He wrote prose comedies which resembled the best of Restoration comedy. His plays however, avoided the immorality and vulgarity of some of the comedies that belonged to the heyday of Restoration drama.
- Sheridan captures the shallow nature of society, but makes their vices appear foolish rather than wicked.
- His plots are intricate and are dependent on the theatrical condition of his day which included grand productions and elaborate staging of plays.
- He is known for his wit and repartee. In fact, his dialogues are so brilliant that they sometimes tend to eclipse the characters.
- He created several immortal characters like Mrs Malaprop, Bob Acres and Sir Fretful Plagiary.

James Thomson (1700–48)

Poetry
'Poem Sacred to the Memory of Sir Isaac Newton' (1727)
'Rule, Britannia' (1729)
The Seasons (1726–30)
Liberty (1734–36)
The Castle of Indolence (1748)

Masque
Alfred (with Mallet, 1740)

Drama
Sophonisba (1730)
Agamemnon (1738)
Edward and Eleonora (1739)
Coriolanus (1749)

Life

Thomson was born in Scotland to a Presbyterian minister. He was the fourth of nine children and was a very average student who did not show any promise. He joined the College of Edinburgh in 1715 and studied the classical languages, Greek and Latin, besides metaphysics, logic and ethics. He did not graduate, but joined Divinity Hall to become a minister.

While at Edinburgh he befriended David Mallet, a poet, whom he followed to London. Through the influence of Mallet, he met prominent English poets of the day like Richard Savage and Alexander Pope. It was while he was in London, that he wrote the four parts of his famous work *The Seasons*—'Winter', 'Summer', 'Spring' and 'Autumn'. He also wrote a few other poems and some plays and tried to make his living through his writing. He died in 1748 and lies buried in St Mary Magdalene's Church in Richmond.

Works

Between 1726 and 1730, the four parts of *The Seasons* appeared. The poems of this volume are all in blank verse and contain several descriptive passages about nature—an unusual practice at that time, as it was more fashionable to write about urban life and the manners of men.

His next important poetical work is *The Castle of Indolence* which was published the year he died. He chose the Spenserian stanza but the poetic gravity and depth of Spenser's writing is missing in his work. Much of the work is imitative and the sentiments expressed are commonplace; but the versification is harmonious and lyrical. The poem describes the idealised lotus land (a pleasant place, where people do not have to worry about anything) into which discounted souls (individuals who have lost their sense of purpose and meaning in life) are summoned to retire. The rest of his poems warrant lesser merit.

Apart from poetry, Thomson tried his hand at drama. His dramatic work includes five tragedies and a masque written in collaboration with his friend Mallet. Thomson was not very successful as a dramatist because he had no stage sense and his characterisation was poor.

Features

- Although Thomson is seen as a poet of transition, in truth he was almost an exact contemporary of Alexander Pope. Thomson wrote little in heroic couplets at a time when the heroic couplet was the popular measure of poetry It is interesting to note that he preferred blank verse and that his poetry contained long passages that described nature at a time when the focus of poetry was on man and court or city life. As a poet, Thomson may not be rated as one of the greats, but his works are an important milestone in the history of English literature since they heralded a new style of writing.
- His use of blank verse influenced the younger generation of poets like Collins. Thomson showed how blank verse could serve as a suitable form to describe nature.
- His descriptions of nature played an important role in the revival of romanticism. His great service to literature was in reviving the poetical treatment of various aspects of nature. He made nature his subject and described it with exactness and charm.
- He wielded great influence on the poets of the next generation.

Thomas Gray (1716–71)

'Sonnet on the Death of Mr Richard West' (1742)
'Hymn to Adversity' (1742)
'Ode on a Distant Prospect of Eton College' (1742)
'Ode on the Spring' (1742)
'Ode on the Death of a Favourite Cat' (1748)
'Elegy Written in a Country Churchyard' (1750)
'The Progress of Poesy' (1754)
'The Bard' (1757)

Life

Thomas Gray was born in London and was the only one of twelve children to survive. He had a troubled childhood as his father was given to fits of violence. It was his mother who was responsible for his education and upbringing. He spent nine years at Eton where he met Horace Walpole, with whom he toured Italy and France. Apart from Walpole, he befriended Richard West and Thomas Ashton at Eton. Gray later continued his education in Cambridge.

West's death in 1742, at the age of twenty-four, came as a great blow to Gray who sought consolation in writing the poem 'Sonnet on the death of Richard West'. He, however, was very shy and reluctant to publish his work. Soon several other poems from Gray followed, including his famous 'Elegy', and in 1757 he was offered the laureateship which he refused to accept.

He spent two years in London studying Old English manuscripts in the newly opened British Museum. From 1762 till he died in 1771, he toured through different parts of England and Scotland. He was made professor of modern history at Cambridge University in 1768 but he never delivered any lectures. He led a very quiet and frugal life and died suddenly. He was buried in a cemetery in Stoke Poges, which he had immortalised earlier in his 'Elegy'.

Works

The volume of his work is very slender, but what he wrote is timeless and exquisite. His work is also remarkable for being representative of the changing taste in literary production. His lyric poems—'Ode to the Spring', 'Ode on the Distant Prospect of Eton College', 'Hymn to Adversity' and 'Hymn to Ignorance'—reveal Gray's mastery of the form. In these poems, he explores human emotions and experiences but in the artificial diction that was popular at the time.

With the publication of the 'Elegy Written in a Country Churchyard', one can discern a definite change in style. The poem is highly successful in evoking the brooding and melancholy atmosphere of a graveyard. The 'Elegy' is the most famous and outstanding poem in the genre of works by **graveyard poets** for several reasons. The term 'graveyard poets' was applied to some eighteenth-century poets who wrote melancholy poems set in graveyards. Gray's use of nature in 'Elegy Written in a Country Churchyard' is both subtle and profound. In it, Gray contrasts the simple life of the peasant with that of the townsman. Finally, the poem draws our attention to the ordinary and unremarkable men and women of an unknown hamlet—a definite slant towards the democratic spirit that was soon to be witnessed in England. The poem is full of memorable lines that are celebrated even today, such as: 'The paths of glory lead but to the grave' and 'Full many a gem of purest ray serene, / The dark unfathomed caves of ocean bear: / Full many a flower is born to blush unseen, / And waste its sweetness on the desert air.'

When Gray attempted the mock heroic in 'Ode on the Death of a Favourite Cat', he succeeded in displaying scholarly wit and a gracefulness of expression. It is in this poem that we find the famous lines: 'A favourite has no friend'; 'Not all that tempts your wandering eyes / And heedless hearts is lawful prize; / Nor all that glisters, gold'.

His Pindaric odes, 'The Progress of Poesy' and 'The Bard', are a rich tribute to the classical Greek form. In the first poem, Gray traces the genealogy of English poetry. He posits a poetic tradition that springs from Greece and Rome and flows to Shakespeare. In the second poem, he highlights the discontinuity of poetry. The poem is based on the legend of Edward I who passed an order against the bards of Wales and how one bard prophesied the end of the Plantagenets and the triumph of poetry under the Tudors. Through this poem, Gray succeeds in fusing the Celtic and English traditions.

The total bulk of his poetical writing is very small and he never attempted to publish his writings, which remained in manuscript form till his death.

Features

- Gray anticipated the Romantic age in several ways—in his approach to nature, in adopting a subjective style and in taking poetry from the urban to the rural.
- His poems contain several truisms. For example, in his poem, 'Ode on a Distant Prospect of Eton College', we have the lines, 'where ignorance is bliss, / 'tis folly to be wise'. This, probably, is one of the most misunderstood phrases in

English as Gray was definitely not promoting ignorance. In the poem, he recalls nostalgically how he was allowed to be ignorant in his youth.

- He was known as one of the graveyard poets who wrote about mortality and the finality of death.
- His influence on the Romantic poets was tremendous.

William Collins (1721–59)

Persian or *Oriental Eclogues* (1742) *Odes* (1746)

Life

William Collins was born in Chichester and was well educated, first at Winchester and later at Oxford. While still a student at Oxford, he published *Persian Eclogues.* In 1744, he went to London with hardly any money and led a hard life of toil and poverty. As a result, he could not write much although he had great dreams of building a literary career. In 1746, he managed to publish a slim volume of twelve odes which found little readership. It was at this stage that he made the acquaintance of James Thomson which developed into a great friendship. His 'Ode on the Death of Thomson', one of his finest poems, bears ample testimony to this fact. By the time he was twenty-eight, he slowly began to sink into depression and died at the age of thirty-eight.

Works

Collins left behind a very slender body of work, of hardly more than two thousand lines. Yet, what he has written is of a high quality and great literary merit.

The poems in *Persian Eclogues* are neoclassical in style although the theme is oriental. They reflect the growing fascination in English society for the exotic and the distant. He won a place for himself in literature with his odes. This collection of twelve odes deals with a variety of subjects like simplicity, fear and pity. His 'Ode to Evening' is one of his best odes and is written in unrhymed verse. Five of the odes have a patriotic theme, the longest of them being 'Ode to Liberty'.

Features

- His work was influenced by Milton's *L'Allegro* and *Il Penseroso*.
- He wrote unrhymed verse at a time when the heroic couplet was reigning supreme.

William Cowper (1731–1800)

Olney Hymns (1779) *Poems* (1782) *The Task* (1785)

Life

Cowper was born in Great Berkhampstead, Hertfordshire. The loss of his mother when he was just six years old left a deep impression on him. After her death, he was sent to a boarding school, where he was bullied by one of his schoolfellows for nearly two years. He studied the classics and made the acquaintance of Warren Hastings at school.

He made an attempt to be a barrister, but his extremely reticent nature prevented him from succeeding as one. In fact, his timid disposition increased to such great proportions that it drove him to contemplate suicide. His extreme shyness proved to be the bane of his entire life.

The latter part of his life was spent among understanding friends at Buckinghamshire. For a while, he was at peace with himself, but again he slipped into depression before he finally died.

Works

He started writing late in life, but he wrote a lot. He was not a serious student of poetry and wrote only to divert his mind and keep himself from brooding too much. His first work was a collection of poems, the *Olney Hymns*, written in collaboration with Reverend John Newton. The hymns are sincere in nature and some of them, such as 'Oh! For a Closer Walk with God', 'Hark, My soul! It is the Lord' and 'God Moves in a Mysterious Way', are still famous.

He was next encouraged to write by another friend, Mrs Unwin, and the result was what may be called his moral satires—'Table Talk', 'The Progress of Error', 'Truth', 'Expostulation', 'Hope', 'Charity', 'Conversation' and 'Retirement'. These and a few more of his short poems, written in the heroic couplets that were popular at the time, were collectively published as *Poems* in 1782.

He next undertook writing *The Task* at the suggestion of Lady Austen, Jane's mother. He used blank verse to describe the rural walks and fireside joys experienced during his stay at Olney. 'God made the country and man made the town' is the theme of this volume of poems. This book reveals him as a complete contrast to Pope who concentrated only on depicting city life. It is in this collection that we find the delightful ballad of John Gilpin which reveals Cowper's humour at its best.

'The Castaway', written shortly before his death, is about man's isolation and helplessness. He used the metaphor of storms and shipwrecks to explain the mysterious ways of God.

Features

- Cowper is a lesser-known poet, but a poet who must be read. His love for nature was one of the most important aspects of his work. He was also extremely sensitive to animals.
- His works were influenced by his strong Calvinist beliefs and exhibit his search for spirituality. This religious strain is seen especially in 'The Castaway' where he is shown grappling with the concept of divine providence.
- He was sympathetic to the difficulties of the poor and scornful of their oppressors.
- His style is full of idiomatic grace and his verse has variety and melody. He is known for his usage of unconventional language.
- Some critics have pointed out that he was a precursor to Wordsworth and Byron in his love for nature and his approach to humble rural life.

PRE-ROMANTICS AND THE ROMANTIC REVIVAL (1780–1837)

The beginning of the eighteenth century witnessed the heydays of neoclassicism with Pope at the height of his career. It was the Age of Reason which turned its back firmly on imagination and inspiration. Importance was given to the mind and intellect over the heart and emotion. The neoclassical poets turned away from nature and focused on urban and court life.

The middle of the century saw a gradual shift in focus with several poets, beginning with Thomson, experimenting with poetry. Reason still held sway but importance was given to sensibility too. This period of transition from the neoclassical to the Romantic also witnessed a reaction in matters of style and form. The strict heroic couplets of Pope gave way to experiments in verse by new poets who were tired of the monotony of writing in just one type of verse. Thomson's *Seasons* was written in blank verse. Blank verse was found to be more suitable to the new generation as it was more elastic and offered greater opportunities for the free movement of the poet's mind. Yet another change that was noticeable was the shift from Augustan urban poetry to rural poetry that was closer to nature.

By the last decade of the eighteenth century, Romanticism firmly took root marked by the publication of *Lyrical Ballads* in 1798.

The Romantic Revival in English literature roughly spans the period between 1798 (when *Lyrical Ballads, with a Few Other Poems* by Wordsworth and Coleridge appeared) and 1837 (when Queen Victoria ascended the throne). It was a turbulent period that was marked on the one end by the revolutions in America and France and on the other by the series of reforms in the English Parliament that gradually transformed Great Britain from a monarchy to a democracy. It was also the period that witnessed the emergence of industrialisation and the birth of the middle class.

The word 'romantic' comes from the term 'romance', one of the most popular genres of the medieval period. The medieval romance typically consisted of tales of chivalry, with knights in shining armour rescuing damsels from imprisonment in far-away castles or from the clutches of fire-breathing dragons. As one can immediately understand, the romance was far removed from the world of reality. Thus, romanticism could be seen as a movement opposed to the classical and neoclassical approaches to life and literature—a literary style that has ebbed and flowed since medieval times. Some of the best romances of England were Sir Thomas Malory's *Le Morte d'Arthur* (1485), Spenser's *Faerie Queene* (1589) and Sidney's *Arcadia* (1590). Romanticism had peaked in the age of Shakespeare and the chivalrous Elizabethans, only to recede in the early years of the seventeenth century to gradually make way for the triumph of classicism. Its revival towards the close of the eighteenth century resulted in one of the best periods in England's literature. Thus, the Romantic Revival of the eighteenth century was not the beginning of a completely new phenomenon, but something that could be traced as far back as the fifteenth century. Towards the close of the eighteenth century, the term 'romance' became synonymous with the flights of fancy and imagination that were so characteristic of the age—something that was abhorred by the neoclassical writers. It was a period that witnessed the revival of ballads, folk-tales and the stories of *The Arabian Nights*.

Romanticism is a term that covers a vast range of developments in the field of art, literature, music and philosophy. The term 'romantic' was a label that was applied retrospectively almost a century later to the age. One of the men who was an inspiration to the Romantics was Jean-Jacques Rousseau who famously declared in *The Social Contract* (1762) that 'Man is born free, and everywhere he is in chains'. The major transitions that were taking place at the time inspired the young poets who upheld individual freedom and denounced the exploitation of the poor. The French Revolution, which witnessed the toppling of monarchy and the creation of a new social order, reached the shores of England. These ideals convinced the Romantics that one should follow one's heart and not be guided by conventions and rules. They felt it was the responsibility of the poets to transform society.

This period in the history of English literature witnessed an extraordinary amount of literary activity. In the field of poetry, there were giants like William Wordsworth, Samuel Taylor Coleridge, Robert Southey, Lord Byron, Percy Bysshe Shelley and John Keats. In the genre of fiction, we have Sir Walter Scott, Mary Shelley and Jane Austen. It was a great period of prose too with writers like Thomas De Quincey, William Hazlitt and Charles Lamb who raised the personal essay to great heights. Historians offer several reasons for this literary outburst:

- Improvement in the art of printing and greater freedom of the press in the late-eighteenth and nineteenth centuries were favourable to the publishing industry.
- The Industrial and Agrarian Revolutions enriched the nation and there was a great improvement in the welfare and economic conditions of England.
- The French Revolution, which represented equality and universal brotherhood, opened the floodgates of passionate energy and filled the young poets with the hope for a brighter future.
- Collections of old ballads like Percy's *Reliques* inspired poets like Coleridge, Scott, Southey and Keats. The romantic ballads from Germany, especially those of Goethe and Schiller, also proved to be a great influence upon Romantic poetry.

Romanticism could be seen as a stage in the cyclic development of societies—a stage when a new generation of people began to question accepted traditions and authority. There was an urge to live without the shackles of conformity and embark on a quest for freedom from the constraints of traditions. In this, Romanticism could be seen as a kind of idealised state of being. Another aspect of Romanticism was the dependence of the individual on his own emotions and instinct in order to discover his identity.

This changed attitude towards life resulted in a new style of writing. Some of the important features of the Romantic Revival in literature are:

- The turn of the century was a period of revolution in the history of politics. The Romantics, who came under its spell, rebelled against traditions, formulas and conventions. Precedence was given to individuality and freedom. As a result, they had great contempt for the prescribed rules, set standards, conventions and traditional laws of the poetry of the Augustan Age. New verse forms were introduced and the Romantics experimented with them. For example, Blake, who anticipated the Romantics, wrote visionary epics; Wordsworth spent a good part of his life writing a poetic autobiography; and Byron's *Don Jaun* (1819) is a curious mixture of a tale of adventure and a burlesque.

- Spontaneity was one of the key features of Romantic poetry. This idea is summed up succinctly by Keats when he said, 'That which is creative must create itself'. Wordsworth also asserted a similar thought in his preface to *Lyrical Ballads* (1800) when he declared that poetry was a 'spontaneous overflow of powerful feelings'.
- There was a sharp swing from the objectivity of neoclassical literature to subjectivity. The Romantics believed in the assertion of the self and their poetry was the product of the emotions and sentiments experienced in their hearts. Much of Romantic poetry is subjective where one is able to delve deep into the inner conscience of the poets. For example, Wordsworth shares his deepest thoughts with us in his 'Immortality Ode':

  Thanks to the human heart by which we live,
  Thanks to its tenderness, its joys, and fears,
  To me the meanest flower that blows can give
  Thoughts that do often lie too deep for tears.

  Similarly, we hear the agonised voice of Shelley when he cries out in dire need in his 'Ode to the West Wind':

  I would ne'er have striven
  As thus with thee in prayer in my sore need,
  Oh, lift me as a wave, a leaf, a cloud!
  I fall upon the thorns of life! I bleed!

- Poetry moved from the city to the countryside. The return of poetry to nature, begun by Thomson and quickened by Gray and Burns, was further advanced to greater heights by Wordsworth and the other Romantics. Although all the

Romantics turned to nature in a big way, each one had his own unique approach to it. While Wordsworth, and Shelley to a certain extent, gave a spiritual flavouring to nature, Byron discovered a reflection of his own moods in the ever-changing aspects of nature. It was the sensuous beauty of nature that had a special appeal to Keats.

- Importance was given to emotion and imagination over intellect and reason. Each of the Romantic poets had his own special view on the role of imagination. Their poems usually present imaginative experiences as being very powerful or moving. This reveals the fact that to them imagination was not merely a special faculty of the mind, but also a kind of desire or a motive to learn things that could not be learnt by rational or logical thinking. We, therefore, understand that imagination is responsible for moving the mind in mysterious ways to imitate nature and the purpose of this imitation is to create new realities in the mind and, as a result, in poetry.
- The Romantics discarded the poetic diction of the early-eighteenth century. Poetry then was written exclusively for the benefit of the rich and the aristocratic who had access to education. The Romantics believed in adopting the language of the ordinary man and, as Wordsworth declared in his 'Preface', a poet was 'a man speaking to men'. One of the reasons for this change was the influence of the war cry of the French Revolution—'Liberty, Equality and Fraternity'—which urged people to adopt a democratic approach to society. Another was the Industrial Revolution which gave rise to the exploitation of the poor through the ruthless *laissez-faire* policy. The Romantics, therefore, turned their backs to the formal verse of the Augustans and wrote in a more intimate and spontaneous manner in order to be able to appeal to the man on the street.
- Another interesting feature of Romantic poetry is their fondness for locations and settings that were far removed from their own time and place. They tried to escape the harsh realities of contemporary life by going back to a

bygone age or to an exotic land far away. This can be seen in the poems like 'Kubla Khan' and 'The Rime of the Ancient Mariner' of Coleridge and the historical novels of Sir Walter Scott. These lines from Keats's 'Ode to a Nightingale' also reflect the Romantics' partiality for exotic locations:

The same that oft-times hath
Charm'd magic casements, opening on the foam
Of perilous seas, in faery lands forlorn.

Fiction

The novel, which emerged as a popular literary form in the eighteenth century, developed further as the century progressed. During the late-eighteenth century, a form of the novel known as the **Gothic novel** became popular. This form was first introduced in England by **Horace Walpole** (1717–97) in his novel *The Castle of Otranto* (1765). The Gothic novel was a very distinct form that combined romance with mystery and horror. The novel was usually set in a haunted castle and portrayed secret passages, dungeons and eerie happenings. Walpole attributed the cause for writing this novel to a nightmare in which he had seen a ghost.

The popularity of the Gothic novel attracted writers like Ann Radcliff (1764–1823), Charles Robert Maturin (1780–1824) and Matthew Gregory Lewis (1715–1818), who wrote historically inaccurate Gothic novels that were also known as 'novels of terror'. These had little literary merit and were a crude form of fiction. Jane Austen satirised these novels in her *Northanger Abbey.*

Mary Shelley, Godwin's daughter and Shelley's wife, wrote *Frankenstein* which captured the imagination of the readers. The novel explores the effect of a monstrous being created by science, which eventually destroys its creator.

Apart from novels of terror, women novelists wrote novels reflecting contemporary society and domestic life. The focus of these novels was on the manners and behaviour of the characters in a given social environment. This type of writing was known as the **novel of manners**. Fanny Burney's *Evelina* (1778) is an excellent example of this type of fiction. Jane Austen's novels, too, offer us a close-up view of the society and manners of her time.

Maria Edgeworth shifted the setting to Ireland in her novels. She was one of the first to paint a realistic picture of the Irish instead of their earlier comic depiction. Her novels inspired Sir Walter Scott to do for Scotland what Edgeworth did for Ireland.

An important form of the novel that became extremely popular was the **historical romance** or the **historical novel**. This was a type of novel that was developed by Sir Walter Scott. Any story that has a historical setting or which describes the events and manners of a bygone age could be known as a historical novel. When a historical novel combined the facts of history with a tale of romance, it could be called historical romance.

Non-Fiction

Verse and fiction dominated the literary scene during the Romantic Age. However, there were a few prominent writers who gave their attention to prose and literary criticism. This was one of the richest periods for literary criticism. Not only did it see professional literary critics like William Hazlitt, but it also had several practicing poets writing criticism and explaining the theories behind their work. Wordsworth's 'Preface' to the *Lyrical Ballads* and Coleridge's *Biographia Literaria* are two important works in the history of literary criticism. Shelley's *A Defence of Poetry* and the letters of Keats, too, are considered as important treatises on the art of poetry. Such writing by practising poets is known as **workshop criticism**.

Apart from literary criticism the **familiar** and **personal essay** saw a new blossoming in the hands of writers like Charles Lamb, William Hazlitt, Leigh Hunt and Thomas De Quincey. These writers were all inspired by the periodical essays of the eighteenth century. Unlike the periodical essay, the personal essay did not have an agenda of reforming society or refining tastes. Personal essays were conversational pieces in which the writer shared his feelings and experiences with the readers. In keeping with the spirit of the age, the personal essays too returned to the past to evoke its charm and focused on man's relationship with nature. The personal essay of the late-eighteenth century marked a significant improvement on its predecessor, the periodical essay. It allowed the writer the perfect freedom to wander wherever his fancy led him. He could begin where he pleased and end where he liked. Reviews, too, became popular during this period. This was later developed in the Victorian Age by authors like Carlyle and Macaulay.

Robert Burns and William Blake completely broke away from the classical tradition and could be considered as the immediate precursors of the Romantics. In their work, we can clearly perceive all the elements of Romanticism. Since they predate the peak of the Romantic movement, they could not be included in the Romantic school.

Robert Burns (1759–96)

Poems (1786) Songs in *Select Scottish Airs* (1792)

Life

Burns was the eldest of a family of seven children born in Ayrshire, Scotland. He attended school for a few years but he was mostly self-taught and was guided by his father. His childhood was spent in poverty and he had to do severe manual labour on his father's small farm when he was fifteen.

He struggled a lot and worked hard in order to improve his financial condition. It was at that time that he started writing poetry and discovered that his poems were received well. At the same time, he became interested in collecting the old songs of Scotland that were slowly disappearing and wished to preserve them. He collected about three hundred songs which he contributed to James Johnson's *The Scots Musical Museum* and *A Select Collection of Original Scottish Airs for the Voice* by George Thomson.

In 1790, appeared his famous poems, 'Tam o' Shanter' and 'The Jolly Beggars'. His lifestyle was frowned upon by the narrow-minded Scottish Calvinists of his times and he often got into trouble. One night, when he was returning home after a drinking spree, he fell into the snow and fell asleep. He never recovered from the after-effects of this episode and died at the age of thirty-seven.

Works

Burns was one of the most important precursors of the Romantics. His poetry played a significant role in reviving and promoting the Scottish language. He was considered one of the leading poets of the century. He was very patriotic yet his sympathies were not restricted to Scotland. He was a poet who was sensitive to the joys and sorrows of common people which was reflected in the spontaneity of his songs. His lyrics were full of warmth and freshness—qualities that were long absent from lyrical poetry.

At the time when he began his literary career, Pope's classical school of writing was still very influential. Blake imitated this in the poems where he did not use his native Scottish dialect. He broke away from this early influence to create a personal poetry that was totally different from its classical predecessor. His poetry was forged from within and gave expression to his passions and feelings and his revolt against Presbyterian tyranny. He made use of several Scottish words and phrases that were typical to the language. Blake also differed from other poets in his turning away from didacticism.

As seen in the list of works by Burns given above, he wrote only one volume of poems which he edited five times. Apart from this he contributed to *The Scots Musical Museum* and to Thomson's *Select Collections of Original Scottish Airs*. His poems reveal a vast variety of emotions ranging from the rollicking wit of 'The Jolly Beggar' to the graceful sentiment of 'O My Love is like a Red, Red Rose'. There is a strong Scottish flavour in all his poems. Poems like 'Auld Lang Syne' and 'Green Grow the Rashes, O!' have the rustic melody that is rooted in Scottish peasantry. His poems also abound in a wealth of natural descriptions of the Scottish landscape and customs.

Burns was loved so much by the people that his birthday, 25 January, is celebrated as Burns Night every year.

Features

- The most outstanding feature of his poetry is its lyrical quality. In this, he anticipated Shelley. The emotional

element in his lyrics had an immediate appeal to the Romantics.
- He is known for the versatility of his imagination, robustness of expression and veracity of description.
- He displays a wide range of emotions in his songs although their theme is mostly love.
- He is the national poet of Scotland. In his poetry, we are able to hear the Highland tones ringing clearly and loudly. His poetry played a crucial role in reviving the fading language and customs of Scotland.

William Blake (1757–1827)

Poetical Sketches (1783)
Songs of Innocence (1789)
The Book of Thel (1790)
The Marriage of Heaven and Hell (1790)
The French Revolution (1791)
The Visions of the Daughters of Albion (1793)
Songs of Experience (1794)
Europe (1794)
The First Book of Urizen (1794)
The Book of Ahania (1795)
The Book of Los (1795)
The Song of Los (1795)
Milton (1804)
Jerusalem (1804)

Life

He was the son of a hosier and was born in London. He was mostly self-taught and was familiar with the works of Shakespeare, Milton and the Bible. Apart from this, he also read about **Gnosticism**. Gnosticism is a Greek term that describes a collection of ancient religions that taught people to shun the material world and embrace the spiritual world. He was apprenticed to an engraver at the age of eighteen and went on to practise engraving throughout his life. At the age of twenty-five, he married an illiterate but affectionate woman of his own rank and set up shop as an engraver. At the same time, he started writing poetry and his first book *Poetical Sketches* was published in 1783.

His finances were poor and he had to lead a humble life. But he seemed to have a mysterious communion with an invisible spiritual world which sustained him in times of difficulty. He was filled with strange visions which had a great impact upon his writing and life. His poetical output was quite substantial and included several poems that are famous even today.

Works

In Blake's poetry the romantic 'vision' is distinct. He gave great importance to imagination and the feelings of the heart. Like Burns, he too sympathised with the poor and believed in using the language of the common man. His own reading of essays on Gnosticism and Druidism influenced his thoughts deeply. The Oriental dualism of Gnosticism led Blake to see the presence of good and evil in life; as he says in the title page of *Songs of Innocence* and *Songs of Experience*, these are 'the two contrary states of the human soul'. Druidism, which was revived in the eighteenth century, proclaimed that the ancient inhabitants of Britain were the direct descendants of Noah and, further, of Adam and Eve and God, himself. All these ideas coloured his writing and made it at times obscure and unintelligible.

He was a professional artist who illustrated almost all his poems. He also printed much of his poetry himself, using engraving methods that he had created. Blake would transfer the written text of his poem to an etched copper plate. He would also add appropriate illustrations or decorations. After printing the page, he would colour it elaborately by hand. Thus, in order to study his poems properly, one needs to interrelate the engraved image with the text. The picture is not a mere representation of the text; neither is the text an extension of the image. Both necessitate an interpretative reading and together they form a total text in which different symbols prove to be either complementary or contradictory.

His first work *Poetical Sketches* was not printed by him and failed to attract any notice. The poems were mostly imitative and uninspired. His next work *Songs of Innocence* contains beautiful lyrics that describe the contrary states of sensation and perception. In it, he portrays his view of the unadulterated state of human society by depicting the joy and innocence of children.

The Book of Thel also celebrates the same theme of love and joy. This was followed by a series of revolutionary and prophetic books—*The French Revolution, The Visions of the Daughters of Albion, America* and *Europe*.

The Songs of Experience, which came later, lacks the spontaneity and joy of *The Songs of Innocence*. Here, we see Blake presenting the duality of nature. An excellent example of this theory is evident in his famous poem 'The Tyger', where the line 'Did he who made the Lamb make thee?' sums it up succinctly.

Taken together, the two texts offer a series of shifting perceptions. The subtitle of the two works—'Showing Two Contrary States of the Human Soul'—suggests not only a falling away from man's original innocence, but also the prospect of advancement towards a Christ-inspired state of higher innocence. The poems have a hymn-like simplicity and rhymes that resemble those of children's lullabies. *Songs of Innocence* contains poems which depict the challenges that the innocent stage of childhood has to face—darkness, wild beasts that threaten lambs, slavery and child labour like that endured by the chimney-sweep. In *Songs of Experience,* the 'wisdom' of the old is seen as a form of oppression. The songs here are more satirical in tone and sometimes even border on the sarcastic. 'The Sick Rose' and 'The Poison Tree' are examples of such poetry.

A bearded representative of a negative god is portrayed as the figure of Urizen in his work, *The First Book of Urizen*. In his incomplete work, *The Book of Los,* he narrates the story of the rebellion against the tyrannical oppression of Urizen led by Los. Orc, the son of Los, is shown as both the rebel and the oppressor in this book. This same Orc is shown as the personification of the revolutions in America and France in his next work, *America: A Prophecy* and *Europe: A Prophecy*.

Milton, A Poem in Two Books, To Justify the Ways of God to Men was written and engraved between 1803–08. In this work, Blake identified himself with both Milton and the fallen and good angels. It was Blake who declared in his work *The Marriage of Heaven and Hell* that Milton was 'a true poet and of the Devil's party without knowing it'.

Features

- His early work is remarkable for its lyrical quality. This made him stand out distinctly from the restrained poetry of the neoclassical period.
- His later poetry is obscure as he used complex symbolism in them.
- He tried to create an experimental mythology, but it was essentially Protestant in nature. He wished to free religion from dogma and suppression.
- Blake was a passionate visionary who gave importance to liberty.
- His works anticipated the Romantic poetry of the coming age.

William Wordsworth (1770–1850)

'An Evening Walk' (1793)
'Descriptive Sketches' (1793)
Lyrical Ballads (1798, with Coleridge)
Poems in Two Volumes (1807)
The Excursion (fragment of *The Recluse*, 1814)
Ladomia (1815)
White Doe of Rylstone (1815)
Miscellaneous Poems (1815)
Peter Bell (1819)
The Waggoner (1819)
Thc Rivcr Duddon (1820)
Memorials of a Tour of the Continent (1820)
Yarrow Revisited (1835)
The Prelude (1850)

Life

Wordsworth was the second of a family of five children born to John Wordsworth and Anne Cookson. He was born in Cockermouth, Cumberland, where he spent his early childhood. He lost his mother when he was just eight and was sent to the free grammar school at Hawkshead. He enjoyed his school life as he had a lot of freedom to read and roam about as he liked. It was Hawkshead that brought him close to nature and made him a poet. It was at this school that he met William Taylor, a teacher who influenced him a great deal and who was commemorated in poems like 'Matthew', 'The Two April Mornings' and 'The Fountain'.

When Wordsworth was thirteen, his father died leaving the family in a financially critical state. His relatives sent him to St John's College, Cambridge, when he was seventeen from where he graduated four years later. In 1790, he went on a walking tour of the Alps and France along with a friend. This resulted in *Descriptive Sketches* which is a poetical account of his travels. While he was at Cambridge, the French Revolution broke out and the young Wordsworth, attracted by its early heady phase, moved to France where he stayed for a year. 'Bliss was it in that dawn to be alive / But to be young was very Heaven', he wrote in *The Prelude*. Wordsworth believed in the ideology behind the Revolution and was eager to join the Girondists (a political group that championed the end of monarchy but were also against the rising momentum of the Revolution, thereby earning the ire of the radical Jacobins; several Girondists were mass executed) and was almost guillotined. He returned to England in 1793. Before long, his political views underwent a change after witnessing the Napoleonic Wars. He was influenced by the views of Edmund Burke and began to believe in England's role as the guardian of freedom against the imperialism of Napoleon.

After he returned to England, he received a small legacy of nine hundred pounds left to him by a friend. This financial independence enabled him to take up a house with his devoted sister Dorothy and pursue his career as poet. He lived first at Racedown, then at Alfoxden in order to be close to where Coleridge lived, before settling down in the Lake District. There he lived first at Dove Cottage and later at Rydal Mount. His finances improved steadily as he received the repayment of a debt of eight hundred pounds owed to his family. He married Mary Hutchinson, a childhood friend.

The honours that came to him in his later years included an honorary degree from Oxford in 1839, a government pension of three hundred pounds in 1842 and the laureateship in 1843. He died a few days after his eightieth birthday and was buried in the Grasmere churchyard.

Works

Wordsworth began writing poetry even when he was in school and his earliest writings were influenced by Pope, who was a dominant influence then. As a university student, he wrote several poems such as 'An Evening Walk' (1793) and 'Descriptive Sketches' (1793) that were published later. These early works, though not very innovative, reflect his keen love for nature.

The *Lyrical Ballads* (1798), a joint production with Coleridge, is often considered by scholars as a milestone marking the birth of the Romantic Revival in England. Its publication changed the course of English literature and poetry. Most of the poems in this collection were by Wordsworth, with only five by Coleridge, which included his celebrated 'The Rime of the Ancient Mariner'. In later editions, Wordsworth included some more poems, a preface outlining his and Coleridge's principles of poetry and an appendix titled 'Poetic Diction'. The two young poets sought to redefine the prudish and stilted style of earlier poetry and recommended the use of normal, everyday language in order to be accessible to the average person. They believed that the best poetry was that which used the simplest words. By bringing poetry down from the ivory tower, they believed that they could assert the universality of human emotions. The title is also indicative of their purpose—'lyrical', which is a spontaneous form of expressing one's emotions, and 'ballads', which are oral methods of narrating tales to a rustic audience.

As far as the subject matter of the poems is considered, it was agreed that Coleridge should focus on the supernatural and the romantic, which would require a 'willing suspension of disbelief for the moment, which constitutes poetic faith' (Coleridge's words from his *Biographia Literaria*) and that Wordsworth would turn his attention on highlighting the charm and originality in everyday things. His themes included commonplace activities of country life and the conversations and thoughts of humble people. At the same time the poems reflect a deep psychological preoccupation of the poets and their constant quest for an elusive 'Truth'. While Wordsworth exalted familiar objects through his reflective sensibility, Coleridge attempted to bring credibility to the supernatural.

This book contains some of the best poems by Wordsworth like 'The Thorn', 'The Idiot Boy', 'Simon Lee', 'Expostulation and Reply', 'Tintern Abbey', 'Michael' and 'The Old Cumberland Beggar'. Coleridge's poems included in the book are 'The Foster Mother's Tale', 'The Dungeon', 'The Nightingale', 'Love' and 'The Rime of the Ancient Mariner'. One of the major themes of *Lyrical Ballads* was the return to the original state of nature when people led a simpler and more innocent life. It was based on the principle of Rousseau who believed in the innate goodness of humanity which was corrupted by the evils of society. This concept was gaining popularity before the French Revolution broke out. *Lyrical Ballads* also explored subjects like instinct and the relationship between man and nature.

After *Lyrical Ballads*, Wordsworth concerned himself less with poetic theory and more with writing sonnets. In 1802, when he was disillusioned with Napoleon, he wrote the sonnet, 'I Griev'd for Buonaparte', where he expresses his pity for the despot for having mistaken thoughts and ideology which made him abuse his power. In the same year, he wrote his other famous sonnets, 'The World is Too Much with Us' (a critique of industrialisation), 'Lines Composed upon Westminster Bridge' and 'It is a Beauteous Evening, Calm and Free'.

In 1807, he published *Poems in Two Volumes*. This contains his best work, where he used every poetic form except the narrative, and is proof of his poetic genius. In the lyric form, we have poems like 'The Solitary Reaper' and 'I Wandered Lonely as a Cloud'; in the philosophical variety, 'Ode on the Intimations of Immortality', 'Resolution and Independence' and 'Ode to Duty'; and in sonnet form the collection includes 'Poems Dedicated to National Independence and 'Liberty'.

The Excursion in nine books, is lacking in the lyrical beauty of his earlier poems and is rather monotonous. It is a didactic poem dealing with the problem of humanity. In it, two friends, the Recluse (the poet himself) and the Wanderer have adventures in the Lake District and have several discussions on nature and human character. It is part of a larger philosophical poem called *The Recluse* which was never completed. After *The Excursion,* Wordsworth's creativity began to ebb, but he never stopped writing. It was followed by works like *The White Doe of Rylstone* (1815), *The Waggoner* (1819), *Peter Bell* (1819), *Yarrow Revisited* (1835) and *The Borderers* (1842), a drama.

The Prelude is his autobiographical poem and was published in 1850 after his death. It was actually meant to be a part of *The Recluse*. This gives the most memorable description of his mind. In it, he records his most intimate experiences and examines the development of his poetic genius since his childhood and youth. Wordsworth acknowledges his debt to nature, his first and best teacher. It is a spiritual autobiography in which Wordsworth emphasises the fact that life is a circular journey that takes us back to the place where we began. It contains fourteen books that vividly trace this spiritual journey. It is considered by critics to be Wordsworth's masterpiece.

Features

- His theory of poetry helped shape the literature of the Romantic Revival. In his redefinition, poetry underwent a metamorphosis with regard to both subject matter and style. His focus on situations from common life as themes for his poems and his use of the language spoken by the ordinary man revolutionised the concept of poetry completely.
- He took subjective poetry to new heights. In any other person, such minute examinations of one's inner thoughts and feelings would have appeared egoistic and self-obsessed, but in Wordsworth, it reached almost epic dimensions.
- In his hands, the Petrarchan sonnet received a new impetus. The Shakespearean sonnet had eclipsed the classical form in England before that. Wordsworth's sonnets reflect a variety of themes such as patriotism, his love for liberty and nature.
- His relationship with nature is the most striking feature of Wordsworth's poetry. He observed nature closely and studied it in all its moods. In nature, he found his true friend and guide and it was the source of all his joys. Nature

to him was a living thing, the expression of a universal spirit which communicated to him through the medium of hills and valleys. In his own words:

... For I have learned
To look on nature, not as in the hour
Of thoughtless youth; but hearing oftentimes
The still, sad music of humanity,
Nor harsh nor grating, though of ample power
To chasten and subdue. And I have felt
A presence that disturbs me with the joy
Of elevated thoughts; a sense sublime
Of something far more deeply interfused,
Whose dwelling is in the light of the setting suns,
And the round ocean and the living air,
And the blue sky, and in the minds of man:
A motion and a spirit, that impels
All thinking things, all objects of all thought,
And rolls through all things.

('Lines Composed A Few Miles Above Tintern Abbey, on Revisiting the Banks of the Wye During a Tour, July 13, 1798')

Samuel Taylor Coleridge (1772–1834)

Poetry	**Prose**
Poems on Various Subjects (1796)	*Lay Sermons* (1817)
Poems (1797)	*Biographia Literaria* (1817)
Lyrical Ballads (with Wordsworth, 1798)	*The Friend* (1818)
	Aids to Reflection (1825)
Christabel and other Poems (1816)	*On the Constitution of Church and State* (1830)
Sibylline Leaves (1817)	*Table Talk* (1836)

Life

Coleridge, the youngest of thirteen children, was born in the parish of Ottery St Mary, in Devonshire. His father who was a vicar died when Coleridge was nine years old. He was educated at Christ's Hospital, London, where Charles Lamb was one of his schoolfellows. Even as a boy, Coleridge had queer tastes in reading and was a dreamer. He was not very ambitious and desired to become a shoemaker. It was his headmaster who sent him to Jesus College, Cambridge, where he studied without much interest for two years. His sympathy with the ideals of the French Revolution displeased the authorities and he was expelled from college.

He enlisted in a regiment named Light Dragoons under the pseudonym Silas Tomkins Comberbach and after about four months, abandoned his military career. Soon after he returned to college, he made his acquaintance with Robert Southey with whom he dreamt of founding an ideal republic in America. In this republic, everyone was to be equal and all were to work with their hands. There would be no priest or king and they would spend their leisure in enjoying literature. The experiment could not be realised as they did not have the money to fund it. It was at Bristol where he lived for a while with Southey, that he married Southey's wife's sister Sarah. The marriage, however, was not a happy one.

Coleridge tried to earn a living through public lecturing and editing a journal of prose and poetry called *The Watchman*. He met Wordsworth and his sister Dorothy in 1797 and the next two years were the most fruitful of his poetic career, when he decided to collaborate with Wordsworth to produce the *Lyrical Ballads*. He wrote 'The Rime of the Ancient Mariner' and a part of *Christabel*.

With financial help from two of his friends, Coleridge went to Germany to study German literature and metaphysics. After he returned to England, he learnt that his two friends, Southey and Wordsworth, were living in the Lake District and decided to join them there. Here, he fell in love with Sara Hutchinson, Wordsworth's sister-in-law. It was in this final stage of his career that he wrote the second part of *Christabel* and 'Dejection: An Ode'. It was a period of pain and despair as his marriage was falling apart and he was heavily addicted to opium. His health was also constantly poor. All these drove him away from home and he went to Malta and Italy from 1804 to 1806. Once he returned, he kept wandering from one place to another.

He became involved with another journal *The Friend*, wrote a play *Remorse* that was a success at Durry Lane and gave brilliant lectures on Shakespeare, Milton and other literary and philosophical topics. He moved to a suburb called Highbury near London in 1816 and was under the care of a doctor, James Gillman. He tried to shake off his habit of taking opium. Coleridge was admired and respected by his contemporaries as a formidable figure and he earned the title 'Sage of Highgate' from Carlyle. He spent the last few years of his life interacting with friends and other visitors. It was here that he met John Keats, who was deeply impressed by Coleridge's intellect.

It was at Highgate that Coleridge breathed his last on 25 July 1834. He had spent the last eighteen years of his life under the care of Dr Gillman. The following lines are an extract from the epitaph on his tomb in St Michael's Church, Highgate, and serve as an apt summary of his troubled life:

O, lift one thought in prayer for S.T.C.:
That he who many a year with toil of breath
Found death in life, may here find life in death!

Works

Coleridge possessed an extraordinary mind and was a multifaceted intellect who was a philosopher, critic, theologian, lecturer and poet. His addiction to opium marred his progress as a young man. The amount of poetry he left behind is very small and some of the poems are fragmentary. Yet, the little that is available is of such exquisite worth that he is ranked as a great poet.

POETRY

His early poetry was collected in the volumes *Poems on Various Subjects* and *Poems*. These poems reflect the poet's personality but lack the intensity of his later poetry. Some of the poems in these collections are 'Songs of the Pixies', 'Lines on a Friend' and 'To a Lady with a Poem'—to mention just a few. After meeting Wordsworth and his sister, the poet in Coleridge emerged fully and some of his most enduring works were produced.

Coleridge contributed five poems to *Lyrical Ballads* while Wordsworth was its major contributor. One of the most important poems by Coleridge in this volume is his famous 'The Rime of the Ancient Mariner'. It is a strange tale of the sea written in irregular measure in which Coleridge uses archaic language probably to create the impression that the 'Rime' is a ballad of ancient times. It is a supernatural poem of unusual length with a long Latin epigraph and strange notes printed in the margin by the poet. The poem explores profound philosophical issues and the theme of crime and punishment. The poem contains the moral that a spiritual presence binds both man and beast together.

He had written the first part of *Christabel* in 1797 and the second part in 1800. He intended to write three more parts but it remained incomplete. The poem was published for the first time along with 'Kubla Khan: A Vision' and 'The Pains of Sleep' by the John Murray Press in 1816. *Christabel* is a narrative poem that tells the tale of a witch who takes the shape of a beautiful lady and wins the confidence of the heroine Christabel. The supernatural element is subtle and suggestive in this poem. *Christabel* is written in lines of four accents, full of skilful rhythmic variations. Coleridge was very innovative in his approach to rhyme and metre. At a time when iambic pentameter was the standard form for writing poetry, Coleridge altered it by using four strong stresses in each line regardless of the number of syllables in the line. This is now known as the 'Christabel metre'.

'Kubla Khan' is a poem which Coleridge saw in a dream. He woke up and rapidly wrote down the lines as they had appeared in his dream, but was distracted by a visitor and could not complete it. It represents the magical element of his poetry and is the most representative of Romantic poetry. In style, it is very different from the other poems of Coleridge as it uses a stylised language. This poem anticipates much of modern poetry that gives great importance to psychological factors like dreams and the subconscious mind. All the poems were collected in a volume entitled *Sibylline Leaves* and published in 1817.

PROSE

An examination of Coleridge's prose reveals the fact that it was of journalistic origin. His first stint with journalism began in 1796 when he began *The Watchman*, which was not very successful. Later, he began to lecture on literary and philosophical topics. During his stay in the Lake District, he began work on *The Friend* that extended into a three-volume collection of essays on politics, morals and religion. *Lay Sermons* (1816–17) illustrate his views on the contemporary debate regarding reform and liberal politics. In it, Coleridge attempted to strengthen the position of Anglican Christianity which was being threatened by radicalism.

His most important prose work is *Biographia Literaria.* The work was intended as just a preface to a collection of his poems, in which he wished to explain features of his style and poetic intention. It, however, developed into an autobiography where he shares information about his education, early experiences and a commentary on Wordsworth's theory of poetry. The work also contains Coleridge's own philosophical views. In this book, we see Coleridge transformed into a critic. Only the first and last parts of the book are of interest to the modern reader as the middle section is full of philosophical material taken from Schelling.

His other prose works are *Aids to Reflection* and *On the Constitution of Church and State.* In the former, he portrays the importance of Christianity and in the latter, he expresses his views on national culture.

Features

- His imaginative power is the most distinguishing aspect of his poetry. Poems, like 'Kubla Khan', 'The Ancient Mariner' and *Christabel*, are fine examples of Coleridge's imagination at its best. In these poems, he takes us through the realms of the magical and the supernatural.
- His insightful descriptions of nature are impressive, especially when he is describing remote atmospheres like the sea and the sky. Like Wordsworth, Coleridge too drew his inspiration from nature.
- His use of simple, everyday language is another distinctive feature of his work. Coleridge is able to convey profound and philosophical ideas in a lucid manner.
- His contribution as a literary critic is significant. In his *Biographia Literaria*, he offers a fine critique of Wordsworth's works besides his eloquent distinction between imagination and fancy. He emphasised the fact that poetry is creative rather than imitative and stressed the priority of imagination

over reason. This work is an important document for its theory of Romantic thought and is seen as the harbinger of much of twentieth-century criticism. His strong rejection of the neoclassical concept of judging a work based on its strict adherence to classical rules, became a beacon light for future critics. Coleridge believed that each work of art should be judged based on its own merit. For him, a poem was an organic unit that could not be paraphrased. Apart from *Biographia Literaria*, his lectures, too, are an important source of literary criticism.

- His contribution to philosophy lies in his introduction of German writers to English readers. He translated the plays of Friedrich Schiller into English and propagated Schiller's ideals through his own literary criticism. While in Germany, he read the works of Kant, Karl Wilhelm Friedrich Schlegel and Friedrich Wilhelm Joseph Schelling and became a passionate religious philosopher.
- He was an innovator in metre and he brought back to English verse its early principle of accentuation. An example of this can be seen in *Christabel* which is written in lines of four accents with a varying number of syllables. Coleridge, thus, became a pioneer in the development of prosody in England.

George Gordon, Lord Byron (1788–1824)

Poetry

Hours of Idleness (1807)
English Bards and Scottish Reviewers (1809)
Childe Harold's Pilgrimage (1812–18)
The Giaour (1813)
The Bride of Abydos (1813)
The Corsair (1813)
Lara (1814)
Hebrew Melodies (1815)
The Siege of Corinth (1815)
Parisina (1815)
Domestic Pieces (1816)
The Prisoner of Chillon (1816)
The Lament of Tasso (1817)
Beppo (1818)
Mazeppa (1819)
The Prophecy of Dante (1821)
The Vision of Judgement (1822)
The Island (1823)
The Age of Bronze (1823)
Don Juan (1819–1824)

Drama
Cain (1821)
Marino Faliero (1821)
Sardanapalus (1821)
The Two Foscari (1821)
Werner (1823)
Heaven and Earth (1824)
The Deformed Transformed (1824)

Life

Byron was born in London in 1788 to Captain John Byron and his second wife, Catherine Gordon, a Scottish heiress. While his father was a reckless and irresponsible man who squandered all his wife's wealth, his mother was a vain and passionate woman who vented her frustration on her disabled son. After the death of his father when he was three, his mother took him to Aberdeen where they had to endure severe financial troubles. When Byron was ten, his great-uncle died and Byron inherited his title and the family estates of Newstead in Nottingham.

He was sent to a preparatory school near London, from where he went to Harrow School and then to Trinity College, Cambridge. He began writing poems even while he was at Harrow and published his first book of poetry *Hours of Idleness* in 1807. He travelled across Southern Europe for the next two years and published the first two cantos of *Childe Harold's Pilgrimage* which made him instantly famous. The next few years saw him publish several more collections of poems. He also entered the House of Lords and made a few speeches. Everything was fine till his marriage to Anne Milbanke which lasted only a year. She left him after accusing him of cruelty and madness. Suddenly Byron lost his popularity and he decided to withdraw from England forever.

He proceeded to Switzerland, where he met Shelley who inspired him to continue writing. He wrote the third canto of *Childe Harold* and *The Prisoner of Chillon* at that time. After Shelley returned to England, Byron left for Venice. He spent the remaining eight years of his life in Italy. In 1819, he married Countess Teressa Gamba Guiccioli, a married woman, but the marriage was not very successful. Byron decided to fight for the Greek struggle for independence. He became seriously ill after sailing wet in an open boat and died at Missolonghi at the age of thirty-six.

Works

His first volume of poems *Hours of Idleness* was immature and was reviewed very harshly by the *Edinburgh Review.* An infuriated Byron lashed back in a satire, *English Bards and Scotch Reviewers,* in a style similar to that of Pope. This work, although juvenile in parts, reflected Byron's sharp wit. It also reflected Byron's skilful use of the heroic couplet that was so popular at the beginning of the eighteenth century.

With the publication of the first two cantos of *Childe Harold,* Byron became a literary celebrity overnight. This semi-autobiographical, narrative poem was the result of his two years of travel. It narrates the adventures of a disillusioned, romantic youth who has a dark past and is living on the edge of society. In it, Byron describes in Spenserian stanzas, several places that he had visited on the continent. The hero of this poem, a world-weary young man who is in search of some distraction in foreign lands, was identified with the poet himself and this contributed greatly to its popularity. It appealed instantly to a generation that was weary of the upheavals of wars. While the first two cantos were completed by 1812, Byron continued to work on the poem and wrote the third in 1816 and the fourth in 1818. The last two cantos show a growth in the poet's attitude to life. They are more intense and without the coldness of the first two cantos.

It is from this poem that the concept of the **Byronic hero** was born. The historian and critic Lord Macaulay defined the Byronic hero in the following words: 'a man proud, moody, cynical, with defiance on his brow, and misery in his heart, a scorner of his kind, implacable in revenge, yet capable of deep and strong affection'. The typical features of a Byronic hero include a high level of intelligence combined with the capacity to easily adapt to new situations. He is also one who is cunning enough to further his own interests. He is portrayed as one who disrespects certain people in authority, leading him to the status of an exile. He is both arrogant and cynical and one who has a history of seducing women. Thus, a Byronic hero is a well-educated, charming and suave young man. He became the prototype for the anti-hero and has been depicted in several novels and films. Much of Gothic fiction in the nineteenth century has this type of hero. Some of the famous Byronic heroes are Paul Frollo from Victor Hugo's *The Hunchback of Notre Dame* (1831), Edmund Dantes from Alexande Dumas's *The Count of Monte Cristo* (1844), Heathcliff from Emily Bronte's *Wuthering Heights* (1847) and Rochester from Charlotte Bronte's *Jane Eyre* (1847).)

After the first two cantos of *Childe Harold* were published, Byron produced a number of hastily written narrative poems like 'The Giaour', 'The Bride of Abydos', 'The Corsair', 'Lara', 'The Siege of Corinth' and 'Parisina'. All these tales have Byronic heroes who have adventures in the East. They were mostly written in the heroic couplet form and the tales were inspired by the works of Sir Walter Scott.

Some of Byron's longer poems include *The Prisoner of Chillon* and *Mazeppa* which are also metrical narratives. While in Switzerland, Byron and Shelley went sailing on Lake Geneva and visited the Chateau de Chillon. Byron was inspired to write *The Prisoner of Chillon* after walking through the dungeon in which Bonivard, a Genevois patriot, was imprisoned. In this poem, he describes the trials of the lone survivor of a family, pining away in a dungeon of a castle.

Mazeppa is a bloodthirsty, narrative poem based on the life of Ivan Mazepa, a Ukranian gentleman who falls in love with a countess married to a much older man. When the affair is discovered, Mazepa is punished by being tied naked to a wild horse that is let loose. The poem narrates the harrowing journey of the hero strapped to the horse.

He next turned his attention to satires. *Beppo*, *The Vision of Judgement* and *Don Juan* are some of the works that belong to this genre. *Beppo* is the story of a Venetian lady whose husband Beppo has been lost at sea for the past three years. She takes on a *cavalier servente* (a professional male escort whom married women could hire), but meets her husband who returns after facing several adventures. The main focus of the poem is in drawing up a comparison of British morals with that of Italy. Byron, through this poem, advocates a more liberal approach towards morality.

The Vision of Judgement is one of the finest political satires. In it, he attacks Robert Southey who had referred to Byron as the head of a 'Satanic School'. The poem is written in ottava rima and is a fine example of Byron's mastery over the satirical style.

Don Juan is often referred to as a 'picaresque novel' in verse form. In it, there is a wandering hero who has several adventures, mostly immoral and bold. It shocked the world and Byron was denounced. This poem, more than any of his other works, is an expression of Byron's wrath and fury. It is a lengthy poem with numerous digressions that narrates the tale of the legendary Don Juan. In Byron's retelling of the legend, Don Juan is portrayed not as a womaniser, but as someone who is easily seduced by women. In this work, Byron combines humour with satire and it was considered by later critics as his masterpiece. It has sixteen cantos with the seventeenth being left incomplete. Byron uses the ottava rima in this poem, too, and writes it in a half-colloquial style that avoids poetical trimmings. Byron turned his back disdainfully on the stylistic innovations of the Lake poets and proved to be a great admirer of Pope and the neoclassical school. The following lines from *Don Juan* serve as a sample of his style and thought:

> Wedded she was some years, and to a man
> Of fifty, and such husbands are in plenty;
> And yet, I think, instead of such a ONE
> 'Twere better to have TWO of five and twenty..

DRAMA

Soon after he left England, never to return, Byron turned his attention to writing plays. In this genre, too, we find him oscillating between the neoclassical and Romantic styles. Plays like *Manfred*, *Cain* and *Heaven and Earth* are romantic in structure and temperament. He resorted to the Romantic style when he had to deal with a Romantic theme. If his theme was historical, Byron tended to fashion his dramas on neoclassical principles. For example, *Marino Faliero*, *The Two Foscari* and *Sardanapalus* are all neoclassical in treatment. All his plays were written in blank verse and in nearly all of them, the Byronic hero is present.

Features

- As a poet, Byron was not in the strict sense, a 'Romantic'. Byron's style of writing deviated sharply from that of his contemporaries. His great admiration of Alexander Pope drew him to the poetic diction and conventions of early-eighteenth-century poetry. He had no ear for melody and lacked the sparkle and wit of the masters whom he admired.
- His plays, written in blank verse, slipped into a rhetorical and declamatory style. He was deeply influenced by the ancients but at the same time experienced the powerful pull of Romantic sensibility.
- The most important feature of his writing is the element of morbidity. These lines from *Childe Harold* reflect the morbid feelings he experienced following the deaths of his loved ones:

  What is the worst of woes that wait on age?
  What stamps the wrinkle deeper on the brow?
  To view each loved one blotted from life's page,
  And be alone on earth, as I am now.
- Byron's art and life are closely interconnected. His alleged incestuous relationship with his half-sister plunged him in guilt and the theme of incest figured strongly in works such as *The Giaour*, *The Bride of Abydos*, *The Crosair*, *Lara*, *The Siege of Corinth* and *Parisina*. Byron used incestuous love as a metaphor for the tragic condition of man—cursed by God, despised by society and agonised by guilt.
- He popularised the concept of the anti-hero through the creation of the popular image of the Byronic hero.
- His satires reveal him as a reforming humourist who uses satire to critique society. He enjoyed scandalising his readers through his cynical remarks. For instance, he gave vent to his anger against religion by making a hero of Cain, who is portrayed as a man who questions God for allowing evil to enter the world.

Percy Bysshe Shelley (1792–1822)

Poetry
Original Poetry by Victor and Cazire (1810)
Queen Mab (1813)
Alastor (1816)
The Revolt of Islam (1818)
Julian and Maddalo (1818)
'Rosalind and Helen' (1819)
The Masque of Anarchy (1819)
'Ode to the West Wind' (1819)
Peter Bell the Third (1819)
'To a Skylark' (1820)
'The Cloud' (1820)
Epipsychidion (1821)
Adonais (1821)

Drama
Prometheus Unbound A Lyrical Drama in Four Acts, with Other Poems (1820)
The Cenci (1819)
Hellas (1822)

Fiction and Prose
Zastrozzi (1810)
St Irvyne or The Rosicrucian (1812)
Address to the Irish People (1812)
A Defence of Poetry (1821)

Life

Shelley was born in 1792 in Sussex to a wealthy baronet. He studied at Eton and then moved on to University College, Oxford. Both at Eton and Oxford, he was a rebel who would not conform. He was sceptical of religion and revolutionary in politics. Even while he was a student, he began his writing career. He published a Gothic novel *Zastrozzi* and a collection of poems called *Original Poetry by Victor and Cazire* along with his sister, Elizabeth. While at Oxford, he published his second Gothic novel, *St Irvyne* and a pamphlet called *The Necessity of Atheism*. He was expelled from Oxford for the heretic views that he expressed in *The Necessity of Atheism*.

Soon after he was expelled, he eloped with a girl called Harriet Westbrook, who was the daughter of a former coffee-house owner. He moved to the Lake District where he made the acquaintance of Robert Southey, who in turn introduced him to William Godwin, author of *Political Justice*, a book that Shelley admired greatly. By then, Shelley's marriage was falling apart and he found himself attracted to Godwin's daughter Mary Wollstonecraft Godwin, whose mother was the famous feminist Mary Wollstonecraft, author of *A Vindication of the Rights of Woman*. Shelley abandoned his wife and ran away with Mary and her stepsister Clare to Switzerland. They returned to England after about six weeks and it was then that Shelley wrote *Alastor*. He also came under the influence of Wordsworth. It was on his second trip to Switzerland that he met Byron and was inspired to write the poem 'Hymn to Intellectual Beauty', after a boating trip on Lake Geneva.

After Shelley and Mary returned to England, his wife Harriet committed suicide. A few weeks later, he married Mary. Shelley lost the custody of his two children with Harriet—a daughter Ianthe and a son Charles, who died in childhood. Shelley continued to uphold his rebellious ideology for which he was frowned upon by society. The publication of his atheist poem *Queen Mab* further damaged his reputation. After writing *Alastor* and *The Revolt of Islam*, he moved to Italy for the rest of his short life.

In Italy, he renewed his friendship with Byron and visited several places and settled finally in Pisa. It was while at Italy, that some of his best poems like 'Adonais', 'The Cloud', 'To a Skylark' and 'Ode to the West Wind' were written. His brilliant poetic career came to a sudden end when Shelley drowned in a boating accident when he was just thirty years old. He was cremated and his ashes were buried in the Protestant Cemetery in Rome.

Works

His first major work of note was *Queen Mab*, a lengthy poem that is a crude expression of his atheism. He used the irregular unrhymed metre that Southey had made fashionable. In it, he expounded his philosophy that a perfect society could be achieved with time, with the evolution of nature and a gradual increase in the number of virtuous people.

His next important work was *Alastor,* which is considered a kind of spiritual autobiography. Written in blank verse, it has several passages of lyrical beauty. It narrates the adventures of a character who resembles Shelley, travelling through a wilderness in search of ideal beauty. This work was followed by *Laon and Cythna*, later renamed *The Revolt of Islam*. In it, the two characters Laon and Cythna are portrayed as waging a war against the tyranny of the despotic ruler of the imaginary kingdom of Argolis. It is a symbolic fable about liberty and radical idealism that is an offshoot of his disillusionment with the French Revolution. Shelley used the Spenserian stanza of eight iambic pentameter lines followed by a single Alexandrine line.

Shelley left for Italy soon after but continued his writing. The important poetical works of this period were 'Julian and Maddalo' and 'The Masque of Anarchy'. 'Julian and Maddalo' was a poem that was the outcome of Shelley's conversation with Byron. Julian, an Englishman, represents Shelley and Maddalo is an Italian nobleman who is supposed to represent Byron. They are shown as taking a ride through Venice, discussing issues like religious faith, free will and progress. In the poem, they visit a friend who has been incarcerated in a lunatic asylum. The poem reflects Byron's cynicism and Shelley's atheism as well as the latter's optimistic belief in the innate goodness of man. In *The Massacre of Anarchy*, Shelley's revolutionary views on politics are given expression. It was a poem that was inspired by the Massacre of Peterloo which took place when people gathered in large numbers to protest in favour of parliamentary reforms in England and were attacked savagely by the cavalry.

In 1820, Shelley went to Pisa where some of his best poems were written. Two important works to follow from this period were *The Witch of Atlas* and *Epipsychidion*. *The Witch of Atlas*, written in ottava rima, has as its theme the quest for the perfect union. In *Epipsychidion*, which explores the nature of ideal love, Shelley advocates the concept of free love. He severely critiques conventional marriage by describing it as 'the weariest and the longest journey'.

The most popular lyrics of Shelley are 'Ode to the West Wind', 'The Cloud' and 'To a Skylark'. All three poems were published along with *Prometheus Unbound*. They best represent Shelley's rebellious spirit and his hope for a better future. 'The Cloud' personifies the perpetual cycle of transformation and change in nature, while 'To A Skylark' is sheer poetry that is unmarred by any melancholy thoughts. In 'Ode to the West Wind', Shelley gives vent to his personal frustration at his inability to change the world:

A heavy weight of hours has chained and bowed
One too like thee: tameless and swift and proud.

It also contains the famous line giving hope:

O Wind!
If Winter comes, can Spring be far behind?

Shelley next attempted a pastoral elegy *Adonais* to mourn the death of the young John Keats. It was modelled on the classical elegy and was written in Spenserian stanzas. It contains some of the finest lines in English poetry such as:

He lives, he wakes—'tis Death is dead, not he;
Mourn not for Adonais—Thou, young Dawn,
Turn all thy dew to splendour, for from thee
The spirit thou lamentest is not gone!

DRAMA

Prometheus Unbound is the story of the rebellious Prometheus who defied the gods and stole fire. It is an epic 'closet drama' that discusses the moral salvation of man. The setting of this play includes such inaccessible places as the sky, the mountains and the sea.

The Cenci is a horrifying tragedy based on the real-life story of a young woman who was executed for the murder of her cruel father. It is a sombre verse tragedy that narrates the story of this family. His next play *Hellas* was inspired by the Greek War of Independence and is modelled after Aeschylus's work *The Persians*. It contains several lyrical passages that are still relevant, as the one quoted below:

Oh, cease! Must hate and death return?
  Cease! Must men kill and die?
Cease! Drain not to its dregs the urn.
  Oh bitter prophecy,
The world's weary of the past,
Oh, might it die or rest at last!

PROSE

His prose writings include two Gothic novels, some pamphlets and a famous essay *The Defence of Poetry.* The novels *Zastrozzi* and *St Irvune* were written when he was still a student and are, therefore, inferior in both theme and style. His pamphlet *The Necessity of Atheism* shocked the authorities in Oxford and Shelley was expelled from college. In the pamphlet, he pointed out that atheism was an involuntary belief and therefore people should not be punished for having such ideas.

His *Defence of Poetry* is representative of the Romantic concept of poetry. In it, Shelley does not give any rules for poetry, but only expresses his philosophical views on poets and poetry. It was written as a rebuttal to Thomas Love Peacock's *The Four Ages of Poetry* in which he argued that poetry was losing its value in a world were science and technology were becoming increasingly more important and central to life. In *The Defence,* Shelley gives us a fine distinction between reason and imagination and points out how it is only through imagination that civilisation is shaped. He elevates the position of poets and calls them the 'unacknowledged legislators of the world'. Shelley's prose style tends to be a little heavy, but is still readable.

Features

- The most important feature of his poetry is his lyrical power. We see evidence of this not only in his shorter lyrics like 'Ode to the West Wind', 'To a Skylark' and 'The Cloud', but also in longer works like his play *Prometheus Unbound* and elegy *Adonais.* The following poem 'Music, When Soft Voices Die' is an excellent example of his lyricism:

  Music, when soft voices die,
  Vibrates in the memory;
  Odours, when sweet violets sicken,
  Live within the sense they quicken.
  Rose leaves, when the rose is dead,
  Are heap'd for the beloved's bed;
  And so thy thoughts, when thou art gone,
  Love itself shall slumber on.

  These lines from 'To a Skylark' are also often quoted:

  We look before and after,
  And pine for what is not:
  Our sincerest laughter
  With some pain is fraught;

Our sweetest songs are those that tell of saddest thought.

Shelley was a visionary poet who dreamt of creating an ideal society. He wished to reform the world through his poems. His 'Ode to the West Wind' is an excellent example of this:

> Drive my dead thoughts over the universe
> Like wither'd leaves to quicken a new birth!
> And by the incantation of this verse,
> Scatter, as from an unextinguished hearth
> Ashes and sparks, my words among mankind!
> Be through my lips to unawaken'd earth
> The trumpet of a prophecy!

- His approach to nature was very different from that of Wordsworth's. Shelley saw nature as being indifferent to man. To him, it was a powerful and sublime entity that was both splendid and fatal, which could never be tamed by man. Wordsworth, on the other hand, looked upon nature as a protective and comforting agent. Yet, we find beautiful descriptions of nature such as 'earthly rainbows stretched across the sweep / Of the ethereal waterfall' in Shelley's poems.
- Shelley's atheism is everywhere evident in his works. He was an erudite scholar who had a voluminous knowledge of philosophy, history and languages. His poetry covered a variety of themes, but behind all his poems one finds a note of radicalism and a challenge to the institutions that he perceived to be tyrannous, such as the monarchy, the government and the church. He was an idealist who wished to bring about a change in society. A half-century after his death, Matthew Arnold referred to Shelley as 'a beautiful and ineffectual angel, beating in the void his luminous wings in vain.'

John Keats (1795–1821)

Poetry
Poems (1817)
Endymion (1818)
Lamia, Isabella, The Eve of St Agnes and Other Poems (1820)

Prose
Letters (1848)

Life

John Keats was the eldest son of a livery-stable keeper and was born in London. He lost both his parents by the time he was fifteen and was apprenticed to a surgeon at Enfield. However, he had no inclination towards the study of medicine and soon gave it up to write poetry full time. He had little formal education and no one to encourage him except Leigh Hunt, who published his poems in his magazine *The Examiner*. Soon he published his first volume of poems, simply called *Poems*.

In 1818, Keats began a walking tour to Scotland with his friend Charles Armitage Brown, his brother George and George's wife. While his brother and his wife migrated to America, Keats proceeded to Scotland where he caught a very bad cold. On returning, he was busy nursing his brother Tom who was down with tuberculosis. This was when Keats became infected with the disease that would eventually take his life.

After the death of his brother Tom, Keats moved to Wentworth Place in Hampstead, owned by Brown. It was while he was here, that Keats wrote some of his best odes. It was also here that he met the love of his life, Fanny Brawne. But the impending doom of his dreaded disease did not allow the young lovers to culminate their passion for each other in marriage. Poems such as 'La Belle Dame Sans Merci' and 'The Eve of St Agnes' reflect his despondency.

Keats was advised by his doctors to move to a warmer climate and Keats left for Rome in 1820, after bidding a sad farewell to Fanny Brawne. His voyage to Italy was very rough and painful, both physically as well as emotionally. It was during this journey that he wrote the sonnet 'Bright Star' in which he laments his separation from Fanny. He died five months later, aged twenty-five, and a devastated Fanny Brawne mourned his death for more than six years and only got married twelve years after his death.

Keats was buried at the Protestant Cemetery in Rome and on his request, there was no mention of his name or any dates on his tomb. At the time of his death, he was greatly pained by the bitter attacks by Lockhart on his poem *Endymion*. So great was his pain that he left instructions with his friend to inscribe the following words on his tomb stone:

This Grave
Contains all that was Mortal
Of a
Young English Poet
Who
On his Death Bed,
in the Bitterness of his Heart
At the Malicious Power of his Enemies
Desired
These Words to be
Engraved on his Tomb Stone:
Here lies one
Whose Name was writ in Water.
24 February 1821

Works

Keats did not have much formal education, but he admired the work of Virgil, Spenser, Chapman and Milton. He was a great admirer of Shakespeare. He developed a love for Greek poetry through reading translated works and seeing the Elgin Marbles. He commemorated this love in the memorable sonnet 'On First Looking into Chapman's Homer'. Keats was attracted to beauty from a very early age and his poetry is proof of this. His first volume of poems, written when he was just twenty-two years old, contains masterpieces such as 'I Stood Tip-Toe Upon a Little Hill' and 'On First Looking into Chapman's Homer'. The influence of Spenser is evident in these poems and reflects the promise of Keats's greatness.

His next important work *Endymion* consists of four books of a thousand lines each. It is based on the Greek story of a youth who was kissed by the moon goddess. It begins with the famous lines:

A thing of beauty is a joy for ever:
Its loveliness increases; it will never
Pass into nothingness; but still will keep
A bower quiet for us, and a sleep
Full of sweet dreams, and health, and quiet breathing.

The poem was not received well by critics and this hurt Keats very badly. Byron, referring to this incident in his *Don Juan*, wrote:

John Keats, who was kill'd off by one critique,
Just as he really promised something great,. . .
Poor fellow! His was an untoward fate;
'Tis strange the mind, that very fiery particle,
Should let itself be snuff'd out by an article.

This view was not very accurate as Keats continued to write some of his best verses after that. His next major collection entitled *Lamia, Isabella, The Eve of St Agnes and Other Poems* contains his best odes: 'Ode to a Nightingale', 'Ode on a Grecian Urn', 'Ode on Psyche', 'Ode to Melancholy', 'Fancy', 'To Autumn' and the incomplete 'Hyperion' apart from the three narrative poems mentioned in the title of the collection. In 'Lamia' he expounds the thesis that knowledge born out of imagination is far superior to that which is an outcome of an argument. 'Isabella' is a retelling of a tale by Boccaccio of the tragic love story of the murder of a girl's lover by her brothers. 'The Eve of St Agnes' is one of the finest poems by Keats that consists of forty-two Spenserian stanzas. It was inspired by the superstitious belief that a girl would be able to see her future husband in a dream if she performed certain rigorous rites like going to bed naked and without any supper. He attempted to write an epic in the mode of Milton and began 'Hyperion'. After abandoning it, he tried to revive it by writing 'The Fall of Hyperion'

The odes stand testimony to the greatness of Keats's brilliance. Each poem is a flawless gem that reflects the poetic genius of Keats. He composed six odes in 1819—'Ode on a Grecian Urn', 'Ode to Indolence', 'Ode on Melancholy', 'Ode to a Nightingale', Ode to Autumn' and 'Ode to Psyche'—in quick succession. These poems show the poet's preoccupation with the concept of beauty and also reflect his longing to escape the pain and suffering that he was going through on account of his ill health. A poignant fact that emerges from the odes, like the one written to a nightingale and the one on a Grecian urn, is the poet's celebration of the immorality of art as opposed to his own short life. The shadow of his impending death was constantly with him.

Among his short poems, 'La Belle Dame Sans Merci' is an outstanding ballad. In his poems, we see a beautiful mixture of classical discipline and sensitive Romanticism. He used different types of metre and verse like the heroic couplet, the Spenserian stanza and the classical Petrarchan sonnet.

PROSE

Keats did not bother to write any prefaces, introductions or theoretical essays defending his poems. In the absence of such explanations, his letters written to various people provide a valuable insight into the workings of a poet's mind. These letters are now an important part of literary criticism and terms from them like 'negative capability', 'truth proved upon our pulses' and 'the egoistical sublime' have become terms that are studied by students of literature. His letters reflect his passionate love for poetry and his opinions about its creation—'if poetry comes not as naturally as the leaves to a tree it had better not come at all'.

His letters also reveal his obsession to make a name as a poet and dwell constantly on the problems of poetic creation. They also reflect the tension between his escape into a different world through his imagination and his brave acceptance of the harsh realities of life. In his letters, Keats bares his soul to the readers and we are able to see the spiritual growth of the poet.

Features

- His love for nature is great and can be seen in almost all his works. Unlike Wordsworth who saw nature as a mystical being, Byron who had a satirical approach to nature or Shelley for whom nature was prophetic, Keats admired nature for its beauty.
- In his descriptions of nature, Keats was very sensuous. The senses of smell, sight, sound and touch are all evoked in his poems. For example,

  Where are the songs of Spring? Ay, where are they?
  Think not of them, thou hast thy music too,—
  While barred clouds bloom the soft-dying day,
  And touch the stubble-plains with rosy hue;
  Then in a wailful choir the small gnats mourn
  Among the river sallows, borne aloft

Or sinking as the light wind lives or dies;

('To Autumn')

I cannot see what flowers are at my feet,
Nor what soft incense hangs upon the boughs,
But, in embalmed darkness, guess each sweet
Wherewith the seasonable month endows
The grass, the thicket, and the fruit-tree wild;

('Ode to a Nightingale')

- His style was distinctively individual. His early works are melodious and decorative, while his later works reveal his belief in the supremacy of the power of beauty.

Walter Scott (1771–1832)

Novels
Waverley (1814)
Guy Mannering (1815)
The Antiquary (1816)
Rob Roy (1817)
Ivanhoe (1819)
The Monastery (1820)
The Abbot (1820)
Kenilworth (1821)
The Pirate (1821)
The Fortunes of Nigel (1822)
Peveril of the Peak (1823)
Quintin Durward (1823)
St. Ronan's Well (1823)
Redgauntlet (1824)
The Betrothed (1825)
Tales of My Landlord series
Old Mortality (1816)
The Black Dwarf (1816)
The Heart of Midlothian (1818)
The Bride of Lammermoor (1819)
A Legend of Montrose (1819)
Castle Dangerous (1831)
The Talisman (1825)
Woodstock (1826)
Chronicles of the Canongate I (short stories, 1827)
Chronicles of the Canongate II (novels *Saint Valentine's Day, or The Fair Maid of Perth*, 1828)
Anne of Geirstein (1829)

Poetry
Minstrelsy of the Scottish Border (1802–03)
The Lay of the Last Minstrel (1805)
Marmion (1808)
The Lady of the Lake (1810)
Rokeby (1813)
The Bridal of Triermain (1813)
The Lord of the Isles (1815)
Harold the Dauntless (1817)

Drama
Halidon Hill (1822)
Macduff's Cross (1823)
The Doom of Devergoil, a Melodrama (1830)
Auchindrane or the Ayreshire Tragedy (1830)

Life

Walter Scott, the son of a lawyer, was born in Edinburgh, Scotland. He belonged to a family of twelve children, of whom six had died before Scott was born. A polio attack when he was just two years old left him lame for life and prevented him from taking part in outdoor activities. As a result, he spent his time reading books, especially border ballads and tales. **Border ballads** are songs collected from the Anglo-Scottish border. Like all traditional ballads, these too were meant to be sung, but did not have the recurring chorus as in most popular ballads. Their themes included the supernatural and recounting of raids and battles. Scott went to Edinburgh High School and University and later studied law and joined his father's office. He was not a very good student, but was keenly interested in history and poetry.

It was the custom of his parents to send him to Tweedside to recover when he was unwell. He spent a lot of his childhood at Sandyknowe, in his grandfather's farm, and at Kelso—both places of great beauty and history. It was there that he read Percy's *Reliques of Ancient English Poetry*. Boccaccio, Spenser and Shakespeare were some of his favourite authors and he also read tales in German, Spanish, Italian and French. Although he was apprenticed at the age of fifteen to his father's law office, his heart was in poetry. He spent all his free time exploring the dales and moors of the Southern Lowlands and interacting with shepherds and farmers. He collected several ballads and legends and explored ruined castles. He revelled in the freedom of the country and had a deep love for romance.

He married Charlotte Carpenter in 1797 and set up house in Lasswade. Scott was appointed as Sheriff-Depute for Selkirkshire at a salary of three hundred pounds. He then moved to Ashestiel where he took up the career of a minstrel. Between 1802 and 1803, he brought out his compilation of border ballads in three volumes. After his publication of *The Lay of the Last Minstrel*, Scott was recognised as a popular poet of the day. He received a promotion in his career, too, which substantially increased his income. Along with poetry, he wrote novels, which made him a celebrity in the literary circle of his time. Apart from his regular career, he entered into a secret partnership with a friend in the business of printing and publishing. He built his dream house at Abbotsford, where he entertained his friends in a grand style.

In 1813, Scott declined the offer of the laureateship in favour of Southey. In 1820, he was made a baronet and enjoyed a period of great success in his career, in both writing and publishing. He was also busy writing for *The Edinburgh* and *The Quarterly.* Unfortunately, his publishing house ran into trouble and he faced a huge debt of about £130,000. This did not, however break his spirit, but instead, he began writing fourteen hours a day in order to pay off his debt. His brain gave way under the terrible strain and he suffered a stroke in 1830 from which he never recovered. But the work he had done was sufficient to repay his debts. After a brief trip to Italy, he came back to his home in Abbotsford where he died in 1832.

Works

The greatest name in Scottish literature is that of Sir Walter Scott. Scott is to Scotland what Shakespeare is to England and Goethe to Germany. He was a prolific writer who was able to churn out absorbing tales of historical romance in a very short time. He wrote *Guy Mannering* in just six weeks, the last two volumes of *Waverley* in the evenings of three summer weeks and *The Bride of Lammermoor* in two weeks. His imagination lived and delighted in the past which to him was a land of inexhaustible romance. Waverley, the principal railway station serving Edinburgh, is the only railway station in the world to be named after a novel. One cannot speak of historical romance without a reference to Sir Walter Scott.

POETRY

Scott began his literary career by translating German poetry. Inspired by Percy's *Reliques*, he published *Minstrelsy of the Scottish Border* in three volumes. These contained ballads compiled by Scott divided under the headings of 'Historical Ballads', 'Romantic Ballads' and 'Imitations of the Ancient Ballad'. The volumes contain many famous ballads like 'The Wife of Usher's Well'. This was soon followed by an original work by Scott which brought him instant fame—*The Lay of the Last Minstrel*. It is a poem in six cantos with irregular lines consisting of seven to twelve syllables. It is a narrative poem based on an old border legend about the goblin Gilpin Horner. This was followed by his masterpiece *Marmion* and he continued to write more poetry till 1817 when his last long poem *Harold the Dauntless* was published.

FICTION

He turned his attention to the novel soon after the publication of *The Lady of the Lake*. The poems that followed were coldly received and Scott anonymously published *Waverley*, which enjoyed public attention. Set in the backdrop of the Scottish Rebellion against England in 1745, it is considered to be the first historical novel in western literature. Scott was most sure of himself when writing about the Scottish traditions and Jacobitism, which were his major themes in *Guy Mannering*, *The Antiquity*, *Old Mortality*, *The Heart of Midlothian* and *Rob Roy*. In these novels, he weaves imagination with his memory of Scottish peasantry. *Waverley* was followed by a series of brilliant historical romances set in different ages and were advertised as being 'by the author of *Waverley*'. These novels, therefore, came to be known popularly as the *Waverley Novels*. They are a reflection of almost eighteen years of dazzling creative activity, consisting of twenty-seven novels covering about eight centuries of history.

In *Ivanhoe* and *The Talisman*, when he moved away from Scotland and wrote about the Middle Ages, he was not at his best as these novels did not have the depth of his Scottish novels. Similarly, his novels *Kenilworth* and *The Fortunes of Nigel*, about the English monarchs Elizabeth I and James I, are superficial.

Scott set the trend for the historical novel by combining fact with fiction in the most absorbing way. The plots were pure fiction and the main characters were imaginary. For instance, in *Ivanhoe* the main focus is not on Richard I but on Ivanhoe. Scott succeeded in bringing history alive by combining it with romance. He was adept at capturing the spirit of the age through his accurate imitation of the nuances of speech, customs and behaviour of the people of the age. He was a good storyteller with a deep love for the legends and battles of a bygone age. *The Black Dwarf*, *The Bride of Lammermoor* and *A Legend of Montrose* are some of his other famous novels. All these works are set against major historical events and his characters are depicted as being caught up in intricate and confusing plots.

Most of his themes were the conflicts between opposing cultures. In *Ivanhoe*, he depicts the struggle between the Normans and the Saxons and in *The Talisman*, he describes the conflict between Christians and Muslims. *Old Mortality* is set against the religious conflict in Scotland in the 1600s. His Scottish novels deal with the differences between the older Scottish culture and the new materialistic English way of life. His novels contrast the earthy vibrancy of the peasants with the artificial language of his aristocratic characters.

Since Scott wrote at a tremendous speed, he often committed mistakes in his recreation of a bygone age. These are known as **anachronisms**—the inclusion of some action or object in a work which does not belong to the historical period that is being depicted in it.

Features

- His contribution to the form of the historical novel is tremendous. He succeeded in bringing alive the dry facts of history and infusing them with a vitalising energy. Before Scott, there had been no attempt to combine romance and realism. It was Scott who blended the two to create a new and popular genre called historical romance. Before Scott, the historical novel was lifeless and dull but after his novels were read, the form gained popularity and in the following decades, several people tried to write this type of fiction.
- As he wrote at a great speed, his plots were at times hastily constructed and carelessly completed. Similarly, his characterisation too suffered, as some of the characters who were developed very well were neglected later.

A good example of this is the character Mike Lambourne in *Kenilworth*.

- His special talent lay in his portrayal of the Scottish peasants who he knew so well. His sense of comedy found expression while dealing with these characters.
- He avoided tragedy as he possessed a sunny temperament himself. He seldom delved deep into the minds of his characters.
- In his approach to history, he was more interested in its colour and pageantry rather than its impact on people.
- Scott has often been compared to Shakespeare in his variety of characters and his search for material. He also possessed Shakespeare's amiable humour but lacked his deep understanding of characters' minds and psychology.
- Scott's style is powerful and assured and he was extremely adept with the Scottish dialect.
- He was not successful with the genre of drama.

Jane Austen (1775–1817)

Sense and Sensibility (1811)
Pride and Prejudice (1813)
Mansfield Park (1814)
Emma (1816)
Northanger Abbey (1818)
Persuasion (1818)

Life

Jane Austen was born on 16 December 1775 at Steventon, in the county of Hampshire in southern England. She was the youngest of seven children and had a very uneventful and peaceful life. Her father Rev George Austen was the rector of Steventon and her mother Cassandra was the daughter of Rev Thomas Leigh. Jane spent most of her life in the countryside with occasional visits to Bath and London.

In 1783, she was sent along with her sister Cassandra to Oxford to be taught by Mrs Ann Cawley, with whom they boarded. A year later, they moved with her to Southampton where both the girls caught typhus. Jane, who suffered a very severe attack, went home and continued her education from there. Most of her education was through the reading of books from her father's fairly large library. She enjoyed reading authors like Samuel Richardson, Henry Fielding and Fanny Burney. Jane's father encouraged his daughters to write by providing them with ample writing material and reading their early, experimental writings.

An interesting aspect of Jane's early life was the family's keen interest in dramatics. As a child, Jane used to perform along with her family members in plays like Sheridan's *The Rivals* for the entertainment of a close circle of friends and relatives.

Her literary career began as early as 1787, when she attempted to write poems, stories and plays for her family. These early writings were later collected by Jane and bound into three notebooks which are now known as *Juvenelia*. These contain her writings between 1787 and 1793.

Around 1793 or 1794, she began writing the novel *Susan* in the epistolary form. This was soon followed by *Elinor and Marianne*, later to be renamed *Sense and Sensibility*.

When Jane was about twenty years old, she fell in love with a neighbour's nephew Tom Lefroy. Lefroy's family, however, discouraged the match since neither of the families was financially sound. Soon after this, she began work on *First Impressions* which she renamed *Pride and Prejudice*—one of the most famous classics ever to be penned in the English language. At the same time, she revised *Sense and Sensibility* and wrote the first draft of *Northanger Abbey*, then known as *Susan*.

After the retirement of her father in 1801, the family relocated to Bath. Between 1801 and 1809, Austen did little writing. The family went through a financially difficult period after the demise of her father. In 1809, her brother Edward came to the aid of his mother and sisters by offering them the use of a large cottage in Chawton village. It was while living at Chawton that four of her novels were published: *Sense and Sensibility*, *Pride and Prejudice*, *Mansfield Park* and *Emma*.

Austen's health began to deteriorate but she continued to write. She completed work on *Persuasion* and wrote the incomplete novel *Sanditon* before she breathed her last. *Persuasion* and *Northanger Abbey* were published posthumously in 1818.

Works

Jane Austen was one of the greatest writers of the novel of manners. In her hands, this type of fiction rose to great literary heights. She did not engage significantly with critical theories while writing her novels nor was she interested in overt didacticism or advocating any strict moral purpose. Contemporary events like the Napoleonic Wars, although ongoing throughout her career as a novelist, did not feature extensively in her novels. She devoted all her time in recreating accurately the society of her time and place.

Any reader approaching the novels of Jane Austen will immediately note that her writing is markedly different from that of her contemporaries. In her writings, she placed intellect above emotion and is, therefore, seen by many critics as being more neoclassical than Romantic. At a time when the novel form was long and rambling, she wrote in a precise manner. While other novels involved a cross-section of society, Austen limited herself to the countryside gentry and the upper middle class. Instead of exposing her heroines to dangerous situations, she merely traces their journey form maidenhood to matrimony. The women novelists of that period were often considered silly and sentimental, but in Austen we have a taste of superb wit, humour and a keen intelligence. Her sense of dialogue is beyond compare and by allowing her characters to speak for themselves, she succeeds in making them lifelike.

Sense and Sensibility is the story of two sisters with opposing temperaments and the upheavals they experience in their quest for love and marriage. While Elinor is practical and down-to-earth, Marianne is the epitome of emotion and sentiment. Both women experience unhappiness in their choice of life partner. Elinor desires a man who is engaged to another woman and Marianne falls in love with a rogue who jilts her. The novel depicts the sisters' closeness and the realisation that both sense and sensibility are necessary for a balanced life.

Pride and Prejudice, too, like the previous novel reveals a symmetry between two emotions—Darcy's pride and Elizabeth's prejudice. The novel traces the story of two strong-willed people who repel one another at the beginning of the story and reach a climax of mutual hostility before they change their views about each other to develop a strong bond of understanding and love.

Mansfield Park traces the journey of Fanny Price from childhood to early adulthood. The protagonist is a girl from a poor family who is sent to live with her rich cousins in Mansfield Park. The novel explores the morality and manners of people through her characters who are allowed to express themselves freely especially through letters.

Emma is an outstanding work by Austen, in which she focuses her attention on a few families and succeeds in bringing to life minor characters like Miss Bates and Mrs Elton. In *Northanger Abbey*, Austen ridicules the tales of romance and terror that were popularised by Ann Radcliffe, by contrasting them with the events of everyday life. In this novel, Austen succeeds in blending social comedy with literary satire.

Published in 1818 after Austen's death, *Persuasion* reaffirms the author's belief in the requirement of love as the basis for matrimony. In this novel, satire and irony are toned down and Austen adopts a serious and tender tone. Critics, reading between the lines, discern the author's own broken engagement being reflected in the story of Anne Elliot.

Features

Jane Austen has continued to be a favourite among novel-readers across the world. There are several factors that have contributed to her popularity.

- A reading of her novels reveals to us the sensitive, observant and ironic humour of their author. Austen is noted for her gentle humour and subtle sense of irony. An excellent illustration of her humour is the famous opening sentence of *Pride and Prejudice:* 'It is a truth universally acknowledged, that a single man in possession of a good fortune, must be in want of a wife.' Mr Bennet's sense of humour is well-known. When his wife accuses him of not having any compassion for her poor nerves, he replies very calmly, 'You mistake me, my dear. I have a high respect for your nerves. They are my old friends. I have heard you mention them with consideration these twenty years at least.'

- Jane Austen, with her keen eye for detail, has successfully captured and presented a slice of the society to which she belonged. She was an artist who believed in writing only about the life of which she had first-hand knowledge. This life, she presented in her novels in accurate detail. Her stories revolve around people belonging to the upper middle-class society of the late-eighteenth and early-nineteenth century. Even this was restricted to the neighbourhood to which she belonged and the people with whom she interacted on a daily basis. Some critics may consider this as a restriction of her art as a novelist, but Austen achieved remarkable success within these narrow walls by giving us a close-up view of her times and society. We get to read about the minute details of daily life as it was lived during her time. It was a society that revelled in sharing nuggets of news—a newcomer to the neighbourhood, a letter from a friend or relative, a new dress, invitations to balls and dinners; all these were of vital importance.
- Her development of character through dialogue is outstanding. Her characters remain in our memory long after we have completed reading her novels. This is because of the dramatic quality of her fiction where Austen allows her characters to reveal themselves in their own voices.
- Being a woman, Austen understood the working of a woman's mind and not that of a man's. Hence, her novels are all women-centric and the male characters, with a few exceptions, are very indistinctly portrayed. The narrative is from the woman protagonist's point of view and we are taken into the most detailed thought process that controls her actions. The male characters, for the most part, do not develop and evolve like her women characters. Mr Collins, Mr Knightley, Mr Bingley and Mr Woodhouse hardly reflect any major changes. One important exception is Mr Darcy

who evolves with the development of the plot in *Pride and Prejudice*.

- Austen's characterisation was so perfect that her readers treated her creations as real people and debated about them. Each of her heroines is different and as a result appeal to different types of readers. For instance, Elizabeth of *Pride and Prejudice* is very different from the self-congratulating Emma.
- As a novelist, Austen avoided the two extremes of heart-wrenching tragedy and rib-tickling comedy. Nowhere in her novels is the reader moved to tears either of sorrow or joy. We only feel either a slight sense of concern at the heroine's plight or experience a gentle desire to smile at Austen's dry and ironic humour.
- Similarly, we do not meet either the extremely rich and the aristocratic nor the poor and the downtrodden in her pages. Compton-Rickett has excellently summed up this quality of Jane Austen in his *A History of English Literature*: 'The tattle, the trivialities of life in a small country town, when tea-time was an exciting event, and a subscription ball a crisis in one's career; when romance expressed itself in country walks (usually with a chaperone), when tragedy hinged upon the non-appearance at the cross- roads of the agreeable young man who danced so well at the ball.' (262)
- Taken as a whole, it is difficult to classify her novels. Sandwiched as she was between the Age of Reason of the early-eighteenth century and the Romantic Age of the late-eighteenth century, she combined in her work the ideals of both the ages—the concept of the correctness of society and the importance of the individual. She never attempted to correct society through harsh satire. She merely stopped to smile at the antics and hypocrisies of the people around her and passed on. To conclude in the words of Compton Rickett: 'There is no didacticism, no philosophy, no propaganda in her fiction. We have a perfect picture of provincial life in the late eighteenth century; a delicate

water-colour to put beside the more vigorous oil-painting of Fielding.' (*A History of English Literature*).

Charles Lamb (1775–1834)

Poetry
Four sonnets in Coleridge's *Poems on Various Subjects* (1796)
Blank Verse (with Charles Lloyd, 1798)
Poetry for Children (1809)
Prince Dorus (1811)
Drama
John Woodvil (1802)
Mr H (1806)
Short Stories
Tales from Shakespeare (with Mary Lamb, 1807)
Mrs Leicester's School (1809)
The Adventures of Ulysses (1808)
Prose
Tale of Rosamund Gray and Old Blind Margaret (1798)
Specimens of English Dramatic Poets who lived about the time of Shakespeare (1808)
Essays of Elia (1823)
Last Essays of Elia (1833)

Life

Charles Lamb was the youngest child of John Lamb, a clerk and personal attendant of the MP Samuel Salt. Salt, who did not have a family of his own, looked upon Lamb's family as his own and allowed them to live in his house. Charles Lamb had two surviving siblings, John and Mary. With the help of Samuel Salt, he got admission into Christ's Hospital, where he received a sound education and the friendship of Coleridge.

After he left Christ's Hospital, Lamb started to work—first in South Sea House and later in East India House, where he stayed for the next thirty-three years. Unfortunately, there was a strain of mental illness that ran in Lamb's family and which attacked him briefly when he was about twenty years old. Although it did not affect Lamb, his sister Mary suffered from frequent bouts of madness and in one such fit, stabbed her mother to death. After that episode, she was admitted to an asylum and would have remained there till her death but for Lamb who brought her home and took care of her till his death. Lamb was just twenty-three when he undertook the task of caring for his sister, his senile father and his sick aunt. As a result, he gave up all hopes of ever getting married although he was in love with a girl called Anne Simmons. As their patron Samuel Salt had died by then, the family had to move out of their comfortable lodgings in the Temple and go to Pentonville. By 1799, both his aunt and his father were dead and the brother and sister continued living together till Lamb himself died in 1843. His sister Mary, who continued to have bouts of insanity, used to keep house for them whenever she was normal. During those periods of lucidity, she even collaborated with her brother as an author. After her brother's death, her insanity became worse and she had to be institutionalised.

Lamb's life was very hard. He worked six days a week in East India House and wrote in the evenings. Apart from this, he had to take care of his sister. His sincerity and humanity endeared him to his friends who mourned his death. He was buried at All Saints' Churchyard, Edmonton.

Works

POETRY

Lamb's friendship with Coleridge resulted in his writing a few sonnets, four of which were published in the latter's *Poems on Various Subjects*. These poems reveal the influence of Burns and William Bowles, a poet who was fairly popular in his day. His next attempt at poetry was *Blank Verse* in collaboration with Charles Lloyd. This included Lamb's most famous poem 'The Old Familiar Faces'. Lamb soon discovered that his true talent lay in prose and not poetry.

DRAMA

Lamb also tried his hand at drama in 1802. He wrote a tragedy called *John Woodvil*, which was a failure as a play but revealed Lamb's knowledge of the sixteenth and seventeenth-century dramatists. His next attempt at drama was the farce entitled *Mr H.* which was hooted out of stage at Drury Lane.

PROSE

Lamb's first attempt at prose was *A Tale of Rosamond Gray and Old Blind Margaret*, a short romantic novel that was highly sentimental. Next, he collaborated with his sister Mary and wrote *Tales from Shakespeare.* This book was very well received as it served as a good introduction, especially for children, to the immortal works of the great Bard. He wrote another book for children known as *The Adventures of Ulysses*, but this did not enjoy the same popularity. His next collection of short stories, again in collaboration with Mary, was *Mrs Leicester's School.* Lamb contributed only three out of the ten stories. Yet another work for children by the brother–sister pair was a book of rhymes—*Poetry for Children*. After *Prince Dorus*, a fairy tale in decasyllabic couplets, Lamb stopped writing for children.

An important prose work by Lamb was *Specimens of English Dramatic Poets who lived About the Time of Shakespeare.* This work is significant for the reason that it reintroduced the Elizabethan dramatists to the contemporary world. It is an important piece of literary criticism as Lamb picked out extracts from the dramatists and supplemented them with insightful notes. He also contributed articles to Leigh Hunt's *Reflector* and magazines like *The Examiner* and *The Indicator*.

ESSAYS

The turning point in his literary career came when his essay 'Recollections of the South-Sea House' signed 'Elia' was published. It became an immediate favourite and Lamb continued to contribute more essays under the same name. It is interesting that the name he chose 'Elia' is an anagram for 'A Lie'—a most suitable name as Lamb loved to mystify and play with his readers. Most of the fifty-three essays collected and published in the two volumes of *Essays of Elia* were written for the *London Magazine* between 1820 and 1823.

Lamb discovered that his true talent lay in his reminiscences, presented with the right mixture of humour, pathos and sentiment. These essays were later published as *Essays of Elia* and *Last Essays of Elia*. The essay form suited Lamb's nature and genius best. In his own words, 'The Essays want no preface: they are all *Preface.* A Preface is nothing but a talk with the reader; and they do nothing else.' In the hands of Lamb, the **personal essay** or the **informal essay** gained immense popularity. This essay is an informal type of literary form in which the writer freely talks with the reader, sharing with him his views on various topics and his personal experiences, likes and dislikes. Lamb's essays serve as little windows through which we can see the personality of the author. In this, the personal essay is like the lyric, which also serves to open up the heart of the writer and bring him close to the reader.

Lamb's *Essays* reveal several aspects about the author. For instance, in 'Dream Children: A Reverie', an extremely sensitive and heartwarming essay written soon after the demise of his brother John, Lamb takes us through a rollercoaster ride of emotions—from humour to pathos to tenderness. He takes us through a typical interaction of a fond father with his little children, and the reader almost forgets that Lamb was unmarried and had no children of his own. The concluding sentence of the essay leaves us with a lump in our throats: 'I found myself quietly seated in my bachelor arm-chair, where I had fallen asleep, with the faithful Bridget unchanged by my side—but John L. (or James Elia) was gone forever.' In another essay, 'A Dissertation Upon Roast Pig', we come across Lamb's shining humour and his lyrical style of writing prose:

> There is no flavour comparable, I will contend, to that of the crisp, tawny, well-watched, not over-roasted, *crackling*, as it is well called—the very teeth are invited to their share of the pleasure at this banquet in overcoming the coy, brittle resistance—with the adhesive oleaginous—O call it not fat! But an undefinable sweetness growing up to it—the tender blossoming of fat—fat cropped in the bud—taken in the shoot—in the first innocence—the cream and quintessence of the child-pig's yet pure food—the lean, no lean, but a kind of animal manna— or, rather, fat and lean (if it must be so) so blended and running into each other, that both together make but one ambrosian result or common substance.

'The Praise of Chimney-Sweepers' reflects his sensitive nature and sympathy for the child labourers tempered with a vein of fine humour. His autobiographical 'The Superannuated Man' is one of his best-known essays. In it, he shares the agony of doing work that was most unsuitable to his natural talent:

> Independently of the rigours of attendance, I have ever been haunted with a sense (perhaps a mere caprice) of incapacity for business … my health and my good spirits flagged. I had perpetually a dread of some crisis, to which I should be found unequal. Besides my daylight servitude, I served over again all night in my sleep, and would awake with terrors of imaginary false entries, errors in my accounts, and the like.

In the same essay, he shares the joy of being relieved from service:

> I do not know the day of the week, or of the month. Each day used to be individually felt by me…I had my Wednesday feelings, my Saturday nights' sensations…the phantom of the next day, with the dreary five to follow, sate as a load upon my poor Sabbath recreations. What charm has washed the Ethiop white? What is gone of Black Monday? All days are the same.

In 'Christ's Hospital Five and Thirty Years Ago', Lamb tugs at our heart strings with the following words:

> I was a poor friendless boy. My parents, and those who should care for me, were far away. Those few acquaintances of theirs, which they could recon upon as being kind to me in the great city, after a little forced notice, …soon grew tired of my holiday visits. They seemed to them to recur too often, though I thought them few enough; and one after another, they all failed me, and I felt myself alone among six hundred playmates…. O the cruelty of separating a poor lad from his early homestead! The yearnings which I used to have towards it in those unfledged years! ... How I would wake weeping…

Features

- Lamb was widely read and had a vast store of knowledge especially of the writers of the seventeenth century, Shakespeare, Milton and the Bible. His essays are full of quotations from these sources. Apart from quoting them, Lamb was also influenced by their style; for example, his fondness for Latinisms, quaint phrases and archaic words.
- He had a keen sense of humour as can be seen in essays like 'A Dissertation Upon Roast Pig', 'A Chapter on Ears', 'Poor Relations' and 'The Praise of Chimney-Sweepers'.

- Lamb was equally good at creating pathos. He had the capacity to bring a lump into his readers' throats. In 'Dream Children', one minute he would evoke an indulgent smile from us and in the next, tug at our heart strings.
- He took the personal essay to new heights and was a great representative of the Romantic period. His essays share all the qualities of the Romantic lyrics—the personal note, the love for the past and empathy for the common man.

William Hazlitt (1778–1830)

An Essay on the Principles of Human Action (1805)
The Eloquence of the British Senate (1807)
Lectures on English Philosophy (1812)
Characters of Shakespeare's plays (1817)
The Round Table (with Leigh Hunt, 1817)
A View of the English Stage (1818)
Lectures on the English Poets (1818)
Lectures on the English Comic Writers (1819)
Political Essays (1819)
Table-Talk (1821–22)`
Liber Amoris (1823)
Characteristics (1823)
The Spirit of the Age (1825)
The Plain Speaker (1826)
Notes of a Journey through France and Italy (1826)
Boswell Redivivus (1827)
Life of Napoleon (1828)
Winterslow
Sketches and Essays

Life

William Hazlitt was born in Shropshire to a Unitarian clergyman. His father was a man of strong views who sympathised with the American colonies in the American War of Independence. Hazlitt inherited his father's penchant for dissent and admired the revolutionary spirit of the working class in the French Revolution, when the rest of his countrymen sympathised with the aristocracy. (Wordsworth, too, had admired the revolutionaries at the beginning of the Revolution, but changed his views when the Revolution turned into a mindless slaughter of the aristocrats. Hazlitt was very disappointed with Wordsworth's change.) This attitude of Hazlitt made him unpopular in England, but he was not bothered and refused to compromise.

The family moved to Ireland in 1780 and from there to America where they stayed for three years. On returning to England, they stayed in Shropshire till 1787 where Hazlitt spent most of his youth. With the intention of joining the clergy like his father, he joined Hackney Theological Seminary in London. He soon discontinued his education when he realised that he was not suitable for the profession. He was attracted to painting after visiting his brother who had settled in London as a painter. On his return to Shropshire, he met Coleridge who introduced him to Wordsworth and Lamb. Friendship with these men of letters inspired Hazlitt and he published his first book *An Essay on the Principles of Human Action.*

This meeting with Coleridge made Hazlitt want to achieve something in life. He visited several art galleries and went to Paris and admired Napoleon's achievements. He took up art seriously and made several copies of pictures and continued to do so even after returning to England. After some time, he realised that it was writing that best suited him and went to London. He married Sarah Stoddart and soon discovered that she was not a suitable wife and got divorced. His second marriage, too, was unsuccessful.

He worked hard at his writing and gave several lectures and made a name for himself. He was an important literary critic of his time and his collected works run into more than six thousand pages. He was however a lonely man who died in solitude. Only Lamb was by his side, to whom he spoke his last words: 'Well, I've had a happy life.'

Works

He began writing about several miscellaneous topics on philosophy and politics which are read by Hazlitt scholars for the insight they give into the writer's mind.

Among his early works are *The Principles of Human Action*, in which he opposed materialistic philosophy, and *The Eloquence of the British Senate* which was a selection of the best speeches of the most eminent English, Irish and Scottish Parliamentary speakers from the reign of Charles I to his own time.

LITERARY CRITICISM

He is remembered today for his essays on literary topics. His lectures which were later published as books are of academic interest. One of his most important works is *Characters of Shakespeare's Plays*, in which Hazlitt adopted the manner of the German critic A.W. Schlegel. This was first delivered as a lecture and was completely opposed to the neoclassical interpretation of Shakespeare's plays by Johnson. It was an important milestone in the increased appreciation of Shakespeare in the nineteenth century. It is the first book to discuss all the plays of Shakespeare and is considered as a good introduction to his plays.

His other works on literary criticism include *The English Poets*, *The English Comic Writers*, *The Spirit of the Age* and *The Dramatic Literature of the Age of Elizabeth*. He had an intimate knowledge of old authors and his critical views on poetry, drama and fine arts were rich and eloquent. He was emphatic in his judgement and forceful in expressing his opinions and proved to have a great influence on the young minds of his day. He based his criticism on his emotional reaction to a work rather than on objective, learned theories. This sometimes resulted in giving a prejudiced account of an author as seen in some of his critiques in his *The Spirit of the Age*. In this work, he discusses almost every English author from Chaucer to his own times. This is, perhaps, his best critical work as he picks out the best writers of the Elizabethan Age and points out the reasons for their greatness.

Again, in his discussion of seventeenth-century writers like Milton, Bunyan, Sir Thomas Browne and Jeremy Taylor, his approach is surprisingly modern. When it came to writing about the authors of the eighteenth century, he was quick to recognise their vitality and his assessment of them is valued to this day. He was one of the earliest critics to recognise the merit of Alexander Pope and look at him as a poet of art as opposed to Shakespeare who was a poet of nature. It was again Hazlitt who recognised the merit of Edmund Burke and his prose style. Hazlitt was most unselfconscious when it came to discussing the authors of his own time. He was not afraid to share his views and what is of importance is that his views were accepted by people for more than a century. The writers whom he thought worthy—Coleridge and Cobbett, Scott who he thought was 'the greatest and wisest' novelist and Wordsworth 'the most original poet now living'—are still considered to be worthy today.

ESSAYS

Hazlitt is best remembered as an essayist. He along with Charles Lamb and Thomas De Quincey are the three most important essayists of the Romantic Age. Hazlitt's *The Round Table*, *The Plain Speaker* and *Table Talk* are some of the best collections of essays on a variety of subjects. His essays are full of proverbs, foreign phrases and quotations from Shakespeare, Southey and Voltaire. He combines Romantic passion with a hearty humour.

Like Lamb, Hazlitt too revealed himself in his essays. He often mused about his past in his essays and gives us a truthful account of it. When he recalls the joys of his childhood and youth, he does so with childlike simplicity and youthful enthusiasm. There is an intense realism in his essays and it is the combination of realism and romance that makes his essays so readable. For instance, in his essay 'On the Pleasures of Hating', he honestly confesses: 'Without something to hate we would lose the very spirit of thought and action. Hatred alone is immortal. Pure good soon grows insipid.'

He is a great lover of nature as seen in his essay, 'On Going a Journey': 'Give me the clear blue sky over my head, and the green turf beneath my feet, a winding road before me and a three hour's march to dinner—and then to thinking!'

Features

- The most important feature of his style is his vigour and energy. When we read his essays, we are impressed with the steady buzz of life that he describes.
- His writing displays a sense of ease and effortlessness. As he says in 'On Familiar Style': 'To write in a genuine, familiar or truly English style, is to write as anyone would speak in common conversation, who had a thorough command and

choice of words, setting aside all pedantic and oratorical flourishes.'

- One should not conclude that Hazlitt wrote plain prose with no embellishments. His writing was full of what he called 'conversational ornaments'—epigrams, paradox, similes, metaphors and apt quotations. For instance: '...the tall rock that lifts its head in the erectness of Wordsworth's spirit' and 'Byron made man in his own image and woman after his own heart'.
- The conversational style had its own drawbacks. Hazlitt was not only careless but also ungrammatical at times and he often misquoted. A planned piece of writing consists of organised paragraphs grouped around an idea arranged in successive sentences. Spontaneous thought cannot be so orderly and organised. Hazlitt's writing, which follows the conversational style, sometimes tends to be difficult to read.

Victorian Age

1837–1901

The nineteenth century is synonymous with the reign of Queen Victoria who ascended the throne on 20 June 1837 and occupied it till her death on 22 January 1901. She held the record for being the British monarch with the longest period of reign of sixty-four years until Queen Elizabeth II broke it with her seventy-year-old reign. The Victorian Age was a period of peace, prosperity and tremendous scientific advancement and was marked by momentous reforms, startling inventions and rapid urbanisation. During her reign, the country reached the zenith of its power and glory and became an empire on which the sun never set. It was the richest country in the world and the first urban industrial society in history. The Age witnessed several inventions such as the steam-powered printing press, the railways, the typewriter, the camera and the telephone to name just a few. It was, in the words of Charles Dickens, 'the best of times' and 'the worst of times', as it also saw the collapse of religion and the rise of materialism. On the one hand, there were people who were immensely prosperous and on the other, those suffering in unthinkable poverty. Progress in science resulted in devastating doubts in religion. In short, it was an age of extremes which proved to be the forerunner of the tumultuous twentieth century.

The term 'Victorian' has several connotations. It was first used in 1851 to celebrate the nation's pride in its institutions and overseas accomplishments. It was the year in which the **Great Exhibition** was organised in a huge 'Crystal Palace' made of iron and glass, to showcase Britain's advancement in industry.

One of the most important historical events of the age includes the passing of the **Reform Bills**. These were a series of bills which empowered the people to select their leaders by casting their vote passed between 1832 and 1928. These Reform Bills transformed the country from being a monarchy to a democracy. This resulted in the social levelling of the people and brought about a great change in their outlook.

Some of the other major historical events of this period were the **Opium War**, the **Crimean War**, India's **First War of Independence** (the **Sepoy Mutiny**) and the **Boer Wars**. These conflicts were viewed by many as being part of what Rudyard Kipling called 'the White Man's burden'. According to this concept, the British felt it was their duty to spread order and culture throughout the world. They believed they were doing a great service by civilising a 'savage' world.

Two men who shook up the sense of complacency of the Victorians were **Karl Marx** and **Charles Darwin**. The rapid strides that industrialised England was taking, resulted in a sharp divide between the rich (the capitalists) and the poor (the working class). The system of laissez-faire which means to 'leave things alone' gave unbridled power to the rich factory owners who indiscriminately exploited the labourers. Marx succeeded in making people analyse issues related to economic injustice and the class system.

Darwin's groundbreaking theories of evolution were in total opposition to the biblical account of Creation. His *On the Origin of Species* and *The Descent of Man* struck at the very foundation of religious thought and succeeded in creating a whole generation of sceptics.

Evangelicalism was a powerful religious movement during the mid-Victorian era. The Evangelicals were a group consisting of 'dissenting' or 'nonconformist' Protestant sects who were Bible-oriented, anti-Catholic and concerned with humanitarian issues. Evangelicalism dominated the religious and social lives of the working and middle-class Britons. They advocated self-denial and frugality and considered most forms of entertainment as sinful. It was largely due to the efforts of the Evangelicals that slavery was abolished. They were also responsible for the strictness of Victorian morality.

The crisis caused in the minds of men due to science had a great impact on Christian beliefs. Many Victorian authors found a way to reassert religious ideas through their writings. George Eliot strongly maintained her faith in the Evangelical sense of duty and morality in her novels. In Tennyson's *In Memoriam*, there is a conflict between religious faith and science-induced despair in which faith emerges triumphant. Similarly, Thomas Huxley confessed that though he had renounced organised religion, he could not ignore spiritual impulses.

The first decade of the Victorian Era was fraught with troubles. It was a time when people, inspired by the French Revolution, began to raise their voices against inequality in society.

An issue that plagued the early-Victorian Age was the rapid growth of cities. London, Manchester and Liverpool expanded rapidly without developing their infrastructure, resulting in filth and slums. The Thames River in London was polluted with sewage and industrial waste.

The period between 1846 and 1868 is generally referred to as the mid-Victorian Era. It was a time when England experienced great prosperity due to the advancement of scientific discoveries, industrialisation and modernised agriculture. Due to its abundant export of textiles and other goods, it earned the title, the 'workshop of the world'. All this led to the development of a feeling of self-satisfaction, popularly known as **Victorian complacency**.

Another quality that characterised the Victorian Age was the growing materialism. People indulged in vulgar displays of wealth by building huge houses and filling them with all kinds of artefacts.

An outstanding feature of the Victorian Age was their obsession with decorum and gentility. The Victorians were often considered to be prudes and publishers and editors had to be extra careful to make sure that there were no passages or words that would make a respectable girl blush. Noble women were seen chiefly as homemakers and if at all they were forced to work due to economic circumstances, they became governesses or teachers.

Women from the poorer sections worked as servants in wealthy households.

Agnosticism is a word that is closely associated with the Age. The term may be defined as the belief that it is not possible to definitively prove or disprove the existence of God. It was coined in 1869 by the biologist, T.H. Huxley , who was one of the major thinkers of the Victorian Age.

Towards the end of the century, there was a gradual decline in people's faith in religion and it never regained its old grasp on society later in the twentieth century. There was also a general slackening of morals and people were less prudish towards the close of Victoria's reign. By the end of the century, Great Britain reached new heights due to her imperialism and colonisation and was considered the most powerful nation on earth.

ଔଡ଼ଓଡ଼

The Victorian Age is an important period in the history of literature. It witnessed a great variety of writing and was particularly renowned for its prose, fiction and poetry. Drama, however, experienced a decline after Sheridan and was only revived towards the end of the nineteenth century, by the plays of Oscar Wilde and George Bernard Shaw (who is considered more of a twentieth-century writer).

Victorian Fiction

Poetry was the predominant genre during the Romantic period, but in the Victorian Age it was the novel that was most popular. There were several reasons for the popularity of the novel. Publishing was a major industry in the Victorian Age. An important factor that contributed to the popularity of the novel was the passing of the Education Acts which made education compulsory. This led to a rapid surge in the size of the reading public resulting in the publication of magazines, newspapers, novels and poems. The majority of readers was from the ever-increasing middle class and there was a growing demand for books. Illustrations were included especially in serialised fiction which was extremely popular during that period. The readers could easily buy the 'penny dreadfuls' and the presence of lending libraries also encouraged more people to take up reading as a hobby.

This practice of borrowing books was the reason behind the extraordinary length of the novels, which were often published in three volumes. This facilitated the lending libraries to receive triple the borrowing fees and also enable three of its customers to borrow a single novel at the same time. By the 1860s, most novels were serialised in weekly or monthly magazines, which greatly increased their sale.

The practice of serialising novels had an impact on the way novels were written. Most of the important novelists of the time whose works were serialised like Dickens, Thackeray, Collins, Gaskell, Trollope and George Eliot had to plan their work in such a way as to leave their readers guessing at the end of each instalment and eager to buy the next issue. Another feature that defined the way novels were written was the practice of reading novels aloud by a family member. Any hint of impropriety, therefore, had to be strictly avoided by the writers. Most of the novels that are classified as classics now were the bestsellers of the Victorian Age.

Women were no longer just passive readers of fiction but actively contributed to the genre, though by using male pseudonyms. George Eliot and the Brontë sisters all wrote in this manner.

Children's Literature

It was the Victorians who first thought of writing for children specifically. They were conscious of the atrocities committed on children in factories and workshops and wished to create public awareness about it. At the same time, they wanted to make education compulsory for all children and encourage them to read. In order to cater to the tastes of the young readers, works for children were produced. Some of the popular children's books were Lewis Carroll's *Alice's Adventures in Wonderland*, Anna

Sewell's *Black Beauty*, R.L. Stevenson's *A Child's Garden of Verses* and *Kidnapped* and Thomas Hughes's *Tom Brown's Schooldays*.

Victorian Poetry

Although it was not as great a period for poetry as the previous one, it still had several distinguished poets. Robert Browning, Alfred, Lord Tennyson and Matthew Arnold were the three giants of the Victorian Age. Gerard Manley Hopkins was a contemporary of these poets but his work was published only in the twentieth century. The Romantic emphasis on self-expression gave way to poetry that aimed at self-examination. Carlyle's admonition in his *Sartor Resartus* is indicative of the literary trend of the times: 'Close thy Byron; open thy Goethe'. What he was trying to convey was that one should turn away from the tormented introspection and alienation associated with the Byronic hero and move towards trying to improve society. This does not, however, mean that Romanticism was dead in the Victorian Age. In fact, Wordsworth's *The Prelude* appeared in 1850, the same year that Tennyson's *In Memoriam* was published. Wordsworth was appointed as the poet laureate in 1843 and the Victorian poets looked up to him as a nature poet whose poetry had a healing power during the changing times. Matthew Arnold considered Wordsworth third only to Milton and Shakespeare—such was his influence.

The new age with its own baggage of spiritual conflict and social upheavals had its impact upon the quality of poetry. Though the essence of Romanticism continued to influence nearly all Victorian poets, there are many changes that gave Victorian poetry a character of its own. The features of Victorian poetry are:

- Victorian poetry is more formally disciplined and steers clear of the self-obsession, bordering on the morbid that was found in some Romantic poetry.
- The scientific spirit that was pervasive in the nineteenth century influenced them to write poems that were analytical and psychological.

- During the late-nineteenth century, a pessimistic tone appeared in much of Victorian prose and poetry. The poets were preoccupied with the intellectual and religious problems of their times and these formed the major themes of their work. Poems like Tennyson's *In Memoriam* and Arnold's 'The Scholar-Gipsy' and 'Dover Beach' are typical examples of such poetry.
- Another feature that distinguished Victorian poetry from that of the previous age, is their fondness for objectivity. Robert Browning, one of the leading poets of the Victorian Age, specialised in a strictly objective style of poetry—the **dramatic monologue**. This is a type of poem in which a single person, who is not the poet, narrates his experiences or shares his inner feelings. Tennyson and Browning were the chief exponents of this form and exhibited great skill in altering their style to reflect the tormented and troubled tones of their protagonists. These poems were usually conversational in tone and psychological in nature. Browning was preoccupied with extreme psychological states and tried to present a character from multiple perspectives.
- They were also drawn towards Greek mythology and the Arthurian legend (for example, Tennyson's *Idylls of the King*).
- A feature that distinguishes Victorian poetry from Romantic poetry is the preference for an ornate style over the simpler methods of the previous generation of poets. This included artistic devices such as alliteration and assonance.
- When we read the poems penned by Victorian poets, we notice the gradual shift from the Romantic preference for solitude to a return to society, from nature to the urban and from spiritualism to pragmatism and agnosticism. These changes in poetic style, reflect the era and the challenges that beset it.

Pre-Raphaelite Poetry

The Victorian Age featured a group of poets, painters and critics known as the **Pre-Raphaelites**. The Pre-Raphaelite Brotherhood was founded by William Holman Hunt, John Everett Millais and Dante Gabriel Rossetti in 1848. They wished to revive the realism, sensuousness and devotion to detail that characterised the art that was popular prior to the Renaissance painter, Raphael. It was, thus, originally an artistic movement and only later did it have its impact upon literature. Rossetti, who was himself a painter, felt an urgent need to save contemporary art which was rapidly becoming unrealistic, formal and too academic. The Pre-Raphaelites believed that it was Raphael who was responsible for steering art towards academics and moving it away from nature. They wished to simplify art and attempted a 'return to Nature'. John Ruskin who was a great champion of this school of art, said that they 'imitate no pictures; they paint from nature only'.

Pre-Raphaelitism was not confined to painting alone, but made its impact on poetry too, as Rossetti was a poet. As far as poetry was concerned, the Pre-Raphaelites revolted against the poetry of Tennyson which they felt was too traditional and involved with the contemporary problems of society. They believed that art should exist only for art's sake and not have any added agenda. To explain their views on art and poetry, they started a periodical called *The Germ* which, however, did not last long. The poets who belonged to this school were Rossetti, Christina Rossetti, William Morris, Algernon Charles Swinburne and Coventry Patmore. The features of Pre-Raphaelite Poetry are:

- The Pre-Raphaelites broke away from the traditional approach of poets like Tennyson who were preoccupied with contemporary socio-political problems. These poets removed themselves from the harsh reality of the day and escaped to an imaginary world of their own or that of a bygone era. They felt that art should exist for its own sake and not be used as a means of propaganda or teaching.
- The dream world that they escaped to was the Middle Ages. This was not something novel as before them the Romantics too set their poems in the past. Poets like Rossetti and Morris were attracted to the chivalry and romance of the Middle Ages.

- To the Pre-Raphaelites, the particular was more important than the general. They concentrated their efforts on minute details, both in their painting as well as their poetry. In painting, the details were visual, but in poetry, it was both visual and auditory. For example:

  She had a mouth
  Made to bring death to life,—the underlip
  Sucked in, as if it strove to kiss itself.
  Her face was pearly pale, as when one stoops
  Over wan water; and the dark crisped hair
  And the hair's shadow made it paler still:—
  Deep-serried locks, the dimness of the cloud
  Where the moon's gaze is set in eddying gloom.

  (Dante Gabriel Rossetti, 'A Last Confession')

- The poems of the Pre-Raphaelites were full of sensuous details. Since most of the poets who followed this school of poetry were painters, we find a certain concreteness in their work which is a characteristic of painting. Referring to this feature, Compton-Rickett observes that these poets thought and felt 'in pigments'. At times, this process of thinking in pigments made them too obsessed with details and a fondness for excessive ornamentation that could be cloying. For instance, the following lines from Christina Rossetti's poem 'A Birthday':

  Raise me a dais of silk and down;
  Hang it with vair and purple dyes!
  Carve it in doves and pomegranates,
  And peacocks with a hundred eyes:
  Work it in gold and silver grapes
  In leaves and silver fleur-de-lys;

  Sometimes these poets interchanged sensory functions to create a startling reaction. Rossetti, for example, talks about 'visible silence' in the poem 'Silent Noon' and in his 'The Blessed Damozel', he writes, 'I heard her tears'.

- The Pre-Raphaelites were fond of making their poems musical and in this too they tended to be excessive. The disproportionate use of alliteration and onomatopoeia detracts from the continuity of thought.

Victorian Prose

Victorian literature is remarkable for non-fiction prose. The criticism and essays of writers like Thomas Carlyle, John Stuart Mill, Cardinal Newman, John Ruskin, Walter Pater and Oscar Wilde raised the reputation of prose writing to new heights and gave it a classic status. These men of intellect wrote in a forceful manner and exhibited inordinate skill in style. Their works are rich storehouses of the English language and display a remarkable usage of similes, metaphors, fable and fantasy. The Victorian essay is known for its ornateness and Ruskin's work stands testimony to this fact. While Macaulay wrote in a style that was both heavy and racy, Carlyle's was often passionate with purple passages of sheer beauty.

Since the Victorian age witnessed several social, religious and political changes, there were a number of subjects that interested the reading public. The prose of this period, therefore, covered a wide spectrum of topics such as politics, religion, science, art and culture. A glance at the quantity of prose written during this period reflects the range of conflicting ideas and issues.

Utilitarianism was another feature of the Victorian Age. This was the philosophy founded by Jeremy Bentham which advocated the concept that one should always do something that would do the greatest good for the greatest number of people. Thinkers like J.S. Mill, Charles Darwin, Herbert Spencer and Thomas Henry Huxley were essentially utilitarian thinkers. The features of Victorian prose are:

- The prose compositions of the Victorian Age are remarkable for their length. Like the bulky novels, the prose pieces too ran into several pages and some of the essays could easily be referred to as either treatises or theses. Sometimes, they were the size of a book. The writers used this medium to discuss in extensive detail any subject that was of interest to the contemporary readers.
- There were no formal rules that these writers observed. The argument was the main thread that held the compositions together.

- There was another group of prose writers who belonged to the Pre-Raphaelite movement. They displayed greater interest in form than the earlier writers who were more interested in the social and religious problems of the age. These writers were not interested in the current affairs and issues that prevailed during the period. They upheld the slogan, 'Art for Art's sake'. There was even a return to nature in their writings. Some of the eminent writers who were associated with this category are Walter Pater and R.L. Stevenson.

Victorian Drama

Drama as a literary form took a backseat in the Victorian Age, with fiction and poetry enjoying the spotlight. This is not to say that there was no drama in the nineteenth century. Theatre-going continued to be popular. The famous drama critic Allardyce Nicoll points out in his book *History of Late Nineteenth Century Drama,* that the theatre was very popular with the rising middle-class audience. The number of theatres increased from a mere nineteen in 1851 to sixty-one in 1899.

In the first few decades of the century, there were no prominent dramatists. The plays of Shakespeare were popular and people flocked to the theatres to watch them. A lot of props and stage settings were used. This resulted in wasting a lot of time between scenes to change the settings. To make up for this, the plays were abridged. Sheridan's plays were also staged occasionally.

Melodrama was very popular and was often alternated with burlesque between the scenes of serious plays. Pictorial drama which gave prominence to elaborate stage design and accuracy of costumes was prevalent. In the second and third decades of the century, the audiences craved for real life horror stories and the dramatisation of popular novels. These were melodramatic in nature and had elaborate sets. After the mid-nineteenth century, melodrama became synonymous with spectacle. Train accidents, storms, sinking boats and chariot races were displayed on the stage. Charles Kean and William Terriss were well-known theatre personalities who churned out melodramas to suit the taste of the day.

In the fifties and sixties, the **problem play** became popular. Thomas William Robertson, professionally known as T.W. Robertson, introduced a new concept in drama by dealing seriously with the issues of contemporary life. His style was innovative and proved to be an inspiration to the problem plays made so popular by George Bernard Shaw. Robertson's plays like *Society*, *Ours*, *Caste*, *Play* and *School* discussed a variety of topics such as marriage between the classes. He tried to make drama as close to reality as possible. Characters were depicted sitting across the table and actually making tea and drinking it, giving rise to the nomenclature 'cup-and-saucer drama'. The settings were realistic compared to the elaborate settings of the earlier melodramas. For example, in the set of a drawing room, sofas, curtains and carpets and real doors with handles were used. If the scene required a character entering the room from a blizzard outside, snow would be blown in from the door. The language spoken on stage, too, was very close to the normal style of speaking. Shaw, who was a great admirer of these plays, called Robertson's play *Caste* 'epoch-making'.

By the late Victorian Age, Oscar Wilde took the theatre by storm with his satirical comedies. He was closely followed by George Bernard Shaw.

William Makepeace Thackeray (1811–63)

Fiction and Prose

The Yellowplush Papers (1837–38)
Catherine (1839–40)
A Shabby Genteel Story (1840)
The Paris Sketch Book (1840)
The Great Hoggarty Diamond (1841)
The Fitz-Boodle Papers (1842–43)
The Irish Sketch Book (1843)
The Book of Snobs (1846–47)
Roundabout Papers (1860–63)
The Luck of Barry Lyndon (1844)
Vanity Fair (1847–48)
The History of Pendennis (1848–50)
The History of Henry Esmond (1852)
The Newcomes (1853–55)
The Virginians (1857–59)
Lovel the Widower (1860)
The Adventures of Philip (1861–62)

Lectures

The English Humourists of the Eighteenth Century (1853)
The Four Georges (1860)

Burlesques
A Legend of the Rhine (1845)
Rebecca and Rowena (1850)
The Rose and the Ring (1855)

Life

Thackeray was the only child of Richmond Thackeray and Anne Becher. He was born in Calcutta (now Kolkata) as his father was associated with the East India Company that was based in that city. After his father's demise in 1815, his mother sent Thackeray to England for his education. It is said that while sailing to England, the ship made a brief stopover at St Helena, where Thackeray had a fleeting glimpse of Napoleon who was a prisoner there.

After reaching England, he studied in Southampton, Chiswick and Charterhouse schools. While at Charterhouse, he befriended John Leech. He was not happy at Charterhouse and later in his writings satirised it by referring to it as a 'slaughterhouse'. He next went to Cambridge but, being an indifferent scholar, left in 1830.

He next attempted to study law at the Middle Temple, but gave it up after a while. Whatever money he inherited from his father, he soon lost through gambling and from funding two unsuccessful newspapers. He was, thus, forced to find a means of supporting himself and tried his hand at art. He was not successful in this field either. It was only after his wedding in 1836 that he took up writing as a career. He wrote some essays on art criticism, some short stories and later a few longer stories for the journal *Fraser's Magazine*. He also wrote for the magazine called *Punch*. Some of these articles were later published as *The Book of Snobs*.

Thackeray suffered a great setback in life when his wife Isabella slipped into depression after their third child was born. He tried every cure and treatment, but could find no permanent cure and finally she suffered a complete breakdown. Isabella outlived her husband by thirty years.

Amidst all these domestic worries, Thackeray managed to write two travel books—*The Paris Sketch Book* and *The Irish Sketch Book*. He became famous after the publication of *Vanity Fair* and visited the United States on lecture tours. He also gave lectures in London and was editor of the journal *Cornhill Magazine*.

In the 1850s, his health began to deteriorate and to add to this he began to indulge in excessive eating. He suffered a stroke in 1863 and was found dead the next morning.

Works

Thackeray is one of the most eminent novelists of the Victorian Age. In his literary leanings, he slanted more towards the eighteenth-century writers like Henry Fielding, whom he admired greatly, than his immediate predecessors, the Romantics. He was a realist who detested affectation.

Most of Thackeray's early writings were humorous and were published in *Fraser's Magazine* and *Punch*. These were collected into a volume that included pieces like *The Yellowplush Correspondence*. This is a fictional diary of a young cockney footman written in his own style. *The Book of Snobs* is a collection of essays originally published in *Punch* and consists of several character sketches. This book reveals Thackeray's gift for creating characters who remain immortal in the readers' minds.

The Luck of Barry Lyndon (renamed *The Memoirs of Barry Lyndon* in a later edition) is a historical work and his first full-length novel that was serialised in *Fraser* in 1844. It is the story of a social climber, a theme he explores more successfully in his famous *Vanity Fair*. His satirical style of writing, later perfected in his renowned work *Vanity Fair*, is evident here. In the two books, *Paris Sketch Book* and *Irish Sketch Book*, he attempted to blend travel notes with a reflection of the two societies, their manners and politics. Although these works reflect his own prejudices, they are examples of his keen sense of observation and humour.

In his next important work *The Book of Snobs*, he is at his best, as Thackeray was totally against any form of affectation. He made the word 'snob' popular by satirising it. The snobbishness of upper-class society came under attack in these essays.

Vanity Fair was the novel that made Thackeray's name immortal in the literary world. It is a social satire that holds up a mirror to the corruption and artificiality of the England of the Napoleonic Wars. Subtitled 'A Novel Without a Hero', it traces the ups and downs of the fortunes of two women who are as different from one another as chalk from cheese. Becky Sharp is a worldly-wise woman who will stop at nothing to reach her goal, while Amelia Sedley is portrayed as a naïve and simple girl who loves George Osborne blindly. The novel first appeared in a serialised form in a magazine between 1847 and 1848 and carried the subtitle *Pen and Pencil Sketches of English Society*. The title of the novel is taken from John Bunyan's *The Pilgrim's Progress* where the central character Christian passes through a town called Vanity in which there is a continuous fair. Bunyan used this concept to represent man's sinful attachment to worldly possessions.

His next major work *The History of Pendennis* is a bildungsroman, a literary genre that focuses on the psychological and moral growth of the protagonist from youth to adulthood—a coming-of-age story. Set in the London of the 1830s and 40s, it presents a satirical picture of human character especially in the aristocratic circles. Following close on the heels of *Vanity Fair*, this novel too maintains a similar atmosphere. One can discern several autobiographical elements in this novel, especially, in the sections dealing with the protagonist's schooldays and his struggles in the field of journalism.

To counter the criticism that *The History of Pendennis* was very loosely constructed, Thackeray took great care in writing his next novel—*The History of Henry Esmond*. Set in the England of Queen Anne, it is the story of an orphaned boy raised by his aristocratic relatives and who later becomes a colonel. It is a historical novel in which real and imaginary characters are woven together. Important historical events such as the Restoration, the Glorious Revolution and the War of Spanish Succession find a place in the pages of this book. Thackeray declared that this was his best work.

The Virginians was a sequel to *Henry Esmond*. In it, Thackeray traces the fortunes of Esmond's grandsons. It is set in both England and America and even includes George Washington as a character.

The ups and downs in the fortunes of a respectable middle-class family is the theme of his next novel *The Newcomes*. The story is set in the 1830s and 40s and follows the characters through several places including France and Italy. In this work, Thackeray refers to several contemporary events and people. One gets a feel of what it might have been to live in the England of those days. He also uses several foreign phrases and words freely without offering any translations.

Features

- Thackeray's main contribution to English fiction is his realism and redefinition of the stock portrayals of characters. For instance, it was standard practice to portray a scoundrel as a one-dimensional wandering hero or a picaro, but Thackeray altered this view. He presents them as complex characters who have their own motives and weaknesses. Similarly, the heartless and cold aristocrat and the idolised poor, too, are portrayed more realistically by Thackeray.
- He was adept at exposing the shortcomings of the middle class. For instance, in his depiction of the Crawleys, the Sedleys and the Osbornes, we are given a very realistic portrait of their lives and their thoughts.
- He was especially brilliant at portraying morally weak characters like Becky Sharp and Rawdon Crawley. He had a talent for delving deep into the psychology of a negative character.
- The moral critic in him made him intrude into the story. This diminished the artistic value of his writings.
- He enjoyed satirising social conventions and snobbery. Several critics, however, have remarked on the scornful edge of Thackeray's cynicism. His ironic portraiture of characters is sometimes marred by his desire to sermonise.

Charles Dickens (1812–70)

Sketches by Boz (1833–36)
The Posthumous Papers of the Pickwick Club (1837)
Oliver Twist (1836–37)
Nicholas Nickleby (1838–39)
The Old Curiosity Shop (1840–41)
Barnaby Rudge (1841)
American Notes (1842)
Martin Chuzzlewit (1843–44)
A Christmas Carol (1843)
The Chimes (1844)
The Cricket on the Hearth (1845)
The Haunted Man (1848)
Dombey and Son (1846)
David Copperfield (1849–50)
Bleak House (1852–53)

A Child's History of England (1851–53)
Hard Times (1854)
Little Dorrit (1855–57)
A Tale of Two Cities (1859)
Great Expectations (1860–61)
Our Mutual Friend (1864–65)
The Mystery of Edwin Drood (1870)

Life

Charles Dickens was born in Portsmouth to Elizabeth and John Dickens. As a boy, he read voraciously, but had an incomplete education due to the imprisonment of his father in the Marshalsea Debtors' Prison. He was forced to discontinue his studies and work in a blacking warehouse, pasting labels on jars of boot-blacking ink.

A small inheritance freed John Dickens from prison and Charles was sent to Wellington House Academy. It was not a well-run school and had a sadistic headmaster William Jones who was later the inspiration for the cruel headmaster Mr Creakle in *David Copperfield*.

Dickens worked for a while in a law office in Gray's Inn and also learnt shorthand. He next became a reporter and gained extensive experience observing legal proceedings and election campaigns. He used all these first-hand experiences in his novels. His first book *Sketches by Boz* was a collection of the articles that he had written while covering election campaigns and was in the form of sketches. This book paved the way for a commission to write a humorous collection of stories which resulted in *The Pickwick Papers*. This book shot him to instant fame and he was recognised as one of the leading authors of the day.

He continued writing steadily by contributing serialised stories to magazines. One novel followed the other in rapid succession. One is awe struck at the quantity and quality of work churned out by Dickens despite his incomplete education. He visited America and delivered several readings of his novels and gave lectures. He was very well received there. After his return to England, he continued to write.

He was not lucky in his personal life, as his marriage was not a happy one. He separated from his wife and was rumoured to have taken a mistress, Ellen Ternan. He died in 1870 while working on his last novel *The Mystery of Edwin Drood*. He was buried in Westminster Abbey, an honour reserved only for the most deserving.

Works

Charles Dickens was a prolific writer, churning out a new novel almost every year. He was a born storyteller, who used his personal experiences to the best advantage. In his capacity for creating immortal characters, he has often been compared to none other than Shakespeare. While being keenly sensitive to the evil ways of man, Dickens never allowed it to cloud his perspective of life. He was able to see and appreciate the comedy behind humanity. He could also observe the struggles of human beings within the various social institutions in a sensitive and philosophical manner.

The very first book to be published when Dickens was just twenty-four was *Sketches by Boz*. This was essentially a collection of fifty-six sketches of everyday life and everyday people that had appeared in various newspapers and journals between 1833 and 1836. The book has four sections under the headings 'Our Parish', 'Scenes', 'Characters' and 'Tales'. Of these, only the pieces belonging to the final section are fictional, the others being non-fictional pen-pictures.

The success of *Sketches by Boz* attracted the attention of a London publisher who was interested in printing a series of comic 'cockney sporting plates' which were basically pictures of hunting and fishing expeditions that have gone wrong. Dickens was asked to provide write-ups to go with the pictures. After doing a couple of pictures, Dickens began to provide the incidents and the artist had to illustrate according to the text provided. Soon the stories began to occupy centre stage and the illustrations became secondary. Dickens created the character Samuel Pickwick who was the founder of the 'Pickwick Club'. He and his three friends travelled throughout the English countryside and reported their findings to the club. The theme of the novel was their travels by coach. These loosely strung incidents were collected together to become *The Pickwick Papers*, Dickens's first novel.

After the success of *The Pickwick Papers*, Dickens began to turn his attention to more serious issues although he never gave up his natural inclination for the comic. His next novel *Oliver Twist* focused on the criminal world of London and the appalling conditions of the workhouse. It is a social novel in which Dickens highlighted the plight of orphans in mid-nineteenth century. He turned the spotlight on the problem of employing children to commit crimes. Through this novel, Dickens makes a veiled attack on poverty and the oppression that prevailed in schools, prisons and workhouses. This novel, too, was published originally in monthly instalments in a magazine.

His third book *Nicholas Nickleby* began to appear as a serial from 1838 to 1839 and is episodic in nature like his earlier works. In this novel, the private schools came under attack for their greed and brutal treatment of students. The book was a result of Dickens's personal visit to a Yorkshire school and witnessing of the cruelty of its headmaster William Shaw who inspired the character Wackford Squeers.

The Old Curiosity Shop was the next book to be serialised between 1840 and 1841. When it first appeared, it was popular, although today it is not rated among the best of Dickens's novels. The death scene of Little Nell, particularly, has come in for a lot of criticism for its excessive sentimentality. This novel was written three years after the death of his sister-in-law Mary Hogarth, who was just seventeen years old. Dickens was affected deeply by this death, which resulted in a number of death scenes in *The Old Curiosity Shop*.

Dickens next tried his hand at the historical novel and wrote *Barnaby Rudge* set against the backdrop of the Gordon Riots of 1780. His next two books *Martin Chuzzlewit* and *American Notes* were written after visiting America. In both these books, he depicted America in a poor light. In his treatment, the country appears to be little better than a wilderness with a few oases of civilisation. The people are shown to be deceptive and hypocritical. These works made him unpopular in America.

After returning from America, he began work on his five Christmas novels of which *A Christmas Carol* is the most famous.

It is the story of the transformation of the miserly Ebenezer Scrooge into a warm and unselfish person after the three ghosts, representing the past, present and future, visit him. The other books that belong to this theme are *The Chimes*, *The Cricket on the Hearth*, *The Battle of Life* and *The Haunted Man*. The last four books, however, are not as popular as *A Christmas Carol*.

As Dickens continued to write, he began to develop as an artist. One finds his novels becoming better structured and there is a greater variety as far as style and tone are concerned too. He also decided to use his novels as vehicles to highlight the evils of Victorian society, of which he had first hand knowledge. Victorian materialism comes in for attack in his *Dombey and Son*. He was disgusted with the love for money that the Victorians had and believed that it was this quality that was at the root of all evils such as the exploitation of the poor and the proliferation of crime.

He turned his attention inwards in his next work, the immortal *David Copperfield*. Many of the events presented in this novel are from Dickens's own life. It is written in the first person and traces the life of David from childhood to middle age. In the preface to the 1867 edition of the book, Dickens declared, 'like many fond parents, I have in my heart of hearts a favourite child. And his name is David Copperfield.'

In *Bleak House*, which followed on the heels of *David Copperfield*, Dickens makes use of the unhealthy London fog as a metaphor for the illnesses of Victorian society. In this book, Dickens focuses his attention to the long-drawn-out legal cases. Such was the effect of his writing that it helped to bring about reforms in the judiciary in the 1870s. It is also a social commentary that touches upon several other issues such as the appalling conditions of the poor, the lack of sanitation and the corrupt clergy and false humanitarians.

Hard Times is a hard-hitting novel in which Dickens lashes out against Jeremy Bentham's philosophy of utilitarianism. Utilitarians believed in the theory that advocated the greatest good for the greatest number. Dickens had visited the factories in Manchester and was horrified at the conditions of the poor factory workers. He believed that it was the prevalence of utilitarian values in education that led to the creation of disdain on the part of the mill and factory owners towards the workers. Dickens felt the suppression of imagination advocated by this kind of education was bad for the emotional growth of people.

In *Little Dorrit*, he highlights the defects of the government and society. He, especially, focuses his attention on the miserable plight of the debtors' prisons where the debtors were imprisoned because they were unable to pay their debts. Once in the prison, they were unable to work and their debts mounted. He fashioned the prison after Marshalsea, where his own father was held captive.

A Tale of Two Cities is Dickens's second historical novel and one of the best books to be written against the backdrop of the French Revolution. It is set in London and Paris. In it, Dickens takes his readers through the different phases of the Revolution—the events leading to the rebellion, the appalling conditions of the poor and the heartlessness of the aristocracy, the horrors of the Reign of Terror and the persecution of the aristocrats, both the guilty as well as the innocent. The reader is fully sympathetic towards the poor when a child is run over by the rash driving of an aristocrat's coach and the rider of the coach contemptuously throws a gold coin at the father of the dead child. The same reader is horrified at the heartless manner in which the bloodthirsty Madame Defarge hunts down Charles Darnay for the sole reason that he belonged to the Evrémonde family. It is also a beautiful love story in which the word sacrifice is given a new definition by Sydney Carton. Of course, it has the most well-known opening sentences that have ever been penned and which serve as an introduction not only to the epoch depicted in the novel, but also to the Victorian Age:

> It was the best of times, it was the worst of times, it was the age of wisdom, it was the age of foolishness, it was the epoch of belief, it was the epoch of incredulity, it was the season of Light, it was the season of Darkness, it was the spring of hope, it was the winter of despair, we had everything before us, we had nothing before us, we were all going direct to Heaven, we were all going direct the other way—in short, the period was so far like the

present period, that some of its noisiest authorities insisted on its being received, for good or for evil, in the superlative degree of comparison only.

Great Expectations is Dickens's second bildungsroman in which he traces the growth and development of an orphan named Pip. Like *David Copperfield*, this novel, too, is completely narrated in the first person. It is set in Kent and London and has several memorable scenes and characters. Dickens explores themes such as the importance of wealth in one's life, poverty, love and rejection and the triumph of good over evil.

His final novel of social criticism was *Our Mutual Friend*. In this novel, he uses the garbage dumps of London as a metaphor for filthy money. He attacks the superficiality of the nouveau riche. Dickens was working on *The Mystery of Edwin Drood*, when he died without completing it.

Features

- He was a great storyteller. Dickens's stories were very popular and the demand for them was great. Since they first appeared in monthly magazines, they are sometimes episodic in nature. Nevertheless, he was adept at creating a plot and holding the readers' interest.
- Dickens is considered to be second only to Shakespeare in the creation of memorable characters. He was able to bring alive on his pages a variety of characters who were comic, kind and villainous. Who can ever forget the inimitable Samuel Pickwick, Miss Havisham, Madame Defarge, Betsey Trotwood, the Artful Dodger, Ebenezer Scrooge and Sydney Carton, to name just a few. Critical opinion was not the same in the first-half of the twentieth century which gave importance to the psychological approach to characterisation. Dickens was often criticised for creating exaggerated characters who were mere caricatures. Today, Dickens is ranked along with authors like Franz Kafka and Fyodor Dostoevsky.
- He was at heart a social reformer who drew his readers' attentions to the plight of the poor and the downtrodden.

He highlighted the evils in several institutions of his time, such as the workhouses, schools and factories. He was able to recreate scenes of horror that would stir people's conscience. At times, this zeal for social reform detracted from the artistic quality of his works.

- Dickens was known for his humour. The broad appeal of his sense of humour made his works enjoyable to a large section of the public. In his very first novel, he succeeded in creating the immensely popular Mr Pickwick. This was followed by other humorous characters like Mrs Gamp, Mr Micawber and Sam Weller.
- The next important feature of his writing is his pathos. Dickens's style, however, appears exaggerated to the modern reader as it, slants towards the melodramatic.
- Another criticism levied against Dickens is that he created flat characters and not round ones. Flat characters represent only one characteristic and do not change or develop. Round characters have many facets to their character and are shown to develop and grow through the story. For example, Uriah Heep is always portrayed as being humble while Barkis is always 'willing' or agreeable.
- Dickens's writings reflect his moral vision. He firmly believed in human goodness and the possibility of a change in social values.

Anthony Trollope (1815–82)

The Macdermots of Ballycloran (1847)
The Barsetshire Novels
The Warden (1855)
Barchester Towers (1857)
Doctor Thorne (1858)
Framley Parsonage (1861)
The Small House at Allington (1864)
The Last Chronicle of Barset (1867)
The Palliser Novels
Can you Forgive Her? (1864–65)
Phineas Finn (1867–69)
The Eustace Diamonds (1871–73)
Phineas Redux (1873–74)
The Prime Minister (1875–76)
The Duke's Children (1879–80)

Life

Anthony Trollope was born in London. His father was unsuccessful as a lawyer and as a farmer. As a result, the family was always poor and when things became very bad, they moved to Belgium. His mother tried to support the family through her writing.

Trollope joined as a junior clerk in the General Post Office in London and was soon transferred to Ireland. His work at the post office involved a lot of travelling to places like Egypt, the West Indies and the United States. Among his achievements in the postal department, an important one is the introduction of the pillar box for letters in Great Britain.

Apart from his duties in the postal department, he wrote novels. Although he is not rated very high in the literary world, the quantity of his writing is quite impressive. He wrote forty-seven novels, and many more biographies, travelogues and short stories.

Trollope passed away in London and was buried at Kensal Green Cemetery.

Works

Trollope's first novel *The Macdermots of Ballycloran* was published in 1847. This work received little notice and it was only with the Barsetshire novels that he was recognised as a novelist. Trollope set six of his novels in an imaginary place called Barsetshire which he was able to visualise so well that he could even draw a map of it. *The Warden* was the first novel set in Barsetshire that made him famous. The five novels that followed deal chiefly with the clergy and the gentry and their manipulations and give us a perfect picture of provincial life. He was preoccupied with the delineation of characters than in the construction of plots. He made his characters move freely between his novels, which made them seem more realistic. The best of this series is *Barchester Towers*. The other novels that belong to this group are *Doctor Thorne*, *Framley Parsonage*, *The Small House at Allington* and *The Last Chronicle of Barset*.

His next series of novels that is worthy of mention is known as the Palliser novels. These novels dealt with the wealthy people and politicians and were earlier referred to as the Parliamentary novels. The wealthy politician Plantagenet Palliser and his equally rich wife Lady Glencora are the central characters in all of the six novels belonging to this series. The first of this series is the novel called *Can You Forgive Her?* and it continued with *Phineas Finn*, *The Eustace Diamonds*, *Phineas Redux*, *The Prime Minister* and *The Duke's Children*.

These two series of novels were written by Trollope over a period of about twenty years.

Features

- Trollope's chief contribution to British fiction is the establishment of the novel-sequence. The reappearance of the same characters in a whole series, a style made popular by Balzac earlier, is an important feature of Trollope's work.
- He was more preoccupied with character than with plot. He believed that an author should know his characters intimately. The characters are multi-dimensional and their emotional and psychological characteristics are portrayed in detail.
- Trollope was a realist who wrote about the daily life that he observed around him. His novels offer a detailed description of the social and political realities of his time. He focused on issues such as class, marriage and politics and used his work to highlight the shortcomings of his age.
- There are no extremes in his depiction of ordinary life although there are both pathos and humour. Trollope was known for his sense of humour, wit and satire.

Charlotte Brontë (1816–55), Emily Brontë (1818–48) and Anne Brontë (1820–49)

Poems by Currer, Ellis, and Acton Bell (1846)

Works by Anne Brontë

Agnes Grey (1847)

The Tenant of Wildfell Hall (1848)

Works by Emily Brontë

Wuthering Heights (1847)

Works by Charlotte Brontë
Jane Eyre (1847)
Shirley (1849)
Villette (1853)
The Professor (1857)

Lives

Charlotte, Emily and Anne were the three surviving daughters of Patrick Brontë, an Irishman who settled down as the perpetual curate of Haworth, Yorkshire. They had a brother, Branwell, of whom they were very fond. They began their literary career under the pseudonyms Currer, Ellis and Acton Bell and became renowned poets and novelists. After the death of their mother, their aunt Elizabeth Branwell was given the responsibility of bringing up the children.

Four of the five daughters were sent to a boarding school at Cowan Bridge. A year later, two of the girls returned home as they had fallen sick and soon died. Charlotte and Emily were taken away from the school and they returned to Haworth. The sisters were naturally traumatised by the death of their siblings and this impacted their writings. In Charlotte Brontë's *Jane Eyre*, Lowood School where Jane Eyre studied was based on Cowan Bridge School and the death of the character Helen Burns is a direct reference to their dead sister Maria.

Once they were back in Haworth, the surviving children pursued their education at home. They were avid readers and lived in a world of fantasy influenced by the works of Byron and Scott and the stories of *The Arabian Nights*. Charlotte and Anne worked for a while as governesses. Most of their time, however, was spent in Haworth and the wild Yorkshire moors. The siblings spent their time writing stories, creating miniature versions of popular magazines and other literary activities. They gathered around a huge table in the evenings and read out to each other what they had written during the day.

The three sisters wrote their novels—*Wuthering Heights*, *Agnes Grey* and *Jane Eyre*— almost at the same time. In the meantime, their brother Branwell's health began to decline and he died in September 1848. In December of the same year, Emily, too, died of tuberculosis and which was followed by her younger sister Anne's death in May 1849.

Charlotte, the lone survivor, married a curate named Arthur Bell Nicholls in 1854. She died the following year at the age of thirty-eight due to a combination of tuberculosis and typhoid fever. She was pregnant at the time and had a few complications, all of which contributed to her untimely death. Their father Patrick Brontë survived all his children and died in 1861 at the age of eighty-four.

Works

The works of the three sisters were inseparably linked with the lonely moors of Yorkshire and were noted for their passion and originality. Their first literary attempt was the book of poems entitled *Poems by Currer, Ellis and Acton Bell* in 1846. It is said that Charlotte discovered several poems written by Emily and, convinced of their worth, decided to give it for joint publication. The book was not too well received.

The three sisters were busy writing their novels in the meantime. Charlotte completed her first novel, *The Professor*, which was rejected by several publishers. The story was a take on her experience of falling in love with her French tutor in Brussels. The novel was published posthumously in 1857.

Wuthering Heights by Emily Bronte was published in 1847 under the name of Ellis Bell. It got a mixed reception from the Victorian readers as they had not come across such a novel earlier. They felt that the stark depiction of physical and mental torture went against the grain of Victorian decorum and morality. It has a fable-like quality, reminding one of the story of 'The Beauty and the Beast' in which the father while leaving his home asks his daughters fondly what each of them wanted on his return. As the novel progresses, it turns into a turbulent and stormy love story between Catherine Earnshaw and the foundling Heathcliff whom her father brings back from his journey. It is a violent story of revenge and savagery, sometimes tottering on the irreligious, as for example in the scene between the housekeeper Ellen Dean and Heathcliff. A hurt Heathcliff promises Ellen (Nelly) that one day he would have his revenge on Catherine's brother Hindley.

When Nelly points out that God would take care of punishing him, Heathcliff gives the classic retort, 'No, God won't have the satisfaction that I shall'. This was the only novel to be written by Emily, who died the following year.

In the same year, Anne Brontë published the first of her two novels, *Agnes Grey*. It is the story of a governess, based on her own experiences as one for five years. She highlights some of the issues that young women who took up jobs as governesses had to face.

Her second novel *The Tenant of Wildfell Hall* is considered to be one of the earliest, sustained feminist novels. It sets out to expose the horrors experienced by the wife of an alcoholic and depraved husband. The novel occupies an important position in mirroring the position of women in Victorian society. It helped in bringing about changes in the outdated laws of England. Until 1870, a married woman could not have an independent legal existence, could not own property, sue for divorce or have custody of her children. In this novel, the protagonist slams the door on her husband and walks out of the house to raise her son independently.

Charlotte Brontë's novel *Jane Eyre* is the story of a plain, but spirited, heroine who works as a governess. Written in the first person, it is based on the author's own experiences. The book brings into focus several issues such as religion, class, feminism and psychological problems. It is a remarkable love story that has elements of the Gothic. It was an immediate success when it was first published and shot Charlotte Brontë to fame.

Jane Eyre was followed by two more novels, *Shirley* and *Villette*. *Shirley*, which was set against the backdrop of the Luddite uprisings in the Yorkshire textile industry, is a less impassioned love story of a young girl named Shirley. *Villette* is based on Charlotte's experiences in Brussels, which has been renamed 'Villette'. Charlotte reworked the material from her first novel *The Professor* and narrated the story of the love of a teacher for her fellow-teacher. The novel blends daily life in Belgium with elements of the Gothic. A hint of the supernatural adds to the depth of the heroine's character.

Features

- The Brontë sisters could be seen as pioneers of fiction as far as the exploration of the human soul in literature was concerned. In their novels, they laid bare the inner workings of their characters' minds and souls.
- They brought the Yorkshire moors to life in their works. Nature is almost a character in their stories.
- Their works often included elements of Gothic literature such as gloomy settings, eerie atmospheres and supernatural experiences.
- The sisters based their novels on their own experiences. While this has its merits, there are some disadvantages too. They were restricted in their imagination as they were anchored to their personal experiences.
- Loneliness and isolation were some of the recurring themes in their novels. The characters, who lived in remote settings, experienced emotional loneliness.
- The high seriousness of their works is unrelieved by humour.
- Their works succeeded in taking the readers to the inner workings of a woman's mind and heart. They were feminists who did not hesitate in giving expression to the true feelings of women.

George Eliot(1819–80)

Scenes of Clerical Life (1857)	*Romola* (1862–63)
Adam Bede (1859)	*Felix Holt, the Radical* (1866)
The Mill on the Floss (1860)	*Middlemarch* (1871–72)
Silas Marner (1861)	*Daniel Deronda* (1876)

Life

George Eliot was the pen name of Mary Ann Evans, the youngest surviving daughter of an estate agent in Warwickshire. As a child, she was particularly close to her brother from whom she was estranged in later years.

Even as a child, she was a voracious reader and read *Aesop's Fables*, *The Pilgrim's Progress* and the books of Dr Johnson and

Scott. She had a good education and was a very intelligent and bright student.

She went to London to work as assistant editor of the magazine *The Westminster Review*. Here she found a soulmate in George Henry Lewes who was also a writer. Although they were not legally married, she considered him as her husband and it was under his encouragement that she became a novelist. After the death of Lewes, she was grief-stricken. One of the first friends allowed to visit her was John Walter Cross—a great admirer of her novels. She married him in 1880. Unfortunately, she died a few months later, in the same year. She was buried in Highgate Cemetery, London.

Works

George Eliot had scant respect for the trifling and outlandish plots of contemporary fiction by women. Instead, she slanted towards the realism of the European novelists. She adopted the penname 'George Eliot' in order to be accepted by her readers without any prejudice and to escape being typecast as a writer of light-hearted romances. She used many of her own personal experiences in her stories and her detailed depictions of rural life were remarkable. She was a serious writer who addressed the moral and social problems of the day.

Her first work of fiction was *Scenes of Clerical Life* which was a collection of three short stories. The stories were set in the imaginary town of Milby in the English Midlands. They touched upon several current issues such as the conflict between the Established Church and the Dissenters, poverty, alcoholism and domestic violence.

After the success of her first work of fiction, she was encouraged to continue writing and soon *Adam Bede* was published. It is a tragic love story of Adam Bede and Hetty Sorrel, set in the fictional community of Hayslope. The novel was very well received and won a lot of critical acclaim for its authentic representation of country life.

The next year, she published *The Mill on the Floss*, one of the most famous novels of the Victorian Age. It has several autobiographical elements and the character Maggie Tulliver resembles the author in several matters. It is the story of the unconventional and intelligent Maggie and her deep attachment to her brother, Tom. In this novel, George Eliot explores the protagonist's conflict between her conscience and her strong longing to be loved.

In *Silas Marner*, George Eliot combines realism with fable to create an extraordinary story of a weaver who is falsely accused of stealing. He, in turn, is robbed of his gold and in a distraught state discovers an abandoned orphan child with golden hair. In this book, we often find the author intruding to point out the effects of good and evil deeds. As a story, although it appears a little contrived at times, it succeeds in holding the reader's interest.

Romola, her next novel, is set in Florence during the period of the Renaissance. Several historical characters make an appearance in the story. It is a well-researched novel that takes us to fifteenth-century Italy and weaves into the plot, the famous Girolamo Savonarola and the downfall of the Medici family.

In *Felix Holt*, the author explores the political unrest caused due to the passing of the First Reform Act of 1832. The story is set in the fictional town of Treby in the English Midlands. It is one of George Eliot's least read novels.

Middlemarch is considered to be her best work and occupies a prominent place in the history of British fiction. This story, which deals with several issues like the position of women, religion, hypocrisy, politics, education and the nature of marriage, is set in the fictitious place called 'Middlemarch' in the English Midlands. It weaves together realism, humour and history. In it, the author includes several current events like the introduction of the railways, the passing of the First Reform Act and the demise of King George IV. George Eliot examines the psychological impact upon the mindset of a community that is threatened by unwelcome changes.

Daniel Deronda, her last work, is set in the contemporary period. It was the most controversial of her works since she set out to examine the position of Jews in British and European societies. It is the story of an aristocrat who comes to the rescue of a young

Jewish girl. Eliot shows through her work that Jews were victims of prejudice. It could be considered a mixture of social satire and moral self-examination.

Features

- George Eliot was adept at portraying the humble virtues and petty vices of human beings accurately. She was able to look at her creations with sympathy and catch the nuances of their speech in her dialogues. Her characters belonged largely to the lower classes and she reveals a great understanding of them. She was adept at delving into the complexities of human nature and their moral dilemmas.
- Her realism was consciously developed and she wrote with an eye for minute details. Her novels provide a critique of the social and cultural issues of her time, such as the status of women, religion and class distinctions.
- Her plots were interesting and she was able to hold the reader's attention through her narration.
- Her preoccupation with morality and the effect of good and bad, often marred her novels, as she tended to intrude into the story at times in order to underline the obvious.
- The moral heaviness of her work was relieved by her humour. She was able to see both the comic side of life as well as the serious side.
- She had a lucid style of writing which tended to grow heavier while dealing with philosophical ideas.

Wilkie Collins (1824–89)

Antonina (1850)
Basil (1852)
The Woman in White (1859–60)
No Name (1862)
Armadale (1864–66)
The Moonstone (1868)

Life

William Wilkie Collins was the son of a landscape painter and was born in London. After a few years of education in a private school in London, he went with his parents to Italy and France for two years. He worked as a clerk under a tea merchant and later joined Lincoln's Inn to study law. Although he completed his legal studies, he did not practise law.

He never married but lived for many years first with a lady called Catherine Graves and later with Martha Rudd, with whom he had three children. He divided his time between the two ladies and led a very unconventional life. He died at the age of sixty-five and was buried in Kensal Green Cemetery, London.

Works

Wilkie Collins occupies a very important position in the history of English Literature as he was the pioneer of the **detective novel**. Although Edgar Allan Poe had written a few short stories in this category in America, Collins's novels served as models for later writers like Sir Arthur Conan Doyle and G.K. Chesterton, to write the detective novel. T.S. Eliot described Collins's *The Moonstone* as 'the first, the longest, and the best of modern English detective novels'.

His first novel *Antonina* is written in a deliberately laborious style. It has a very confusing plot with several descriptions of ancient Rome. It also has several passages of horror and violence. In spite of all these shortcomings, the novel was well received and was reprinted throughout the lifetime of the author.

Collins's next work *Basil* is considered as the first **sensation novel**. A sensation novel is a type of fiction that was popular in Great Britain in the 1860s. It was fashioned to arouse strong emotions like shock or controversy. There are a few autobiographical elements in it such as the snobbish father of Basil, who bears a resemblance to Collins's own father, who could never understand him. It is a psychological thriller about a secret marriage, madness, betrayal and violence, that upset the strict morality and decorum of the Victorians.

The Woman in White is a detective novel with multiple narrators. It is a chilling story about a man's exploitation of a woman. The legal education that Collins had at Lincoln's Inn clearly had an impact on his writing, as Collins himself states in the book's preamble: 'the story here presented will be told by more than one pen, as the story of an offence against the laws is told in Court by more than one witness'. The novel combines Gothic horror with psychological realism.

In *No Name*, Collins explores the theme of illegitimacy. It is the story of two sisters who make the traumatic discovery that their parents were not married when they were born. As a result, they are not allowed to inherit their father's property and name. This novel, too, created a sensation when it was first published. *Armadale* is a melodramatic novel about murder and revenge. It was considered to be too sensational for Victorian taste.

It was his final novel that brought lasting fame to Collins—*The Moonstone,* which is regarded as the first full-length detective novel in English. The novel is written in the first person, but includes multiple narratives by the characters in the story. It tells the story of the theft of a huge diamond and the search for it. The novel is outstanding for its psychological ingenuity and brilliant characterisation. Sergent Cuff, the professional detective, with his calm reasoning and keen sense of observation, set the stage for later detective figures like Sherlock Holmes. This novel has appealed to the Victorian as well as the modern readers.

Features

- He made the sensational novel famous. He was adept at creating the right atmosphere of horror and creating terror in the minds of the reader.
- Collins's novels are known for their use of multiple narrators which allows the readers to get multiple perspectives.
- His novels featured strong female characters like Marian Halcombe in *The Woman in White*. She is portrayed as a strong and intelligent character who does not conform to the typical conventions of women of the nineteenth century.
- He combined the supernatural with the real to keep his readers on edge.
- His contribution to English literature is the introduction of the genre of the detective novel. His character Sergeant Cuff in *The Moonstone* is one of the earliest fictional detectives in literature.

Thomas Hardy (1840–1928)

Fiction

Desperate Remedies (1871)
Under the Greenwood Tree (1872)
A Pair of Blue Eyes (1872–73)
Far from the Madding Crowd (1874)
The Hand of Ethelberta (1876)
The Return of the Native (1878)
The Trumpet-Major (1880)
Two on a Tower (1882)
The Mayor of Casterbridge (1886)
The Woodlanders (1886–87)
Tess of the d'Urbervilles (1891)
Jude the Obscure (1894–95)
The Well-Beloved (1897)

Short Stories

Wessex Tales (1888)
A Group of Noble Dames (1891)
Life's Little Ironies (1894)
A Changed Man and Other Tales (1913)

Poetry

Wessex Poems (1898)
Poems of the Past and the Present (1901)
Time's Laughingstocks and Other Verses (1909)
Satires of Circumstance (1914)
Moments of Vision and Miscellaneous Verses (1917)
The Dynasts (1904–08)

Life

Thomas Hardy was the son of a stonemason in Dorset. After a few years of education in the local schools, he went to London and studied in King's College. He worked as an architect for three years, but was more interested in writing poems and novels. At the same time, he lost his faith in religion. While on an architectural mission to Cornwall, he met Emma Gifford, whom he married.

Hardy had begun writing novels which brought him both fame and money. After the success of *Far from the Madding Crowd*, he gave up architecture completely and concentrated on his writing. He and his wife moved to Max Gate, a house designed by Hardy. Although their marriage was not a very happy one, he was distraught after the death of his wife in 1912. He married Florence Dugdale but kept brooding over his first wife. Harsh critical reviews of his novels made him turn his attention to poetry.

Hardy became ill with pleurisy and he died after dictating his last poem to his wife. His heart was buried at Stinsford along with his first wife and his ashes were preserved in the Poets' Corner, Westminster Abbey.

Works

Firmly rooted in the rural back ground of his native district of Dorset, Hardy's work is devoted to provincial life. Most of his stories are set in the imaginary county of Wessex which is full of gloomy landscapes—a background well-suited to the pessimistic nature of his novels. He believed firmly in the inevitable nature of fate and his characters are depicted as fighting a losing battle against it. In many of his novels, we find that a mysterious and invincible force seems to be steering the course of his characters who are mere victims of circumstances. Hardy's works appear to go against the spirit of Victorian optimism. He believed that human downfall was caused not due to any individual weakness, but as a result of a conflict with an intimidating universe.

His first published novel was *Desperate Remedies*, which did not get very good reviews. He, however, continued to write, completing thirteen more novels in the next twenty-five years. His second novel, *Under the Greenwood Tree*, shot Hardy to fame. The first of the Wessex novels, it continues the old English pastoral tradition of Shakespeare and Fielding. It contains excellent descriptions of nature and rural life and gives expression to Hardy's unhappiness at the ongoing modernisation that was destroying the traditional English country life.

A Pair of Blue Eyes, though not included in the list of major works by Hardy, is important as it contains much of Hardy's characteristics as a novelist. It is set is Cornwall and has several autobiographical elements. It combines romance, strong passion and the inevitability of destiny.

Far from the Madding Crowd is again set in Wessex and deals with the themes of love, tragedy, betrayal and madness. It is the story of the beautiful Bathsheba and her three suitors—Gabriel Oak, William Boldwood and Sergeant Troy. The wrong choice of the heroine lands her in a lot of misery, but the novel has a happy ending with Bathsheba marrying the right person—Gabriel Oak.

In *The Return of the Native*, Hardy describes the disastrous marriage of Eustacia Vye and Clym Yeobright. The novel deals with the contrast between the glittering life of Paris and the gentle countryside of Egdon Heath in Wessex. This novel is about relationships, betrayal, death and guilt.

The Trumpet-Major was a historical novel set in Weymouth during the Napoleonic Wars. During his childhood, Hardy had heard several tales about these wars from his grandparents. He researched extensively for the novel and created the story of Anne Garland and her three suitors, blending the fictional story with the general history of that time. Although the novel does not have a tragic ending, there is a note of ominous doom in the probable fate of one of the main characters.

His next novel *Two on a Tower*, now considered as one of his unimportant works, is a combination of romance and fantasy. *The Mayor of Casterbridge* is one of Hardy's most widely read novels. It is based on a true incident of wife-selling in early-nineteenth-century England. It is the story of Michael Henchard, his rise to greatness and his downfall. It is almost like a Sophoclean tragedy where one is confronted with the complex character of the hero, Henchard.

The Woodlanders is a love story set in the wooded country of Blackmoor Vale in Dorset. It is one of Hardy's best and most powerful novels and, as mentioned by the author himself, his favourite story.

His next novel *Tess of the d'Urbervilles* created an uproar when it was first published as it departed violently from conventional Victorian fiction. The frank treatment of sexuality and religion upset the strictness of Victorian sensibilities. The story was set in the Depression of the 1870s and narrates the tragic story of Tess who is exploited by the rich villain Alec d'Urberville. Once again fate is shown as overshadowing the lives of the characters. It is one of Hardy's most frequently read novels today.

Jude the Obscure with its sexual frankness, upset the public so much that it led to the burning of the book by the Bishop of Wakefield. The public outcry against his fiction was so great that Hardy decided to stop writing novels altogether.

Apart from novels, Hardy wrote several short stories that were received quite well. They include the collections *Wessex Tales*, *A Group of Noble Dames*, *Life's Little Ironies* and *A Changed Man and Other Tales*.

In the next phase of his literary career, he continued to recreate in his poetry, the same landscape that had figured prominently in his fiction. This was a harsh landscape that seemed to represent the indifference of a malicious universe. His first collection of poems was *Wessex Poems*, a collection of fifty-one poems. His poems anticipate the modernists in their exploration of the workings of memory and the perception of the individual. His poems have several references to contemporary events. The theme is again man's futile struggle against cosmic forces.

Poems of the Past and the Present, his second collection of poems, was published in 1901. It is divided into five sections and contains some of Hardy's lasting works. He next wrote *The Dynasts*—a verse drama in three parts and nineteen acts. It is a historical story, again set in the era of the Napoleonic Wars. The stories that he had heard as a child were used extensively by Hardy in this work.

This was followed by a succession of collections of poems such as *Time's Laughing-stocks*, *Satires of Circumstance*, *Moments of Vision and Miscellaneous Verses*, *Late Lyrics and Earlier*, *With Many Other Verses*, *Human Shows*, *Far Phantasies*, *Songs and Trifles*, *Winter Words* and *Collected Poems*. Most of the poems were short lyrics and reflect great technical skill and a love for experimentation.

The pessimistic strain found in his novels continued in his poems. His hatred of wars, the materialism of the contemporary age and a longing for the past are some of the themes that one discovers in his poems. Some of his famous poems are 'The Darkling Thrush' written on 31 December 1900, 'On the Departure Platform', 'Hap', 'Neutral Tones' and 'Wessex Heights'.

Features

- Hardy altered the realist novel of manners into tragic chronicles about the transformation of rural England. His work reflects the declining religious faith and the tension between the classes and the sexes. Hardy depicted the harsh realities of rural life and highlighted the challenges faced by ordinary people.

- There is an overuse of coincidences in his novels.
- A recurring theme in many of his novels is the concept of fate and destiny. His characters are portrayed as helpless victims struggling against forces beyond their control. Hardy is often guilty of intruding into his stories, ranting against cruel destiny and sympathising with his characters.
- His characters are all from everyday life and some of them like Tess, Eustacia Vye and Jude are unforgettable. Hardy was adept at creating complex characters and taking us into their minds to witness their inner conflicts.
- As a regional novelist, Hardy was a great success at creating the imaginary county of Wessex. He was very familiar with the landscape of the countryside and nature is used not just as a backdrop in his stories, but as a character. He blended the settings with the narration in such a way that they played a role in the shaping of the story.
- His mood was one of pessimism. He very poignantly writes at the conclusion of his novel *The Mayor of Casterbridge*, '...happiness was but the occasional episode in a general drama of pain'
- The same pessimistic tone can be seen in his poetry too. For example, the bitterness of the lines of his poem, 'Neutral Tones':

  > The smile on your mouth was the deadest thing
  > Alive enough to have strength to die;
  > And a grin of bitterness swept thereby
  > Like an ominous bird a-wing…

- He uses the same locations that he had used in his novels, for his poems too—the countryside that he was so familiar with.

Alfred, Lord Tennyson (1809–92)

Poetry

Poems by Two Brothers (1827)
Poems, Chiefly Lyrical (1830)
Poems (1833)
Poems (1842)
The Princess (1847)
In Memoriam (1850)
Maud, and Other Poems (1855)
Idylls of the King (1859–85)
Enoch Arden (1864)

The Holy Grail and Other Poems (1869)
Ballads and Other Poems (1880)
Tiresias and Other Poems (1885)
Demeter and Other Poems (1889)

Drama
Queen Mary (1875)
Harold (1876)
The Cup; and The Falcon (1884)
The Foresters (1892)
Becket (1884)

Life

Tennyson was born in Somersby and was the third surviving son of a rector. His early education was under his father, and later, he was sent to Trinity College, Cambridge, where he became a friend of Arthur Hallam. He became a member of a society of undergraduates called the Apostles, that included several men who later dominated the intellectual horizon of the Victorian Age. In 1832, he travelled to the Continent with his friend, Hallam. Hallam died in 1833 and Tennyson began his *In Memoriam*, to mourn his death.

He got married in 1850 and had a son, whom he named after his friend, Hallam. His career as a poet was progressing very well and he was appointed poet laureate after the demise of Wordsworth. He settled down in Farringford on the Isle of Wight. Many famous writers of the day used to visit Tennyson in his house. He later built his second house at Aldworth. He was awarded the title of Baron Tennyson in 1884 by the Queen. He died in 1892 and was buried at the Poets' Corner of Westminster Abbey.

Works

While at university, he wrote a poem called 'Timbuctoo' for which he was awarded the Chancellor's Gold Medal. The first volume entitled *Poems by Two Brothers* was a collection of poems by him and his brother, Charles. Tennyson, which were not reprinted after they were published in 1827.

His second book, *Poems, Chiefly Lyrical* contains some famous poems like 'Mariana' and 'A Spirit Haunts the Year's Last Hours'. This was followed by *Poems* in 1833 which included the popular poems, 'The Lotos-Eaters' and 'The Lady of Shalott'. Both these volumes were not received well. It was only with the publication of his third volume in 1842, *Poems*, that he began to be accepted by readers. This contained outstanding poems like 'Break, Break, Break', 'Ulysses' and 'Morte d' Arthur'. His popularity could be due to the fact that his poems held up a mirror to the divergent moods of the age—pessimism and optimism. In 'Lotos-Eaters', he mournfully asks: 'Death is the end of life; ah, why / Should life all labour be?'

He concludes the poem with the following lines:

Surely, surely, slumber is more sweet than toil, the shore
Than labour in the deep mid-ocean, wind and wave and oar;
Oh rest ye, brother mariners, we will not wander more.

In 'Ulysses' he echoes the exact opposite:

Yet all experience is an arch wherethro'
Gleams that untravell'd world, whose margin fades
For ever and for ever when I move.
How dull it is to pause, to make an end,
To rust unbyrnish'd, not to shine in use!
As tho' to breathe were life…

The same poem calls out to his compatriots:

… Come, my friends,
'Tis not too late to seek a newer world…
…for my purpose holds
To sail beyond the sunset, until I die.

The Princess, a narrative poem in blank verse, was not received well as it had a poor story of a heroic princess who turns her back on men and creates a university in which men are not allowed. In spite of its weak narration, the poem is memorable for asserting the cause of women's education and for its beautiful lyrical breaks.

Tennyson's next major work was *In Memoriam*, begun as early as 1833 but completed only in 1850. It is an epic contemplation on mortality, evolution and the ultimate triumph of inner faith. It is a requiem for his friend, Arthur Hallam written in the four-line stanza form of iambic tetrameter. It has 133 cantos and discusses several topics ranging from the spiritual to the nostalgic and philosophical. It reflects the moral and religious conflicts of the age. It was an instant success and with the death of Wordsworth in the same year, Tennyson was made poet laureate. The memorable line, 'He seems so near and yet so far...' is from this immortal work.

Maud and Other Poems, his next volume. contained 'The Charge of the Light Brigade', 'Ode on the Death of the Duke of Wellington' and 'Maud', a **monodrama** which was the title piece of the volume. A monodrama is a theatrical piece played by a single actor who portrays one character.

A trip to Wales fuelled his interest in Arthurian legends and he embarked upon his great work, *Idylls of the King*. He based his story on Thomas Malory's *Le Morte d' Arthur*. In the poem, Tennyson blended his friend Arthur Hallam with the literary character Arthur. It is an epic in twelve books. It is a pessimistic piece about King Arthur's attempt to create an ideal kingdom. It is about betrayal—being cheated on by his wife, Guinevere, and his murder by the traitor, Mordred. It has several individual poems about Lancelot, Galahad, Merlin and the Lady of the Lake. It is considered by critics to be a commentary on the social conflicts in England during the nineteenth century.

In his later years, he turned his attention to drama. He wrote three historical plays—*Queen Mary*, *Harold* and *Becket*. These were not very successful on the stage, although they were skilfully crafted. He tried his hand at comedy and wrote *The Falcon*, which was based on a story from Boccaccio's *The Decameron*, and *The Cup*, inspired by a story by Plutarch. *The Foresters* was a play about Robin Hood and was produced in America.

Features

- His greatness lay in mirroring the anxieties and desires of his era. Many of his poems, such as 'Ulysses', *In Memoriam* and *Idylls of the King*, portrayed the high energy and idealism of an industrial society which was, at the same time, tormented by doubts about materialism and the existence of God.
- He was ahead of his times in advocating the cause of women's education which he did in his poem, *The Princess*. He wrote about the exploitation of the poor long before Marx and Engels became popular.

- He gave to English language several sayings and quotations: ''Tis better to have loved and lost / Than never to have loved at all', 'The old order changeth, yielding place to new', 'Knowledge comes, but wisdom lingers' and 'Theirs not to reason why, / Theirs but to do and die'.
- His favourite forms of poetry were the idyll, the lyric and the elegy. In his early poems, we see his skill in handling these forms. Later in his career, he moved to narrative poetry. He was adept at using alliteration and assonance.
- His descriptions have a pictorial quality and his poems are full of ornate and detailed images.

  Lo! In the middle of the wood,
  The folded leaf is woo'd from out the bud
  With winds upon the branch, and there
  Grows green and broad, and takes no care,
  Sun-steep'd at noon, and in the moon
  Nightly dew-fed; and turning yellow
  Falls and floats adown the air.

Robert Browning (1812–89)

Pauline (1833)
Paracelsus (1835)
Sordello (1840)
Bells and Pomegranates (1841–46)
Christmas-Eve and Easter-Day (1850)
Men and Women (1855)
Dramatis Personae (1864)
The Ring and the Book (1868–69)
Dramatic Idylls (1879-80)
Asolando (1889)

Drama
Strafford (1837)

Life

Robert Browning was the only son of a bank clerk and was brought up in Camberwell, a pleasant suburb of London. His father had an excellent collection of books which was the chief source of education for the poet. The early influences on him were the poems of the Romantics and his mother's strong nonconformist piety. With the exception of a year spent in London University, he lived with his parents and only sister till he was thirty-four years old.

His parents doted on him and encouraged him in trying to discover his true calling. After watching a stage performance of *Richard III*, he was impressed by the objectivity of the performer in bringing out the character of Richard III. This inspired him to write poems in which different characters were brought alive and who revealed themselves to the readers while their creator remained hidden.

His courtship of Elizabeth Barrett and their subsequent marriage is one of the most celebrated ones in the literary world. She was an established poet and was almost seven years older than him. They lived in Florence, Italy. After the death of his wife in 1861, he returned with his son to England. His writing gained popularity and he enjoyed the attention of the literary circle. He died at his son's house in Venice and was buried at Westminster Abbey in the Poets' Corner.

Works

Browning was deeply interested in studying the workings of the human mind. He enjoyed getting into the minds of complex and controversial characters living in distant times and places. By presenting their cases through their points of view and in their own voices, he tried to decode the relationship between the characters' souls and their environment.

His first work *Pauline*, a long romantic poem, was published anonymously. In it, he speaks through a narrator who confides: 'I will tell / My state, as though 'twere none of mine'. This work did not meet with success. His second book, *Paracelsus*, is about the career of a Renaissance doctor whose practice is based on science as well as quackery. The poem is a study of an ambitious mind that rejects emotion and love, in its quest for life-changing truth. This book, too. was not received very enthusiastically by his readers.

Sordello narrates the experiences of an obscure Italian painter and is one of the most difficult poems to understand in the English language. Tennyson's famous retort after trying to read it was, 'There were only two lines in it that I understood, and they were both lies; they were the opening and closing lines, 'Who will may hear Sordello's story told', and 'Who would has heard Sordello's story told!'.

Browning next turned his attention to drama. He wrote six plays including *Strafford*. These plays did not go down well with the audience as they found them to be too hampered with debates and discussions. Browning was more interested in portraying characters rather than in the development of the plot.

Bells and Pomegranates is a collection of eight volumes of lyrical and narrative poems that had been published earlier. The opening piece was the famous play in verse *Pippa Passes*.

Gradually, Browning discovered what best suited his talent—combining his theatrical instincts with lyric poetry. He began to write his famous dramatic monologues in which idiosyncratic personalities presented their cases in their own style and language. *Dramatic Lyrics* and *Dramatic Romances and Lyrics* reveal Browning's true talent as a poet. *Dramatic Lyrics* contains poems like 'The Pied Piper of Hamelin', 'My Last Duchess' and 'Porphyria's Lover'. Some of the well-known poems in his *Dramatic Romances and Lyrics* are 'Home Thoughts, from Abroad', 'How They Brought the Good News from Ghent to Aix', 'The Bishop Orders His Tomb at St Praxed's Church', 'Meeting at Night' and 'Parting at Morning'.

Some of Browning's best work could be found in *Men and Women*. It contains his most famous works like 'Fra Lippo Lippi', 'Andrea del Sarto' and 'Cleon'. Most of them are dramatic monologues in blank verse. Although the dramatic monologue was in existence even before Browning's time, it was Browning who infused new life into the form. We find, in his pieces, characters who are situated in specific historical places and periods. At times they are real characters like Andrea del Sarto, Fra Lippo Lippi or Child Roland. These characters are caught at moments of great intensity and are shown trying to explain their behaviour. Through his skilful handling of their arguments, Browning steers the readers to sympathise with these speakers of dubious character. His gallery of speakers includes a duke who is suspected of murdering his wife, an artist whose wife cheats on him and a dying bishop who recalls his fleshly delights.

He continued to win his way into the hearts of his readers with his next collection, *Dramatis Personae*. In it one can find 'Caliban upon Setebos', 'A Death in the Dessert', 'Rabbi Ben Ezra' and 'Abt Vogler'. All these poems reveal interesting characters caught in crucial moments of their lives, trying to defend themselves.

His last major work that has stood the test of time is *The Ring and the Book*. It is a verse novel that revisits a sensational murder of a woman called Pompilia by her abusive husband, which had taken place in 1698. It narrates the story of the trial of Pompilia who is accused by her husband of adultery. Ten different witnesses give their testimony, each repeating the same story which reflects their own character. Through this sordid tale of marital abuse, Browning explores issues such as the rights of women and the role of religion in determining earthly actions.

His long career ended with *Asolando*, whose epilogue best describes the poet:

> One who never turned his back but marched breast forward,
> Never doubted clouds would break,
> Never dreamed, though right were worsted, wrong would triumph,
> Held we fall to rise, are baffled to fight better,
> Sleep to wake.

Features

- Browning's contribution to the form of the dramatic monologue is significant. In his hands it rose to new heights.
- Whatever theme he chose, Browning advocated the philosophy that the aim of life was a constant reaching out towards the better. His poems are all an affirmation of this faith, that life's inadequacies and strivings are only a prelude to the perfection of afterlife. Andrea del Sarto declares: 'Ah, but a man's reach should exceed his grasp, / Or what's a heaven for?'
- He was intensely optimistic and believed that 'God's in His Heaven—All's right with the world!'. Another of his famous lines reassures us: 'Grow old along with me! / The best is yet to be.'

- He was adept at using both blank verse and rhyme. 'My Last Duchess' and 'Andrea del Sarto' are good examples of poems in which blank verse was used and 'Child Roland to the Dark Tower Came' of rhymed verse.

Elizabeth Barrett Browning (1806–61)

The Battle of Marathon (1820)
An Essay on Mind and Other Poems (1826)
The Seraphim and Other Poems (1838)
Poems (1844)
A Drama of Exile (1845)
Sonnets from the Portuguese (1850)
Casa Guidi Windows (1851)
Aurora Leigh (1857)
Poems before Congress (1860)

Translation

Aeschylus: Prometheus Bound (1833)

Life

Elizabeth Barrett was the eldest of twelve children of Edward Moulton Barrett, a wealthy man who had an inheritance from his family's plantations in Jamaica. She was educated at home and was well-versed in the classics. After the death of her mother and a decline in family fortunes, they moved first to Devon and later to London. She had serious health issues and the death of her brother in a boating accident added to this. As a result, she became a recluse.

She spent all her time writing poems which established her reputation as a poet. It was then that her correspondence with Browning began, and eventually blossomed into a romance. They had to keep their romance a secret from her tyrannical father who had forbidden his children from marrying. They eloped to Italy and settled in Florence. They lived very happily and had a son. Her health also improved greatly. Both of them enjoyed the friendship of eminent people like Tennyson, Ruskin, Carlyle and Rossetti. After some years, her health began to decline again and she died in her husband's arms in 1862.

Works

Elizabeth Barrett Browning was the most celebrated female poet of the Victorian Age. She wrote on diverse topics ranging from love poems to poems on radical political issues and women's liberation. She was famous in England and America and was a great influence on Emily Dickenson and Edgar Allan Poe. She is best remembered today for her lyric, 'How Do I Love Thee' and her magnum opus, *Aurora Leigh*.

Her first book was written when she was just twelve years old—the four-book epic, *The Battle of Marathon*. Her next work, at the age of twenty, was *An Essay on Mind, with Other Poems*. She also translated Aeschylus's *Prometheus Bound*.

It was with the publication of *The Seraphim and Other Poems*, that her reputation as a poet was established. The two volume *Poems* placed her on the top rung of eminent literary figures of the day. It was this work that attracted the attention of Browning who began a correspondence with her.

Sonnets from the Portuguese, a sonnet sequence of forty-four sonnets tracing the development of her romance with Browning, contain some of her most memorable lyrics, including 'How do I love thee? Let me count the ways'.

Her greatest achievement was her verse novel *Aurora Leigh*. It is a combination of epic romance and bildungsroman. Often compared to Wordsworth's *The Prelude*, it traces not only the growth of a woman poet, but also a woman's struggle to attain artistic and economic independence. It was a great success in spite of its radical departure from the conventional Victorian ideals of femininity. Through her work, she showed how women and men could work together. She was the first to prove to English readers that women could occupy an equal place in the poetic tradition of the country.

Features

- She had an excellent and spontaneous diction and rhythm, although some of her works might appear a trifle sentimental now.
- She wrote on a number of social issues, as for instance, child labour in the poem 'The Cry of the Children'. She also addressed political problems like the freedom of countries like Italy, from foreign control.

Matthew Arnold (1822–88)

Poetry
The Strayed Reveller and Other Poems (1849)
Empedocles on Etna and Other Poems (1852)
Poems: A new Edition (1853)
Poems, Second Series (1855)
Merope (verse tragedy, 1858)
The New Poems (1867)

Prose
The Popular Education of France (1861)
On Translating Homer (1861)
Essays in Criticism: First Series (1865)
On the Study of Celtic Literature (1867)
Culture and Anarchy (1869)
St Paul and Protestantism (1870)
Friendship's Garland (1871)
Literature and Dogma (1873)
God and the Bible (1875)
Last Essays on Church and Religion (1877)
Essays in Criticism: Second Series (1888)

Life

Matthew Arnold was the oldest son of Thomas Arnold, headmaster of the famous English school, Rugby. He studied in Rugby and Oxford University and became inspector of schools for poor children and served in this capacity for thirty-five years. This enabled him to travel extensively throughout England and gain first-hand knowledge of its social conditions. He used this knowledge in his later critical writings.

In 1851, he married Fanny Lucy Wightman and had six children. In 1857, Arnold was elected Professor of Poetry at Oxford University. Through this post, he was able to deliver several lectures in English as against his predecessors who lectured only in Latin. Many of his lectures were later published as books. His fame as a critic grew steadily and he was invited to deliver lectures in America. He died in Liverpool, while waiting for the arrival of his daughter Lucy from America.

Works

Matthew Arnold was one of the most influential writers and thinkers of the Victorian Age. He was a multifaceted personality who excelled as a poet, essayist, literary critic and theoretician, orator, educationist and social reformer. His writings not only offered useful guidelines to a society that was going through a metamorphosis, politically and culturally, but also presented instructions on refining literary taste. His contribution to Victorian poetry and prose were of equal measure.

POETRY

His poetic works, though very few in number when compared to his contemporaries, Browning and Tennyson, are of a very high quality. No other poet of his age was more concerned with the problems besetting their age and his poetry reflects his deep anguish. He believed that literature must directly address the moral needs of readers.

Arnold was a poet with a mission. Through his writings, he wished 'to animate and ennoble' his readers. This driving force behind his writings made Arnold write the most distinctive poems about alienation and doubt. His best friend was the poet, Arthur Hugh Clough, with whom he shared his anguish about the spiritual bankruptcy of the Victorian age. He dealt with this dissatisfaction by writing about it in his poems. Some of the works that belong to this period of his literary activity were his first volume of poems *The Strayed Reveller and Other Poems* followed by the second collection called *Empedocles on Etna, and other Poems*. His famous poem 'Dover Beach' also belongs to this period but was published much later in the collection entitled *Poems, Second Series*.

Arnold had great love for the countryside and he tried to explore the relationship between his emotions and external objects. He was on a constant quest for identity and there is a note of nostalgia for the past and a lost childhood in his poems. We hear his melancholy voice clearly in the famous lines from 'Dover Beach' that follow:

> …for the world, which seems
> To lie before us like a land of dreams,
> So various, so beautiful, so new,
> Hath really neither joy, nor love, nor light,
> Nor certitude, nor peace, nor help for pain;
> And we are here as on a darkling plain
> Swept with confused alarms of struggle and flight,
> Where ignorant armies clash by night.

PROSE

Arnold firmly believed that the Victorian Age offered no creative material to the poets as it was 'an age wanting in moral grandeur… an age of spiritual discomfort'. He urged his contemporaries to turn to Sophocles and Aeschylus to draw inspiration for the universal 'great actions'. Unable to follow his own advice, Arnold turned away from poetry after the mid-1850s. He became increasingly frustrated with both his society as well as his poetry. He was unhappy with his poetry as he felt that it merely presented 'a continuous state of mental distress … unrelieved by incident, hope, or resistance, in which there is everything to be endured, nothing to be done'.

From an anguished poet, Arnold emerged as a social reformer who tried to mend the ways of a hopelessly materialistic society after he joined Oxford University. He delivered several lectures, which he published as essays, in which he urged the people to go back to Greek classical literature in order to reform their taste. Arnold believed that going back to the classics could save the Victorians from the morally depraved state into which they had slipped. Some of the important books that emerged during this period of his life included *On Translating Homer* (1861) and *On the Modern Element in Literature* (1869).

LITERARY CRITICISM

The publication of the canonical book *Essays in Criticism* in 1865, proved to be an important milestone in the history of literary criticism. The first essay 'The Function of Criticism at the Present Time' contains the main theme of his concepts. It expounds the idea that the function of criticism 'is a disinterested endeavour to learn and propagate the best that is known and thought in the world, and thus to establish a current of fresh and true ideas'. He placed on the critics the responsibility of guiding their readers by reforming their taste. A greater knowledge of the literatures of other countries was also advocated by Arnold. A look at the topics discussed in this book reflects Arnold's wide spectrum of knowledge. In the second essay, 'The Literary Influence of Academics', he criticises the provinciality of English writers. One can gauge the extent to which Arnold attempted to widen the intellectual horizon of criticism by a mere glimpse at the contents of this book. He deals with various writers and thinkers like Spinoza, Tolstoy and Guerin apart from poets like Milton, Keats and Wordsworth.

The second volume of *Essays in Criticism* appeared in 1888. 'The Study of Poetry' is the first essay in this volume in which he says poetry will have to serve the role of religion in an age of rapidly deteriorating religious beliefs. He said people will be looking to poetry to 'interpret life' for them. It is therefore of vital importance for one, to be able to distinguish good poetry from bad. In order to be able to do this without any prejudice of biographical or historical influence, he advocated the 'touchstone' method. He selected some passages of 'high seriousness' which were admirable for their style, diction and movement and used them as a benchmark with which a work could be compared and evaluated. This method of criticism was found defective by later critics as it focused only on high seriousness, ignoring the humourous, satirical or the lyrical. Another drawback to this method, was that it does not take into account the poet's age, background or intent.

In *Culture and Anarchy*, he severely criticised his contemporaries for being selfish and for not having the greater good of society in mind. He felt that the English aristocracy was 'barbarian' and the middle class were 'philistines'. He believed that only education could unite the antagonistic factions of British society, by inculcating a respect for 'sweetness and light'—a phrase taken from Swift's *The Battle of the Books*.

His books of religion *St Paul and Protestantism* (1870), *Literature and Dogma* (1873) and *God and the Bible* (1875) gave rise to a lot of protests from both the religious as well as the agnostic.

Features

- Arnold was neither a prophetic critic like Carlyle nor a visionary poet of social reform like Elizabeth Barret Browning. He merely gave a prescription to society to

overcome the issues thrown up by the introduction of democracy and the sudden scientific revelations.
- His poetry accurately captures the conflict, doubt and pessimism of the age.
- He had a classical style of writing poetry, which had a formal and stately beauty.
- As a literary critic, he played a very important role as he gave to the genre a significance and dignity hitherto unknown. His wide knowledge and vast reading made him one of the great intellects of not only his own times, but of future generations too.
- Although there is a lot of criticism of his touchstone method and comparative criticism, he proved to have a great influence on later poets and critics like T.S. Eliot, F.R. Leavis and Lionel Trilling.

Dante Gabriel Rossetti (1828–82)

Poetry

'The Blessed Damozel' in *The Germ* (1850)

'My Sister's Sleep' in *The Germ* (1850)

Sixteen sonnets in *The Fortnightly Review* (1869)

Poems (1870)

Poems (1881)

Ballads and Sonnets (1881)

Prose

'The Stealthy School of Criticism' in *The Athenaeum* (1872)

'Hand and Soul' in *The Germ* (1850)

Translation

Dante and his Circle (1874)

Life

Rossetti was the son of an Italian political refugee who was not only a poet but also a scholar of Dante. Rosetti's sister, Christina Rossetti, was also a poet who started composing poems even before she could write. Rosetti himself showed signs of genius and was sent to study art at the Royal Academy of Arts. It was there that he befriended William Holman Hunt and John Everett Millais and founded the **Pre-Raphaelite** group.

His personal life was unconventional and unpredictable. His first wife committed suicide which devastated him. Overcome by sorrow, he buried some of his unpublished poems along with his wife's body. A few years later, he had the poems exhumed and published. Next, he fell hopelessly in love with William Morris's wife. Finally, he married a woman called Fanny Cornforth and lived with her. During his later years, he suffered from ill health and depression. In 1882, he died in the house of a friend and was buried at Birchington-on-Sea, in Kent.

Works

Rossetti had a double career as artist and poet. As one of the founders of the Pre-Raphaelite Movement, he aimed to reject the contemporary conventions of painting and return to the natural light and realistic detail of the fourteenth and fifteenth century painters, who preceded Raphael. Although his paintings were not accepted initially, later he found admirers and he was able to make a modest living out of them. Rossetti once said, 'If any man has any poetry in him, he should paint it.' Like William Blake, Rossetti was skilled both as a poet and a painter.

He published his early poems 'The Blessed Damozel' and 'My Sister's Sleep' in the Pre-Raphaelite journal, *The Germ*. These poems reflect the conflict in his mind between the mystical and the factual, ultimately culminating in the triumph of the sensual. He was attacked by critics for being immoral in his emphasis on sensual details. He recreated a dream world which was intangible and magical. In 'The Blessed Damozel', he combines the spiritual with the sensual—something he could not achieve in his own life. The poem is based on genuine Christian faith, but totters on heresy in suggesting that the loss of earthly love could cause dissatisfaction in Heaven. In it, Rossetti made full use of symbols. This style, known as symbolism, refers to the usage of a concrete image to convey an emotion or an abstract idea. 'The Blessed Damozel' is replete with symbols that are religious in nature. For example, the three lilies in the Damozel's hand symbolise the Holy Trinity—Father, Son and the Holy Spirit; the gold bar is the symbol of a gate separating the Damozel from her earthly lover and the stars signify the fact that she has become a guiding star to the earthly lover. The Symbolist poets of the late nineteenth century were greatly influenced by Rossetti.

After the publication of his *Poems* in 1870, a critic called Robert Buchanan attacked the poems in his essay entitled 'The Fleshly School of Poetry'. Rossetti gave a counter-argument to this in his essay 'The Stealthy School of Criticism'. He continued to write and paint and became an inspiration to a new generation of aesthetics led by writers like Walter Pater and Oscar Wilde. Rossetti can be considered as an important figure in the promotion of Aestheticism. His aestheticism combined the erotic with the ideal and the sensuous with the poetic. This unique blend was a decisive force in the shaping of English aestheticism.

Ballads and Sonnets was published in 1881. He drew his inspiration for his ballads from the poets of the Middle Ages to which he gave a contemporary twist with his artistic sensibility. He made continual use of the refrain but the end result was one of artificiality. This volume also contained a sonnet sequence called 'The House of Life' which had forty-seven sonnets. These sonnets express his love for his wife. They use mystic symbolism and have a subtlety which sometimes is obscure. The Italian influence is evident in much of his poetry which has a warm and sensuous quality.

Features

- His poems are representative of the Pre-Raphaelite style of writing in their deliberate, semi-mystical quaintness of language and use of mysterious symbols.
- Both his paintings as well as his poems combine the spiritual with the erotic.
- Unlike Arnold, Rossetti distanced himself from the problems besetting his age. His work presents a world far removed from the Victorian Age as he firmly believed that art should exist only for art's sake and have no other agenda.
- He had a great influence on the writers of the next generation.

Christina Rossetti (1830–94)

Verses (1847)
'Up-Hill' in *Macmillan's Magazine* (1861)
'A Birthday' in *Macmillan's Magazine* (1861)
Goblin Market and Other Poems (1862)
The Prince's Progress and Other Poems (1866)
Sing-Song, a Nursery Rhyme Book (1872)
A Pageant and Other Poems (1881)
Time Flies: A Reading Diary (1885)
New Poems (1896)

Life

Christina Rossetti was born in London in 1830 and was the youngest of the Rossetti children. She was the sister of the famous Dante Gabriel Rossetti. She was educated at home and was raised in a very intellectual atmosphere. During her childhood, her home was the meeting place for a passionate group of Italian exiles. Christina and her two brothers, Dante and William showed signs of their poetic abilities and art at a very early age.

Her life changed drastically when her father became an invalid and the family had to face severe financial difficulties. As a teenager, she suffered from ill health herself, and turned to religion. She, along with her mother and sister, was a devout High Anglican and broke off her engagements a few times due to religious differences. She lived with her mother and sometimes modelled for her brother's drawings. She lived a religious life and never married. She died in 1894 and was buried in the family grave at Highgate Cemetery.

Works

Christina Rossetti was a gifted writer who began composing poems ever since she was a child. Being a woman, she could not become a member of the Pre-Raphaelite group but she contributed poems to their journal, *The Germ*. Although she was shy by nature, she had a social life that included some of the literary luminaries of the day like Browning, Ruskin, Lewis Carroll, Swinburne and the Pre-Raphaelites.

Goblin Market and Other Poems was published in 1862 and this brought in its wake a lot of critical acclaim. Mostly regarded as a children's tale, the poem is now being examined as a representation of the struggle between the self and the soul. Impressed by her outstanding technique and keen observation, Edmund Gosse called her the 'high priestess of Pre-Raphaelitism'. This volume was followed by *The Prince's Progress and Other Poems*, *Sing-Song*, *A Nursery Rhyme Book* and *A Pageant and Other Poems*. Her work ranged from fantasy poems for the young to ballads, love sonnets and religious poetry.

She wrote a lot of prose, especially of a devotional nature. These included *Time Flies: A Reading Diary*, which consists of a passage of prose for each day of the year.

Features

- Christina Rossetti expressed herself equally eloquently in both prose and verse. She attempted a vast range of literary forms and was comfortable in all of them.
- There is a preoccupation with the theme of death in her works, probably caused by years of caring for dying family members.
- She was a spontaneous writer who could express herself lucidly.
- A sense of melancholy can be seen throughout her work, which sometimes borders on the morbid.
- There is a religious austerity in her style of writing.
- Many of her poems deal with the theme of failure in love.

Algernon Charles Swinburne (1837–1909)

Poetry
Poems and Ballads (1866)
A Song of Italy (1867)
William Blake (1868)
Songs before Sunrise (1871)
Poems and Ballads Second Series (1878)
A Study of Shakespeare (1880)
Mary Stuart (1881)
Tristram of Lyonesse and Other Poems (1882)
Marino Faliero (1885)
Poems and Ballads third Series (1889)

Drama
The Queen Mother and Rosamund (1860)
Chastelard (1865)
Atalanta in Calydon (1865)

Bothwell (1874)
Erechtheus (1876)

Prose
A Study of Ben Jonson (1889)

Novel
A Year's Letters(1877)
Lesbia Brandon (1952)

Life

He was born in London and spent most of his childhood on the Isle of Wight. His father was an admiral and his mother was the daughter of an Earl. From an early age, he was obsessed with the sea and earned the nickname, 'seagull'. He was educated in Eton and Oxford. His friends were Rossetti and Morris and he became a close associate of the Pre-Raphaelite Movement.

He lived a wild and bohemian life in London impressing people with impromptu recitations of his own erotic verse. When his beloved cousin, Mary Gordon got married, he was devastated and spent the next fourteen years in self-destruction. He had several breakdowns after drunken sprees and was finally taken by a friend to the rural suburb of Putney, where he spent the last three decades of his life.

Works

He took the Victorian world by storm with his poetry, which depicted love that was not only passionate but also often perverted and sadistic. He replaced the delicate sentiments and declarations of love, that the restrained Victorians were used to, with frenzy and brutality.

DRAMA

Swinburne began his literary career as a dramatist. He wrote in a lyrical and poetic style that reflected the influence of the Elizabethan dramatists. His first drama *The Queen Mother and Rosamund* is about Catherine de Medici, the Queen consort of Henry II, King of France. It was his second drama *Atlanta in Calydon* that attracted public notice. Based on a story from Greek mythology, Swinburne wrote a play styled on the Greek tragedy, complete with a chorus, lyrical odes and high seriousness.

His next drama *Chasteland* was about Mary, Queen of Scots. This play raised doubts about the morality of his verses, as it narrates the story of a French courtier, Chasteland, who falls passionately in love with the Queen.

POETRY

His collection of poems published in 1866, *Poems and Ballads*, contained sixty-two lyrics that reflected his metrical genius and also at the same time, his scandalous themes. These include dramatic monologues whose speakers include a necrophiliac lover, a sadist and an incestuous mother. Understandably, this book provoked the staid Victorians and there was public outrage.

His next two works, *A Song of Italy* and *Song before Sunrise* express his views on Italy's struggle for independence and his hatred for authority. The second series of *Poems and Ballads* was more subdued than the first and contained poems like 'A Forsaken Garden'. After moving to the countryside, he continued to write, but his writing lacked the force and vigour of his earlier work.

PROSE

Apart from creative writing, Swinburne was preoccupied with literary criticism throughout his life. In some of his writings, his views were marred by his personal prejudice. His keen sense of discernment was revealed in many of his critical pieces, especially in his studies on the Elizabethan and Jacobean dramatists. Among his critical writings, *William Blake*, *A Study of Shakespeare* and *A Study of Ben Jonson* rank the highest.

Features

- While the other Pre-Raphaelites were painters and wrote poetry that had richness of detail, Swinburne was more interested in music. He focused more on sound effects than images. He was essentially lyrical, even in his drama.
- Swinburne was most admired for his style. We find in his poctry, his attempt to convey all the senses, especially that of sound.
- His favourite theme was love which he expressed without restraint.
- His poems abound in descriptions of the sea, for which he had a great passion.

- His critical writing was original but erred in its excess of both praise and fault. He had a tendency to overuse superlatives which irked the reader. One should make a note that his critical writings were founded on direct knowledge and close reading of the authors concerned.

Thomas Carlyle (1795–1881)

Life of Schiller (1825)
Sartor Resartus (1833-1834)
French Revolution (1837)
On Heroes and Hero-Worship and the Heroic in History (1841)
Past and Present (1843)
Oliver Cromwell's Letters and Speeches (1845)
Life of Sterling (1851)
The History of Frederick II of Prussia (six volumes, 1858–65)

Pamphlet

Chartism (1839)

Satire

Latter-Day Pamphlets (Series of Satires) (1850)

Translation

Wilhelm Meister (1824)

Life

Carlyle was born in a small village in Scotland and was the son of a stonemason. He had a strict Calvinist upbringing and was taught the value of hard work from a very early age. He was sent to the University of Edinburgh to study for the ministry. He was however filled with religious doubts and gave up his aim of joining the church, to become a school teacher. He did not find this vocation suitable either and finally turned to a literary career. He also devoted himself to German studies.

He married Jane Welsh, a woman with literary interest, and they lived together for nearly forty years. They lived for a few years in a remote farm, where he wrote some of his famous essays. Later, they moved to London, where they spent the rest of their lives. After the demise of his wife, he suffered from ill health and a growing dissatisfaction with all the changes that were taking place at that time—industrial, political and scientific. He died in London and was buried in the small village in Scotland where he was born.

Works

The writings of Carlyle had a great impact on his contemporaries. He was among the prominent intellectual leaders of his time who tried to shake his age from its complacency. He opposed the materialism of the utilitarians and placed his trust on the individual and the organisation of society. Although he rejected a career in the field of religion, there was a mysticism and a Puritanical spirituality in him which made him write about guiding England from a pious country to a new state of independent morality. He was against mere material progress and pointed out that the prosperity of the Victorian Age was shallow and that it concealed a terrible pauperism beneath it.

He was also very critical of democracy. While he upheld the right of every citizen to vote, he pointed out that literacy was a necessary prerequisite for responsible participation in democracy. He believed that granting franchise to the illiterate would only lead to disaster. These ideas were vehemently discussed by him in his various writings which influenced his fellow Victorians like Mill, Tennyson, Browning, Dickens and Ruskin.

He began his literary career with translations, essays and biographies. A great admirer of German literature, he translated Goethe's *Wilhelm Meister's Apprenticeship*. Being a Calvinist, he was troubled by the conflict of good and evil. It was at this troubled time that he wrote *Sartor Resartus*, a kind of allegorical autobiography. The novel is a biography of a German philosopher, but serves as a means of expressing Carlyle's own spiritual struggles in his youth.

Carlyle next turned his attention to historical writing. His *French Revolution* written in the most passionate and vivid style, brought to the forefront the horrors of the Reign of Terror. His descriptions of the storming of the Bastille and the death of Robespierre are unequalled. His approach to history was very unconventional. In a highly fervent style, he traced the downfall of the callous French aristocracy which had to be replaced by a better society. In their destruction, he read a warning for England which was rapidly abandoning the country to democracy and laissez-faire capitalists. After the publication of *The French Revolution*, he received widespread public recognition. People looked up to him as a sage and prophet and he was often referred to as the 'Sage of Chelsea.'

He was invited to give a series of lectures which were later published as *On Heroes and Hero-Worship*. His heroes were Odin, Mahomet, Dante, Shakespeare, Luther, Knox, Johnson, Rousseau, Burns, Cromwell and Napoleon. Before Carlyle elevated them to the status of heroes, most of them were not considered to be heroic. Carlyle believed that by studying history's heroes, one could understand one's true nature. He said, 'The history of the world is but a biography of great men.'

The essays that were written by him in the first few years of his literary career were mostly on German subjects. He was a great admirer of Goethe and looked up to him to guide his troubled soul from the Age of Machinery. He contributed his essays to journals in order to earn his living. These essays were later collected and published as books. Examples of these were *Chartism; Past and Present* and *Later-Day Pamphlets*. In these essays, he deals with a number of topics like politics, biographical sketches, literary and social criticism and history. He found the essay form a suitable vehicle to address the problems of his times.

Oliver Cromwell's Letters and Speeches reintroduced the much-maligned historical character. One could, for the first time, hear the voice of Cromwell himself through his speeches and letters. Through his book, Carlyle was able to reinvent the character of Cromwell who was looked at as a usurper and regicide.

His *Frederick the Great*, published in six volumes, was hailed as Carlyle's masterpiece. He spared no pains in elevating his hero to heroic proportions. *Life of Sterling* was a more modest biography and has some remarkable reminiscences of Coleridge.

Most of his ideas, lauded during his time, are considered to be irrational today. To quote Hudson, 'Anti-scientific in his reading of history, Carlyle is also anti-democratic in the practical lessons he deduces from it.' He believed that the masses could not be trusted to solve for themselves the intricate problems that they had to face.

Features

- Carlyle was considered a social prophet and critic and had a tremendous influence on his contemporaries. However, his thoughts and teachings, so highly valued in his time, seem exaggerated to the present readers.
- Carlyle's approach to history was unconventional. He wrote in a dramatic style and tried to bring the past to life by focusing on details. His history was essentially biographical as he believed that only the hero could transform society.
- He was a moral critic who attempted to stir his contemporaries from their complacency. He tried to lead his country back to a more spiritual life.
- He was against democracy and the rapid developments in science. He attacked materialism and utilitarianism.

John Stuart Mill (1806–73)

Essays
'Bentham' (in *London and Westminster Review)* (1838)
'Coleridge' (in *London and Westminster Review*) (1840)
'What is Poetry?' (1833)
'On Liberty' (1859)
Prose
System of Logic (1843)
Principles of Political Economy (1848)
Thoughts on Parliamentary Reform (1859)
Dissertations and Discussions (1859)
Representative Government (1861)
Utilitarianism (1861)
Auguste Comte and Positivism (1865)
The Subjection of Women (1869)
Autobiography (1873)

Life

John Stuart Mill was born in London in 1806. He was the son of James Mill, a Scottish political theorist and philosopher. He was home-schooled by his father who wanted to prove that a child could learn a great deal at a very young age. He began teaching his son Greek when he was just three years old and made him memorise several Greek words and their English translations. He also taught him history, geography, calculus, psychology, political economy and several more subjects. His father declared that he had completed his education when Mill was fourteen. Mill acknowledged in his autobiography that by that age, he had acquired the knowledge and intellectual maturity of a forty-year-old man.

This experiment that his father tried on him proved to be very costly. Mill was deprived of the usual pleasures of childhood which led to a nervous breakdown in 1826. He recovered from his depression by reading the poems of Wordsworth.

He got a job in the East India Company through his father's help. At the same time, he began to show interest in writing and politics. He formed the Utilitarian Society that met for a few years to read essays and discuss them. He met and fell in love with Harriet Taylor, a married woman with three children. He could marry her only twenty years later, after her husband died. She shared his views on women's rights and Mill gave her equal credit for his works.

After the East India Company ceased to exist in 1858, Mill was elected member of parliament, in which capacity he made some excellent speeches. He died in 1873.

Works

Mill turned to Wordsworth during his extreme state. Wordsworth's poetry aroused in Mill an interest in the everyday thoughts and feelings of the common man. His essay 'What is Poetry?' argues that true poetry expresses the passionate and solitary meditations of the poet. He famously said that these thoughts recorded in poetry are not heard but 'overheard'.

Gradually, he began to move away from the teachings of Bentham. Although he did not completely break away from him, Mill's views were more liberal compared to those of Bentham. Mill expanded the principles of utilitarianism with elements of idealism, justice and moral progress. He also emphasised the importance of personal liberty. This shift is reflected in his early essays, 'Bentham' and Coleridge'. These were followed by *System of Logic* and *Principles of Political Economy*, which were recognised as standard works on the subject. He also wrote several influential books on philosophy, politics and economics such as *Thoughts on*

Parliamentary Reform, *Utilitarianism*, *Representative Government* and *Auguste Comte and Positivism*.

His essay 'On Liberty' is an oft-studied piece of literature. In it, he defended the rights of the individual in a society dominated by bureaucracy and mass culture. Another famous work of Mill's was *The Subjection of Women* in which he insisted on granting perfect equality to women. In his final work *Autobiography*, he detailed his intellectual and moral journey from his early childhood and onwards.

Features

- Mill expressed himself with clarity and tried to counter probable objections to his theories by giving examples to support his arguments.
- His contribution to the concept of freedom of speech and women's equality was monumental.
- His best work was in the examination of social life.
- He wrote in a clear and simple prose that resounded with sincerity.
- His views were considered radical by Victorian standards, because he advocated equal rights for women, the right to divorce, universal suffrage and free speech. He was a leading philosopher of his age.

John Ruskin (1819–1900)

Modern Painters (five volumes, 1834–60)
The Seven Lamps of Architecture (1849)
The Stones of Venice (1851–53)
The King of the Golden River (1851)
Pre-Raphaelitism (1851)
Lectures on Architecture and Painting (1853)
The Political Economy of Art (1857)
The Two Paths (1859)
Sesame and Lilies (1865)
Ethics and the Dust (1866)
The Crown of Wild Olives (1866)
Fors Clavigera (1871–87)
Unto this Last (1860)
Munera Pulveris (1862)
Lectures on Art (1870)
Aratra Pentelici (1872)
The Relation between Michael Angelo and Tintoret (1872)
The Eagle's Nest (1872)

Love's Meinie (1873, 1881)
Ariadne Fiorentina (1873–76)
Praeterita (1885–1900)
Time and Tide (1888)

Life

Ruskin was the only child of middle-class parents and was born in London. He grew up in Surrey and was educated at home. He had a strict upbringing and a sheltered life. Later, he went to Christ Church College in Oxford.

Ruskin and his parents loved travelling which took them to several parts of Europe. He was fascinated by the architecture and art that he saw there, especially in Italy. These travels resulted in making him one of the most insightful art critics of the nineteenth century.

In 1869, he was appointed as the first Slade Professor of Fine Art at Oxford (the oldest professorship of art and art history at the universities of Oxford, Cambridge and London), which he had to give up after ten years due to ill health. He resumed the post after a break and worked for a few years more. His lectures were immensely popular and most of them were published. He spent his retired life in the Lake District, where he lived till his death.

Works

Ruskin's parents inculcated in him a deep reverence for the Bible, firm political views, a love for romantic literature and an interest in art. He began his career as an art critic. He looked at art as being a mirror of the moral disposition of the age which produced it. To Ruskin, art criticism was thus the same as social criticism. He fervently denounced the ugliness and materialismof the Victorian Age, which was experiencing a rapid decline in spirituality. His mission in life was to create a taste for the lovely and harmonious life that was free from the tyranny of the machine.

He was appalled by the apathy around him, which he believed, sprang from cowardice. He was repelled by the ugliness of the industrial world and the absence of good taste. In this campaign, he was a disciple of Carlyle.

He began writing *Modern Painters* in a series of five volumes. He praised Turner as being a great artist who captured nature better than the Dutch realists. These volumes were published over seventeen years and reflect Ruskin's transition from his preoccupation with art and nature to humanism and society.

In *The Seven Lamps of Architecture* and *The Stones of Venice*, he praised Gothic art and shared his contempt for Renaissance art. He believed that the former was the product of genuine faith while the latter was the product of Paganism.

Unto this Last is about economics, where he rages against the injustice of laissez-faire capitalism and urges employers to care for their workers. This book was not received well by his contemporaries, but succeeded in influencing the radical political thinkers who became the founders of the British Labour Party. Mahatma Gandhi after reading this book wrote, 'All Ruskin's words captivated me … I lay awake all night and there and then I decided to change my whole life.'

Among the most popular of his shorter works is *Sesame and Lilies*. In this book, he combined the two lectures 'Of King's Treasuries' and 'Of Queen's Gardens'. In the former lecture, he criticises Victorian men and in the latter, he advises women to take their role as the moral guides of men very seriously. He urges parents of girls to educate their daughters, keeping this end in view. In present times, these ideas appear outdated and chauvinistic.

In 1871, he began *Fors Clavigera*, a collection of letters addressed to the working men of England. Towards the end of his life, he started writing his autobiography *Praeterita*. In it, he chose to record only whatever gave him pleasure in remembering.

Features

- Ruskin's prose style was poetic and beautiful. There is a biblical eloquence in his early works. Later, he changed his style to a simpler one.
- He had a great influence on his contemporaries such as Charlotte Bronte and George Eliot. His constant demand for moral sincerity in art in an age of commercialism, immediately appealed to several of his readers.

- He was respected for his critical views on art and architecture. He believed that art should reflect nature and emphasised the importance of detailed observation. His writings helped in reviving the Gothic architectural style which he considered to be superior to other styles. His book *The Stones of Venice* especially played a significant role in popularising the Gothic Revival Movement.
- He was a social critic who drew people's attention to the exploitation of the labourers and the disappearance of traditional craftsmanship.

John Henry Newman (1801–90)

Contributions to *Tracts for the Times* (1840–41)
The Idea of a University Defined and Illustrated (1873)
Apologia pro Vita Sua (1864)
The Grammar of Assent (1870)

Novel

Loss and Gain (1848)
Callista (1856)

Poetry

Lyra Apostolica (poems by six authors, 1834)
'The Dream of Gerontius' (1866)
Verses on Various Occasions (1868)

Life

Cardinal Newman was born in London and studied at Oxford University. He was a famous theologian and poet who influenced people through his sermons and writings. He was an Anglican clergyman and an important member of the **Oxford Movement**, a movement begun in Oxford by a group of men to revive faith at a time of disillusionment and despair. Newman, in his struggles to discover the authority of the Anglican Church in early church history, became convinced about the authenticity of Catholicism. His conversion to Catholicism sent shock waves throughout England.

He went to Rome and was ordained. After returning to England, he settled down at Birmingham and established an oratory there. He served as rector of the new Catholic university in Dublin in which capacity, he delivered several lectures on university education. In 1879, he was made cardinal. He continued to preach and write all his life. He died of pneumonia in Birmingham in 1890.

Works

Newman's earliest literary work consisted of several poems that were a part of *Lyra Apostolica*. The most well-known of these was the famous and evergreen hymn 'Lead Kindly Light'. In the same year, he began *Tracts for the Times*, which was an important tool of the Oxford Movement, of which Newman was a prominent member. Gradually, Newman began to move towards the Roman Catholic Church.

While serving as rector in the Catholic University of Ireland, his lectures and essays were collected and published as *The Idea of the University Defined and Illustrated*. In these lectures, he advocated theological teaching and the tutorial system.

Apologies pro Vita Sua was written by Newman in response to an attack on his teachings by Charles Kingsley. It is a sincere account of his spiritual journey and is an admirable example of his formidable powers of argument. This book had a great impact on even those who did not share his views on religion.

'The Spread of Gerontius' is a poem depicting the journey of a pious man's soul. It includes the famous hymn, 'Praise to the Holiest in the Height'. He expounded his thoughts on the nature of belief in *The Grammar of Assent*.

He wrote two novels, *Loss and Gain* and *Callista*. The former reflects the religious fervour of the Oxford Movement, and traces the gradual conversion of its protagonist to the Catholic religion. *Callista* narrates the tale of the persecution and martyrdom of a Christian sculptor in the third century.

Features

- Newman's chief contribution lay in his theory of religious belief. He opposed the purely rational attitude that was becoming rampant in the mid-nineteenth century.
- Newman had a strong and elegant diction and knew how to use irony.
- He had the gift of giving expression to the most complex conflicts of the heart in a lucid manner.

Oscar Wilde (1856–1900)

Poetry
Poems (1881)
'The Sphinx' (1894)
'The Ballad of Reading Gaol' (1898)

Fiction
Lord Arthur Savile's Crime and Other Stories (1887)
The Canterville Ghost (1887)
The Picture of Dorian Gray (1890)
The Happy Prince and Other Stories (fairy tales, 1888)
The House of Pomegranates (fairy tales, 1891)

Drama
Salome (1892)
The Duchess of Padua (1883)
Lady Windermere's Fan (1892)
A Woman of No Importance (1893)
An Ideal Husband (1895)
The Importance of Being Ernest (1895)

Literary Criticism
Intentions (1891)
De Profundis (1905)

Life

Oscar Wilde was born in Ireland. His father was a surgeon and his mother a fairly well-known writer. He studied in Trinity College, Dublin, and later at Magdalene College, Oxford. While at Oxford, he was influenced by the Pre-Raphaelite poets. He was also equally influenced by both Ruskin, who claimed that all good art was moral art, and Walter Pater, who believed in the art for art's sake concept. He displayed his literary abilities while at Oxford by winning the Newdigate Prize for his poem 'Ravenna'.

He went to London, where he soon became the centre of the social scene. He was greatly admired for his witty and conversational skills. The opera *Patience* by Gillbert and Sullivan satirised the **'fleshly poetry'** (a derogatory term hinting at the sensuality and moral laxity of the Aesthetic Movement) of Rossetti and Swinburne by exaggerating aesthetic mannerisms. Though Wilde was not the intended target of the satire, he came to be identified with the character Bunthorne of the opera. Wilde, however, was not insulted by this and used this to his own advantage. He even published a book of poems called *Poems* in 1881, mimicking the aesthetic style of the characters in *Patience*. The New York production of *Patience* led to an invitation for Wilde to lecture in the United States. He stayed there for a year and returned to England, rich and famous. He got married and had two sons for whom he wrote some fairy tales. His marriage, however, did not last long.

When he was at the peak of his career, his homosexual relationship with Lord Alfred Douglas landed him in trouble and he was prosecuted and sentenced to two years in jail. While in jail, he wrote a long letter, *De Profundis*, to Douglas blaming him for his selfishness. He chose to have this letter published only after his death.

He was a broken man, both mentally as well as financially. He left England and changed his name to Sebastian Melmoth and died in Paris.

Works

Wilde made a name for himself in poetry, prose and drama and one can discern the spirit of the **decadent school** of the 1890s. This was a movement that began in Europe and was characterised by a disillusionment with the world, a spirit of skepticism and a delight in perversion. The movement rejected Victorian morality and displayed a fascination with the macabre and the erotic. It shared the ideology of Aestheticism which emphasized the importance of beauty and art for its own sake and believed in the superiority of human creativity.

POETRY

His early poetry was clearly influenced by the Pre-Raphaelites. The poems were far removed from the realities of life and lacked any emotional depth. They were highly decorative in style. *Poems* and 'The Sphinx' were not very well received. 'The Sphinx' is the best example of Wilde's decadent style of poetry. 'The Ballad of Reading Gaol' written after his imprisonment reveals a more mature style. It narrates the sad tale of heartbreak caused by betrayal.

FICTION

Wilde wrote a collection of fairy tales, *The Happy Prince and Other Stories*, for his sons. Though these stories were for children they had a message for adults, too. This was followed by *Lord Arthur Savile's Crime and Other Stories* and *The House of Pomegranates.*

His only novel was *The Picture of Dorian Gray*. This novel reflected Wilde's aestheticism in all its aspects. He established the fact that for the artist, his art was his whole life and was above the rules of society and morality. In the preface to the novel, he said: 'The nineteenth century dislike of Romanticism is the rage of Caliban not seeing his own face in a glass.'

DRAMA

Wilde found his true calling in drama. His plays are all comedies of manners, full of intrigue and witty repartee. His *Lady Windermere's Fan* was a huge success. The sparkling wit and humour which reflected the foibles and superficiality of Victorian society, took London by storm. It is the story of a mother's secret sacrifice for her daughter. The play is a refined social satire that attacks the hypocrisy of the Victorians. The oft-quoted line, 'I can resist everything except temptation', is from this play.

A Woman of No Substance and *An Ideal Husband* followed in quick succession. Wilde in these two plays, like in the earlier one, juxtaposes an intolerant young idealist with a character guilty of a social sin. The plot set against a social backdrop that gave great importance to mere appearances, mocks at Victorian society's rigid ideals and proves that an honest acceptance of one's weakness is preferable to a false pretence to be flawless.

Wilde's masterpiece was *The Importance of Being Earnest*. The title of the play alludes to the Victorian obsession with earnestness as a moral ideal. Wilde said that its philosophy was 'We should treat all trivial things very seriously and all the serious things of life with sincere and studied triviality.' The play is replete with witty dialogues like 'To lose one parent may be regarded as a misfortune; to lose both looks like carelessness.'

PROSE

Wilde chronicled his aesthetic ideas in a series of long prose pieces which were published in the important literary journals of his day. He believed in the autonomy of art and opposed the idea of using art or literature as tools for moralising. Two of his essays, 'The Decay of Lying' and 'The Critic as Artist', were in the form of dialogues. In 'The Decay of Lying', Wilde reveals his preference for romanticism over realism. 'The Critic as Artist' discusses the role of criticism in promoting literary and artistic appreciation. These and a few more essays were collected and published in the volume called *Intentions* in 1891.

Wilde's final piece *De Profundis*, a long letter written while in prison and published after his death, was an anguished autobiography. He reflected on the betrayal and selfishness of Douglas, who did not stand by him when he was prosecuted, and tried to find his own peace of mind in forgiveness.

Features

- Oscar Wilde is one of the best social critics of his age. His comedies serve as an accurate reflection of the hypocrisy of the Victorian Age, especially of the upper classes.
- He breathed new life to the comedy of manners that was so popular in the plays of Congreve and Sheridan. His plays drew audiences back to the theatre, which had become almost defunct in the nineteenth century.
- Wilde is remembered for his witty one-liners and dialogues. His humour and wordplay are hallmarks of his style.
- He was a part of the Aesthetic Movement which emphasised the importance of beauty and art for art's sake. He rejected the notion of art having a moral or utilitarian purpose.

Robert Louis Stevenson (1850–94)

Essays

An Inland Voyage (1878)
Travels with a Donkey in the Cevennes (1879)
Virginibus Puerisque (1881)
Familiar Studies of Men and Books (1882)
New Arabian Nights (1882)
The Silverado Squatters (1883)

Poetry

A Child's Garden of Verses (1885)
Underwoods (1887)

Novels

Treasure Island (1883)
Prince Otto (1885)
The Dynamiter (1885)
Dr Jekyll and Mr Hyde (1886)
Kidnapped (1886)
Underwoods (1887)
The Black Arrow (1888)
The Master of Ballantrae (1889)
The Wrecker (1892)
Catriona (1893)
The Ebb Tide (1894)

Life

Stevenson was the son of an engineer and was born in Edinburgh, Scotland. As he was a sickly child, he could not follow the strenuous career of his father and was initiated into law. Although he became an advocate, his heart was in writing and he had begun to write several essays.

Due to his poor health, he was advised to travel to various places in search of a cure. In France, he met Mrs Fanny Osbourne who was ten years older to him and eventually married her after she obtained a divorce from her husband. While on his travels, he wrote *An Inland Voyage*, describing a canoe trip in Belgium and France and *Travels with a Donkey in the Cevennes.*

He left for California and this trip resulted in *The Silverado Squatters.* After returning to England, he settled down at Bournemouth for the next three years and continued to write essays, travel pieces and short stories. It was during that period that he wrote his famous novels. He set off on a long sea voyage to the Pacific and settled down in the island of Samoa. He died there suddenly from a brain hemorrhage.

Works

His early writings include the travel books *An Inland Voyage* and *Travels with a Donkey in the Cevennes.* Next came the two books of moral essays and criticism—*Virginibus Puerisque* and *Familiar Studies of Men and Books.* The essays in these books belong to the personal essay tradition of Lamb and Hazlitt.

His next publication *New Arabian Nights* was a collection of short stories. Some of the stories from this collection are rated very highly by critics.

The book that brought him great fame and recognition as writer of adventure books was *Treasure Island.* It is a gripping adventure story that has created lasting images of pirates, buried treasure, maps marked with an 'X' and lame seamen carrying parrots on their shoulders. Set in faraway tropical islands, the book is enjoyed by both adults and children even today.

Stevenson's next book *The Strange Case of Dr Jekyll and Mr Hyde,* was the story of a person with a split personality presented as a terror mystery. It is the story of the fine doctor Jekyll and the evil Edward Hyde. The influence of this novel was so great that the phrase 'Jekyll and Hyde' has now become a part of the English language.

Stevenson, then, turned his attention to historical fiction. His treatment was very different from that of Sir Walter Scott. The first of these was *Kidnapped* originally written for young boys. It was based on the real incidents that took place during the Jacobite risings of 1745 in Scotland. One can feel the effects of Stevenson's research into the eighteenth-century Scottish history in the book. This was followed by the other historical novels: *The Black Arrow*, *The Master of Ballantrae* and *Catriona*.

His collection of poems *A Child's Garden of Verses*, *Underwoods* and *Collected Poems* explore a number of themes such as childhood, illness and solitude.

Features

- The works of R.L. Stevenson introduced the novel of adventure which was highly appreciated by Victorian readers. The range of genres attempted by him was remarkable—essays, travel writing, short stories, novels, romances, poems, plays, biography and children's writing.
- He developed a romantic style as a reaction to realism which was the preferred style of the day. His works stand out as a stark contrast to the gloomy and pessimistic atmosphere of Hardy's novels. His optimistic view of life appealed to both adults as well as children.
- He was a good storyteller and could narrate an adventure story without any tedious digressions. He gave greater importance to plot over character in his stories.
- He was familiar with the culture and manners of Scotland and recreated in his stories, the Scottish landscape.
- As an essayist, the subjectivity of his style is close to that of Charles Lamb. The writer's personality comes through in his essays. There is a happy mingling of irony with an acceptance of the harsh truths of reality.

- His poems were simple pieces and could be easily enjoyed. They reveal a sensitive soul that had the power to understand the nuances of life.

Lewis Carroll (1832–98)

Fiction	**Poetry**
Alice's Adventures in Wonderland (1865)	*Phantasmagoria and Other poems* (1869)
Through the Looking-Glass and What Alice Found There (1871)	*The Hunting of the Snark* (1876)
	Silvie and Bruno (1889, 1893)

Life

'Lewis Carroll' is the pen name of Charles Lutwidge Dodgson. He was the third of a family of eleven children and was born in Cheshire. His early education was at home during which time he read a lot of books including *The Pilgrim's Progress.* He was later sent to Richmond Grammar School and Rugby. After leaving Rugby, he went to Christ Church, Oxford, where he studied mathematics. He remained in Oxford working in various capacities as a teacher and sub-librarian.

He suffered from stammering from his childhood and was acutely conscious of it. He died of pneumonia in 1898 and was buried in Gilford.

Works

Lewis Carroll is remembered today for his remarkable *Alice* books. The books, originally meant for children, are widely read today by both children and adults alike. Children's literature, as a genre, was enriched by the stories of Carroll, who could appeal to the imagination of young minds through his tales of fantasy.

He loved spending time with children and created the character of Alice on a rowing expedition on the River Isis with the daughters of the Dean of Christ Church. What began as an oral story narrated on-board, was developed first as a short story and then as a full-length book. *Alice in Wonderland*, as it is more popularly known, is about the adventures of a little girl who finds herself in a secret underground world, after she accidentally falls down a rabbit hole. The book has several characters who have become famous such as the Cheshire Cat, the Mad Hatter, the Queen of Hearts and the Mock Turtle.

Through the Looking-Glass soon followed and it introduced some more interesting characters like the scary dragon Jabberwock, the ridiculous twins Tweedledum and Tweedledee and the Walrus. Both his *Alice* books had interesting illustrations and were a great hit with children. Unlike the usual stories for children, Carroll did not attempt to impart any moral lesson. This was the chief reason for their success apart from the highly creative imagination of the author.

Apart from his novels for children, he also wrote verse. *Sylvie and Bruno* is a fairy tale which combines prose and verse. The poem 'The Hunting of the Snark' is a nonsense poem in which ten characters, all with names starting with 'B', go in search of a Snark, an imaginary animal. It is now considered to be an allegory for the search for happiness.

Features

- His contribution to children's fiction and verse is great. His works are not weighed down by any moral or didactic intentions. His aim was only to amuse and entertain and, in that, he was very successful.
- He was famous for creating a world of fantasy in his books in which there was no room for logic or realism. His stories challenged traditional storytelling conventions.
- He was good at creating new words and phrases. In *Through the Looking Glass*, he combined two words, 'chuckle' and 'snort' to create 'chortle'; 'fabulous' and 'joyous' to form the new word, 'frabjous' and 'mimsy by blending 'miserable' and 'flimsy'.
- He introduced several memorable and quirky characters like the Queen of Hearts and the White Rabbit. Some of his characters are so popular that their names have become part of everyday speech. For example: 'to grin like a Cheshire Cat' and 'as mad as the March Hare'.

Twentieth Century

1901–2000

House of Saxe-Coburg and Gotha
Edward VII (1901–1910)
George V (1910–1917)
House of Windsor
George V (1917–1936)
Edward VIII 1936 (abdicated)
George VI (1936–1952)
Elizabeth II (1952–2022)
Charles III (2022–present)

The nineteenth century was very eventful and succeeded in bringing about far-reaching changes not only in social life, science, transport and communication, but also in literature. With the death of Queen Victoria in 1901, a new era began in the history of Great Britain. Edward VII, her eldest son, ascended the throne and was king till his death in 1910. The Victorian way of life continued to linger with all its class distinctions and moral rigidities during his reign. It was the last period of peace preceding the First World War, which would shatter all human values and beliefs.

Edward VII was succeeded by George V. The Georgian Era (1910–36) was a tumultuous period with the First World War and the Irish Rebellion. With rapid advances in science and technology, people gradually began to question the established Victorian values and ideas. The First World War (1914–18) and the horrors that it ushered in, completely devastated the mental condition of the people. This had a tremendous impact upon the literature of the period. The conventional and realistic style of writing, characterised by linear narrative, was questioned and replaced by experimental forms that reflected the complexities of the modern world.

In 1936, George VI ascended the throne after the abdication of his elder brother Edward VIII. Even as the people were recovering from the ravages of the First World War and the Great Depression that followed on its heels, the Second World War (1939–45) broke out. This had a devastating effect on Britain and its economy was destroyed. The two Great Wars resulted in a loss of life hitherto unseen even during the worst plagues. This period also witnessed the decline of the British Empire as several colonies began to demand their independence. All these events resulted in a new cynicism that replaced Victorian complacency forever.

After the demise of George VI, his daughter Elizabeth II became the queen and was on the throne till 2022. The present monarch is King Charles III who was crowned after the long reign of his mother came to an end. Monarchy, however, has taken a backseat in England after the rise of democracy in the nineteenth century. The two major political parties, the Conservatives and Labour, are the main power-holders. The twentieth century witnessed their alternating regimes and a series of eminent prime ministers.

The second-half of the twentieth century brought about sweeping changes not only in the UK, but all over the world. It was the period when old buildings gave way to skyscrapers and urban motorways snaked their way into the beautiful countryside. Gradually, but steadily, mankind had begun destroying nature in the name of progress.

Scientifically, the world was taking giant strides. Communication, especially, witnessed an incredible revolution. After the letters and early telephones of the Victorian Age gave way to fax, email and mobile phones, the world has not been the same again. There were similar developments in other fields such as transportation, medicine and the invention of several household gadgets. In short, the twentieth century was a century of great change, some of which, one may argue, was definitely not for the better.

Twentieth-Century Prose

The twentieth century saw the revival of the short periodical essay. The innumerable monthly and weekly journals offered great opportunities to several writers. The last few years of the Victorian Age saw the proliferation of this genre, which continued in the twentieth century. Writers like G.K. Chesterton, E.V. Lucas, who wrote on a variety of topics, were popular. H.H. Munro (Saki), Lytton Strachey, Arthur Symons, Robert Lynd and J.B. Priestley are some of the important writers who contributed to this genre.

Many distinguished authors published collections of essays on both serious and informal topics. T.S. Eliot's *Selected Essays* (1932), George Orwell's *Selected Essays* (1946), Graham Greene's *The Lost Childhood and Other Essays* (1951), Aldous Huxley's *Adonis and the Alphabet* (1956) and W.H. Auden's *The Dyer's Hand* (1963) are some renowned examples.

In the last few decades of the century, the informal essay began to decline as there were fewer periodicals to publish them. At the same time, academic publications increased in number, as literary and critical essays became more popular. Criticism evolved into a complex discipline in the hands of scholars like F.R. Leavis, William Empson and I.A. Richards. These writers expounded various approaches to the study and appreciation of literary texts.

The twentieth century witnessed a great diversity in the genre of prose. The essay as a form was extensively used to discuss a variety of subjects such as politics, literature and culture. Some essayists used this form to comment on important cultural and historical events too.

Twentieth-Century Fiction

The literature of the twentieth century is as varied and complex as the century itself. The three thinkers whose work undermined the hitherto held political, religious and psychological ideas were Karl Marx, Charles Darwin and Sigmund Freud respectively. The writers of the twentieth century began to reject Victorian values and literary styles. The two wars further contributed to the destabilisation of the beliefs that formed the bedrock of British society.

Fiction in the twentieth century could be divided into four broad stages: before 1910, from 1910 to 1930, from 1930 to 1945 and 1945 to 1999. This is not a strict division as there is a lot of overlap and some writers spanned more than one of the time periods mentioned above.

Before 1910

Novelists like Arnold Bennett and H.G. Wells continued to write at the beginning of the new century. Arnold Bennett wrote in the realistic tradition, which came under a lot of criticism from the modernists who came later. H.G. Wells wrote science fiction and political and satirical fiction. John Galsworthy was another famous writer of the period who wrote novels as well as plays. He wrote mainly about upper-class lives and social issues. These novelists and many more who wrote at that time employed the traditional, realistic style. Yet another characteristic was the use of the techniques of realism and naturalism. This meant dealing with subjects previously considered to be trivial or taboo for art and literature. **Realism** focused on the details of everyday life, without idealising them, while **naturalism** examined the social and economic problems of human beings. Naturalism believed that man was a victim of the forces of nature that were within him such as sexual desire, hunger and greed.

Joseph Conrad, who wrote during this period, pioneered the use of psychological realism, exploring the individual's struggle against nature in tales of the sea. His works, however, were far ahead of his times and anticipated the modernists.

Modernist Fiction (1910–30)

Modernism is the term used to distinguish a certain style of writing. Modernism was influenced by several intellectual movements like Symbolism, Impressionism, Dadaism and Surrealism. **Symbolism**, in the words of Mallarme, is the art of evoking an object 'little by little so as to reveal a mood'. **Impressionism** is a term applied to a school of painters who were preoccupied with the transitory effects of light and attempted to capture the fleeting impression created by an object. This is a very subjective mode of art. **Dadaism** was a nihilistic movement in art and literature which believed in absolute freedom from rules and traditions. In literature one can see its effects in the creation of a collage of unrelated objects and words. **Surrealism** was an attempt to capture, in art and literature, the workings of the unconscious mind and to yoke these workings with the conscious mind. Of these, modernism was chiefly influenced by the Symbolist movement which originated with poets like Charles Baudelaire and Stephane Mallarme. They used a number of imaginative symbols to evoke emotions in the readers' minds.

The most characteristic feature of modernism is its experimental quality. A radical breaking away from the traditional way of writing could be discerned in fiction, poetry and drama. Ezra Pound's bold slogan 'Make it New' was the catchphrase of the modernists. One strategy for making literature new was to experiment with the standard forms and conventions of writing. This sometimes made the works difficult to comprehend, but modernists believed that greater artistic value could be derived from transforming traditional forms and approaches to literature. This was in response to the proliferation of popular entertainment during the early-twentieth century.

It is impossible to categorise the features of modernism as none of them are common to more than a few writers. Modernist works often contained non-linear narratives and they gave importance to the autonomy of the literary piece. In fiction, they departed from simple chronological narration. Presenting multiple points of view was another favourite with the modernists. They experimented with interior monologues and stream-of-consciousness techniques. Unlike the Victorian novels, there were seldom any definitive closures to the plots in modernist works. While the traditional novels ended with either a marriage or a death or a financial windfall, the modernist novels usually had ambiguous endings. Sandwiched between the two Great Wars, the modernist writers agonised over the individual pain of isolated characters. They were preoccupied with finding the means of uniting these individuals into a community once again. This concept can be felt powerfully in Woolf's novel *Between the Acts* where the characters sing the refrain 'Dispersed are we', which, ironically, is the only time they come together.

One cannot say exactly when the modernist movement began. The quarter century from 1914 until the onset of the Second World War in 1939 is now conventionally accepted as the modernist period. However, a transformation in all the fields of art can be noticed even at the beginning of the century. A new school of painting called **Post-Impressionism** had a great impact upon writers and artists. Inspired by French painters, its artists aimed at producing the impression left on the mind by the subject rather than its outward appearance. This style was in sharp contrast to the Victorian's attempt to reproduce faithfully the object that was being studied. Virginia Woolf famously announced soon after the Post-Impressionist exhibition of paintings in London, 'On or about December, 1910, human character changed'.

Picasso, the Spanish painter and sculptor, made **Cubism** popular after his landmark painting *Les Demoiselles d'Avignon* was displayed in 1907. In the same year, the Irish playwright J.M. Synge's *The Playboy of the Western World*, which was seen as an offence to public morals, was premiered. Concurrently, the Irish novelist and poet James Joyce's *A Portrait of the Artist as a Young Man*, which used interior monologue and stream of consciousness, was published. All these works challenged traditional notions of aesthetics and order, thereby opening new and unexplored avenues of expression.

At about the same time, a group of writers and artists met in an area in London called Bloomsbury to discuss intellectual questions. They were known as the **Bloomsbury group**. Virginia Woolf, J.M. Keynes, E.M. Forster and Lytton Strachey were some of the most famous members of this group. They believed in emphasising 'the importance of personal relationships and the private life' in literature and the significance of aesthetics. They discussed questions of art, morality, philosophy and religion and dedicated themselves to the pursuit of truth through the path of reason. Although they did not take a stand on any one particular view as a group, they were critical of the conservative approach of English society towards religion and morality.

From 1930 to 45

Social and political issues began to capture the attention of writers in the 1930s and 1940s. In the aftermath of the international financial depression of the 1930s, Marxism, fascism and totalitarianism had become popular. **Marxism** is a philosophy that follows the principles set forth by Karl Marx. This philosophy severely criticises capitalism for exploiting the working classes and advocates communism. **Fascism** and **totalitarianism** are forms of dictatorship in which people are not allowed to question their government. In the late thirties, people began to protest against fascism and totalitarianism after the rise of Adolf Hitler in Germany and Benito Mussolini in Italy. The modernist movement began to decline along with the changing social and political order.

Writers like Aldous Huxley used satire to attack the misuse of science in a totalitarian society. George Orwell satirised communism in his famous novels *Animal Farm* and *1984*. Other famous writers include Graham Greene, Evelyn Waugh, C.P. Snow and Elizabeth Bowen, to mention just a few.

From 1945 to 1999

During this period, a group of younger writers began to emerge. They shared a common antipathy towards the pretensions and superficial lives of the newly prosperous middle class. These writers became known as the **Angry Young Men**. This group included novelists like Kingsley Amis, John Wain and John Braine.

There was a great diversity in British fiction in the second-half of the twentieth century, both in subject matter and style. They concerned themselves with global issues like the destruction of the environment and the threat of nuclear war. Some writers focused on the problems of the working class or turned inward to explore the individual's attempt to cope with modern urban life.

British fiction was influenced by a number of new stimuli. Translations of books by many foreign writers were easily available and were avidly read by the British readers. Writers like Kafka, Gunter Grass, Boris Pasternak, Aleksandr Solzhenitsyn,

Jean-Paul Sartre, Albert Camus and Simone de Beauvoir had a great impact on British thinking. Apart from translations, novels from the USA were also easily available. John Steinbeck, Saul Bellow, Carson McCullers, J.D. Salinger, Norman Mailer, Truman Capote, John Barth and John Updike were some of the authors who were read widely.

Women Writers

Women began to write in large numbers. Prominent among these were Jean Rhys, Margaret Drabble, A.S. Byatt, Muriel Spark, Iris Murdoch and Nadine Gordimer. Although some of them would fervently deny it, most of them wrote in a style that could be called 'feminist realism'. They did not follow the modernist experimentalism of Virginia Woolf, but used the traditional tools of fiction to give expression to their experiences as women.

Post-Colonial Writers

A significant development in the history of British fiction at this stage, is the appearance of writers from Britain's former colonies. An offshoot of colonisation was the spread of the English language across the globe. This resulted in several writers using this medium to express themselves. A host of writers from different corners of the earth gained rapid recognition. To mention just a few—V.S. Naipaul and Derek Walcott from the Caribbean; Doris Lessing, Wole Soyinka, Nadine Gordimer, Chinua Achebe and Ben Okri from Africa; and Salman Rushdie, Ruth Prawer Jhabvala and Mulk Raj Anand from India.

Twentieth-Century Poetry

Poetry of the twentieth century could be studied under the following headings:

Edwardian Poetry

A bird's eye view of twentieth-century poetry reveals the evolving styles of the literature of the period. The Edwardian Era roughly corresponds with the first decade of the twentieth century and marked the transition between the Victorian and the modernist movement in literature. The poets of this period were inspired by nature and the countryside and looked back to earlier periods in time with nostalgia. Edwardian poetry is known for its simplicity and clarity as opposed to the elaborate style of the Victorians. It also witnessed the continuation of the work of poets like William Butler Yeats and Thomas Hardy who would later be associated with the modernists. Yeats's earlier poetry was a blend of the Romantics' love for nature and his own interest in Celtic mythology. In his later poetry, he began to adopt the colloquial diction of the modernists.

Georgian Poetry

In the second decade of the century, pastoral poetry continued to be popular. The poets of this decade wrote in an idealistic and traditional style. The publication of five anthologies of poems called *Georgian Poetry* by Edward Howard Marsh, elevated the early years of George V's reign to a cultural 'golden age'. Some of the Georgian poets were Rupert Brooke, Edmund Blunden, W.H. Davies, Walter de la Mare and Lascelles Abercrombie. The **Georgian School** of poets rejected the 'art for art's sake' concept of the Decadents of the 1890s. They followed the techniques and forms of traditional poetry. Their love for nature and the English countryside was seen abundantly in their work. They emphasised the importance of clear and lyrical language and traditional forms. The Georgians were criticised for being escapists who sought to find a refuge from the harsh realities of a rapidly changing world in literature. With the growing influence of the modernists, the Georgian School began to decline.

War Poetry

The advent of the First World War had a great impact upon the poets. The term 'war poets' refers to a group of poets who emerged during and after the war and who wrote about their experiences of the battlefield. Their poetry which expressed the horrors and sufferings caused by war had a great impact on the public.

To begin with, there were poets like Rupert Brooke who wrote idealistically and patriotically about the war. After the First World War came to an end, the poets who survived, echoed the feelings of the 'lost generation'. This term was coined by Gertrude Stein to refer to a group of American writers, poets and musicians of the 1920s.

The English poets who fought in the First World War, popularly known as the war poets, include Wilfred Owen, Siegfried Sassoon, Ivor Gurney and Robert Graves. They wrote about the horrors of the war, which was in sharp contrast to the patriotic verse of Rupert Brooke. These poets ushered in a new approach to war by honestly talking about the devastating effects it had on people. They challenged the traditional concepts about war that were generally prevalent.

War poetry is an important milestone in the history of British literature. The war poets shared their experiences in the front and highlighted the realities and horrors of the war. These poems were a source of inspiration for contemporary writers. A few of the poets were killed in action, but left behind poignant memories of themselves. The features of war poetry are:

- The poets who belong to this school of poetry described the trauma and pain that they had experienced in the war. Through their accounts, they wished to give readers a true picture of the brutal conditions of war and correct the romantic misconceptions of war that were prevalent till then. The poems were personal accounts of their experiences in trench warfare.
- Many of these poets criticised the politicians who were responsible for causing the war.
- War poetry had a profound impact on literature and played an important role in creating an anti-war sentiment.

Modernist Poetry

After the First World War, poetry changed in both subject matter and form. With the world literally falling apart before their eyes, the poets could not continue to write in the earlier, idealistic manner.

A number of poets began to revolt against the conventional poetic forms. This reaction was accompanied by a physical and moral exhaustion after the First World War came to an end, leaving in its wake untold destruction and loss of life. Ezra pound's clarion call to the poets to 'make it new', was met with a certain amount of pessimism—that there was nothing new left to make or write. T.S. Eliot gave an explanation to this injunction in his essay 'Tradition and the Practice of Poetry': 'The perpetual task of poetry is to *make all things new*. Not necessarily to make new things ... It is always partly a revolution, or a reaction, from the work of the previous generation.'

Imagism could thus be seen as a reaction against the long-winded style of Victorian poems like Tennyson's *Idylls of the King* or Browning's *The Ring and The Book*. Imagism was a literary movement of the early-twentieth century, whose followers believed that a sharp, clear image was vital to poetry. They also strongly felt that poetry should use the language of everyday speech. The fundamental ideas of the movement were developed by T.E. Hulme years before they were popularised by Ezra Pound. Pound's poem 'In a Station of the Metro' is the most quoted example of an imagist poem. The poem creates a striking visual by comparing the faces of the crowd waiting at a metro station with the dark petals of a tree, drenched in rain.

These concepts rekindled an interest in the metaphysical poetry of the seventeenth century. T.S. Eliot, especially, found a similarity between the techniques of metaphysical poetry and those of imagism. He put these techniques to good use in his celebrated poem 'The Love Song of J. Alfred Prufrock'.

> Let us go then, you and I,
> When the evening is spread out against the sky
> Like a patient etherised upon a table.

T.S. Eliot, who was the most representative poet of this period, captured the ugliness and despair of the times in his magnum opus *The Wasteland*. The jagged style, complex symbols and cross-references to other texts completely revolutionised poetry writing. Modernist poetry was difficult to comprehend due to its usage of techniques like intertextuality, collage and fragmentation and complex symbols. One reason for the use of this new style was to counter the proliferation of popular literature and the complacent taste of the growing middle class.

Poets of the 1930s

An interesting development in the early 1930s was the emergence of four poets who were initially known as the Pylon Poets. The name 'Pylon' refers to the frequent use of industrial imagery in their work. A pylon is a tall metal structure which is used to hold electric wires high above the ground. Spender wrote a poem titled 'The Pylons', Day-Lewis' poem 'The Magnetic Mountain' features pylons and skyscrapers and Auden, too, wrote about power stations.

These poets were also popularly referred to as 'Macspaunday'. This was the name created by Roy Campbell for the poets Louis MacNeice, Stephen Spender, W.H. Auden and Cecil Day-Lewis by fusing together parts of their names. These poets believed that the devastation of the First World War and the Depression that followed were a result of capitalism. The 1930s was pre-eminently Marxist in outlook when most of the poets adopted extreme left-wing views. It was a period when more and more people were looking at socialism as a better alternative to capitalism. The poets of the Thirties were attracted to Marxist ideas but at the same time were wary of growing fascism. The following declaration by Stephen Spender sums up the ideology of the Thirties Poets:

> The qualities which distinguished us from the writers of the previous decade lay not in ourselves, but in the events to which we reacted. These were unemployment, economic crisis… fascism, approaching war…. The older writers were reacting… to the exhaustion and hopelessness of a Europe in which the old regimes were falling to pieces. We were a 'new generation,' but it took me some time to appreciate the meaning of this phrase… that we had begun…in circumstances strikingly different from those of our immediate predecessors and that a consciousness of this was shown in our writing…. We were the 1930s.

The poets of the Thirties wrote in a variety of poetic forms ranging from sonnets to free verse. They were not very noted for any innovations, except Auden.

Late-Twentieth-Century Poetry

In the 1940s, there was a group of poets who called themselves the **New Apocalypse**. In their view, it was time to stop British poets' tendency of being concerned with politics and psychology, as they felt that poetry was being turned into a platform for intellectual debate. Instead, they wished to return to the language of the Romantics. These poets were also influenced by the surrealists and their use of the dream imagery of the subconscious. As a result, the poetry of this group was at times frenzied and made use of surreal imagery. Their works appeared in three anthologies, *The New Apocalypse* (1940) edited by James Findlay Hendry, *The White Horseman: Prose and Verse of the New Apocalypse* (1941) edited by Hendry and Henry Treece and *The Crown and the Sickle* (1945) also edited by Hendry and Treece. Of the poets belonging to this group, only Dylan Thomas stood the test of time.

The term the **Movement** was coined by the editor of *The Spectator*, J.D. Scott, in 1954. Modern critics have questioned the notion of this title but the term caught on to identify the poets who rejected the experimental nature of modernist poetry. Some of the poets who belonged to the Movement were Philip Larkin, Kingsley Amis, Elizabeth Jennings, Thom Gunn and D.J. Enright. These poets reacted against modernism and romanticism. They believed in writing in a down to earth style that was not sentimental and which would reflect an English identity. After the excesses of modernist poetry, the simple and down to earth style of the Movement poets was a welcome change. At the same time, a number of modernists were still publishing their work in the 1950s and 1960s, chief among these were T.S. Eliot and Ezra Pound.

As the century progressed, British literature was infused with new stimuli from writers of other countries as well as new voices from within the British Isles. Welsh, Scottish and Irish writers were rapidly becoming a significant presence. The Nobel

Prize-winning Irish poet Seamus Heaney, the Welsh poet R.S. Thomas and the Scottish poet Carol Ann Duffy enriched the poetry of Great Britain in the second-half of the last century.

Twentieth-Century Drama

Drama at the turn of the century was gradual and turned its back to the sentimental romances and melodrama that was popular until the last quarter of the 1800s. Some of the playwrights of this period were James Barrie, Oscar Wilde, John Galsworthy and George Bernard Shaw. These dramatists were interested in highlighting the social issues of the age in a realistic and humorous style. The influence of the Norwegian playwright Henrik Ibsen was great. His play *A Doll's House* was an important milestone in the history of drama. Shaw especially was influenced by Ibsen to write plays that discussed the political, social and religious issues of the day. The twentieth century witnessed sweeping changes in both the content and form of drama. Censorship of the stage in England ended in 1968, throwing open new subjects to be explored.

Irish Literary Revival

The Revival, also known as the Irish Literary Renaissance or Celtic Renaissance, began in the late-nineteenth century and flourished until the 1920s. Its aim was to breathe new life into the dying Gaelic language and to revive early Celtic history and literature. Some of the books that prompted this revival were translations and retelling of Irish legends, folklore and poetry.

In 1899, W.B. Yeats and Lady Gregory were instrumental in founding the Irish Literary Theatre. This later developed as the Abbey Theatre which produced several plays about Ireland and its culture. Some of the dramatists whose plays were performed at the Abbey Theatre were Sean O'Casey, J.M. Synge, and Yeats. These writers wished to showcase Irish experiences, legends and traditions. The Abbey Theatre played a very significant role in the development of British drama in the twentieth century.

Apart from drama, the poetry of Yeats, the prose writings of G. Moore and the fiction of James Joyce added to the stature of Irish writing.

Poetic Drama

Poetic drama or verse drama had declined in the Victorian Age. Yeats attempted to revive it, but Yeats was more a poet than a dramatist. Synge's plays had a poetic quality about them although they were not written in verse. After the Second World War concluded, there was a brief attempt by dramatists like T.S. Eliot and Christopher Fry to revive verse drama. Some of the famous plays that belong to this genre are *A Cocktail Party*, *Murder in the Cathedral* and *The Lady's Not for Burning*.

Theatre of the Angry Young Men

In the 1950s, a group of British novelists and playwrights from middle-class and working-class backgrounds began to raise their voices against the sordid state of England after the Second World War. Their works were a reaction to the well-made play which was known for its artificiality. They also wished to break the stereotypical portrayal of the working class by the upper-middle-class writers. They questioned the injustice of the British class system, which they believed was rendered redundant. Urbanisation, increased access to education and economic changes, brought about significant changes in the social landscape. These writers, who were critical of traditional hierarchy, came to be known as the 'angry young men'. With its focus on a realistic portrayal of working class, their type of drama also came to be known as **kitchen sink drama**. John Osborne's *Look Back in Anger* is the most well-known drama of this genre.

Theatre of the Absurd

The term 'Theatre of the Absurd' was coined by Martin Esslin in 1960; this became an important movement in drama. Based on the bleak view that man was essentially an isolated creature living in a world that no longer had any meaning, it captured the imagination of the war-weary writers of the time. This type of drama broke away from the traditional theatre of the preceding four hundred years and did away with the linear development of plot and the traditional mode of dialogue. Man was seen as struggling in a world that had no meaning or purpose. The absurdists did not want to tell a story with characters arguing about the emptiness of life. They wanted instead to shock the audience with this emptiness, moment by moment, so that they could actually feel it. The Absurdist Movement was anti-literary as they believed that language could no longer convey meaning. Important playwrights who belonged to this school included Samuel Beckett, Eugene Ionesco, Jean Genet, Harold Pinter and Tom Stoppard.

These ideas however were not new to the twentieth century. The German philosopher Fredrich Nietzsche had pointed out in the previous century that traditional religion had been undermined by the advances made in science. Therefore, all ideas of morality and ethics, which had sprung from such faiths, were also declared superfluous by him. According to Nietzsche, all values were 'constructed' rather than given truths. Logically, therefore, all truths were merely opinions and all identities merely roles. The profound shock of the two world wars further added to these ideas and shaped the drama of the period.

Absurd theatre was also influenced by existential philosophy. Albert Camus's essay 'The Myth of Sisyphus' asked the question why a man should not commit suicide when faced with a meaningless and absurd situation. He used the myth of Sisyphus to demonstrate this idea. According to the myth, Sisyphus was condemned to push a boulder up a mountain for eternity, only to have it roll down each time. The absurd dramatists did not offer any solution to man's meaningless situation. It merely represented an attitude towards life.

> A world that can be explained by reasoning, however faulty, is a familiar world. But in a Universe that is suddenly deprived of illusion and of light, man feels a stranger … This Divorce between man and his life … truly contributes to the feeling of absurdity.
>
> (Albert Camus, *The Myth of Sisyphus*)

George Bernard Shaw (1856–1950)

Drama

Widowers' Houses (1893)
Arms and the Man (1894)
Candida (1894)
You Never Can Tell (1898)
Mrs Warren's Profession (1898)
The Devil's Disciple (1901)
Man and Superman (1903)
Major Barbara (1905)
The Doctor's Dilemma (1906)
Misalliance (1910)
Fanny's First Play (1911)
Androcles and the Lion (1912)
Pygmalion (1913)
Heartbreak House (1919)
Back to Methuselah (1921)
Saint Joan (1924)
The Apple Cart (1929)
Too True to be Good (1932)
Village Wooing (1934)
The Simpleton of the Unexpected Isles (1935)
Plays Pleasant and Unpleasant (collection of plays) (1898)
Three Plays for Puritans (1901)

Prose

The Perfect Wagnerite (1898)
The Quintessence of Ibsenism (1891)
Common Sense About the War (1914)
The Intelligent Woman's Guide to Socialism and Capitalism (1928)
Everybody's Political What's What (1944)

Life

George Bernard Shaw, born in Dublin, was the youngest of three children. His parents separated when he was sixteen years old. His father was a drunkard who neglected his family and his mother, who was a talented singer, moved to London with her daughters and supported herself and her daughters. Shaw completed his schooling in Dublin and worked as a clerk and cashier for a few years before joining his mother in London.

The initial years in London were a great struggle. He earned little money as a critic of music, art and books. Apart from this, he was a drama critic too and wrote for *The Saturday Review*. Being a great admirer of Ibsen, he attacked the artificiality of the London theatre and advocated the discussion of social and moral problems through drama. Shaw joined the **Fabian Society** which believed in democratic socialism. (The Fabian Society, founded in 1884, is a British organization whose aim is to promote the principles of social democracy through reforms rather than revolution.) Shaw gave up the Christian religion and, although he refused to call himself a Christian, he conducted himself as a man of religion. He became a vegetarian at the age of twenty-five and was a teetotaller. Shaw was also interested in reforming the English alphabet and simplifying the spelling and pronunciation of English words.

When he was forty-two, he attempted creative writing. The five novels that he published in the next few years were unsuccessful. He next turned to writing plays and, in this genre, found great success. He was married to Charlotte Payne-Townshend in 1898 and they lived together till her death in 1943. He continued to write well into his nineties till his death.

Works

In his long life, Shaw wrote fifty plays. With the exception of some of his early plays like *Widowers' Houses* and *Mrs Warren's Profession*, his plays have stood the test of time. His great contribution to the world of drama earned him the greatest recognition of the Nobel Prize in the year 1925. His works are still relevant today as the evils and follies that he had attacked in his plays are still with us. Shaw used the stage to discuss and debate several social, religious and moral problems of the day. Critics, therefore, refer to his plays as **problem plays**.

His first play *Widowers' Houses* was an ironical exposure of the evil practices of slum landlords. This play did not meet with success as the English audiences found the subject totally new. This was followed by *Arms and the Man,* where he debunked the romantic view of war. Shaw exposed the hollowness of Sergius both as a lover as well as a soldier. In Captain Bluntschli, he portrayed a realist who filled his pockets with chocolates instead of cartridges. The contrast between the two men allows Raina to understand the truth about war and have a more realistic approach towards life. The change in the romantic Raina served as an eye-opener to the audience as well. In *Candida,* Shaw continued to question Victorian ideas of love and marriage.

You Never Can Tell was a light-hearted comedy set in the seaside. It contained several arguments about marriage, society and parenthood that are still relevant today. *Mrs Warren's*

Profession focused on prostitution. Shaw wished to highlight the fact that prostitution was not a moral failure but rather was the result of economic necessity.

The Devil's Disciple was published along with two more plays, *Captain Brassbound's Conversation* and *Caesar and Cleopatra*, in his collection entitled *Three Plays for Puritans*. In *The Devil's Disciple*, Shaw wrote about the religious intolerance of people and the plight of the protagonist who was treated as an outcast.

Man and Superman was a play in which Shaw introduced a kind of dream in which Don Juan was depicted as having a lengthy conversation with the Devil. In it, Don Juan counters the Devil's prediction that no one could save mankind as they were so stupid as to believe that Man could rise above his predicament and become Superman. This philosophical argument was a concept hitherto unknown to the contemporary audience. His wit and humour engaged the attention of his audience, although the matters discussed were of a serious nature.

John Bull's Other Island was another play that found success in London. It is a play that was about the relationship between Britain and Ireland and though it was popular soon after it was produced, it is rarely revived now. One reason for this could be the topicality of much of the dialogue.

In *Major Barbara*, Shaw portrayed an idealistic woman serving as a major in the Salvation Army. The play centred around the conflict between the idealistic protagonist and her estranged and rich father who was engaged in manufacturing munitions. Finally Major Barbara, who had scorned her father's money as it was earned by selling munitions, learnt that it was the same that was supporting her Salvation Army. This is typical of Shaw's art of anticlimax. After leading us to expect a conventional conclusion, he pulls the rug from under our feet.

The Doctor's Dilemma explored the moral struggle created by the demands generated by limited medical resources and the large number of patients needing treatment. The doctor had to decide who was more worthy of being saved.

In *Androcles and the Lion*, Shaw used an old Roman story about Androcles to explore the theme that one should have something worthy to die for. He combined the techniques of miracle play and Christian pantomime to produce a philosophical farce about true and false religious exaltation.

Shaw was deeply interested in the English language and its pronunciation and often expressed his disgust at the sloppy speech of the English people. He felt that the quirky nature of English spelling was at the root of this problem. Such was his passion for this cause that he left a huge part of his fortune to be spent in replacing the English alphabet with a new one based on phonetic principles. He believed that uniformity in pronunciation would help pave the way to the disintegration of class distinctions. This deep interest in phonetics was behind the brilliant comedy *Pygmalion*. The play portrayed an experiment conducted by the Professor of Phonetics Higgins, to prove that he could train an uneducated cockney-speaking flower girl to blend with cultured and aristocratic people. It is to the author's credit that a play dealing with such a dry theme as phonetics became such a delightful hit. It was also made into a musical called *My Fair Lady* and, later, into a film of the same name.

Saint Joan was the only tragedy that Shaw wrote. Through his retelling of the story of the martyr Joan of Arc, Shaw wished to show that the people involved in the trial of Joan were not villains but merely people acting according to their own beliefs.

In *The Apple Cart,* Shaw turned to political satire. The play depicted the conflict between a fictional king and a prime minister who wished to limit the powers of the king.

Features

Shaw occupies a very elevated position in British drama, second only to Shakespeare. He had a long career spanning the last decade of the nineteenth century to the middle of the twentieth century. Such was his influence that the word 'Shavian' was coined to describe his wit and ideas. Ibsen had a great impact upon Shaw who championed his ideas at a time when many considered them outrageous. Some of the important features that paved the way for his greatness are as follows:

- Shaw was a rationalist and anti-romantic in his views. He rejected the artificiality and shallowness of Victorian morals and values.
- He did not believe in the concept of art for art's sake. For Shaw, art was a medium to convey ideas and influence people. He strongly felt that the stage could be put to good use to discuss the problems of the day such as attitudes towards war, class discrimination and the false sense of morality and heroism prevalent in contemporary society.
- He had a great sense of the comic and a quick wit which left his comedies, however drab the topic in discussion may be, highly entertaining. He used his talent to debunk conventional ideas such as the glorification of war and the false heroism of soldiers.
- He excelled in the use of irony and paradox. For instance, in *Arms and the Man* Raina is shown protecting Captain Bluntschli whose duty as a soldier is to give protection.
- He was interested in the English language and bemoaned the fact that it was not spoken correctly. He also believed that the different dialects being spoken played a part in causing class distinctions.

John Galsworthy (1867–1933)

Fiction

From the Four Winds (1897)
Jocelyn (1898) (unpublished)
The Island Pharisee (1904)
Fraternity (1909)
The Dark Flower (1913)
The Forsyte Novels
I *The Forsyte Saga* (1922)
II *A Man of Property* (1909)
III *In Chancery* (1920)
IV *To Let* (1921)
A Modern Comedy
I *The White Monkey* (1924)
II *The Silver Spoon* (1926)
III *Swan Song* (1928)
On Forsyte Change (1931)
End of the Chapter
I Maid in Waiting (1931)
II The Flowering Wilderness (1932)
III Over the River (1933)

Drama

The Silver Box (1906)
Strife (1909)
Justice (1910)
The Skin Game (1920)
Loyalties (1922)
Old English (1924)

Life

Galsworthy was born in Kingston Hill, in Surrey. He belonged to a well-to-do family and attended Harrow and New College. He studied law and trained as a barrister but gave it up to go to Europe to look after his family's trans-European shipping agency. While in Europe, he made the acquaintance of Joseph Conrad and developed a close friendship with him.

Galsworthy's literary career included several novels, but it was his drama that stood the test of time. He won the Nobel Prize for literature in the year 1932.

Galsworthy fell in love with his cousin's wife and married her after she got a divorce from her husband. He died of a brain tumour and was cremated at a place called Woking.

Works

FICTION

Galsworthy began his literary career with fiction. His first volume of stories *From the Four Winds,* appeared in 1897. This was followed by his first full-length novel *Jocelyn* the next year. As a novelist, he was interested in portraying the social problems of the day. *The Island Pharisee* reflects Galsworthy's constant interest in the effects of social constraints and poverty on people. This novel was received very well and was followed by several more. In *Fraternity*, Galsworthy highlighted the superficiality of urban life and in *The Dark Flower*, the positive and negative effects of love.

The Man of Property was the first novel in a series about the Forsyte family. The central character of the Forsyte novels was Soames Forsyte, a person from an upper-middle-class family. Through the Forsyte novels, Galsworthy traced the decline of this class from the 1880s to the years after the First World War. The first trilogy, *The Forsyte Saga,* consisted of three novels—*The Man of Property*, *In Chancery* and *To Let.* He continued the story of the Forsyte family in a second trilogy called *A Modern Comedy* consisting of *The White Monkey*, *The Silver Spoon* and *Swan Song.* These novels capture the relentless passage of time and also the eternal conflict between idealism and materialism.

His final collection of novels, which was published posthumously was *The End of the Chapter.* This contained three novels, *Maid in Waiting, The Flowering Wilderness* and *Over the River.* In this trilogy, he related the family history of the Charwells who were the cousins of the Forsytes.

DRAMA

Galsworthy was a successful dramatist. He began his career as a dramatist in 1906 with *The Silver Box.* It explored the difference between an employed man and the son of a prosperous politician. The play features two thefts, one of a prostitute's purse by a rich young man from an affluent family and another of a silver cigarette case from the rich man's house by a poor man. Though justice was done, in each case the repercussions were very different. Through this play, Galsworthy attempted to expose the attitudes of different social classes and the law's discriminative treatment of the rich and the poor. In *Strife*, Galsworthy focuses on the hardships of workers' families due to a prolonged strike at a factory. It basically depicted the conflict between the capitalists and the workers.

Justice was a play that paved the way for improving the conditions of British prisons. Galsworthy painted a grim picture of solitary confinement in prisons in this play. It also highlighted the plight of a woman trapped in a marriage with a violent husband. British law did not recognise domestic violence as grounds for separation at that time and as a result, she was forced to become a destitute, selling her body to maintain herself and her children. This play had a great impact on the audience.

In *Loyalties*, Galsworthy discussed social conduct and racial prejudices. He tried to show how, sometimes, loyalty and justice could not coexist. This play also discussed issues like discrimination between the different sections of society and the perpetual conflict between Christians and Jews.

Features

- His fiction depicted the upper middle class to which he belonged and he tried to portray their lives as faithfully as he could.

- He wrote in a traditional, realistic style at a time when modernist fiction was becoming popular. As a result, his work came under severe criticism by contemporaries like Virginia Woolf who referred to him as a materialist in her essay 'Modern Fiction'. His work, however, continued to be popular with readers.
- Galsworthy used drama as a tool to reform society. His plays touched on several moral and social issues of the day.
- His dialogues were simple and direct. He was adept at creating effective scenes.

James Matthew Barrie (1860–1937)

Fiction
When a Man's Single (1888)
Auld Licht Idylls (1888)
A Window in Thrums (1889)
Tommy and Grisel (1900)
The Little Minister (1891)
Sentimental Tommy (1891)
The Little White Bird (1902)
Peter Pan in Kensington Gardens (1906)

Drama
Richard Savage (1891)
Quality Street (1901)
The Admirable Crichton (1902)
Peter Pan (1904)
Alice Sit-by-the-Fire (1905)
What Every Woman Knows (1906)
The Twelve-Pound Look (1910)
Peter Pan and Wendy (1911)
A Kiss for Cinderella (1916)
Dear Brutus (1917)
Mary Rose (1920)
The Boy David (1936)

One-Act Plays
The Old Lady Shows her Medals (1917)
Shall We Join the Ladies? (1921)

Biography
Margaret Ogilvy (1896)

Life

Barrie was born in Scotland in a weaver family. He was the ninth of ten children. After completing his studies in Scotland, he became a journalist and later moved to London. He began his literary career writing novels and later moved to drama.

In 1894, he married an actress whom he divorced in 1909. He was deeply attached to the five sons of his friends Arthur and Sylvia Llewelyn Davies and entertained them with his stories. His famous creation Peter Pan had its genesis in these stories.

Works

FICTION

Barrie began writing novels in the 1890s. His first successful work was *The Little Minister,* a romantic story about a shy preacher and a rebellious girl. It was set in Thrums, a Scottish village, where Barrie grew up. His earlier novels *Better Dead*, *When a Man's Single* and *My Lady Nicotine* were not received well as they were too sentimental.

Two other novels that he wrote merit a mention here. Known as the Tommy Books, *Sentimental Tommy* and *Tommy and Grisel* trace the travails of the eponymous Tommy as a twelve-year-old boy and as a young man. These two books are supposed to be most revealing about their author.

DRAMA

As a dramatist, Barrie set off on a path of his own. At a time when his contemporaries, like Shaw and Galsworthy, were using the stage to discuss social issues in a realistic manner, most of Barrie's plays created a world of make-believe and fantasy. He wrote more than thirty-five plays.

His first play *Richard Savage* was a biography and was not a success on the stage. After a few more plays that were not successful appeared *The Admirable Crichton*. In it, a group of upper-class English men and women are shipwrecked on a deserted island. Barrie demonstrates how the British class system is turned completely topsy-turvy when the butler, Crichton, becomes the head of the group as he was the only one who had the knowledge required to survive under harsh conditions. This play, an excellent combination of fantasy and realism, reveals Barrie's cynical view of the society of his day.

Barrie is remembered mostly as the creator of Peter Pan, the boy who refused to grow up. The character first appeared in Barrie's novel, *The Little White Bird*. This was later developed by him into the play *Peter Pan*. It is the story of Peter Pan who runs away to Never-Never Land to escape growing up. On returning to the human world once again, he encounters the three Darling children—Wendy, John and Michael. He convinces the children to fly back with him and the fairy Tinker Bell to Never-Never Land. On reaching the fantasy world, they have several adventures with other characters, that include an Indian princess named Tiger Lily, the evil pirate Captain Hook and a crocodile. Peter Pan, Tinker Bell, Tiger Lily and Captain Hook are immortal characters of children's fiction even today.

Later he followed this up by dramatising several chapters of the novel as *Peter Pan in Kensington Gardens*. Driven by the success of the character Peter Pan, Barrie wrote the novel *Peter Pan and Wendy*.

Of his other plays which are more realistic than *Peter Pan*, a mention has to be made of *What Every Wife Knows*. In it, Barrie touched upon the sensitive subject of a wife's role in a marriage. The play features a meek wife who is portrayed as guiding the political career of her husband.

Barrie's other plays are *Quality Street*, *Alice Sit-by-the-Fire*, *The Twelve Pound Look*, *A Kiss for Cinderella*, *Dear Brutus* and *Mary Rose*.

Features

- His novels were highly sentimental and romantic.
- In his fantasies, he was at his best. The delicacy of his touch delighted his audiences.
- He created immortal characters like Peter Pan and Captain Hook who have remained popular over the decades.
- His grasp of theatrical conditions made him a successful dramatist.
- His dialogues were memorable and are quoted even today. For example: 'All the world is made of faith, and trust and pixie dust.', 'The moment you doubt you can fly, you cease forever to be able to do so.' and 'It not in doing what you like, but in liking what you do that is the secret of happiness.'

John Millington Synge (1871–1909)

The Shadow of the Glen (1903) *The Well of the Saints* (1905)
Riders to the *Sea* (1904)

The Playboy of the Western World (1907)
The Tinker's Wedding (1908)
Poems and Translations (1909)
Deirdre of the Sorrows (1910)

Life

Synge was born in a well-to-do Anglo-Irish family that lived near Dublin. His father, who was a barrister, died when Synge was still an infant. Synge had his early schooling at home as he suffered from poor health. His interest in music led him to Trinity College in Dublin from where he graduated.

When he visited Paris, he met Yeats who influenced him to write about Irish life and culture. At this time, Synge grew increasingly interested in poetry. He visited the Aran Islands several times to get first-hand knowledge of Irish peasant life. He confessed in the preface to his play *The Playboy of the Western World:* 'When I was writing *The Shadow of the Glen,* some years ago, I got more aid than any learning could have given me, from a chink in the floor of the old Wicklow house where I was staying. That let me to hear what was being said by the servant girls in the kitchen.'

Apart from his interest in music and poetry, Synge developed a keen interest in Irish history and became a member of the Irish League. He, however, left the League because he did not want to be part of the political revolution which was on its agenda.

In 1899, he along with Yeats, Lady Gregory and William Russell, formed the Irish National Theatre. Synge spent five summers in the Aran Islands collecting stories and folktales. The rest of his year was mostly spent in Paris. He suffered from Hodgkin's disease and succumbed to it when he was just thirty-seven years old. His final play *Deirdre of the Sorrows* was completed by Yeats and his ex-fiancée Molly Allgood.

Works

His first play *In the Shadow of the Glen* is a one-act drama that was set in an isolated farmhouse in rural Ireland. It is a comedy in which an elderly husband pretends to be dead in order to test the fidelity of his wife.

Riders to the Sea, his next play, is a poetic tragedy that depicts the struggle of the Irish peasants and the relentless sea that swallows up all the members of the protagonist's family. The play captures the poetic speech of rural Ireland accurately. The plot was inspired by the stories that Synge had gathered during his annual visits to the Aran Islands. In the play, Synge weaves pagan beliefs and superstitions with the Roman Catholic faith. The sea, too, is shown playing a dual role, both as a source of livelihood as well as a death trap.

His next play *The Well of the Saints*, a three-act drama, was performed at the Abbey Theatre in 1905. The setting is a remote mountainous area and the story takes place in a bygone age. This story, too, was based on an Irish folktale that Synge had heard during his visits to the place.

The Playboy of the Western World is his most well-known play. The story revolves around a character who boasts of killing his father in a quarrel. The women of the village, used only to the mild nature of their local men, are shown as being in awe of his daredevil act. The play triggered riots and protests for glorifying patricide. The play is an excellent example of how Synge is able to portray the Irish in a comic and satirical manner. This treatment of the Irish resulted in antagonising the people of Ireland.

Features

- Most of Synge's plays revolved around the lives of rural Irish peasants.
- He captured the conflict between the pagan and Christian beliefs of the rustic folk and highlighted their everyday struggles, superstitions and traditions.
- Synge used a language that was rhythmic and lyrical in order to capture the mood of his characters. He was skilful in capturing the cadences of the Irish dialects.
- Synge made good use of symbols in his work to add depth to his narratives. For example, in *Riders to the Sea*, the sea itself is a powerful symbol of both life and death.
- Yeats called Synge 'the greatest dramatic genius of Ireland'. He helped to immortalise the lives of the simple peasants of

the Aran Islands. He influenced later dramatists like Sean O' Casey who wrote for the Abbey Theatre.

Sean O'Casey (1880–1964)

The Shadow of a Gunman (1923)
Juno and the Paycock (1924)
The Plough and the Stars (1926)
The Silver Tassie (1928)
Within the Gates (1933)
Purple Dust (1940)
Red Roses for Me (1942)
Cock-a-Doodle Dandy (1949)
The Bishop's Bonfire (1955)

Life

Sean O'Casey was born in the Dublin slums to Protestant parents. He was mostly self-educated and worked from the age of fourteen at a variety of jobs. He was drawn into the Irish nationalist movement and changed his name from the original Sean Casey to its Irish form. He joined the Gaelic League and the Irish Republican League and also learnt Irish. Gradually, he moved away from politics and became interested in theatre. Encouraged by Lady Gregory, his first three plays were staged at the Abbey Theatre and were received well.

His play *The Plough and the Stars* provoked rioting as the people felt that the play was an insult to Irish patriots and Irish women. O'Casey left Abbey Theatre after that and moved to England. He married an Irish actress and had three children.

Works

Deeply rooted in the Irish cause, O'Casey's plays depict the violence that Ireland was subjected to between 1916 and 1924—the years of turmoil when Ireland was fighting for independence and their aftermath. In these early plays, he attacks the empty sloganeering and the idealised concept of patriotism. Most of the heroes of his early plays were rebels and called for a radical transformation of society.

The Shadow of a Gunman is a two-act play set in the slums of Dublin that O'Casey was familiar with. The plot is set against the backdrop of a guerrilla war between the Irish Republican Army (IRA) and the Black and Tans of the British police force.

His most popular play *Juno and the Paycock* is set in the working-class tenements of Dublin during the Irish Civil War period. The play, which is a tragicomedy, portrays an Irish family which is shattered by poverty, alcoholism and the Irish Civil War. It has a blend of grotesque humour and deep tragedy.

The Plough and the Stars is the third play of O'Casey's Dublin Trilogy. The play is set just before and during the Easter Rising of 1916. The title refers to the Starry Plough flag of the Irish Citizen Army. The play created riots as the audience felt that the flag was disrespected.

The Abbey Theatre refused to stage his next play *The Silver Tassie*. This play portrays war as the destroyer of individuality and heroism. O'Casey employed expressionistic features in this play. In his later plays, one notes the growing use of symbolism and expressionism.

His later plays include *Within the Gates*, *Red Roses for Me*, *Cock-a-Doodle Dandy* and *The Bishop's Bonfire*. These plays were not as popular as his 'Abbey' plays, but continued to create both controversy and appreciation. These plays reflected the idea that independence only shifted the domination from the British to the Roman Catholic Church. He used expressionistic techniques extensively.

Features

O'Casey used his own experiences which enabled him to assess the life of the Irish peasantry. He is considered as one of the important dramatists of the theatre of the inter-war period.

- He had the gift of combining comedy with tragedy. Although comedy is seldom absent in his plays, one is made aware of the grim underlying gloom. He was skilled at conveying the sordid realism through a racy local idiom which prevented his work from slipping into melodrama.
- He drew his themes from his hometown, especially during the times of the Irish Civil War.
- His characters were weak men and women whose fate was to suffer tragedy. These characters too were etched from the people he was familiar with in the outskirts of Dublin.

- His prose had a poetic style. Some of the lines from his plays are proof of this: 'All the world's a stage and most of us are desperately unrehearsed.' and 'It's my rule never to lose my temper till it would be detrimental to keep it.'
- O'Casey was a serious literary artist who endeavoured to explore the range and depth of modern theatre.

Noel Coward (1899–1973)

Drama
The Vortex (1924)
Fallen Angels (1925)
Hay Fever (1925)
Cavalcade (1931)
Private Lives (1933)
Design for Living (1933)
Blithe Spirit (1941)
Screenplay
This Happy Breed (1942)
Brief Encounter (1944)
Fiction
Pomp and Circumstance (1960)
Collected Short Stories (1962)
Bon Voyage (1967)
Poetry
Not Yet the Dodo (1967)
Autobiography
The Noel Coward Diaries (1982)

Life

Noel Coward was born in Teddington, near London. His father was a piano salesman and his mother encouraged him in his theatrical ambitions, even when he was a mere boy. He began acting on the stage from the age of twelve and later started writing plays. His plays were popular in the period between the two world wars. He was knighted in 1970 and spent the later part of his life in the Caribbean and Switzerland and died in Jamaica.

Works

Coward is best remembered for his sparkling comedies of manners. His works emerged in the 1920s, a time when the country was limping out of the ravages of the First World War. He had a flippant and cynical style of writing which appealed to his contemporaries.

He took the London theatre by storm with *The Vortex*, his first play to become popular. Coward himself acted as Nicky Lancaster, a young drug addict who was traumatised by his mother's adulterous life.

The success of *The Vortex* was quickly followed by *Fallen Angels* and *Hay Fever*. *Fallen Angels* is a witty comedy about two bored wives eagerly anticipating the arrival of a mutual past lover. The play focused on two women who seemed ahead of their conservative times and created quite a stir. *Hay Fever*, set in an English country house, is about the Bliss family. Each of the four members of the family invites a guest to spend a weekend at the house. But the Blisses are so preoccupied with fighting and arguing with each other that the guests quietly slip away. The play has elements of farce and comedy of manners.

Cavalcade traces the lives of an upper-middle-class family and their servants through the first three decades of the twentieth century. Major historical events such as the demise of Queen Victoria, the sinking of the *Titanic* and the First World War are mentioned in the play.

His next play *Private Lives* is a comedy about two divorced couples on a honeymoon with their new spouses. They discover that they are staying in adjacent rooms. In spite of their earlier bitterness for each other, they find themselves being drawn towards one another.

Design for Living is a scandalous story about three artistic characters and their questionable three-way relationship. Since the subject matter would not have been approved by the official censor of London, it was first performed in Broadway, New York. It was only seven years later that it was presented by a London production.

Coward described his play *Blithe Spirit* as 'an improbable farce in three acts'. In it, a famous novelist in search of material for his next novel invites an eccentric medium and clairvoyant, Madame Arcatt, to conduct a séance. As a result of this exercise, the ghost of his temperamental first wife starts to haunt him and causes a disruption in his second marriage.

Apart from drama, Coward wrote a number of songs, screenplays, short stories and a novel.

Features

- Noel Coward was a prominent dramatist who excelled in the genre of the comedy of manners.

- In his plays, he exposed the shallowness and triviality of the younger generation. He satirised the *nouveau riche* and conservative morality.
- He wrote comedies of manners, farce, domestic and patriotic melodramas and musical comedies.
- His plots usually revolved around couples in a romantic relationship and their verbal fencing.
- His dialogues were epigrammatic and dazzling, exposing the hypocrisy and shallowness of the upper class. For instance in the play *Blithe Spirit,* a character remarks, 'It's discouraging to think how many people are shocked by honesty and how few by deceit.'
- His characters were not fully developed as their motives were not made clear.

Christopher Fry (1907–2005)

The Boy with a Cart (1939)
The Firstborn (1946)
A Phoenix Too Frequent (1946)
Thor with Angels (1949)
The Lady's Not for Burning (1949)
Venus Observed (1950)
A Sleep of Prisoners (1951)
The Dark is Light Enough (1954)
Curtmantle (1962)
A Yard of Sun (1970)
One Thing More (1986)
A Ringing of Bells (2000)

Life

Christopher Fry was born in Bristol, England. His father was an American lay preacher and his mother belonged to the Quaker sect. He lost his father at a very early age and adopted his mother's surname. He first started working as a schoolteacher and later moved on to becoming an actor, director and reviewer of plays.

His career as a dramatist was given a boost when he was commissioned by the vicar of Steyning to write a play about the life of the local saint St Cuthman. The play was titled *The Boy with a Cart* and Richard Burton acted in it. He continued writing plays which enjoyed popularity through the 1940s and 50s.

Fry continued to write in the following decades, but his style of poetic drama was eclipsed by the plays of the Angry Young Men. He started to write plays for both radio and television.

He busied himself with writing screenplays, too, and he collaborated on the screenplay of the famous film *Ben Hur.*

Works

Fry attempted to recreate in his plays the beauty and eloquence of Elizabethan drama. Along with T.S. Eliot, Fry ushered in a renaissance of poetic drama. He achieved the height of his popularity in the 1940s and 1950s.

The Boy with a Cart is a mystical and religious drama written in the style of mystery plays. It narrates the legend of St Cuthman and his miracles. His next play *The Firstborn* is set in Egypt at the time of the Biblical plagues and is about Moses getting the Jews out of Egypt. *Thor with Angels* and *A Sleep of Prisoners* are also religious plays.

Although his religious plays were received well, the theatre-going audience preferred the exuberant wordplay of his comedies. *A Phoenix Too Frequent*, a light-hearted comedy in one act set in ancient Greece, is the story of a mourning widow torn between her attraction for a young soldier and her desire to join her husband in the underworld.

His most well-known play is *The Lady's Not for Burning*. It is a three-act play about a world-weary man who confesses to a crime he has not committed in order to be hanged. It is set in the Middle Ages when witch-hunting was rampant. While waiting to be hanged, he meets a woman accused of witchcraft but he does not want her life to end by being burnt at the stake. The play depicts the love blossoming between the two.

Venus Observed is another historical verse drama that is about an aging Duke who asks his son to find a bride for him. When they see the beautiful girl Perpetua both father and son wish to marry her. The play stands out for its subtle humour.

In *A Sleep of Prisoners*, Fry symbolically portrays the problems of four prisoners of war who are locked up in a church in the enemy territory. An ensuing fight between two of the inmates results in one of them almost killing the other. When they finally go to sleep, each of them has a dream revealing his inner response to the event. Fry takes the story to a spiritual plane and the attempted murder is seen successively in the stories of Cain and Abel, David and Absolom and Abraham and Isaac. The story of Shadrach is reflected in the dream of the fourth prisoner.

Fry gave the subtitle 'A Winter Comedy' to his play *The Dark is Light Enough* to hint at the tragic nature of the work. Set against the backdrop of the Hungarian Revolution of 1848, it reflects the impact of the revolution on the inhabitants of an Austrian country house.

Curtmantle is about Henry II's famous quarrel with Thomas Becket, the Archbishop of Canterbury. It is written in the form of a character's memory which is acted out on the stage. In his later years, Fry was less active as a playwright and focused more on screenplays.

Features

- Fry's religious background is reflected strongly in his works. In all his plays, he explored the problem of man's existence in a world of horror and cruelty. He had unshakeable belief in God and this is reflected amply in his work.
- His contribution to poetic or verse drama is tremendous. His plays helped to revive the blank verse that was popular in the Elizabethan Age.
- His plays discussed philosophical and religious themes. He explored questions of morality and dilemmas of life through his characters.
- He had a gaiety and an inclination for banter which appealed to his audience. His work slanted more towards the comic rather than the tragic.
- Many of his plays had a historical setting. Setting a story in a bygone era enabled Fry to explore timeless themes like human relationships.

John James Osborne (1929–94)

Look Back in Anger (1956)
Epitaph for George Dillon (1957)
The Entertainer (1957)
Luther (1961)
Inadmissible Evidence (1964)
A Patriot for Me (1965)

West of Suez (1971)
A Sense of Detachment (1972)
Watch it Come Down (1976)

Autobiography
A Better Class of Person (1981)

Life

John Osborne was born in London. His father was a commercial artist and his mother a barmaid. He lost his father when he was barely twelve years old. He studied briefly in a boarding school but was soon expelled. He joined his mother in London and worked as a trade journalist and later joined a touring company as an actor. This early exposure to the theatre was instrumental in making him a dramatist.

His personal life was not very happy. He was married five times and his last wife lived with him till his death. He was a vegetarian which was something unusual at the time. He died leaving behind a lot of debt in 1994.

Works

John Osborne took the theatre by storm with his land mark play *Look Back in Anger* in 1956. This play broke away from the drawing-room comedies and middle-class dramas of dramatists like Noel Coward and the verse drama of T.S. Eliot and Christopher Fry. Osborne's plays were not revolutionary in form but were startling in their subject matter. He focused on the working-class and the lower-middle-class life, with an emphasis on domestic realism. This type of drama later came to be known as **kitchen sink drama**.

Osborne portrayed in this play, the anger, frustration, confusion and despair of a generation of young people who had not been in World War Two, but who suffered from its after-effects. Osborne and a few more playwrights who shared his angst came to be known as the **Angry Young Men**. The hero Jimmy Porter is a frustrated young man who is struggling to find a footing in a society where the traditional possessors of privilege hold better jobs. He vents his anger out on his middle-class wife Alison. *Look Back in Anger* proved to be a landmark in the history of theatre. Structurally, it is a conventional well-made play in three acts but the style and mood are different. The essence of this type of drama is a kind of left-wing lashing out at the establishment. This attack upon a whole section of society appealed to the younger post-war intellectuals. The treatment was not genteel but caustic and rough. For example, read the following lines of dialogue from Osborne's *Look Back in Anger*:

> Jimmy: One day, when I'm no longer spending my days running a sweet stall, I may write a book about us all. It's all here. *(Slapping his forehead)* Written in flames a mile high. And it won't be recollected in tranquility either, picking daffodils with Auntie Wordsworth. It'll be recollected in fire and blood, my blood.

His next play *The Entertainer* written mainly for the actor Laurence Olivier, is about a shabby music hall comic. Its main character is a middle-aged comedian who was once a great success but has now fallen on bad times. Archie Rice, the protagonist, refuses to accept the reality that his days on the stage are over and vents his frustration on his family. Osborne uses this situation to portray the decline of Great Britain in the second-half of the twentieth century. Through this play, Osborne shows the impact of the German playwright Bertolt Brecht on his work; Brecht was becoming a strong influence on the English playwrights in the 1960s, 70s and 80s.

Luther is a three-act historical play about Martin Luther, who protested against the Roman Catholic Church. Osborne portrays him as an angry man caught between his belief in the church and doubts about its practices. This play reveals an individual in conflict with authority, a favourite theme with Osborne.

Bill Maitland, the protagonist of the play *Inadmissible Evidence,* is a middle-aged lawyer who is in search of the meaning of his life. It is a disturbing play that compels us to witness a desperate man tearing up his life.

A Patriot for Me was refused a performance license since it dealt with a subject that was controversial in the 1960s—homosexuality. It is based on the true story of Alfred Redl who worked in the Austro-Hungarian intelligence service. Redl is blackmailed by the Russians into revealing several state secrets. Through this play too, Osborne highlights the plight of a non-conformist who is being persecuted.

His later plays such as *West of Suez*, *A Sense of Detachment*, *A Better Class of Person* and *Watch it Come Down* are more offensive in attitude. Osborne's outbursts of fury against contemporary society were appealing to his audience—a generation of war-weary people. At the same time, one notes a nostalgia for the past in the dramatist.

Features

- John Osborne was known for his critical depiction of contemporary British society. Though not too experimental with the form of drama, his subject matter was completely novel.
- One of the most important contributions to British drama was his depiction of the Angry Young Man. This was a term coined by the critic Kenneth Tynan to describe Osborne's protagonists. These characters vent their frustration with the social and economic restrictions of the contemporary times.
- His plays also dealt with psychological studies of complex characters. For example in *Inadmissible Evidence,* Bill Maitland is a lawyer struggling with depression and the play portrays his psychological state skilfully.
- Osborne's plays were also a political critique of post-war Britain. In *The Entertainer,* he critiques Britain's failure to accept the truth of its declining colonial empire.
- Osborne was adept at using a realistic and colloquial style of language in his plays. The dialogues of his plays often shocked the audience for their usage of slang and profanity.
- His plays were characterised by their realism, psychological insights and social commentary.

Samuel Beckett (1906–89)

Drama

Waiting for Godot (1955)
Endgame (1958)
Krapp's Last Tape (1959)
Happy Days (1961)
Come and Go (1967)
Breath (1969)
Not I (1973)

Footfalls (1976)
Rockaby (1981)
Catastrophe (1982)
What Where (1983)

Poetry

Collected Poems in English and French (1977)

Non-Fiction

'Dante...Bruno,...Vico...Joyce' (1929)
'Proust' (1931)
'Three Dialogues' (1949)
'Disjecta: Miscellaneous writings and a Dramatic Fragment' (1929–67)

Fiction

More Pricks Than Kicks (1934)
Murphy (1938)
Watt (1953)

The Trilogy

Molloy (1951)
Malone Dies (1958)
The Unnameable (1960)

Life

Samuel Beckett was born in an upper-class Protestant suburb of Dublin, Ireland. His parents were quite well-to-do and he had a comfortable childhood. After his schooling, he studied at Trinity College, Dublin, where he received his BA degree.

He then proceeded to Paris on a fellowship. While in Paris, he became a close friend of James Joyce, who had a tremendous influence on him. It was at that time that he wrote the essay entitled 'Dante...Bruno...Vita...Joyce', the first work of Beckett's to be published.

After returning to Dublin, he briefly taught at Trinity College but found himself unsuitable for the job. After spending five restless years in Germany, France, Ireland and London, he went back to Paris and settled down there. Most of his writing was originally in French which he translated into English. He was awarded the Nobel Prize in 1969.

Works

Samuel Beckett was a very well-read person and his writing reflected several subtle references to the books that had impacted him. Intellectuals like Dante, René Descartes and James Joyce had a deep influence on Beckett's thinking and writing. Beckett was not merely depicting the sordid and dreary view of life but, rather, was deeply concerned with discovering the true meaning of our existence on this earth.

Beckett began his literary journey with critical essays, reviews, short stories and poems. *More Pricks Than Kicks,* a collection of ten short stories, appeared in 1934. The stories were about the experiences of an Irishman, Belacqua Shuah. This was soon followed by his first full-length novel *Murphy.* Highly influenced by James Joyce, the novel displays an exuberant style of writing. The protagonist is an Irishman who flees from a girl he is about to marry, to become a nurse in a mental asylum.

His next novel *Watt* is a play on words. The protagonist Watt ('what?'), is preoccupied with trying to understand the various characters around him and he fails to meet his employer Mr Knott ('not') who does not appear in the novel. It is an absurdist novel presenting an Irishman's impressions of London.

Molloy, Malone Dies and *The Unnamable* are collectively referred to as 'The Trilogy'. All three books were initially written in French and later translated into English. In these books Beckett tried to focus on the problem of identity of the human self. The famous and oft-quoted phrase, 'I can't go on, I'll go on' is from the novel *The Unnamable.* Another example is when Molloy, struggling to discover his identity, cries out: 'And I was there, a man. Now I'm a heap of memories…and all those things at hand without which I could not bear being a man.'

Beckett's most well-known play is *Waiting for Godot*. It has a symmetrical, mirror image-like two-act structure. It broke away from every convention of the well-made play. The Irish critic Vivian Mercier described the work as a play in which 'nothing happens, twice'. *Godot* represents Man's expectation for something to happen at some time. Beckett tried to highlight our predisposition to lead a habitual existence. People keep themselves busy everyday with small habitual activities to prevent themselves from agonising over their loneliness and the emptiness of life. The play is about two characters Vladimir and Estragon who are waiting for someone called 'Godot'. They are not sure when he is supposed to meet them, or exactly where. They are not even sure which day of the week it is: 'And is it Saturday? Is it not rather Sunday? (Pause) Or Monday? (Pause) Or Friday?'. The tramps are joined by a bizarre pair, Pozzo and Lucky, one a master, the other a slave on the end of a rope. Act II is almost a repetition of Act I, except for Pozzo and Lucky. In Act II, Pozzo is blind and Lucky is dumb.

Endgame is Beckett's bleakest stage production. It gives expression to the extreme futility of human life and man's helplessness at this emptiness. It describes the breakdown of the relation between a master, Hamm, and his servant, Clov. This breakdown could be symbolically interpreted as the break of the physical body from the soul at the time of death.

In *Krapp's Last Tape,* the protagonist who is an old man listens to revelations made by him when he was younger. One learns about his self-inflicted isolation through the tapes, recorded during several periods of his life. The name of the character 'Krapp' suggests that his whole life has been 'crap'. The fact that the protagonist suffers from digestion problems and is shown eating bananas throughout the play heightens the irony of his name.

Happy Days is a play about a woman called Winnie who is shown buried to her waist and sinking further into the ground, but still talking about the trivial things in her handbag. Beckett is symbolically trying to convey that even as we get closer to dcath, we behave as if we are immortal and continue to be attached to material things.

Beckett's later works inclined towards extreme brevity and concentration. *Come and Go*, a playlet, containing just 121 words, has three women characters. Beckett referred to this work as a 'dramaticule'. *Breath* is an even briefer play, with a duration of just thirty seconds. It is a recording of a birth cry, followed by the slow breathing of somebody. There is a second identical cry and the play comes to an end. There are no characters to be seen on the stage and Beckett gave instructions that the stage should be littered with rubbish. Through this play, Beckett brilliantly highlights the fragility and transience of life. In *Not I*, a monologue is delivered by an actor of indeterminate sex, with only the actor's mouth illuminated.

He wrote a number of poems, too, which were published in 1977 as *Collected Poems in English and French.*

Features

- Beckett succeeded in holding up a mirror to the hollowness and meaninglessness of life in the twentieth century after the two world wars uprooted old values and beliefs. He was the chief exponent of the genre called 'absurd drama' which sharply turned its back upon conventional drama.
- His work was a sustained attack on the realistic tradition in literature. In his novels and plays, he showed us that one could dispense with plot, setting and dialogues and still be able to convey the human condition.
- He was a master of minimalism. He was adept at using the minimum of characters, words and setting.
- He used the technique of repetition in his plays. This showed the repetitive nature of human action and also succeeded in breaking away from the linear progression of action as everything is depicted as ending where it began.
- In spite of his dismal assessment of life, Beckett made use of farce and comedy. In his plays we see characters struggling to put on and take off shoes, trousers falling down and failed attempts at committing suicide. One could describe his humour as dark comedy.
- He was a realist in his usage of dialogues. He duplicated the language spoken in our daily lives and he achieved a poetic effect through his fidelity to real speech.

Harold Pinter (1930–2008)

The Room (1957)	*The Homecoming* (1965)
The Birthday Party (1958)	*Old Times* (1971)
The Dumb Waiter (1960)	*No Man's Land* (1975)
The Caretaker (1960)	*Betrayal* (1978)
A Night out (1961)	*Moonlight* (1993)
The Lover (1963)	*Celebration* (2000)

Life

Harold Pinter was born into a working-class family in East London. His father was a Jewish tailor. Pinter displayed an interest in the theatre at a very early age and acted with many touring companies. He began to write poetry and he published some of his poems in periodicals before he turned twenty.

He began his career as a dramatist writing one-act plays, before he moved on to full-length dramas. Apart from drama, Pinter wrote screenplays for films such as *The French Lieutenant's Woman*. He also wrote extensively for radio and television.

He married an actress, Vivien Merchant, and had a son, Daniel. The marriage was turbulent because Pinter was involved first with Joan Bakewell, which inspired his play *The Betrayal*, and later with Antonia Fraser whom he ultimately married.

He was honoured with several awards, the chief of which was the Nobel Prize in 2007. He died after battling cancer for several years.

Works

Harold Pinter is considered to have been one of the most influential modern British dramatists. His style of writing was so unique that it has been included in the English language as an adjective, 'Pinteresque'. His plays were influenced by Samuel Beckett, in that they could be described as absurd drama. Pinter's plays differ from those of Beckett's, however, as they deal with real settings and identifiable characters.

His plays have often been described by critics as **comedies of menace**. He presents to us on the stage a world which is very real and frightening. Pinter made good and effective use of pregnant pauses and banal speech to add to the terror on the stage.

The Room, Pinter's first play, is a good example of the comedy of menace. The dialogue, though appearing to be familiar, is at the same time ominously unfamiliar. The mood is both menacing and comic. His play is layered with symbolism. The central characters are visited by a young couple called Sands (meant to symbolise the sands of time). They are intruded upon by a blind black man—symbolising death which is blind in claiming its victims. The room which is the setting of the play, symbolises a secure place that is threatened by the cold and by death lurking outside.

His next play *The Birthday Party* is a play in three acts. Stanley is the central character, who is a boarder in a house. He is paranoid about meeting strangers and little is revealed about his past. Two strangers, Goldberg and McCann, arrive looking for him on what is supposed to be his birthday. What begins as a celebration, turns into a nightmare with Stanley being taken away by the two men. The play is a study in fear and terror.

The Caretaker is a tragicomedy about two brothers who offer the job of a caretaker to a tramp. The play, which depends more on dialogue than action, is about the characters' inability to communicate with each other. Isolation and deceit are other major themes of the play. Pinter deliberately leaves the time, place and language ambiguous and the characters, in all probability, may continue to go on without any change even after the curtains come down.

After *The Caretaker,* his next important play was *The Homecoming*. It is about two characters Teddy and Ruth who return to England after a long absence of six years to meet the former's family. Pinter demonstrates how human beings are overpowered by their primeval instincts when Ruth and Teddy's brothers and father give in to their sexual instincts. Pinter shows the breakdown of human society in this play.

Betrayal was inspired by Pinter's own extra-marital affair. It follows the events in the lives of two lovers, Emma and Jerry. The uniqueness of this play is that it narrates the story in reverse chronological order, which was very new to the contemporary theatre.

Moonlight is about a character on his deathbed who drifts in and out of consciousness. His disjointed recollections reveal the troubled history of his family. The play is full of pauses and obscure dialogues, a style for which Pinter was famous. His last play *Celebration* is set in a high-end restaurant and is a biting satire of modern society. The play focuses on ideas such as the erosion of communication, the meaninglessness of social rituals and the cruelty of humans.

Features

- Pinter avoided the conventional dramatic development and plot evolution. Instead, he focused on presenting an arresting situation and creating an aura of mystery and suspense.

- His settings were always simple, usually a drawing room. One is able to immediately identify with the familiar setting.
- Pinter was adept at capturing the nuances of colloquial speech which were made more effective through the use of pauses and silence. Pinter explained his approach to language in his well-known speech made at the National Student Drama Festival in Bristol: 'There are two silences. One when no word is spoken. The other when perhaps a torrent of language is being employed. The speech we hear is an indication of that which we don't hear.'
- Pinter was an expert at using symbols. The cold outside the room in his play *The Room* is symbolic of death and the uncertainty of life. In *The Birthday Party,* the initial, rhythmic beating of the drum becomes gradually erratic until Stanley beats it in a 'savage' and 'possessed' manner. This serves as an indication that the peace of the boarding house was soon to descend into chaos.
- Pinter's themes were usually centred around a nameless fear, mental disturbances, sexual fantasy and obsession.

Tom Stoppard (1937–2025)

Drama

A Walk on the Water (1963)
Rosencrantz and Guildenstern Are Dead (1966)
The Real Inspector Hound (1968)
Jumpers (1972)
Travesties (1974)
Dirty Linen (1976)
Every Good Boy Deserves Favour (1977)
Night and Day (1978)

Novel

Lord Malquist and the Moon (1965)
The Real Thing (1982)
Arcadia (1993)
The Coast of Utopia (2002)
Rock and Roll (2006)
Leopoldstadt (2019)
Professional Foul (1977)

Television

Parade's End (2013)

Life

Tom Stoppard was born in Czechoslovakia but moved with his family to Singapore in 1939 to escape from the Nazis. After his father Dr Eugene Straussler was killed during the Japanese invasion, his mother escaped to India with her two sons. He studied for three years in an Indian boarding school in Darjeeling and later settled with his family in England. After his mother married a British officer, he took his stepfather's name and called himself Tom Stoppard. He began his career as a journalist before he started to write plays.

He was married three times and had four sons, two from each of his first two wives. Neither he nor his brother knew anything about their history in Czechoslovakia. It was only after his mother died in 1996 that he visited the place where he was born and learnt that his grandparents on both sides were Jewish and that they had died in the concentration camp at Auschwitz.

Stoppard was knighted in 1997 and lived in Dorset with Sabrina Guinness, his third wife, till his death in 2025.

Works

Tom Stoppard's first play was *A Walk on the Water* which was televised in 1963. It was later staged in London in 1968 as *Enter a Free Man*. His next play *Rosencrantz and Guildenstern Are Dead* won for Stoppard immense fame. In this play, two minor characters in Shakespeare's famous play *Hamlet* are the main characters. The action of the play is in the wings of the stage where *Hamlet* is being performed. In *Hamlet*, these characters who are summoned by the king to spy on Hamlet are not sure about the nature of their task and are ultimately killed. Stoppard uses the technique of metatheatre to completely transform the Elizabethan revenge tragedy to a twentieth-century absurd drama. (**Metatheatre** draws attention to itself as a theatrical performance, reminding the audience that they are watching a play. The term was coined by Lionel Abel in 1963.) In this play, Stoppard explores the theme of man's solitude and his lack of control over his life, reminiscent of Beckett's style.

Jumpers is a play about a professor of moral philosophy George Moore. Stoppard draws a parallel to G.E. Moore, who was a professor of philosophy and who had a great influence on the Bloomsbury group. The play is about a comparison between the physical acrobatics of the jumpers and the verbal gymnastics of Moore's long speeches. It is a brilliant parody of academia and the media.

In *Travesties,* Stoppard presents a fictional meeting between three important people who had a tremendous impact upon twentieth-century thinking and values. The action takes place in Zurich in the year 1917. The three people are the communist leader Lenin, the Dadaist poet Tristan Tzara, and the modernist author James Joyce. Henry Carr, who was an acquaintance of Joyce in real life, is the narrator of the events. Through this play, Stoppard cleverly explores the theories of Marxism, Dadaism and modernism.

His next important play was *The Real Thing*. It is a marital tragicomedy that revolves around an actress and a man fighting to free a Scottish soldier imprisoned during a protest. Stoppard once again uses the technique of a play within a play.

Arcadia is a drama that explores the meeting between two modern academics and the residents of a country house in Derbyshire. It is set in the nineteenth century amidst a cast of aristocrats and tutors. It also includes the invisible presence of Lord Byron.

Stoppard continued to write in the twenty-first century. His next work was a trilogy of plays under the title *The Coast of Utopia.* The three plays were *Voyage*, *Shipwreck* and *Salvage* and they were about philosophical discussions between the revolutionary Russian figures of the nineteenth century.

This was followed by *Rock and Roll* which was about the pop culture of the 1960s and a limited series called *Parade's End*. The series was about a love triangle between an aristocrat, his socialite wife and a suffragette.

His most recent play *Leopoldstadt*, written in 2020, was about Jews living in Vienna in the early-twentieth century.

Features

- His work could be described as belonging to the absurd theatre that was popular in the mid-twentieth century. His plays reflect the meaningless state of human beings.

- Stoppard tried to demonstrate through his plays the unreliability of language in a meaningless world. In his plays, human beings are unable to communicate as they are no longer certain of the meaning of words.
- An important feature of absurd drama is the use of verbal games. Most characters in absurd theatre indulge in verbal tennis to apparently pass the time. *Rosencrantz and Guildenstern Are Dead* is full of such verbal games.
- His plays make several references to other texts. For example, he refers to well-known works by Shakespeare, Oscar Wilde and T.S. Eliot.
- His plays displayed a technique known as metatheatre, in which the fourth wall is broken in order to remove the boundary between the audience and the actors.

Arnold Bennett (1867–1931)

Fiction

A Man from the North (1898)
Anna of the Five Towns (1902)
The Old Wives' Tale (1908)
Clayhanger Series
I Clayhanger (1910)
II Hilda Lessways (1911)
III These Twain (1911)
IV The Role Call (1918)
The Pretty Lady (1918)
Riceyman Steps (1923)
Lord Raingo (1926)
Mr Prohack (1927)
The Strange Vanguard (1928)
Accident (1929)

Short Stories

The Grim Tale of the Five Towns (1907)
The Matador of the Five Towns (1912)
Imperial Palace (1930)
The Night Visitor (1931)

Drama

Gates of Wrath (1903)
What the Public Wants (1909)
Milestones (with E. Knoblock, 1951)
The Great Adventure (1913)
The Love Match (1922)
London Life (with E. Knoblock, 1924)

Life

Arnold Bennett was born in Staffordshire, England, and his father was a solicitor. Bennett went to London when he was twenty-one and worked as a clerk and journalist before he became a writer. For a few years, he lived in France where he married a French woman. He moved back to England after ten years and separated from his wife after about fifteen years of marriage. He began writing a highly successful weekly article on books, which he continued until his death, for the *Evening Standard.*

He was a prolific writer and contributed several articles and short stories for journals. Bennett had more than thirty-four novels and thirteen plays to his credit. He believed that the common people should be able to enjoy literature and his writings, therefore, had a great appeal to people. He was criticised by the modernist writers, especially Virginia Woolf, for his style of fiction. He died in 1931 of typhoid fever.

Works

Arnold Bennett was a prolific writer who churned out several novels, short stories, essays, articles and plays, but it is as a novelist that he is remembered today. Of the novels, his reputation rests only on a few of his books. One could consider him as a regional and realistic novelist, who set most of his work in the Black Country, an area in the West Midlands County which had a lot of coal mines and iron foundries. He continued in the tradition of Charles Dickens and George Eliot and wrote realistic fiction which appealed to the common people. Bennett wrote in a detailed and realistic style about the lives of ordinary folk. His novels were set in a drab and unromantic world and he drew his characters from the lower-middle class of shopkeepers and clerks. Bennett was influenced by the work of Flaubert and Balzac. George Moore also had a great impact on Bennett.

Bennett strongly believed that literature should be accessible to ordinary people. Although he admired the complex works of the modernists, his own fiction was more popular and sold in large numbers. Unfortunately, this style of writing came under severe criticism from Virginia Woolf in her famous essay 'Modern Fiction' where she criticised Bennet, Wells and Galsworthy for writing about unimportant things.

Bennett's best works are *The Old Wives' Tale*, the *Clayhanger* trilogy, *Hilda Lessways* and *These Twain*. All these books are set in in the Black Country which Bennett depicts in a detached and mildly ironic manner. *The Old Wives' Tale* chronicles the lives of two sisters, daughters of a draper, through their girlhood, disillusionment and death. Bennett brings to life the drab and uninteresting life of the draper's shop.

His trilogy *The Clayhanger* series is about the Clayhanger family. This series of novels is set in the fictionalised 'Five Towns', modelled on the six towns of the Staffordshire Potteries where Bennett grew up. He gives a detailed account of provincial life and the culture of the region. This trilogy has many memorable characters like Darius Clayhanger, Auntie Hamps, Edwin Clayhanger and Hilda Lessways.

His two volumes of short stories *The Grim Tale of the Five Towns* and *The Matador of the Five Towns* are again set in the same region and reveal his concern for the ordinary and obscure lives.

The best novel of his later period is *Riceyman Steps*. It narrates the story of a miserly second-hand bookseller and is set in a place called Clerkenwell in London. It covers one year in the life of the protagonist. Bennett wrote a number of novels that were in a lighter vein and which displayed a love of luxury and fantasy. Some of them were *The Grand Babylon Hotel*, *The Card* and *Mr Prohack*.

Bennett wrote a few plays but it is as a novelist that he is remembered today.

Features

- Arnold Bennett was a realistic writer whose novels forged an important link between British fiction and European realism. He focused on portraying the everyday lives of the ordinary middle-class folk.
- He could be considered as a regional writer who set many of his stories in a fictional place evocative of his hometown.
- He was not interested in propaganda or in expounding any particular philosophy. This prevented his work from suffering from any distortions that a reformer was susceptible to.

- His characters were provincial middle-class people with average intelligence. They were not socially refined, but through them Bennett succeeded in representing a whole class of people in an era of rapidly growing industrialisation.
- On the downside, Bennett's novels are very slow-moving and heavy. They also lack poetic language and imagination.

Rudyard Kipling (1865–1936)

Novels
The Light that Failed (1890)
The Naulahka: A Story of West and East (1892)
Captain Courageous (1897)
Kim (1901)
Life's Handicap (1891)
The Jungle Book (1895)
The Second Jungle Book (1895)
Stalky and Co. (1899)
Just-So Stories (1899)
Rewards and Fairies (1910)
Debits and Credits (1926)

Short Story
Plain Tales from the Hills (1888)
Soldiers Three (1888)
The Phantom Rickshaw and Other Tales (1888)
Wee Willie Winkie and Other Stories (1888)
In Black and White (1889)
Under the Deodars (1889)

Poetry
Puck of Pook's Hill (1906)
Departmental Ditties (1886)
Barrack-Room Ballads (1892)
The Seven Seas (1896)
The Five Nations (1903)

Life

Rudyard Kipling was born in Mumbai and spent the first five years there before he was sent to England along with his younger sister. They spent the next five years separated from their parents, with an English family who were paid to look after them. The children were treated badly and they did not see their parents for those five years. These years were later recalled with bitterness in his short story 'Baa, Baa, Black Sheep'. From there he went to a boarding school about which he wrote in *Stalky and Co.* When he was about seventeen, he returned to India to work as a journalist.

He married an American woman and lived in Vermont for many years, before settling down in Sussex. Kipling wrote: 'I am slowly discovering England which is the most wonderful foreign land I have ever been in.'

He was regarded as the unofficial poet laureate and, in 1907, became the first English writer to receive the Nobel Prize. He continued to write till the early 1930s and died in 1936.

Works

FICTION

Rudyard Kipling belonged as much to the Victorian Age as he did to the twentieth century. He wrote a number of poems, novels and stories for children. He is remembered particularly as the creator of Mowgli, a child raised by wolves in the jungle.

A prolific writer, he gained popularity when he was in his early thirties. His stories about life in India were expressed in vigorous prose that combined the vernacular speech of the region with formal language. This style helped in bridging the gap between the characters and his readers. Somerset Maugham, speaking about the magic of his Indian stories said, 'They give you the tang of the East, the smell of the bazars, the torpor of the rains, the heat of the sun-scorched earth, the rough life of the barracks.'

Kipling was an imperialist who infused the idea of the British Empire in the minds of the people. Louis Cazamian in his *History of English Literature* says, 'It is from Kipling that to the majority of Englishmen the existence of the Empire dates.' Being an imperialist who gave the world the phrase, 'the White Man's burden', he was against Home Rule in India. (White Man's burden refers to the supposed duty of white people to educate and civilise the subjects of their colonies.)

He began his literary career with poetry and short stories. His earliest work consisted of a collection of verses *Departmental Ditties* and a book of short stories *Plain Tales from the Hills.* The success of these early works prompted him to write several volumes of short stories. His stories were mostly set in India and some in different parts of the British Empire. *Plain Tales from the Hills* is a collection of forty stories based on Kipling's own experiences as a journalist.

His next volume of short stories was *Soldiers Three* which is about three British soldiers in India. The three men are portrayed as being deeply loyal to the British Army, in spite of their personal quirks. These stories provide an insight into the lives of British soldiers during the colonial period.

In *The Phantom Rickshaw and Other Stories,* there is a blurring of the line between reality and fantasy. The titular story is about a British man who is haunted by the ghost of his lover who died in a rickshaw accident. These stories are remarkable for their vivid descriptions of India.

Kipling published several collections of short stories like *Wee Willie Winkie and Other Child Stories*, *The Day's Work*, *Stalky and Co.*, *Just So Stories for Little Children*, *Puck of Pook's Hill* and *Rewards and Fairies*. Most of these stories were for children. *Just So Stories,* for example, is a collection of funny stories which explain how animals came to be as they are.

The Jungle Book and *The Second Jungle Book* are the most famous collections of short stories by Kipling. These stories are set in the jungles of India and feature a young boy called Mowgli who is raised by wolves and other wild animals. Most of the characters in these stories are animals such as Shere Khan, the tiger, Baloo, the bear, and Bagheera, the black panther. The stories discuss ideas such as the importance of family, the struggle between man and nature and loyalty. These stories, describing the exploits of Mowgli, have become extremely popular and have been made into several animated films.

The success of his short stories encouraged Kipling to write novels. His first novel *The Light that Failed* is mostly set in London. It is the story of an artist who loses his sight and whose love for his childhood friend remains unrequited.

His novel *Kim* narrates the story of an orphaned boy, Kimball O'Hara, who grows up in Lahore. He meets a Tibetan lama and decides to follow him, but is soon captured by British soldiers who find his parents and decide that he should be raised as the Englishman that he is. The British officers discover his potential to act as a spy in their interactions with the Russians and Kim is trained suitably. The book is rich in its descriptions of India of the colonial period.

POETRY

He was a genius at capturing the language of the common folk and his first volume of poems *Departmental Ditties* excels in depicting the ordinary life as lived in the different parts of the British Empire. *Barrack Room Ballads*, a collection of poems about the lives of soldiers, gives us a sympathetic account of the soldiers.

Kipling's poetry was seldom introspective, preferring more public-oriented themes that dealt with the empire. Some of his well-known poems are 'If', 'Gunga Din', 'The Last of the Light Brigade' and 'Land of our Birth'.

Features

- In his poetry, he was influenced by Sir Walter Scott, Swinburne, and the American, Mark Twain.
- Kipling captures the nuances of everyday speech in many dialects—Indian, cockney, Yorkshire and Irish. He was adept at assuming the narrative voices of a vast range of people like soldiers, sailors and Muslim sages.
- His writings often reflected an imperialist attitude that was prevalent at that time. Kipling tended to glorify British colonialism and considered it as a boon to, what were considered, 'uncivilised' colonies.
- Kipling's contribution to children's literature is significant. His *Jungle Book* stories have continued to fascinate children through the decades.
- His descriptions of Anglo-Indian and native life during the colonial period are accurate and detailed.
- As a poet, he slanted toward the realistic style of writing and succeeded in capturing the nuances of common people.
- Some of the phrases we use today such as 'the female of the species', 'but that is another story' and 'the White Man's burden' were coined by Kipling.
- Some of his works have been criticised for expressing imperialist and racist views. His characterisation of native characters has also been viewed as being stereotypical and offensive.

Herbert George Wells (1866–1946)

Science Fiction
The Time Machine (1895)
The Stollen Bacillus and Other Stories (1895)
The Wonderful Visit (1895)
The Island of Dr Moreau (1896)
The Invisible Man (1897)
The War of the Worlds (1898)
When the Sleeper Wakes (1899)
The First Men of the Moon (1901)
The Food of the Gods (1904)
The War in the Air (1907)
Sociological Novels
Kipps (1905)
Tono-Bungay (1909)
Ann Veronica (1909)
The History of Mr. Polly (1910)
Social Treatises and Pamphlets
Mankind in the Making (1903)
Socialism and the Family (1906)
New Worlds for Old (1908)
An Englishman Looks at the World (1914)
The War that will End War (1914)
The Fate of Homo Sapiens (1939)
The New World Order (1940)
Mind at the End of its Tether (1945)
The New Machiavelli (1911)
Mr Britling Sees it through (1916)
The World of William Clissold (1926)

Life

H.G. Wells was born in Bromley, Kent. His father was an unsuccessful shopkeeper and Wells had to start working from the age of thirteen. He was apprenticed to a chemist and then a draper. He then taught at a grammar school and while he was teaching, he studied at night and won a scholarship to the Norman School of Science. Here, he met the famous Thomas Huxley who influenced him greatly.

After completing his studies, he went back to teaching and writing articles, but ill health made him give up teaching and take up writing as a full-time career. He joined the Fabian Society but left it after six years.

As he grew older, he became ill and the Second World War undermined his confidence in the human race. His last work *Mind at the End of Its Tether* reflects his pessimistic view of the world in which humankind is ultimately destroyed.

Works

Wells was a prolific writer who is best known for his science fiction. Apart from science fiction, he also wrote a number of sociological novels, especially focusing on the lower-middle class. In his later years, he preferred to write pamphlets and treatises which made him one of the most influential voices of the age.

SCIENCE FICTION

His first novel *The Time Machine* catapulted him to instant fame. The post-apocalyptic science fiction work is a social allegory set in the year 802701. It describes a society divided into two classes—the Eloi and the Morlocks who are the distant descendants of the contemporary upper and lower classes respectively. The whole story is narrated by a time traveller who travels to different periods of time.

The Stolen Bacillus and Other Stories is a collection of fifteen fantasy and science-fiction short stories. This was followed in quick succession by the novels *The Wonderful Visit* and *The Island of Dr Moreau.* In *The Wonderful Visit*, the protagonist is an angel visiting contemporary England. The tone is slightly satirical, and mocks some of the customs of Victorian England. *The Island of Dr Moreau* recounts the experiences of a shipwrecked man stranded on a Pacific Island, which is under the control of Dr Moreau, who uses science to turn animals into human-like beasts.

Wells's next famous work in the genre of science fiction is *The Invisible Man.* This narrates the tale of a scientist who stumbles upon the secret of making himself invisible. Unfortunately, he is not able to reverse it. The invisible man turns violent, terrorising people until he is cornered and savagely beaten by a mob. Only after he dies does his body gradually become visible.

The First Men on the Moon, inspired by Jules Verne, is a story of the journey of two men to the moon and their subsequent experiences there with the 'Selenites', who are insect-like creatures inhabiting the moon.

Yet another novel by Wells which proved to be prophetic is *The War in the Air.* It was written only four years after the Wright brothers made their historic flight and about two years prior to their design being accepted.

SOCIOLOGICAL NOVELS

Kipps was H.G. Wells's first important novel that was not in the genre of science fiction. This novel is an important document of England at the turn of the century. Kipps is a working-class hero who rises from humble beginnings to become a successful businessman. *The History of Mr Polly* is the story of an unsuccessful and unhappy shopkeeper who frees himself by setting his shop on fire. These novels are known for their comic and realistic style of narration.

Other novels in this genre were *Tono-Bungay*, *Ann Veronica*, *The New Machiavelli*, *Mr Britling Sees it through* and *The World of William Clissold*. These novels give us graphic pictures of contemporary society and focus on the distinctions between the classes.

Apart from fiction, Wells wrote a lot of prose in the form of pamphlets, expounding his views on politics and society. His books *The Rights of Man* and *Universal Declaration of Human Rights* reveal his preoccupation with social equality and human rights. His other important works in this category are *Mankind in the Making*, *Anticipations*, *New Worlds for Old*, *A Short History of the World* and *Mind at the End of Its Tether*. In the last work, Wells's tone is pessimistic as he expresses his despair at the probable destruction of the human species.

Features

- H.G. Wells is widely accepted as the father of science fiction. Writing as he did, at the turn of the twentieth century when science and technology were taking giant strides, Wells's books fired up the imagination of his readers.
- In his science fiction, he gave many convincing details born out of his study of science. He explored concepts like time travel, space travel and air travel.
- He was deeply concerned with man and society. He highlighted the problems besetting contemporary society and he was particularly concerned with the lower-middle class. As a result, his later novels were discussions of social or political issues.
- He had a rich imagination and could create entire worlds and universes with unique creatures and laws of their own.
- He is considered a futurist as he anticipated several important scientific achievements of the twentieth century.

Somerset Maugham (1874–1965)

Fiction
Lisa of Lambeth (1897)
Of Human Bondage (1915)
The Moon and Sixpence (1919)
The Painted Veil (1925)
Cakes and Ale (1930)
The Razor's Edge (1944)

Short Stories
The Trembling of a Leaf (1921)
Six Stories in the First-Person Singular (1931)

Drama
A Man of Honour (1903)
Lady Frederick (1907)
Mrs. Dot (1908)
Jack Straw (1908)
The Land of Promise (1914)
Home and Beauty (1919)
Caesar's Wife (1919)
The Circle (1921)
East of Suez (1922)
The Constant Wife (1927)
For Services Rendered (1932)
Christmas Holiday (1939)

Life

Somerset Maugham was born in Paris and lost both his parents by the age of ten. He was brought up by a relative and educated in Canterbury, England. He became a qualified doctor and used this knowledge in writing his first novel.

After his first novel was accepted, he gave up his medical career and took up writing. He began his literary career with plays which were very popular. After writing more than thirty plays, he turned his attention to fiction.

He loved travelling and he used his travel experiences in his novels and short stories. Towards the end of his life, he became senile and died at the age of ninety-one.

Works

FICTION

Somerset Maugham began his literary career as a novelist and then turned to drama, but his fame rests on his short stories and novels. He made good use of his experiences as a doctor and his extensive travels to far-flung places, in his fiction. His simple and realistic style of writing had an immediate appeal to people. He was a realist who was keenly interested in human nature. He is noted for his slightly cynical and detached style of writing.

His first novel was *Lisa of Lambeth* where he used his experiences while on duty in the obstetric ward. Set in a slum, Maugham, captures accurately not only the details of the lives of the slum dwellers but also their language. This was followed by his autographical novel *Of Human Bondage.* The protagonist Philip Carey is a thinly veiled version of Maugham. Carey, like Maugham, loses his mother at the age of nine, has a handicap and lives with his uncle and aunt. Maugham, however, stated that 'This is a novel, not autobiography; though much of it is autobiographical, more is pure fiction.'

The Moon and Sixpence, based on the life of the artist Paul Gaugin, explores the nature of creativity and the sacrifices it demands. The protagonist Charles Strickland a stockbroker in London, suddenly gives up his job to pursue a career as an artist. He abandons his wife and children and finally settles in Tahiti where he creates his greatest works.

The next important novel by Maugham, *Cakes and Ale*, is a satire on the literary world. Two of its principal characters were said to be inspired by the novelists Thomas Hardy and Hugh Walpole. It is a witty and genial novel that gives us a glimpse of the novel form in the early-twentieth century.

The Razor's Edge is a philosophical novel about a disillusioned young man who returns from the First World War. He goes on a quest to discover the true meaning of life. This journey takes him to Paris where he meets a Hindu guru and ultimately goes to India. Maugham used his experience of meeting the great sage Ramana Maharishi when he visited India in 1938. The following lines, translated into English, are from the Katha Upanishad, from where Maugham got the title for his novel.

> Get up! Wake up! Seek the guidance of an
> Illumined teacher and realise the Self.
> Sharp like a razor's edge is the path,
> The sages say, difficult to traverse.

Apart from these and several more novels, Maugham wrote many short stories. Many of these stories were set in the Far East and the Pacific Islands. He was able to evoke the atmosphere of these places in an economical and remarkable way. Most of his stories were narrated in the first person in which he shared his meetings with various interesting people across the globe. His stories were well known for their unexpected twist in the end. *The Trembling of a Leaf: Little Stories of the South Sea Islands* is another collection of six stories. Maugham had travelled to the Pacific Islands along with his secretary in 1916–17. Some of the best stories in this collection are 'Red', 'Mackintosh' and 'Rain'. Other famous short stories by Maugham are 'The Verger', 'Mr Know-All', 'The Man with the Scar' and 'The Ant and the Grasshopper', to mention just a few. Maugham has written about a hundred short stories.

DRAMA

Maugham was a very successful dramatist, who wrote more than thirty plays between 1904 and 1933. His keen eye for detail and observation of human beings and their quirks contributed to his success as a dramatist. One of his earliest plays was *A Man of Honour* a realistic tragedy. It is about the tragic life of a well-educated man who has to marry a barmaid he had got pregnant, but whose heart belonged to another.

His later plays were mostly light-hearted comedies of manners. *The Circle* explores the theme of marital infidelity and questions the institution of marriage. *The Constant Wife* is another play dealing with the same theme. In this play a woman, upon discovering the unfaithfulness of her husband, decides to pay him back by having an affair herself. Maugham raises questions on gender equality, fidelity and other social issues in this play.

For Services Rendered is an anti-war play that explores the lives of a family dealing with the after-effects of the First World War and the Great Depression.

Features

- Somerset Maugham was a born storyteller. His style of writing in the first person gave his stories an air an authenticity. His realistic style and lucid prose made his fiction popular.

- Maugham had a keen psychological insight and he used this gift to flesh out lifelike characters. He was skilled at creating complex characters with interesting characteristics. His work is dotted with memorable characters with unique characteristics. For example, Philip Carey, Rosie Gann and Charles Strickland.
- His writing is known for its satire. He treated many social issues in a satirical and ironic manner.
- His stories which dealt with interesting people were known for a twist at the end of the plot.
- He was a realist with a keen interest in human nature. At a time when the genre of fiction was undergoing several changes and writers were experimenting with the form, Maugham wrote in the realistic tradition.

Joseph Conrad (1857–1924)

Novel
Almayer's Folly (1895)
The Nigger of the 'Narcissus' (1897)
Lord Jim (1900)
Youth—A Narrative and Two other Stories (1902)
Typhoon, and other Stories (1903)
Nostromo (1904)
Under Western Eyes (1911)
Chance—A Tale in Two Parts (1914)
Victory—An Island Tale (1915)
The Shadow Line—A Confession (1917)
The Rescue (1920)
The Rover (1923)

Non-Fiction
The Mirror of the Sea—Memoirs and Impressions (1906)

Short Stories
Tales of Unrest (1898)
A Set of Six (1908)
'Twixt Land and Sea—Tales (1912)
Within the Tides—Tales (1915)

Autobiography
A Personal Record (1912)

Life

Joseph Conrad was born to Polish parents and his original name was Teodor Josef Konrad Korzeniowski. He was a lifelong exile from his homeland. Due to his father's political views, his family was exiled to Volagda in northern Russia. He lost his mother when he was seven and his father when he was twelve years old.

The young Conrad imbibed his father's passion for translating French and English works into Polish.

He was raised by his uncle who also had strong political leanings and a love for literature. Unhappy with his school education, Conrad opted for a life on the seas at the age of seventeen. He served first in the French merchant navy and later in the British merchant navy for about twenty years. In 1894, he changed his name to the well-known 'Joseph Conrad' and settled in England to become a full-time writer. He got married in 1895.

During his career in the navy, he had gone to several parts of the world such as Indonesia, the Philippines, Venezuela and Africa. He used his experiences as a sailor in his novels.

By the end of the nineteenth century, the various nations of Europe were busy consolidating their empires. Conrad became keenly interested in this political activity and was conscious of the fact that he was witnessing history in the making. He made use of this interest in many of his novels. He suffered from poor health and died in Kent.

Works

Joseph Conrad's writing, which appeared at the turn of the century, heralded a new style of fiction which was considered by many critics to be modernist and experimental. In most of his novels, the protagonist is confronted with the complexities of the modern world. Well-known fiction critic, Ian Watt, saw Conrad's *Heart of Darkness* as 'the obdurate incompatibility of the self and the world in which it exists'—a theme often explored by the modernists.

Almayer's Folly, Conrad's first novel, is set in Indonesia. It is the story of a European on a quest for a hidden gold mine, his marriage with a local woman and relationship with his mixed-race daughter. This was followed in quick succession by *An Outcast of the Islands* which is also about a character's tragic end due to his own folly. In this novel, too, the protagonist is a European living in a tropical region.

His next novel *The Nigger of the 'Narcissus'* is a story set on a ship. The protagonist in this work is an Afro-Caribbean man on-board a ship named 'Narcissus'. Conrad paints a vivid and graphic picture of life on a ship, something he had first-hand knowledge of. He explores the conflicting themes of isolation and harmony in this novel.

Tales of Unrest is a collection of five stories and it was followed by one of Conrad's best-known novels *Lord Jim: A Tale.* It is a psychological study of guilt where Jim, the central character, is haunted by the incident of abandoning his ship in a moment of distress, along with other crew members. The whole novel is about how Jim tries to make amends for his mistake. Although he earns the respect of the local people in a remote village for his services to them, Jim continues to be haunted by the ghosts from his past. Conrad introduces his famous narrator Marlow for the first time in *Lord Jim.* The entire story of the protagonist is revealed to us through the eyes of Marlow, whose role could be compared to that of the Greek chorus.

Conrad's next two collections of short stories are *Youth—A Narrative; and two other Stories* and *Typhoon, and Other Stories.* His renowned novella *Heart of Darkness* is one of the stories in the collection *Youth.* Though written in the Victorian Age, this work is a forerunner of modern British literature and had a tremendous impact on the writers of the twentieth century. Adopting the age-old theme of the quest, it summarises in its pages the entire subject of empires treating their subjects as uncivilised savages, the clash of values and a hero's personal quest.

As with most of his other works, this too was based on Conrad's personal experiences. Being fascinated with maps from early childhood, Conrad had been intrigued with a blank space in the centre of the map of Africa. When he had the opportunity to command a steamboat in River Congo, he grabbed it and witnessed first-hand, the effects of the exploitation of local people by imperialistic Belgium. In *Heart of Darkness,* Conrad's narrator tells his tale to a few Englishmen as they sail on a ship on the Thames. He compares the upstream journey through the river to a backward journey into the darkness that lies at the heart of the English people, who are exploiting the colonies in the name of civilising them. In a profound passage, Conrad recalls centuries of history where the same mistakes have been made again and again:

> The tidal current runs to and fro in its unceasing service, crowded with memories of men and ships it has borne to the rest of home or to the battles of the sea. It had known and served all the men of whom the nation is proud, from Sir Francis Drake to Sir John Franklin … and the commissioned 'generals' of East India fleets. Hunters for gold or pursuers of fame, they had all gone out on that stream, bearing the sword, and often the torch, messengers of the might within the land…the dreams of men, the seed of commonwealth, the germs of empires.

The story of *Heart of Darkness* explores the exploits of the Belgian King Leopold II in the Congo Free State. He stripped the place of its natural treasures like ivory, but claimed to be civilising the locals and suppressing savagery. Conrad's nested narrative blurs the boundaries between darkness and light and poses a challenge to our understanding of our motives and the self. Another telling sentence from the same story further emphasises the above idea: 'The conquest of the earth, which mostly means the taking it away from those who have a different complexion or slightly flatter noses than ourselves, is not a pretty thing when you look into it too much.'

Nostromo is a multilayered novel about man's vulnerability and corruptibility. It follows the tyranny, corruption and revolution in an imaginary place called Costaguana in South America. The story revolves around a silver mine which is the country's main source of wealth. Nostromo is an Italian sailor who wants to smuggle silver out of the country. At the end of the novel, the silver that so many of them had longed to possess is lost. This novel, too, reiterates the recurring theme of regret caused by shattered dreams and failed duties.

The Secret Agent and *Under Western Eyes* are novels that have a political theme. The former is set in London and is about a spy working for an unnamed country. The latter is set in Russia and Switzerland and is often seen as Conrad's response to the troubles his father faced as a Polish independence activist, persecuted by Russia.

His other novels include *The Mirror of the Sea*, *Victory*, *The Shadow Line*, *The Rescue* and *The Rover*.

Features

- Joseph Conrad, who began his literary career in the Victorian era but continued to write in the twentieth century, displayed a marked movement away from his contemporaries. Much of his fiction deals with the modernist themes of alienation and loneliness. His novels display a shift from a preoccupation with society to a focus on individual introspection.
- His prose has a visual nature which makes his readers 'see'. Critics like Ford Madox Ford called Conrad an impressionistic writer, although Conrad himself disagreed with the description. When we read his novels, especially the early ones, we note that the narrators are telling us what they had seen. They are mostly a recreation of impressions conveyed through senses.
- Although most of his novels were based on his personal experiences, they cannot be considered as straightforward and realistic. He wrote in a complex and symbolic style and used new narrative methods. Marlow, who was a recurring narrator in many of his stories, was not the typical narrator. He makes the reader participate in the gradual development of the story and undergo the experience of the protagonist almost physically.
- He made good use of his experiences as a sailor and his travels to far flung places.
- His contempt for imperialism and colonialism is evident. *Heart of Darkness* stands testimony to this. In this, his views were directly opposed to those of Rudyard Kipling who was an imperialist who believed that it was the white man's burden to 'civilise' a 'savage' world.
- He was preoccupied with the themes of morality and guilt. His novels are psychological studies of characters that take us deep into the workings of their minds.

- His work had a significant impact on the development of modern fiction and influenced several writers, including T.S. Eliot.

E.M. Forster (1879–1970)

Novels
Where Angels Fear to Tread (1905)
The Longest Journey (1907)
A Room with a View (1908)
Howard's End (1910)
A Passage to India (1924)

Short Stories
The Celestial Omnibus (1911)
The Story of the Siren (1920)
The Eternal Moment (1928)

Literary Criticism
Aspects of the Novel (1927)
Arbinger Harvest (1936)
Two Cheers for Democracy (1951)

Life

Edward Morgan Forster, more popularly known as E.M. Forster, was born in London. He lost his father when he was just one year old, but the legacy he had left behind enabled Forster to go to a good public school. Forster hated his school and he criticised the public school system severely in his writings. His childhood days, which he spent with his mother and great-aunt at a house called 'Rooksnest', were the happiest years of his life. This house had such an impact on him that he evoked it in the description of the country house in his novel *Howards End.*

He enjoyed his time at King's College, Cambridge, which was responsible for shaping his personality and thinking. He was particularly inspired by the Professor of Philosophy G.E. Moore. He became a part of the Cambridge Apostles, which was an exclusive intellectual society, and later of the famous Bloomsbury group.

Forster travelled with his mother for a year, visiting Italy and Greece. These travels provided him with good material for his early novels. He also visited Egypt, Germany and India. He spent his last years in King's College and died in Coventry.

Works

E.M. Forster attempted to create a fictional world as close to reality as possible. He did not believe in fixed patterns but, as he pointed out in his *Aspects of the Novel*, a story should not seek to find closures, but rather focus on 'opening out'. Unlike the realists who were writing at the turn of the century, Forster disregarded the conventional plot structure. He was a modernist who turned his back on the ways of the Victorian middle class.

His one year of travel in Italy and Greece provided ample material for his early novels. In most of these, he satirised the English snobbery towards foreigners. In his first novel *Where Angels Fear to Tread* Forster demonstrates the destructive power of pride and a clash of cultures. He contrasts the suffocating world of Edwardian England, represented by Swaston, with the carefree and passionate life in the Italian town Monteria.

His next novel *The Longest Journey* recalls his days in his beloved Cambridge. This novel is considered by critics as being one of Forster's most autobiographical works. This was followed by *A Room with a View* and *Howards End*. In *A Room with a View*, Forster critiques the English society of the early-twentieth century. The novel is about a young English woman who is touring Italy with a fussy chaperone and the novel follows their experiences there and the romantic involvements of the heroine.

Howards End captures accurately a picture of English society before the First World War. The house bearing the name 'Howard's End' evokes 'Rooksnest', Forster's childhood home in Stevenage. It tells the story of two families—the Wilcoxes and the Schlegels. The former represents the rich upper class while the latter represents the intellectual middle class.

A Passage to India is a symbolic book that explores colonial India. It is considered to be one of those rare novels by English authors where Indians have been portrayed in an acceptable manner. It explores the themes of racism, imperialism and religion. It focuses on the attitudes of the British towards native Indians through the story of a visiting Englishwoman falsely accusing a respected Indian doctor of attacking her in a cave.

Apart from the above five novels, Forster wrote several short stories. Some of his well-known stories include 'The Other Side of the Hedge', 'The Road from Colonus' and 'The Machine Stops'. He explores complex themes and ideas in these stories.

LITERARY CRITICISM

Forster is equally respected as a literary critic. In his *Aspects of the Novel,* he talks about the structure and technique of fiction and points out that the genre of fiction is a suitable vehicle to convey the complexity and depth of human experience. He also discusses the importance of characters in fiction and invented the terms 'flat' and 'round' characters. A round character is one who changes and develops in the course of the novel, while a flat character is built around a single idea and does not change. His essays on various contemporary writers examined the impact of the zeitgeist to which they belonged. His essays on D.H. Lawrence and Virginia Woolf are especially important. In his essay 'The Modern Man', Forster talks about the intellectual and cultural changes and the decline in religious values in his time. He was basically a moralist who was interested in the trials and tribulations of an individual when confronted with values contrary to one's own.

Features

- His literary criticism reveals him as a humanist who was concerned about the relationship between literature and life. He was not supportive of the 'art for art's sake' theory of literature. He believed that the best literature should be able to connect with the readers emotionally.
- Forster was interested in exploring the social and political issues of his time. Unlike Kipling, Forster did not believe in imperialism and strongly condemned the imperialistic attitudes of the British.
- He was critical of Victorian snobbishness. He hated the public school system of the late-nineteenth century which inculcated these values. He attacked this as the 'materialism of the English school system' in his works.
- One of his important themes was the study of the relationship between the individual and society and how one could be limited by social conventions and restrictions.

- He gave a lot of importance to characterisation. His characters are complex and multilayered with psychological nuances.
- Forster was adept in the use of symbolism. For example, the Marabar Caves in *The Passage to India* serve as a metaphor for the mysteriousness of India and the house in *Howards End* symbolises the changing values of English society.
- Forster was interested in studying the cultural clashes between Western and non-Western cultures. He was particularly interested in examining the impact of colonialism on both the coloniser as well as the colonised.

Virginia Woolf (1882–1941)

Novel
The Voyage Out (1915)
Night and Day (1919)
Jacob's Room (1922)
Mrs Dalloway (1925)
To the Lighthouse (1927
Orlando, a Biography (1928)
The Waves (1931)
Flush (1933)
The Years (1937)
Between the Acts (1941)
The Moment (1947)

Short Story
A Haunted House (1943)

Literary Criticism
'Mr Bennet and Mrs Brown' (1924)
The Common Reader (1925)
A Room of One's Own (1929)
The Second Common Reader (1932)
Three Guineas (1938)
Roger Fry (1940)
The Death of the Moth (1942)

Life

Virginia Woolf was born into an intellectual family in London. She was brought up amidst books and was exposed to an atmosphere of intellectual sophistication. As she was too frail to attend school, she was tutored at home.

After her father's death, she moved along with her sister and two brothers to an area in London called Bloomsbury. This became the hub of literary activity where several intellectuals used to meet and discuss art and literature.

She began writing at a very early age and, by the time she was twenty-three, started to contribute reviews to the *Times Literary Supplement*. She married Leonard Woolf, an author and social reformer, and became involved in the Hogarth Press which was founded by them.

Virginia Woolf continued to suffer from poor health and her delicate mental condition required constant care. She had to be institutionalised several times. She died by drowning herself in a river at the age of fifty-nine.

Works

Virginia Woolf was a brilliant literary figure whose works popularised the technique of **stream of consciousness** in twentieth-century fiction. Her essay 'Mr Bennett and Mrs Brown', in which she made the famous statement 'on or about December 1910 human character changed', is an important milestone in modern fiction. In this essay, she attacked the realism of Arnold Bennett and proposed a more fluid and internalised approach to portraying characters in fiction.

Her first two novels *The Voyage Out* and *Night and Day* were written mostly in a conventional style. The first is a story that describes the voyage of an Englishwoman to South America, her romantic involvements and subsequent death. *Night and Day*, set in London, focuses on the daughter of a well-known literary family.

It was only with her third novel *Jacob's Room* that she was recognised for her distinct techniques of storytelling. This work completely shattered the conventions of fiction-writing. It narrates the story of a young man's life after his death entirely through the examination of his room and its chaotic contents by his sister. This work is evocative of her own brother's death. We never actually get to meet the character, but we come to know a great deal about him through the artistic arrangement of photographs. We are taken through a series of disconnected impressions shared mainly through the consciousness of the people he had come into contact with. Woolf makes brilliant use of the internal monologue in this novel.

She continued to refine this style of writing in her next few novels, *Mrs Dalloway, To the Lighthouse* and *The Waves.* These novels established her firmly as an architect of modernist fiction.

The entire time span of the plot of *Mrs Dalloway* is just one day in the life of Clarissa Dalloway. She is preparing for a party and as she goes about it, her thoughts fly back and forth. This book is best known for Woolf's use of the stream-of-consciousness technique that allows the reader to experience the character's thoughts and emotions in real time. It has no definite plot and whatever happens takes place in the characters' consciousness. The author succeeds in capturing the fleeting moments of everyday life.

To the Lighthouse is another important novel by Woolf where she experiments with narrative structure and technique. The book has three parts dealing with different time periods and different characters. The first part deals with Mrs Ramsay, the matriarch of the family, and her husband, a philosopher, and their eight children. Their plans of visiting the lighthouse are thwarted by the weather conditions and other reasons. The second section, which takes place after ten years, shows the house, once the setting of a happy home, now in a dilapidated condition. Many of the characters are dead. Woolf uses the house as a symbol for the passage of time and the transience of human existence. In the last section, the remaining members of the family return to complete the long-awaited trip to the lighthouse. In this novel, Woolf gives a haunting portrait of her own parents.

In her next novel *The Waves* there is hardly any plot. It presents a series of internal monologues which take us into the consciousness of six characters. Woolf captures the changing moods of these characters in a sensitive and almost poetic way. Some critics refer to this work as a prose-poem.

Her next two novels *Flush* and *The Years* are generally not listed among her major works. The former is a 'biography' of E.B. Browning's spaniel, while the latter is a more conventional novel which traces the events of the Pargiter family over the course of fifty years. The novel deals with several themes like the decline of the class system, rise of feminism and the First World War. *Between the Acts*, her final work, is again a highly experimental novel. The novel is in three parts and each part is marked by the ringing of a bell. It was published posthumously.

Orlando is an imaginary biography inspired by her friend Vita Sackville-West. It describes the life of a poet through four centuries, in both male and female manifestations. It is considered as a feminist classic.

ESSAYS

Woolf has written several essays and reviews. She occupies a prominent place as a literary critic and journalist. Among her important essays is *A Room of One's Own,* which is a book-length essay. It is a feminist manifesto in which she examines the discrimination that women have been facing down the ages. Her famous and oft-quoted words 'a woman must have money and a room of her own if she is to write fiction' is from this essay. This was followed by a sequel *Three Guineas* which is also a book-length essay. It is in the form of a letter to an unnamed correspondent who had sought her help in his efforts to prevent war. This essay was written against the backdrop of the rising fascism across Europe.

Her other important essays were collected in the volumes *The Common Reader* and *The Common Reader: Second Series.* Her essays cover a wide range of topics ranging from literature, art and history to social issues.

Features

- Virginia Woolf is one of the most influential people of the twentieth century literary world. Her thoughts and approach to fiction, feminism and biography have had a tremendous impact on novelists and critics.
- She brought about a revolution in the genre of fiction by questioning accepted concepts of realism. In her famous essay 'Modern Fiction' she pointed out: 'Life is not a series of gig lamps symmetrically arranged; but a luminous halo, a semi-transparent envelope surrounding us from the beginning of consciousness to the end.' She was against the 'materialistic' fiction of writers like H.G. Wells and Arnold Bennett, in whose novels, she felt, 'life escapes'.

- She pioneered the narrative device of stream of consciousness, which allows the reader to listen-in on the thoughts of the characters. It is non-linear unlike traditional fiction where one event or idea follows another in a logical order. It is a narrative style that tries to capture the non-linear way in which our brains work.
- Her contribution to feminism is significant. She drew attention to the discriminatory ways in which women were treated socially, culturally and physically. *Three Guineas* is a major feminist work apart from *A Room of One's Own*. In this work, she argues that it is impossible to prevent war without addressing the patriarchal system.

James Joyce (1882–1941)

Novels
A Portrait of the Artist as a Young Man (1916)
Ulysses (1922)
Finnegan's Wake (1939)
Short Story
Dubliners (1914)

Drama
Exiles
Poems
Chamber Music (1907)
Pomes Penyeach (1927)

Life

James Joyce was born in a suburb of Dublin and was the eldest of a large family of several children. He was educated at Jesuit schools and the University College, Dublin, in preparation for priesthood in the Roman Catholic Church. His scepticism towards Catholicism made him give up this idea and he left for France. He began to study medicine, but had to return to Ireland as his mother was dying. He gave up his medical career and began teaching in a school and thought of becoming a writer.

He fell in love with Nora Barnacle in 1904 and lived with her for many years before they got married in 1931. They lived in Trieste for a few years where they had two children. During the First World War, they lived in Zurich and then moved to Paris where he focused on a career in writing. He was encouraged by

Yeats and Pound who saw great potential in him. Pound helped him get his work published when he was being turned down by several publishers. Joyce received a grant from the Royal Literary Fund, which somewhat relieved him from financial difficulties. As his financial troubles began to improve, his health began to suffer. He had a severe attack of glaucoma and had to undergo many operations and suffer a lot of pain. Within a span of about thirteen years, he underwent twenty-five operations for glaucoma and cataracts. He had periods of blindness, but he kept his spirits up. Some of his most comical passages in *Ulysses* were written when he was in the greatest pain.

He became severely ill and was diagnosed with duodenal ulcer. He died on January 13, 1941.

Works

James Joyce is regarded as an avant-garde writer who shaped modern fiction in the twentieth century. Although his oeuvre consists only of one volume of short stories and three novels, his position in the history of modern fiction is enormously significant.

Joyce began his writing career with poetry. He published two volumes of poems, *Chamber Music* and *Pomes Penyeach.* He also wrote a play, *Exiles,* which is hardly remembered today. His attempts at poetry and drama were not very successful and he realised that prose fiction was his strength and focused only on that genre for the rest of his life.

He published a collection of short stories called *Dubliners* that depicts the lives of the people of Dublin. This collection of deceptively simple tales focuses on people who appear ordinary, but whose minds are in a state of psychological and emotional turmoil. He used the device called 'epiphany' in each of the fifteen stories of this collection. (**Epiphany** is the moment when a character is suddenly struck with a life-changing realisation.) The characters in this collection experience, in some way, a self-awareness that leads to the climax of the story. Joyce structured the stories to reflect the life cycle of an individual, beginning with childhood and ending with death. Some of the characters who appear in *Dubliners* appear also in *Ulysses*. These stories were written at a time when Irish nationalism was at its peak.

At the same time, he began writing a novel called *Stephen Hero*. Unsatisfied with what he had written, Joyce rewrote it a few years later as *A Portrait of the Artist as a Young Man*. This is a fictionalised account of his own life from infancy to the age of twenty. It is a kunstlerroman that reflects the intense conflict of the protagonist Stephen Dedalus who is torn between his religious upbringing and his desire for sensuousness. A **kunstlerroman** is a novel that focuses on the development of an artist or writer. Stephen, like Joyce, finds himself in conflict with his family, the Roman Catholic Church and the nationalistic fervour of his countrymen. H.G. Wells called it 'by far the most living and convincing picture that exists of an Irish Catholic upbringing'.

The novel is notable for its use of stream-of-consciousness narration. The reader experiences the entire narration through the consciousness of Stephen. It is divided into five sections, each of which represents a different stage in the development of Stephen. Beginning with childhood, Joyce explores his early years in school and his doubts regarding religion. In the second section, where the focus shifts to adolescence, the novel follows Stephen as he becomes aware of his sexuality and his desire to become a writer. In the third section, we see Stephen in university, where he becomes disillusioned with the Irish nationalist movement and the social values of Ireland. We see the rebel in Stephen emerging when he decides to break free from the social norms that had held him back. In the last section, Stephen leaves Ireland and sets out on a journey of self-discovery in Europe. The novel concludes with a powerful epiphany in which Stephen realises that he must break free from the shackles of his past and pursue his identity as an artist.

His magnum opus *Ulysses* is a challenging and complex work that is difficult to comprehend. The novel is structured loosely on the eighteen episodes from Homer's *Odyssey*, but set in the squalor of Dublin. Leopold Bloom, Molly Bloom and Stephen Dedalus are the characters who could be compared to Homer's Ulysses, Penelope and Telemachus respectively. Joyce experimented with a variety of styles in the writing of each chapter. The entire action of the novel takes place on a single day, 16 June 1904, the anniversary of Joyce's first walk with the love of his life, Nora Barnacle. This date is now celebrated as 'Bloomsday' by admirers of James Joyce. Leopold Bloom is a Jewish salesman who visits several places in Dublin such as a public bath, a newspaper office, a library, public houses, a maternity hospital and a brothel. In the course of his day, he meets Stephen whom he invites home. The novel ends with an extended stream-of-consciousness soliloquy by Molly Bloom. This work attempts to mirror and interpret our own lives in the twentieth century, similar to that of Homer's effort to mirror the world of the ancient Greeks in his epic.

His last novel *Finnegans Wake* is the story of a Dublin tavern-keeper, Humphrey Chimpden Earwicker. He is referred to by several names, most of them bearing the initials H.C.E. The book is apparently about the dream of the tavern-keeper who has fallen into a drunken stupor. It reflects the flow of his unconscious mind through the course of one night. Joyce coins several new words which are an amalgam of more than a dozen modern and ancient languages. In *Ulysses,* Joyce had attacked the form of the novel. In this novel, he targeted the very structures of the English language. When questioned about this, Joyce replied, 'I'd like a language which is above all languages, a language to which all will do service. I cannot express myself in English without enclosing myself in a tradition.' Interest in this novel has increased a great deal after the advent of post-structuralist criticism.

Features

- James Joyce influenced several prominent writers like Hemingway, Faulkner and Virginia Woolf. His writing style varied with each of his works as he made remarkable use of diction and narrative techniques.
- He used interior monologues and stream of consciousness in his novels. Through this process, he was able to take his readers into the hearts of his characters.
- He experimented with short prose sketches that he called 'epiphanies'. In *Dubliners,* each of the characters experiences

this moment of self-awareness. This process was further developed in *A Portrait of the Artist as a Young Man*.

- Joyce made use of myths to narrate a modern tale. In *Ulysses*, Stephen Dedalus, estranged from his real father, is evocative of Telemachus who is in search of his father.
- Joyce employed Irish slang, especially in *Finnegans Wake*. He used several foreign words to create puns and symbols. He experimented a lot with language as he felt that the English language, as it existed, did not meet his needs.

David Herbert Lawrence (1885–1930)

Novels
The White Peacock (1911)
The Trespasser (1912)
Sons and Lovers (1913)
The Rainbow (1915)
Women in Love (1920)
The Lost Girl (1920)
Aaron's Rod (1922)
Kangaroo (1923)
The Plumed Serpent (1926)
Lady Chatterley's Lover (1928)

Poetry
Love Poems (1913)
Amores (1916)
Look! We Have Come Through (1917)
Birds, Beasts and Flowers (1923)
Pansies (1929)

Short Stories
The Prussian Officer (1914)
England, my England (1922)
The Ladybird, The Fox, The Captain's Doll (1923)
The Woman who Rode Away and Other Stories (1928)
The Virgin and the Gypsy (1930)

Literary Criticism/Non-Fiction
Twilight in Italy (1916)
Sea and Sardinia (1921)
Studies in Classical American Literature (1923)
Reflections on the Death of a Porcupine (1925)
Mornings in Mexico (1927)

Life

David Herbert Lawrence, one of five children of a coal miner, was born in Nottinghamshire. He was quite a sickly child and grew up in considerable poverty. He witnessed his parents quarrelling often and he grew very close to his mother, who encouraged him to pursue his education. A scholarship allowed him to study at Nottingham High School for a few years, but he had to discontinue when he was fifteen years old.

He began working in a surgical goods factory and later as a pupil teacher. He spent several years as a teacher before turning to writing as a livelihood. In 1912, he decided to leave his teaching job and go to Germany. He sought the help of his former French teacher to get a job in Germany and fell in love with his wife Frieda. Frieda was six years older than Lawrence and was the mother of five children, but decided to elope with Lawrence to Germany. In the next few years, both of them travelled extensively to Italy, Malta, Ceylon (now known as Sri Lanka), Australia, California and New Mexico. His nomadic life provided him with ample material for his stories.

Lawrence returned to England with Frieda briefly in 1913 and they got married in 1914. The German roots of his wife caused a lot of difficulty for the couple during the war years and they were forced to leave England. They travelled extensively and lived in New Mexico for a few years. Subsequently, the couple moved to Italy and he continued to write in spite of his deteriorating health. He suffered from tuberculosis and died on 2 March 1930.

Works

His first novel *The White Peacock*, which narrates the story of unhappy relationships and their consequences, is set in the Eastwood region where Lawrence grew up. Although the book does not rank among Lawrence's major works, it still displays his keen eye for detail and lyrical style. Another early work *The Trespasser* deals with the adulterous affair of a married man. The story is based on Lawrence's friend Helen Corke's affair with a married man and who had later committed suicide.

These initial novels were followed by the well-known *Sons and Lovers* which has autobiographical overtones. This was written after the death of Lawrence's mother with whom he shared a close relationship. The novel delineates the experiences of a young man who was socially and economically deprived like the author himself. It studies the relationship of a mother and son and pays a tribute to the mother who saves the protagonist from the dismal life of a miner.

The Rainbow narrates the story of three generations of the Brangwen family. The first two generations have unhappy marriages and the story focuses on the third-generation character, Ursula. The novel ends with Ursula's break-up with her lover as she finds him too conventional. The appearance of the rainbow at the end of the novel is symbolic of hope. The book was banned as it was considered to be obscene. This was followed by *Women in Love* in which the same character, Ursula, finds fulfilment in Rupert Birkin and marries him. In contrast, her sister has a disastrous love affair. The novel focuses on the story of the two sisters and their encounter with modern life when they move out of their countryside. In this novel, Lawrence expresses his disillusionment with British industrial capitalism and turns to the classical culture of Europe.

Lawrence continued to write at a rapid pace. His next few novels were *The Lost Girl*, *Aaron's Rod*, *Kangaroo* and *The Plumed Serpent*. He wrote a number of short stories and poems too.

Lady Chatterley's Lover, the novel that Lawrence is best known for, is his last novel. It is the story of an aristocratic lady, Constance, who lives in a large manor house with her paralysed husband and has an affair with the gamekeeper of the estate. Lawrence's portrayal of the husband as an industrialist and intellectual (both groups of people he hated) and the gamekeeper as a 'natural' man reflects the author's views on society. He shows the futility of living a life that is only of the mind. In the union of Constance and Mellors, the gamekeeper, there is a perfect balance of the mind and the body. The book was banned for its obscenity and was published in unexpurgated editions in the USA and England only thirty years later.

POETRY

Lawrence began his literary career as a poet with several of his poems appearing in magazines. Although he wrote numerous novels, he also continued to write poems throughout his life. In his poetry, he expresses his belief in the natural and primitive instincts of human beings. His well-known poem 'Snake" is an excellent example of this. In it we hear the regret in his voice when he exclaims, 'I thought how paltry, how vulgar, what a mean act! / I despised myself and the voices of my accursed education.'

In his poetry, we note his marked departure from the well-crafted poetry of the previous generation. He writes in a spontaneous and simple style in which we can hear the natural voice of the poet. His poetic collections include *Love Poems and Others*, *Amores*, *Look! We Have Come Through*, *New Poems*, *Tortoises*, *Birds, Beasts and Flowers*, *Pansies* and *Last Poems*.

Features

- D.H. Lawrence was deeply influenced by the theories of Sigmund Freud and Friedrich Nietzsche. A remarkable poet, an insightful essayist and a powerful novelist, Lawrence is a force to reckon with in twentieth-century literature. Although his writing was severely criticised for its obscenity, they are now admired for their vivid settings and psychological insight.
- In his writings, we discern his hatred for modern industrial civilisation and a leaning towards the primitive and natural. He had little regard for merely intellectual faculties and gave importance to natural instincts and the senses.
- His novels explore psychological relationships between characters. In *Son and Lovers*, for example, he explores the complicated bond between a mother and her son.
- Lawrence hated the materialism of the modern world and the havoc caused by industrialisation.
- He was adept at capturing the distinct dialects of different characters. For example, the rough dialect of Australia in *The Boy in the Bush* and the dialect of the Nottinghamshire mining villages in novels like *Sons and Lovers* and *Lady Chatterley's Lover*.
- Most of his characters bear a resemblance to the author himself. Lawrence projected himself in his characters, thus giving expression to his own views and feelings.
- In his poetry, Lawrence wished to break free from the chains of rhyme and metre. He used *vers libre* in his poems which added to the spontaneity and naturalness of his style. (*Vers*

libre, a French term meaning 'free verse', refers to poetry that does not follow regular metre or rhyme but which focuses on the natural rhythm of the spoken language,)

Graham Greene (1904–1991)

Novels
The Man Within (1929)
Stamboul Train (1932)
It's a Battlefield (1934)
England Made Me (1935)
The Power and the Glory (1940)
The Heart of the Matter (1948)
The End of the Affair (1951)
The Quiet American (1955)
A Burnt-Out Case (1961)
The Honorary Consul (1973)
The Human Factor (1978)

Short Stories
The Basement Room (1935)
Nineteen Stories (1947)
A Sense of Reality (1963)

Entertainments
A Gun for Sale (1936)
Brighton Rock (1938)
The Confidential Agent (1939)
The Third Man (1950)
Loser Takes All (1955)
The Ministry (1958)
Our Man in Havana (1958)
The Comedians (1966)

Autobiography
A Sort of Life (1971)
Ways of Escape (1980)

Drama
The Living Room (1953)
The Plotting Shed (1957)
The Complaisant Lover (1959)

Life

Graham Greene was born in Hertfordshire, England, to well-to-do parents. His father was the headmaster of Berkhamsted School which Greene attended. Greene hated school and tried to run away. He was sent to London for psychoanalysis and later attended Oxford University.

Greene was an agnostic till he converted to Catholicism after his engagement to Vivien Dayrell-Browning. Although he was not very religious, his interactions with the priest Father George Trollope made him believe in the existence of God. His Catholic faith proved to be an important influence in his writing.

Much of his early working life was spent as a journalist and travel writer. He worked for the *London Times*, the British Foreign Office and later became a director of a publishing house. He also served as a foreign correspondent and was sent to Malaysia, Indochina, parts of Africa and Cuba.

Greene suffered from manic depression throughout his life. This had a great impact on his writing. He left Britain in 1966 and lived in Antibes and later in Switzerland. He died of leukemia and was buried in Switzerland, where he had spent his final years.

Works

Graham Greene is known both for his light 'entertainments' and realistic novels dealing with the psychology of human character. '**Entertainments**' was the name Greene gave to some of his thrillers. His oeuvre consists of a number of these entertainments as well as serious novels, plays and travel books.

Greene's first published novel was *The Man Within*, a story about a man who testified against his fellow smugglers. This was followed by two more novels *The Name of Action* and *Rumour at Nightfall*, which are not ranked among his best work. His thriller *Stamboul Train* won him fame and money and was also made into a film. He wrote three more entertainments that were also very well received—*A Gun for Sale*, *The Confidential Agent* and *Ministry of Fear*. These are adventure stories and spy thrillers with secret service and hot pursuits.

Brighton Rock, although listed by Greene as an entertainment, is a serious work that highlights the religious concerns of the author. In it, Greene explores the nature of good and evil and the mysterious workings of divine grace. It is one of Greene's finest novels in which he portrays the plight of an immoral teenager whose tragic situation is intensified by his Roman Catholic upbringing. In *The Power and the Glory*, the Catholic theme is more direct. The protagonist is an alcoholic priest in Mexico during a time when the Mexican government was trying to suppress the Catholic Church.

In his most well-known novel, *The Heart of the Matter*, Greene gives us an in-depth view of the downfall and eventual suicide of a benign British colonial officer in Sierra Leone due to his pity for both his wife and his mistress. Greene draws our attention to the fact that the hero was led to his ruin and damnation due to his kindness and compassion.

Greene revealed an unorthodox kind of Catholicism in which naturally sinful men and women, living in a sinful world, are often given a last-minute chance at redemption. They are people without roots or beliefs who confront moral dilemmas. While *The Brighton Rock* and *The Heart of the Matter* are set in Africa, his next novel, *The End of an Affair* is set in London around the end of the Second World War. A story of jealousy and obsession, it is based on Greene's own affair with Catherine Walston. The novel brings to the forefront many contradictions in Catholicism that Greene questions—a religion he struggled to live with.

The Quiet American is a novel written against the backdrop of America's involvement with Vietnam. It is narrated in the first person by a British journalist who is living in Saigon and traces his relationship with an idealistic American undercover agent. The novel focuses on the conflict that results between these two men over politics and other issues.

A Burnt-Out Case is about an architect who is 'burnt out'. He no longer finds any meaning in art or beauty. Set in a leper colony in the Congo region, it narrates the tragic story of the protagonist who is killed for no reason.

Although Greene is primarily known for his fiction, he had written a few plays as well. His plays dealt with themes such as moral ambiguity and conflict of faith. *The Living Room* is set in the living room of a middle-class British family and focuses on the tensions and secrets that exist in the family. *The Potting Shed* is a psychological play that highlights the trauma of a man who goes back to his childhood home and recalls his past. His other notable plays are *The Complaisant Lover* and *Carving A Statue.*

Features

- Graham Greene is a rare author who is equally well-known as a serious writer dealing with contemporary moral dilemmas as well as a writer of thrillers and spy stories. He was quick to realise that if he wanted to write about religion, he would have to sugar-coat it in such a way as to make it the least expected. For this, he found the thriller a useful tool. He was able to slip in metaphysical questions in the midst of exciting intrigue and mystery.

- Greene used a wide range of settings in his stories, ranging from Africa to London. He excelled in recreating exotic locations. These settings were usually hot and decaying. The parched and crumbling landscapes reflected the troubled souls of the characters.
- There is a strong Catholic element in several of his works, where he discusses questions of right and wrong, good and evil. He shows us through his stories that there are grey areas that cannot be categorised neatly under the above heads.
- He often chose as his protagonists, life's losers or those whom the world thinks of as losers. These people are portrayed realistically and Greene succeeds in arousing our sympathy for them.

William Golding (1911–93)

Drama
The Brass Butterfly (1958)

Novels
Lord of the Flies (1954)
The Inheritors (1955)
Pincher Martin (1956)
Free Fall (1959)
The Spire (1964)
The Pyramid (1967)
The Scorpion God: Three Short Novels (1971)
Darkness Visible (1979)
Rites of Passage (1980)
The Paper Man (1984)
Close Quarters (1987)
Fire Down Below (1989)

Life

William Golding was born in Cornwall and grew up in Marlborough, Wiltshire. He attended a school in which his father was the science master. After completing his education at Oxford, he worked as a writer, actor, and producer briefly and then as a teacher. During the war, he served in the British Royal Navy and after the war, worked as a teacher and writer.

He was married to Ann Brookfield and they had two children. Unfortunately, Golding was an alcoholic which, in later years, affected his literary output. He died of heart failure in 1993. He was awarded the Nobel Prize for his works in 1983.

Works

William Golding's novels explore the conflict between intellect and instinct. His work emphasises the importance of conscience, without which, there would be chaos and destruction. His first and most famous book is *The Lord of the Flies*. This novel shows us how centuries of civilisation can be reversed in a very short time and that it takes little for us to regress to a savage stage. It follows the adventures of a group of boys stranded on a deserted island after their plane crashes. The book portrays their rapid descent into savagery when they are removed from civilisation. All moral constraints are given up as the boys turn completely savage and commit murder.

The Inheritors is set in prehistoric times. In it, Golding describes the extinction of the last of the Neanderthal tribes by the more refined Homo sapiens. Through this novel, Golding illustrates the fact that innocence and instinct were both destroyed after the development of the Homo sapiens. The Neanderthals are portrayed in a lovable manner and earn the reader's sympathy.

His third novel is *Pincher Martin,* an existential novel. The protagonist, who is a survivor of a torpedo destroyer, suffers from anxiety and stress. The novel explores the themes of sanity and insanity as we witness Martin, the protagonist, who is at first very resourceful and intelligent, sinking into a delusional state. The ending comes as a shock to the reader when we are made to realise that Pincher Martin had actually died as soon as his ship had sunk. This revelation makes the novel an allegorical story about the afterlife. In an interview, Golding explained that Martin's greed for life made him continue to exist in another dimension.

Novels like *Free Fall* and *The Scorpion God* explore the destinies of people who turn their backs on heaven and are gradually sucked into hell. Golding was filled with a sense of wonder as he gazed upon the spire of the Salisbury Cathedral from his classroom window. This admiration for the engineering skill of its builder resulted in the novel *The Spire*. This book narrates the story of a man who is driven to build a spire as he believed that God had given him that task. He continues in his mission in an obsessed manner, ignoring the disturbance his work was causing to others. Golding raises the question as to whether the protagonist is driven by God or by the Devil to complete his task.

Features

- William Golding often focused on isolated individuals or small groups of people in extreme situations. In novel after novel, he talks about man's instinct to cause physical and spiritual destruction.
- His novels can be read as fables portraying the omnipresence of evil and the difficult task of being good.
- He uses a variety of remarkable settings such as the prehistoric world and unnamed deserted islands.
- His characters are portrayed in a realistic manner in spite of their extraordinary conditions. They are multidimensional and are portrayed as grappling with moral dilemmas.
- Through his novels, he takes us into the innermost aspects of human nature and exposes man's inherent potential for evil. He focuses on the effects of isolation on people and the fragility of civilisation. His experiences during Second World War exposed to him the depths of human cruelty.
- Golding's thought-provoking novels prompt readers to examine questions of morality and human behaviour.

Kingsley Amis (1922–95)

Novels
Lucky Jim (1954)
That Uncertain Feeling (1955)
I Like it Here (1958)
Take a Girl Like You (1960)
One Fat Englishman (1963)
The James Bond Dossier (1965)
The Anti-Death League (1966)
Colonial Sun (1968)
The Green Man (1969)
The Riverside Villas Murder (1973)
Ending Up (1974)
The Alteration (1976)
Jake's Thing (1978)
The Old Devils (1986)

Poetry
Bright November (1947)
A Frame of Mind (1953)

Life

Kingsley Amis was born in London and educated at the City of London School and Oxford University. He had to discontinue his studies to serve in the Royal Corps of Signals during the Second World War. After the war ended, he went back to complete his education.

He worked as a lecturer in English at the University College of Swansea and devoted a lot of time to his writing. He married Hillary Bardwell and they had two children. After more than fifteen years of marriage, the couple separated due to Amis's infidelity. He was knighted in 1990 and a few years later, suffered a stroke and died.

Works

Kingsley Amis is popularly known as a comic novelist, although he wrote in many genres. His first and most well-known novel *Lucky Jim* is a satire of academic life. Its protagonist is an anti-hero who rises from lowly origins to become a faculty member in a university, only to be disgusted by the falseness of his colleagues. He understands finally that he has to compromise with the status quo as he is not able to change it. This novel was a great success as the readers were able to identify with the anti-hero, Jim Dixon, who through hard work rose from the working class. Amis shows through this novel that the higher levels in academia were, however, reserved for the upper and wealthier classes. This aspect of his writing prompted readers to classify Amis with the Angry Young Men.

His next novel *That Uncertain Feeling* is about a married librarian who has an affair with a married woman. It is a satire of the Welsh obsession with culture. After visiting Portugal, Amis wrote his next novel *I Like it Here*. It is mostly an autobiographical account of Amis's experiences in Portugal.

He used his experiences in America, where he had gone twice on teaching assignments, for the novel *One Fat Englishman*. It is the story of an English publisher who is a gluttonous and philandering alcoholic and critical of everything.

Later, Amis began writing detective and spy fiction. Using the name Robert Markham, he wrote *The James Bond Dossier* and *Colonel Sun.*

Features

- He was a comic novelist known for his witty and satirical style of writing. He had the ability to make his readers think while making them laugh.
- He was a social critic who highlighted the shortcomings of British society and culture, especially that of the middle class.
- He wrote in a realistic style and about ordinary characters with whom the common reader could identify.
- Amis was interested in exploring the relationships between men and women and studying the psychological reasons behind their actions.
- Amis is known for the unexpected twists that he gave to his stories.

Iris Murdoch (1919–99)

Novels

Under the Net (1954)
The Flight from the Enchanter (1956)
The Sandcastle (1957)
The Bell (1958)
A Severed Head (1961)
An Unofficial Rose (1962)
The Unicorn (1963)
The Red and the Green (1965)
The Time of the Angels (1968)
Bruno's Dream (1969)
An Accidental Man (1971)
The Black Prince (1973)
The Sacred and Profane Love Machine (1974)
A Word Child (1975)
The Sea, The Sea (1978)
The Philosopher's Pupil (1983)

Non-Fiction

Sartre, Romantic Rationalist (1953)
The Sovereignty of Good (1970)

Life

Iris Murdoch was the only child of a Presbyterian father and a mother who belonged to the Church of Ireland. Born in Dublin, she was raised in London, where she attended school. She studied the classics, history and philosophy at Oxford University. After completing her education, she joined the British Treasury and worked in London, Brussels, Innsbruck and Austria.

She resigned from her job to continue her studies and did her postgraduation in philosophy at Cambridge University. She took up a teaching job at Oxford University, where she taught philosophy. She married a literary critic, John Bayley, and lived with him till her death.

She was a prolific writer who wrote twenty-five novels, several works on philosophy as well as poetry and drama. She was made a Dame Commander of the Order of the British Empire in 1987. She suffered from Alzheimer's and died in 1999.

Works

In the fiction of Iris Murdoch, we see a fusion of tradition and innovation. Her books, which have been described as psychological and philosophical stories, reflect the complex and troubled relationships between the characters. Her first novel *Under the Net* is a first-person narrative by an 'angry' hero who makes several attempts to escape from his current situation. It is a comic novel written in the popular formula of a struggling hero who finds himself in a number of comic situations.

Her next novel *The Flight from the Enchanter* is likewise admired for both its wit and high seriousness. It is the story of a group of people who are under the spell of a mystic. The story is set in post-war London and Murdoch highlights current issues such as immigration and women's liberation.

The Sandcastle is a story about love, guilt and art. It narrates the story of the disruption in the quiet life of a middle-aged schoolmaster caused by the arrival of an artist. *The Bell,* one of her best-loved works, depicts an ordinary community with characters struggling to come to terms with their sexual and personal desires. It is a complex story that highlights the conflict between spirituality, morals and physical attraction. Murdoch uses a lot of symbols to give her novel a multilayered significance. She raises several philosophical questions through this complex tale. As a student of philosophy, Murdoch's forte was in the study of moral conflicts and ethical questions. Her approach to these issues is intellectual rather than emotional and she uses symbolism to enhance her themes.

In *A Severed Head*, Murdoch deals with adultery, incest, abortion and suicide. The tone is both funny as well as serious. It is considered the most entertaining of her novels. *The Unicorn* is a Gothic novel that has castles set in isolated locations, daunting cliffs and a rough sea. In *Bruno's Dream*, the protagonist is a dying man who is recollecting his past and regretting his mistakes. Her other important novels are *The Black Prince*, *The Sea, The Sea*, and *The Good Apprentice*. *The Sea, The Sea* which is about a theatre director and his childhood love won the Booker Prize. Murdoch also wrote three plays.

Features

- Iris Murdoch is known for her philosophical novels in which the characters face difficult moral choices.
- Her stories reflect complex and sophisticated sexual relationships, involving intricate networks of love affairs. Her characters are portrayed as possessing morally ambiguous natures as Murdoch wished to challenge the traditional notions of good and evil. They are often multifaceted and have complicated psychological profiles.
- Her plots have a symbolic structure in which she combines the comic, the bizarre and the gruesome.
- Her portrayal of twentieth-century middle-class life is rich in detail.
- Her novels reveal her preoccupation with religion, the nature of morality and love.
- Her knowledge and exposure to philosophy is revealed in her deep engagement with existentialism. She explores the individual's search for meaning in a chaotic world and emphasises the need for a moral choice.

John Fowles (1926–2005)

Novels
The Collector (1963)
The Magus (1966)
The French Lieutenant's Woman (1969)
Ebony Tower (1974)
Daniel Martin (1977)
Mantissa (1982)

Non-Fiction
The Aristos (1965)

Life

John Fowles was born in Essex and lived there till the outbreak of the Second World War. He was educated at Bedford School and Oxford University and taught for a few years in England, France and Greece. While teaching in Greece, he met Elizabeth Christy whom he married a few years later. After moving back to England, they finally settled down at Belmont, in Lyme Regis.

His wife died of cancer after only a few years of marriage which affected him very deeply. After about eight years, he married Sarah Smith. He died of heart failure at the age of 79.

Works

John Fowles, who wrote in the second-half of the twentieth century, demonstrates elements of both postmodernism and modernism in his works. His works often challenge traditional literary conventions.

His first novel *The Collector* is a psychological thriller in the first-person. It narrates the tale of a lonely and psychotic butterfly collector who kidnaps a female art student. Fowles's next work *The Aristos: A Self-Portrait in Ideas* is a collection of essays on subjects such as art, politics and evolution. *The Magus* is his next work of fiction. It is set on a Greek island and is about a schoolmaster who is hounded by a series of mysterious apparitions. The novel has a complex narrative and a mythological dimension that is faintly evocative of **magic realism** (a chiefly Latin-American narrative strategy in which fantasy or mythical elements are introduced into seemingly realistic fiction).

The French Lieutenant's Woman is a semi-historical novel that is set mostly in Lyme Regis, where Fowles resided. It is the story of a wealthy gentleman's obsession with a socially ostracised woman. The novel is notable for the intrusive commentary of the author and its multiple endings. *Daniel Martin* is the story of a successful screenplay writer who ponders about his life and relationships and *The Ebony Tower* is a collection of short stories about art, love and identity.

Features

- John Fowles was known for his interest in philosophy and his belief in the freedom of the individual. His work is difficult to categorise into conventional literary categories.
- He is often considered to be a postmodernist writer as he flouted traditional literary conventions. In his works, there is a blurring of boundaries between fiction and reality. He rejected the idea of a single, objective truth and his works are marked by a parodic tone. He frequently made use of multiple endings for his novels.
- Fowles's works have metafictional elements in it. **Metafiction** is a literary technique that deliberately draws the reader's attention to the fact that the story is a work of fiction and not something real.
- Fowles often addresses the reader directly.
- There is a preoccupation with the psychological aspects of his characters. His characters are often portrayed as complex and multi-dimensional people in search of love and romantic relationships.
- The settings in his novels are very evocative. The stories often take place in coastal towns or rural areas.
- His novels raise philosophical questions such as free will versus destiny. He used his works to comment on social and moral issues.

Arthur Conan Doyle (1859–1930)

Novel

A Study in Scarlet (1887)
The Sign of Four (1890)
The Adventures of Sherlock Holmes (1892)
The Hound of the Baskervilles (1902)
The Firm of Girdlestone (1893)
The Final Problem (1893)
The Memoirs of Sherlock Holmes (1894)

The Stark Munro Letters (1895)
Round the Red Lamp (1894)
Spiritual Books
The New Revelation (1918)
The Vital Message (1919)
The Wanderings of a Spiritualist (1921)
History of Spiritualism (1926)
The Land of the Mist (1926)
Historical fiction and Fantasy
Micah Clark (1889)
The White Company (1891)
The Exploits of Brigadier Gerard (1896)
Rodney Stone (1896)
Sir Nigel (1906)
The Lost World (1912)
Sir Nigel (1906)
Non-Fiction
The Great Boer War (1900)
The British Campaign in France (six volumes, 1916–20)
The Crime of the Congo (1909)
Science Fiction
The Lost World (1912)
The Poison Belt (1913)

Life

Arthur Conan Doyle was born in Edinburgh, Scotland and was second of ten children. After seven years of education in Lancashire and one year in Austria, he returned to Edinburgh. He studied medicine in Edinburgh where he deeply admired his professor Dr Joseph Bell, after whom his famous character Sherlock Holmes was modelled.

He married twice and had five children. Conan Doyle was knighted in 1902. He was deeply involved in spiritual and psychic matters and believed in the existence of spirits and fairies. He died in 1930.

Works

Sir Arthur Conan Doyle wrote extensively and in a variety of genres like detective fiction, science fiction, historical fiction, non-fiction and fantasy. However, it is as the creator of the immortal detective Sherlock Holmes that he is remembered today. Conan Doyle made the detective novel extremely popular and Holmes and his friend Dr. Watson became legendary characters. The author modelled the character of Holmes on his medical college professor, Dr Joseph Bell, who had a keen sense of perception and observation.

Sherlock Holmes made his first appearance in the novel *A Study in Scarlet*. With his trademark cloak, cap, pipe and magnifying glass, he became a cult figure. Dr Watson serves as the narrator of many of the Sherlock Holmes stories. He gives us a firsthand account of Sherlock Holmes's excellent methods of detecting a crime. The stories appeared in the monthly journal *The Strand Magazine*. The character, Sherlock Holmes, was so popular that when the author got bored with him and wished to kill him in one of the stories, there was a vehement protest by the readers and Conan Doyle was forced to revive him. To this day, several letters are addressed to Sherlock Holmes at his famous address 221B Baker Street.

Some of the best stories dealing with Sherlock Holmes are: *A Study in Scarlet, The Sign of Four, The Adventures of Sherlock Holmes, The Hound of the Baskervilles* and *The Valley of Fear.*

HISTORICAL FICTION

Conan Doyle believed that his historical fiction deserved greater recognition than his detective fiction, but that it was overshadowed by the characters Sherlock Holmes and Dr Watson. His historical novels were set in time periods ranging between the medieval times to the nineteenth century. *Micah Clarke* was his first historical novel. Set in seventeenth-century England against the backdrop of the Monmouth Rebellion, it narrates the story of a gallant young man fighting a lost cause. *The White Company* and its companion piece *Sir Nigel* received a better response from readers. *The White Company,* set in the time of the Hundred Years' War, is about a group of mercenaries who become entangled in the conflict between England and France. The stories represent a microcosm of English society in the Middle Ages. Conan Doyle tried to establish the fact that one should be judged not by birth but by their accomplishments. *The Refugees,* another historical novel by Conan Doyle, is set during the French Revolution.

These historical novels reveal Conan Doyle's craft as a writer and researcher. They offer a unique perspective on a variety of famous historical times and events.

NON-FICTION

In addition to his works of fiction, Conan Doyle wrote on a number of other topics, such as his experiences as a doctor during the Boer Wars and about the First World War. *The British Campaign in France and Flanders*, is a series of essays written by him for *The Strand Magazine*. The first four of the six volumes of essays is about a single year of the First World War and give a graphic account of the experiences of the soldiers.

SCIENCE FICTION

He wrote a number of books of science fiction that feature the eccentric, but brilliant, Professor Challenger. The first of this series is *The Lost World*. It tells the story of an expedition to a remote plateau on the Amazon basin where the explorers come across a world inhabited by dinosaurs. The novel focuses on the exploitation of animals by human beings. In *The Poison Belt*, Professor Challenger and his team discover that the Earth is about to pass through a cloud of poison gas and attempt to prevent the disaster. *The Land of Mist* focuses on spiritualism and the occult. In this novel, Professor Challenger plays a secondary role following a journalist investigating paranormal phenomena.

His other notable works in this genre are *The Maracot Deep* about the discovery of the sunken city of Atlantis by a team of explorers led by Professor Maracot.

SPIRITUAL BOOKS

Conan Doyle was keenly interested in spirituality and the paranormal and believed that supernatural beings could be contacted. He firmly believed that the spirits of the departed continued to exist in the afterworld and wrote several books on this subject. Some of them are *The New Revelation*, *The Vital Message*, *The Wanderings of a Spiritualist* and *History of Spiritualism*.

Features

- Conan Doyle was a prolific writer who excelled in several genres. His contribution to the world of fictional characters is great in that he has given us the iconic characters Sherlock Holmes, Dr Watson Professor Challenger.

- He made the detective novel popular. Although there were several books written in this genre before, Conan Doyle's novels and short stories infused new interest in it. His detective stories are known for their intricate plots and attention to minute details.
- Conan Doyle's attention to detail while describing his settings is noteworthy. Most of his detective stories are set in Victorian or Edwardian London and the detailed descriptions of the place lends a sense of authenticity to the stories.
- His stories reveal a strong sense of justice and morality. Criminals are caught and justice is appropriately rendered.
- He was adept at other genres like science fiction, historical fiction and fantasy too.

Agatha Christie (1890–1976)

Novel

The Mysterious Affair at Styles (1920)
Murder of Roger Ackroyd (1926)
The Murder at the Vicarage (1930)
Murder on the Orient Express (1934)
Death on the Nile (1937)
Ten Little Niggers (1939)
And Then There Were None (1939)
The Body in the Library (1942)
A Murder is Announced (1950)

Play

Black Coffee (1930)
The Mousetrap (1952)
Witness for the Prosecution (1953)

*This list is not exhaustive

Life

Agatha Christie, whose full name is Dame Agatha Mary Clarissa Christie née Miller, was born and brought up in Torquay. She was educated at home by her mother and, in 1914, got married to Archibald Christie. Her service as a nurse during the First World War, provided her with a knowledge of poisons, which she later made use of in her detective novels.

Her first marriage with Archibald Christie ended in 1926 and she married Max Mallowan who was an archaeologist in 1930.

She accompanied her husband in his archaeologic trips and used this experience, too, in her fiction. She died peacefully in 1976.

Works

Agatha Christie was a prolific writer who wrote several detective novels and plays. Her work has been translated into over hundred languages and she has sold more than a hundred million copies of her books.

She introduced Hercule Poirot, the famous Belgian detective settled in England, in her first novel *The Mysterious Affair at Styles*. He appeared in about thirty novels and many short stories before the author killed him in 1975. He appears in some of her best-known works such as *Murder on the Orient Express*, *Death on the Nile* and *The Murder of Roger Ackroyd*. Christie portrays Poirot as a fastidious character with unique mannerisms such as an obsession with symmetry.

While *The Mysterious Affair at Styles* takes place in an English country house, *Murder on the Orient Express* is set in a train. Poirot, who is a passenger on the train, is called upon to find the murderer of a man killed on the journey. The novel has an intricate plot with an unexpected twist at the end.

Death on the Nile takes place on a cruise along the River Nile and Poirot is once again called upon to solve a murder. Christie gives us a vivid description of Egypt in this novel. *Murder of Roger Ackroyd* is another famous novel by Christie. The story is set in a small English village and Poirot is assigned the task of investigating the murder of a wealthy businessman. This novel is notable for its unreliable narrator and its unique narrative structure.

Miss Jane Marple, or Miss Marple as she is better-known, is another detective in Christie's novels. Miss Marple, who appears in about fifteen novels, is an amateur elderly private detective who lives in the village of St Mary Mead. *The Murder at the Vicarage* is the first book in which Miss Marple is introduced. She is described as being naturally good at solving problems and accurate in assessing human nature and behavior. Some of the novels in which she is the detective are *The Body in the Library*,

A Murder Is Announced, *A Pocket Full of Rye* and *The Mirror Crack'd from Side to Side*.

Christie's novels usually followed a set formula of a murder, an investigator, a plethora of characters, several misleading clues and, finally, a culprit who is suspected the least.

PLAYS

Agatha Christie wrote several plays apart from novels. *The Mousetrap* is her most famous play; it opened in London's West End in 1952 and ran continuously till March 2020, when the theatres were closed due to Covid. It is a murder mystery that takes place in a remote guest house, where a group of strangers are forced to spend their time due to bad weather and subsequently one of them gets murdered. *Witness for the Prosecution* is another famous play by Christie. It is adapted from one of her short stories and narrates the story of a man who is on trial for murder. His wife is the key witness for the prosecution and the play ends with an unexpected twist. Her other well-known plays are *And Then There Were None*, *The Unexpected Guest* and *Spider's Web*.

Features

Agatha Christie is one of the best-loved authors of detective fiction. There are several reasons for her popularity.

- Christie's novels are well-known for their intricate plots and unexpected twists at the end. Her stories often have several suspects and the reader is baffled by the mystery till the detective unravels it.
- Her novels have memorable characters like Hercule Poirot and Miss Marple and several realistic villains.
- She usually sets her stories in a closed setting where the characters are not allowed to leave till the mystery is solved.
- Christie shared all the clues with her readers and gave them an equal opportunity to solve the crime.

Aldous Huxley (1894–1963)

Crome Yellow (1921)	*Antic Hay* (1923)
Mortal Coils (1922)	*Those Barren Leaves* (1925)

Point Counter Point (1928)
Brave New World (1932)
Eyeless in Gaza (1936)
After Many a Summer (1939)
Island (1962)
The Devils of Loudun (1952)
The Doors of Perception (1954)
Heaven and Hell (1956)

Life

Aldous Huxley was well-connected on both his father's as well as his mother's side. He was the grandson of Thomas Huxley who was a close associate of Charles Darwin and the grand-nephew of Matthew Arnold. He was born in Surrey, England, and studied in Eton and Oxford. He suffered from two major setbacks that affected him deeply—he lost his mother at the age of nine and he suffered from an eye problem that almost blinded him.

He taught French at Eton for a year; George Orwell was one of his students. Later he worked in a chemical plant which provided rich material for his novels. He worked as a farm labourer in a manor house near Oxford during the First World War. There he met and married a Belgian refugee and lived in Italy during the twenties.

He moved to America in 1937 where he lived until his death in 1963. He earned a good income as a Hollywood screenwriter. His friend, Gerald Heard introduced him to Vedanta and Eastern philosophy. Huxley met Jiddu Krishnamurthi who influenced him profoundly and he became a Vedantist. Huxley wrote a book expressing his spiritual values and concepts, named *The Perennial Philosophy*.

In 1956, he got married again after the demise of his first wife the previous year. Huxley was diagnosed with cancer and died at the age of 69.

Works

Aldous Huxley has to his credit poetry collections, essays, short stories, plays, travel narratives and novels. He is, however, best remembered for his utopian satires or dystopian novels. Some of his best novels in this genre are *Brave New World*, *Ape and Essence* and *Island*.

His early novels *Crome Yellow* and *Antic Hay* ridicule the pretentions of contemporary British intellectual and literary coteries. *Those Barren Leaves* set in an Italian palace is about the affectations of a group aspiring to belong to the cultural elite and *Point Counter Point* is his longest and most complex novel.

Huxley is best remembered for his dystopian fiction. *Brave New World* which is set in a futuristic world where the citizens are controlled by a hierarchy based on a scientific system. Human beings are ranked from the highest intellectuals to the lowest manual labourers and are hatched from incubators. This world is built upon the assembly line popularised by the car manufacturer Henry Ford. In this work, his description of the factory workers is very lifelike as it was based on his actual visit to a factory.

Huxley used several techniques like cinematic montages and intertextuality. He used multiple references to several well-known texts to enrich the meaning of his works. *The Brave New World* is full of references to Shakespeare which help develop the theme. He also made use of the technique of bathos, that is contrasting high culture with 'low' popular culture. He brought in jingles that were popular at the time in order to highlight the fall in musical and literary standards.

Eyeless in Gaza has several autobiographical elements, describing the four periods in the life of the protagonist named Anthony Beavis. It examines the ups and downs in his life and his search for meaning and concludes in the character's discovery of pacifism and mysticism. His last utopian novel is *Island* in which he tells us how to construct a good society. It is a counterpart to his *Brave New World* in which he explores concepts such as overpopulation, ecology and democracy.

Features

- Huxley believed in the freedom of the individual and questioned traditional beliefs, religion and authority. He was especially interested in philosophical and ethical questions and in examining the impact of scientific advancement on human nature.

- He was keenly interested in examining the impact of technology on human behaviour and society. He was also concerned about the effects of mass media and consumerism on people.
- He used satire and irony to highlight the dehumanising effects of consumerism.
- He was known for his use of symbolism and a rich prose style.

George Orwell (1903–50)

Novels
Burmese Days (1934)
A Clergyman's Daughter (1935)
Keep the Aspidistra Flying (1936)
Coming up for Air (1939)
Animal Farm (1945)
Nineteen Eighty-Four (1949)

Autobiography
Down and Out in Paris and London (1933)

Non-Fiction
Down and Out in Paris and London (1933)
The Road to Wigan Pier (1937)
Homage to Catalonia (1939)

Essays
'Shooting an Elephant' (1936)
The Lion and the Unicorn (1941)

Life

'George Orwell' is the pen name of Eric Arthur Blair. He was born in Bengal Presidency, India and educated in England. He served in the Indian Imperial Police in Burma for about five years. He resigned as he was disgusted with imperial domination. He made ends meet by working in poorly-paid jobs in Paris and London.

He then began to pursue his writing career and published his first novel and a few essays. He served in the Spanish Civil War and was a member of the British Home Guard during the Second World War. He was politically very involved and was against imperialism, totalitarianism and social injustice. He died of tuberculosis in 1950.

Works

George Orwell is a writer in whom we see the coming together of the middle-class intellect and the zeal of a social reformer. In his writings, we see a reflection of his life and experiences. In his first novel *Burmese Days* he uses his experiences as an officer in the Imperial Police in Burma.

Orwell spent some time living on the streets of Kent in order to understand the difficulties of the poor. He used this experience in his next novel *A Clergyman's Daughter*. It is a story about the adventures of a spinster who loses her memory and escapes from her life of restriction to join the tramps. Orwell used realism with modernism in this work. His next novel *Keep the Aspidistra Flying* is a sardonic novel that reflects his contempt for the upper-middle class.

Orwell became a political writer and began to see himself as a democratic socialist who hated totalitarianism. His *Animal Farm* is a savage fable that is an attack on fascism and communism. In it, the animals of Mr Jones's farm revolt against their human masters and drive them out. The pigs, who soon become the new leaders, gradually become corrupted by power and a new tyranny replaces the old. The cynicism of their slogan says it all—'All animals are equal but some animals are more equal than others.'

Nineteen Eighty-Four is Orwell's next famous novel that narrates a nightmare story of totalitarianism in the future. It describes a society where there is no privacy and people who do not conform are put to death. The book warns the reader about the deceitful manipulation of the past in order to suit the present. The official language of Oceania, the totalitarian state in which the novel is set is 'Newspeak' which is depicted as progressively narrowing the range of ideas and independent thinking. It is a society dominated by slogans like 'War is Peace, Freedom is Slavery, Ignorance is Strength'. Worship of the head of the ruling party, Big Brother, is made compulsory. This novel, along with *Animal Farm* had a tremendous impact on people. These two novels mark him as an important author of **dystopian fiction**.

ESSAYS

His essays cover a vast range of subjects ranging from politics to literary criticism in a lucid and straightforward style. In 'Politics and the English Language', he highlights the effects that the decline of society had upon the English language. He argues that the government is able to cover up the terrible things it has done by using language in an ambiguous way.

In 'Shooting the Elephant', he talks about his experience living in Burma. The essay explores issues such as imperialism, power and morality and is one of his best-known essays. His essays reveal a strong moral sense and his concern for social justice and the difficulties of the working class.

Features

- His writings are marked by their preoccupation with social justice and his antagonism towards totalitarianism.
- His novels *Animal Farm* and *Nineteen Eighty-Four* are excellent examples of dystopian fiction. Through his imagination and eye for detail, Orwell paints an alarming picture of the future of society if totalitarianism is left unchecked. He was highly critical of totalitarianism and censorship. In his writings, he highlighted the dangers of absolute power and the resulting erosion of personal freedom.
- He was an advocate of clear and accessible writing and hated the use of jargon and clichés.
- Orwell used allegory and satire to drive home his message to his readers.
- Orwell is also known for his literary criticism. His essays on literature reveal his belief that literature should be accessible to everyone and his dislike for works that were complex and obscure.

A.G. Gardiner (1865–1946)

Prophets, Priests and Kings (1908)
Pillars of Society (1913)
Pebbles on the Shore (1916)
Leaves in the Wind (1920)
Windfalls (1920)
Many Furrows (1924)

Life

Alfred George Gardiner was born in Chelmsford. He began working at the *Chelmsford Chronicle* when he was very young. He joined the *Northern Daily Telegraph* and worked there for a few years. He became editor of *Daily News* in 1902, but resigned in 1919 due to a disagreement. He contributed to *The Star* under the pseudonym, Alpha of the Plough (Alpha is the brightest star in the constellation 'the Plough').

Works

Gardiner was a prolific writer, known for his witty and thought-provoking essays. He had the gift of converting day to day subjects into insightful topics. For example, in essays like 'On Habits', 'On Being Tidy' and 'On the Rule of the Road', he discusses common topics and draws our attention to their importance.

Most of his essays were published in the leading newspapers and magazines and were read by people outside Britain too. He had the unique ability to combine humour with his social observations. His style of handling societal issues influenced subsequent essayists and is relevant to this day. Some of his best collections of essays are *Pebbles on the Shore* and *Leaves in the Wind*.

Features

- His essays are filled with wit and humour. His essay 'On Shaking Hands' is a humorous piece that discusses different types of customary greetings around different parts of the world and concludes that shaking hands is a happy mean between the oriental salaam and the Russian bear hug.
- His essays are filled with everyday instances. For example, in the essay 'On the Rule of the Road' he points out that individual freedom would result in anarchy if we do not respect the liberty of others. He illustrates this concept by narrating an anecdote of a stout lady walking in the middle of a busy street, claiming that she had the liberty to walk anywhere.
- Gardiner was a keen social commentator. In his essay 'The Suicide of Thought' he critiques the education system of his day which gave importance to learning by rote and neglected individual thinking.

E.V. Lucas (1868–1935)

The Life of Charles Lamb (1905)
Fireside and Sunshine (1906)
Character and Comedy (1907)
Old Lamps for New (1911)
A Little of Everything (1912)
Only the Other Day (1936)

*This list is not exhaustive.

Life

Edward Verrall Lucas was born in a Quaker family. Most of his education was self-acquired while working in a bookshop. He later became a journalist and worked in Brighton. He was commissioned to write the biography of a Quaker poet, Bernard Barton and later to edit the works of Charles Lamb.

He wrote essays for the famous magazine *Punch*, which was renowned for humour and was a member of its staff for some time.

Works

E.V. Lucas wrote several books that included novels, collections of essays and travel books. He is remembered chiefly for his work on Charles Lamb and is recognised as the foremost editor of Lamb's works and as his biographer. Lucas devoted several years to his research on Lamb and was chiefly responsible for popularising him in the twentieth century.

The essays of Lucas were characterised by wit, a light-hearted treatment of subjects, irony and humour. He could write about a number of topics in an interesting way, but avoided writing about himself. Most of his essays were written for periodicals like *London Times, Spectator* and *Punch.* These were later collected and published as books. Lucas had an anecdotal style, which kept his readers engaged.

Apart from essays, he wrote a number of novels, children's books and travelogues. Lucas was interested in fine art and many of his travel writings discussed the works of European masters like Michelangelo, Rembrandt and Leonardo da Vinci.

Features

- He was known for his wit and humour. For example, in his essay, 'On Aging', he says, 'Youth is when you are allowed to stay up late on New Year's Eve. Middle age is when you are forced to.'
- Lucas's work on Lamb is unrivalled and played an important role in making Lamb popular to new readers.
- Lucas wrote in a number of genres and was a prolific writer. He wrote on several subjects including travel, literature, art and society.

Hilaire Belloc (1870–1953)

Essays
On Nothing and Kindred Subjects (1908)
On Everything (1910)
Pongo and the Bull (1910)
The Servile State (1912)
First and Last (1911)
Hills and the Sea (1913)
This and That and the Other (1912)
Europe and Faith (1920)
The Jews (1922)
Biographies
Danton (1899)
Marie Antoinette (1909)
Cromwell (1927)
Charles II (1940)
Poetry
A Bad Child's Book of Beasts (1896)
Cautionary Tales for Children (1907)
Sonnets and Verses (1923)
Histories
The French Revolution (1911)
History of England (1915)
Travel Books
The Path to Rome (1902)
The Pyrenees (1909)
Novels
The Green Overcoat (1912)
Belinda (1928

*This list is not exhaustive

Life

Hilaire Belloc was born in France but educated in England. He arrived in England when he was a child and after he completed his schooling, served in the military. He later studied at Oxford University and belonged to its well-known debating society. He was a prolific and versatile writer who published several books of poetry, essays, biographies, fiction and travel writing. He is chiefly remembered for his essays which cover a wide range of topics.

Works

He wrote more than a thousand essays and was a master of the genre. Through his writing, he was able to convey complex ideas in a simple manner. His essays reveal his great love for the countryside and contain several passages describing the beauty of nature. He firmly believed that modernity had disconnected people from nature and that their happiness lay only in their reconnection with it. 'The Mowing of a Field' is an example of an essay dealing with this subject, where Belloc talks about the joys of working the land and the satisfaction that comes from a hard day's work.

His travel books emphasise the importance of travelling in order to get to know about different cultures. They contain detailed descriptions of his travels abroad. 'The Path to Rome' recounts Belloc's journey on foot from Toul in France to Rome.

He was equally interested in politics. His essays on politics reveal his deep concern for the people and a commitment to social justice. For example, in his essay 'The Servile State' he critiques the modern capitalist system and points out that it has resulted in creating a class of paid slaves, no better off than medieval serfs.

Belloc's essays show us the vast range of his interests. He was able to write with passion, wit and earnestness on many topics.

Features

- He had a keen sense of humour. For example, to quote him, 'When I am dead, I hope it may be said: "His sins were scarlet, but his books were read."'
- He was a versatile writer and wrote in various forms such as prose, poetry, essays and travelogues.
- Belloc's Catholic faith was a recurring theme in his works. He defended the Catholic Church in works like The Great Heresies.
- He wrote verses and stories for children. *Cautionary Tales for Children* is a delightful book of satirical verses that was written to entertain and teach children. It has memorable characters like Jim who was eaten by a lion for ignoring his parents' advice and Matilda who was punished for her excessive curiosity.

G.K. Chesterton (1874–1936)

Fiction
The Napoleon of Notting Hill (1904)
The Man who was Thursday: A Nightmare (1908)
The Innocence of Father Brown (1911)
The Wisdom of Father Brown (1914)
The Incredulity of Father Brown (1926)
The Secret of Father Brown (1927)
The Scandal of Father Brown (1935)

Essays
Heretics (1905)
Orthodoxy (1909)
The Crimes of England (1916)
The Everlasting Man (1925)
On Running After One's Hat and Other Whimsies (1933)

Poetry
The Wild Knight (1900)
Poems (1915)

Life

Gilbert Keith Chesterton was born in London and began his career as a journalist. He was a close friend of Hilaire Belloc and contributed several articles to *The Spectator*. He studied at St Paul's School and the Slade School of Art. He was married to Frances Blogg who was a devout Anglican. Chesterton credited her for awakening the religious spirit in him. After a few years, however, Chesterton converted to Catholicism as he felt that the Anglican religion was 'a pale imitation' of the original faith.

He worked in a publishing house and also contributed articles regularly. He was invited by BBC to give talks on the radio and he gave several talks from 1932 till the very end of his life. He died of heart failure at his home in Buckinghamshire.

Works

Chesterton was a prolific writer who had thousands of essays to his credit. Apart from essays, he also wrote several poems and short stories. He is remembered today for his immortal creation, the detective Father Brown.

FICTION

He attacked capitalism, technology and the monolithic state in his first novel *The Napoleon of Notting Hill.* It is a fantasy novel set in a future in which medieval nostalgia combines with street warfare. Chesterton glorifies the romantic 'Merry England' in this book. These themes were repeated in his other novels too.

DETECTIVE FICTION

Chesterton is known for his Father Brown stories. Father Brown is a fictional Roman Catholic priest, who is also an amateur detective. He is portrayed as a man with penetrating insight and a gift for careful observation. He solves crimes by identifying with the suspects and thinking from their points of view. Father Brown was a celebrated detective along with Sherlock Holmes, Poirot and Miss Marple. One major difference in his detective fiction is the fact that Chesterton used the genre to introduce philosophical ideas.

Father Brown appears in five collections of stories. In these stories, one is able to discern the effects of Chesterton's conversion to Roman Catholicism in 1922.

ESSAYS

Chesterton is universally acknowledged as the master of the essay, having written over five thousand essays. He wrote on a wide range of topics ranging from philosophy and theology to literature and social issues. In his works, we find enduring truths that continue to be relevant to readers even today. He wrote on a variety of topics in a witty and humorous style. He had the gift of being able to present complex thoughts in a simple and entertaining way.

An important feature of his essays is irony and paradox, which he used to convey philosophical and religious ideas. For example, in his essay 'Heretics', he asks, 'When we were children, we were grateful to those who filled our stockings at Christmas time. Why are we not grateful to God for filling our stockings with legs?' 'On Running after One's Hat', another essay that continues to be anthologised even today, has the well-known quote, 'An adventure is only an inconvenience rightly considered. An inconvenience is only an adventure wrongly considered.'

Features

- Chesterton is known for his wit and humour. For example, in his essay 'The Diabolist', he wrote, 'The world will never starve for want of wonders; but only for want of wonder,' playing on the double meaning of 'wonder'.

- Chesterton was a deeply religious writer and his works were influenced by his Catholic faith.
- He had a lucid and simple style and could convey complex ideas easily to his readers.

Robert Lynd (1879–1949)

The Pleasures of Ignorance (1921)	*In Defence of Pink (1937)*
The Green Man (1928)	Contributed essays to *Daily News*

Life

Robert Wilson Lynd was born in Belfast, Ireland, and educated at Queen's College. He belonged to a Presbyterian family and his father was a Presbyterian minister. He went to England in 1901 and worked as a freelance journalist before he joined the *Daily News*. He wrote weekly articles for the *Nation* and later in the *New Statesman*. After he got married, he settled down in Hampstead, London, and lived there till his death.

Works

Robert Lynd was an Irish essayist who breathed new life into the genre with his wit and humour.

He used the pseudonym 'Y.Y.' (that is, Ys or 'wise') while writing for the *New Statesman*. His weekly essays which ran from 1913 to 1945 were eagerly read by his readers and when the paper's editor tried to replace him with another writer, it proved to be a dismal failure.

In his essay, 'The Money Box', he narrates how a gift of a money box to a child could have two repercussions—one, it could turn the child into a miser as he eagerly tries to fill his box or it could make him a spendthrift when he opens it frequently to indulge himself.

His weekly essays were collected and published in various volumes such as *The Pleasures of Ignorance, The Green Man* and *In Defence of Pink*.

Features

- Lynd wrote on a vast range of themes ranging from literature to culture and human nature. His writing was characterised by his sharp power of observation and his gift for discovering humour and irony in day-to-day situations.
- He was interested in social issues such as the undercurrents of social hierarchy and the intricacies of human behaviour.
- Lynd was adept at approaching any subject in a humorous and witty manner. He found irony and absurdity even in ordinary situations.
- His Irish background drew him to explore the Irish identity and culture in some of his works.
- Being primarily a journalist, one notes the journalistic slant in his style. Lynd wrote on a wide range of subjects. He could easily move from the serious to the frivolous. His essays were scattered with wit, epigrams and irony and filled the reader with a delightful experience. He used anecdotes to explain his concepts.

Lytton Strachey (1880–1932)

Landmarks in French Literature (1912)
Eminent Victorians (1918)
Queen Victoria (1921)
Elizabeth and Essex: A Tragic History (1928)
Portraits in Miniature (1931)

Life

Giles Lytton Strachey was born in London. His father was an eminent scholar who had served as an administrator in India for more than thirty years. Strachey was educated at Trinity College, Cambridge and became a member of The Apostles. There he made lifelong friends with illustrious people like G.E. Moore, M. Keynes and Leonard Sidney Woolf. Later, he became a prominent member of the Bloomsbury group. He died of stomach cancer at the age of fifty-one.

Works

Strachey revolutionised the genre of the biography. George Sampson, in his *The Concise Cambridge History of English Literature*, observed that 'Strachey cannot be seriously considered either a biographer or a novelist, either an historian or a writer of fiction, but rather some curious species between the two—which we can call either "biographical novelist" or "fictorian".' In the Victorian Age, it was customary for a biographer to gloss over certain truths as they firmly believed that one should not say anything bad about the dead. Exceptions to this were some of the works by Thomas Carlyle like *The Life and Times of Frederick the Great*.

Strachey, however, did not believe in turning a blind eye to the faults of the subject he was writing about and indulging in mere panegyric. He did not hesitate to criticise and expose the shortcomings of his subjects and wrote in a style that combined wit, humour and irony.

He began his literary career by writing several essays for periodicals such as *The Spectator*, *The Edinburgh Review*, *The Nation* and *The Athenaeum*. His first book *Landmarks in French Literature* is an attempt at introducing the French classics to English readers. The book is a survey of French writers from the Middle Ages to the nineteenth century.

His first great success was *Eminent Victorians*. The book reveals his views on biography as a genre. It contains the biographies of four people—Cardinal Manning, Florence Nightingale, Thomas Arnold and General Gordan. Except for Nightingale, the lives of the other three people are presented in a derisive and malicious way, highlighting their weaknesses. This book brought about a great change in the style of writing biographies and this new style was called **debunking**.

Strachey, however, did not indulge in debunking in his next work on Queen Victoria and presented a sympathetic portrait of the erstwhile queen. It is a very useful book that sheds light on the life of the queen and on the people around her. In *Elizabeth and Essex: A Tragic History*, Strachey displays the impact Freud had on him. The book focuses on Elizabeth's relationship with her father and the impact this had on her treatment of Essex.

In his last book *Portraits in Miniature*, Strachey goes back to writing character sketches in his own, inimitable style. His witty style and psychological insight enrich the biographies of various historical figures in this work.

Features

- Strachey brought about a revolution in the genre of biography by using a modern, satirical and almost irreverent style while writing about prominent Victorian figures like Cardinal Manning and Dr Arnold. This paved the way for future biographers to look at their subjects in a more psychologically nuanced manner.
- He was one of the members of the Bloomsbury group which had a great impact on twentieth-century thought and writing.
- Strachey possessed a fine sense of character which enabled him to portray the subjects of his biography as lifelike human beings rather than the hitherto projected idealised models of virtues.
- He had a witty and ironic style which gave the genre of biography a fresh lease of life.
- His writing was influenced by Freud and French literature.
- Strachey's biographies created controversy as his portrayal of prominent historical figures did not go down well with many of his readers.

Gerard Manley Hopkins (1844–1889)

'Felix Randal' and 'Spring and Fall' (1880-81)
'Carrion Comfort'
'Harry Ploughman'
'Thou art indeed just, Lord'
Poems of Gerard Manley Hopkins (1918)
The Wreck of the Deutschland (1875)
'The Windhover' and 'Pied Beauty' (1877)
'The Loss of Euridice'

Life

Gerard Manley Hopkins was born in Essex and was the eldest son of Anglican parents who were deeply interested in art and literature. He studied at Highgate School and Balliol College. He began writing poetry and was a good friend of Robert Bridges, who later published his works posthumously. While at college, he came under the influence of the Oxford Movement and, after a severe mental conflict, converted into the Roman Catholic faith. In 1868, he decided to become a Jesuit novitiate and burnt some of his poems as he believed writing poetry was sinful. He did not write any more poems in the next few years and devoted himself to the life of a novice and was ordained in 1877. He spent the next four years preaching in different parts of England. Later, he taught Latin and Greek at Stonyhurst College and was appointed the Chair of Greek and Latin at the Royal University of Ireland, Dublin.

While in Dublin, he found himself overwhelmed with work and his health suffered. He became very depressed and shared his frustration with his friend, Bridges. The last poem he wrote was 'Thou art indeed just, Lord', just three months before he died.

Works

Hopkins showed promise as a poet early in his life. He wrote poems even while at school and continued to do so in college. When he came under the influence of the Oxford Movement, he experienced great mental conflict before he finally converted to Roman Catholicism. He decided to become a Jesuit priest and this created a tension within him. He was torn between his intense appreciation of natural beauty which he expressed in a sensuous manner, evocative of Keats, and the asceticism that the Jesuit order demanded. In 1868 just before he joined the Jesuits, he burnt all his poems except a few that survived by accident. He resolved not to write any more poetry and to devote his life to being a devout Jesuit.

In 1875, when his training as a Jesuit novice was nearing its end, an incident happened which led to his writing poetry once again. A ship named 'Deutschland' was wrecked and five

Franciscan nuns died. Encouraged by a Jesuit superior, Hopkins wrote his 'The Wreck of the Deutschland' after maintaining a poetic silence of seven years. It is a long ode in thirty-five stanzas, commemorating the death of the five nuns who had been exiled from Germany. The poem focuses on one particular nun and Hopkins compares her final moments of agony to the Passion of Christ. It is an extremely religious poem in which Hopkins meditates on God and acknowledges His omnipotence and omnipresence.

It was the first poem in which Hopkins used his technique of 'sprung rhythm'. **Sprung rhythm** is a term invented by Hopkins to describe his own metrical system. This is a system of versification in which accented syllables are grouped in emphatic patterns somewhat like that of the Anglo-Saxon alliterative verse. This type of metre is different from the conventional English metre, in which accented and unaccented syllables alternate in regular patterns. Sprung rhythm is based on the number of stressed syllables in a line and permits an indeterminate number of unstressed syllables. Its unspecified and flexible character makes it a bridge between the regular English metre and free verse. In conventional metrics, a foot consists of a prescribed number of stressed and unstressed syllables. For example, an iambic foot consists of one unstressed syllable followed by a stressed syllable. In sprung rhythm, the poet is not required to use only one kind of foot. In Hopkins's poems, a line may consist of many kinds of feet: iambic, trochees, dactyls and spondees. Sprung rhythm had a great influence on the development of English poetry. Apart from sprung rhythm, 'The Wreck of the Deutschland' is rich in alliteration, assonance, and unconventional syntax.

In 1877 when he was ordained a Jesuit priest, Hopkins composed some of his famous poems like 'The Windhover' and 'Pied Beauty'. In these poems, he celebrated the presence of God in nature through his theories of **instress** and **inscape**. These concepts were derived from the medieval philosopher Duns Scotus. Inscape and instress are two key concepts developed by Hopkins to describe his unique approach to capturing the beauty and individuality of the natural world. By 'inscape', he meant 'the individual or essential quality of the thing'. According to Hopkins, each individual entity possesses a unique inscape that sets it apart from everything else. Hopkins believed that by perceiving and expressing the inscape of things, he could reveal the divine presence of God. Instress is the act of perceiving and capturing the inscape of an object. These twin concepts were central to the poetic vision of Hopkins.

He referred to 'The Windhover' as 'the best thing I ever wrote' and dedicated the poem to Christ. It abounds in alliterations like 'dapple-dawn-drawn' and compound epithets like 'blue-bleak embers'. The poem's language is rich and vibrant and is an excellent example of his ability to find divinity in the natural world. 'Pied Beauty' is another brilliant sonnet by Hopkins in which he gives praise to God for all the beautiful things he has created such as 'skies of couple colour as a brinded cow', 'Fresh-firecoal chestnut-falls' and 'Landscape plotted and pierced—fold, fallow, and plough'. The poem reflects Hopkins's deep spiritual connection to nature and his belief in God's presence in all things.

In 'God's Grandeur', he focuses on man's tendency to exploit and spoil nature. He points out, 'The world is charged with the grandeur of God…' and bemoans, 'Why do men then now not reck his rod? / Generations have trod, have trod, have trod; / And all is seared with trade; bleared, smeared with toil; / And wears man's smudge and shares man's smell…'

Some of his other well-known poems are 'Binsey Poplars', 'Felex Randal', '*As Kingfishers Catch Fire*', 'Carrion Comfort' and 'Thou Art Indeed Just, Lord'. All his poems were published posthumously in 1918 by his good friend Robert Bridges.

Features

- The foremost aspect of his poetry is his great love for nature and his celebration of God through nature. In the early days of his priesthood, he experienced a conflict between his enjoyment of nature and his ascetic life. He later learnt to reconcile the two by worshipping God through nature.
- Hopkins had a very unique approach to language. His knowledge of Latin, Greek, Welsh and other archaic

languages enriched his vocabulary. He made excessive use of compound epithets like 'drop-of-blood-and-foam-dapple bloom'.

- He introduced several techniques like sprung rhythm, inscape and instress which had a great influence on modern poetry.
- His poetry is sensuous like that of Keats. His use of language has an immediate appeal to our senses.

William Butler Yeats (1865–1939)

Poetry

The Wanderings of Oisin and other Poems (1889)
The Land of Heart's Desire (1894)
The Wind among the Reeds (1899)
The Shadowy Waters (1900)
In the Seven Woods (1903)
The Green Helmet and other Poems (1910)
Responsibilities (1914)
The Wild Swans at Coole (1917)
Michael Robartes and the Dancer (1921)
Seven Poems and a Fragment (1922)
The Cat and the Moon and Certain Poems (1924)
October Blast (1927)
The Tower (1928)
The Winding Stair and other Poems (1933)
New Poems (1938)
Last Poems (1939)

Drama

The Countess Cathleen (1892)
The Land of Heart's Desire (1894)
The Shadowy Waters (1900)
Cathleen ni Houlihan (1902)
On Baile's Strand (1904)
The King's Threshold (1904)
The Hour-glass (1904)
Deirdre (1907)
The Resurrection (1913)
At the Hawk's Well (1917)
The Only Jealousy of Emer (1919)
Calvary (1921)
The Cat and the Moon (1926)

Prose

Fairy and Folk Tales of the Irish Peasantry (1888)
The Celtic Twilight (1893)
The Secret Rose (1897)
The Ideas of Good and Evil (1903)
Reveries over Childhood and Youth (1915)
The Trembling of a Veil (1922)
A Vision (1925

Life

William Butler Yeats was born near Dublin, in Ireland. His father was a painter who did not make much money and, as a result,

Yeats and his family lived in a financially difficult situation. They moved to London when he was three and remained there for a few years before returning to Ireland. He studied painting for three years before he gave it up for a literary career in London. He was keenly interested in the Romantic poets and the Pre-Raphaelites. He became friends with Arthur Symons who awakened in him an interest in the French Symbolists.

Through his mother's family, he developed a close connection with the countryside of Ireland. His frequent visits to Sligo, a town in the Irish countryside, kindled in him an interest in local folklore and legends. He also began to take an active interest in mysticism and occultism which had a major impact on his life and works. He attended meetings of the Hermetic Order of the Golden Dawn, which was a secret society that was devoted to the study and practice of the occult. All these impacted his later poetry which was firmly based on the belief that there was a storehouse of all human experience and knowledge. He referred to this storehouse of knowledge as the 'Spiritus Mundi' or 'Anima Mundi'.

Another important event in his life which coloured his poetry was his unrequited love for Maud Gonne. He proposed to her several times, but was turned down each time. When she finally married an Irish nationalist, John MacBride, he was totally dismayed. The main reason for Maud Gonne rejecting him was his reluctance to join the Irish nationalist movement. He finally married a long-time friend, Georgiana Hyde-Lees, who shared his interest in mysticism. With his wife, Yeats created a highly complex philosophical system of his own. In a nutshell, the core of this system could be represented through a simple diagram of two interpenetrating cones, placed in such a way that the tip of each cone touches the centre of the base of the other. These two cones describe the paths of two turning gyres or coils representing two alternating and antithetical ages which make up human history. According to Yeats, human history was composed of cycles of about two thousand years. After a cycle of the first two thousand years, there would be a cycle of an antithetical age that would be hostile to the Christian era.

Yeats played an important role in establishing the Irish Literary Society in London in 1892 and the Irish National Literary Society in Dublin. He helped Lady Gregory maintain the high standards of Dublin's Abbey Theatre and was greatly interested in the artistic revival of Irish literature. Yeats was made a senator of the new Irish Free State and was awarded the Nobel Prize for literature in 1923—the first Irish writer to receive the award. On his seventieth birthday, he was hailed by his nation as the greatest living Irishman. He died in the south of France at the age of seventy-four.

Works

POETRY

Yeats's early works are heavily influenced by the late Romantics and the Pre-Raphaelites. *Poems and Ballads of Young Ireland*, a collaborative anthology to which several poets contributed, belongs to this period of his poetic career. Yeats wrote poems that were based on Irish myth and folklore. In these poems, Yeats combines the delicate and smooth grace of the Pre-Raphaelites with a dreamlike, mystical quality of his own. This was followed by *Poems* and *The Wind Among the Reeds*. He also wrote many lyric poems like 'The Lake Isle of Innisfree'. All these early works reflect his urge to escape from the vulgar materialism of the contemporary Victorian age to a mystical time in the past.

He began to move away from his early influences and abruptly entered a new phase after he was advised by Ezra Pound. His poetry changed from dreaminess and became stark and chiselled. One can see the increasing realism in his style in *The Green Helmet and Other Poems* and *Responsibilities*. The outbreak of the First World War and the Irish uprisings further shook him out of his sojourns in a romantic world. In this phase, the poet's voice reflects greater maturity and confidence.

Michael Robartes and the Dancer is another collection that reflects the mature Yeats. Some of the famous poems that belong to this collection are 'Easter 1916', 'The Second Coming' and 'A Prayer for my Daughter.' His concept of the gyres and of history occurring in two-thousand-year cycles can be seen in the poem,

'The Second Coming', where he writes: 'Turning and turning in the widening gyre/ The falcon cannot hear the falconer; … but now I know/ That twenty centuries of stony sleep/ Were vexed to nightmare by a rocking cradle.'

The poems in *The Tower* reveal Yeats at the height of his poetic abilities. The poems in this volume reflect Yeats's disillusionment with the physical world. He attempts to rise above the conflict between the mind and the body by lifting his poetry into a world of vision rather than one of reality. 'Sailing to Byzantium' is the most famous poem that belongs to this collection. *The Winding Stair and Other Poems* offers a parallel and opposite point of view to *The Tower*. While the earlier volume offers a bleak outlook of eternity, the latter expresses a desire for rebirth after death. 'Byzantium' is a sequel to the earlier 'Sailing to Byzantium'.

DRAMA

His early plays like *The Countess Cathleen* and *The Land of Heart's Desire* illustrate his fascination with Celtic mythology. *The Countess Cathleen* is a one-act play that narrates the story of a noblewoman's sacrifice during a famine in Ireland. She sells her soul to the devil to save her starving tenants.

Some of his well-known plays are *On Baile's Strand, The King's Threshold, The Hour-glass* and *At the Hawk's Well.*

PROSE

Yeats wrote several essays and books to explain his philosophy, ideas and beliefs. His prose showcases his preoccupation with the cultural and political issues of his day and also his deep understanding of literature. He wrote extensively on theatre, politics and literary criticism. *The Celtic Twilight*, *The Trembling of the Veil* and *A Vision* are three important works by Yeats in which he explores the themes of mysticism, mythology and the occult. In *The Celtic Twilight*, he highlights the rich Irish tradition of oral storytelling. He captures the twilight period, where the boundaries between the physical and the spiritual worlds blur. He presents a vision of Ireland as a place imbued with magic and mystery.

The Trembling of the Veil is one of the autobiographical works by the poet and covers the period of his life from the late 1880s to the early 1900s. In it, he gives an account of his experiences as a poet, his involvement in Irish nationalism and his meetings with several literary figures of his time. He also talks about his exploration of the occult and his belief in the existence of hidden forces. The title refers to the concept of a veil separating the visible world from invisible realities.

A Vision is a complex and esoteric work that explains Yeats's metaphysical system and his theories on history, symbolism and the cycles of existence. The book draws heavily from mystic and occult sources as well as Yeats's own experiences and visions. It explores the ideas of gyres or spiralling cycles of time and the interplay between opposing forces.

Features

- Yeats is one of the important Irishmen who revived the declining glory of Ireland and gave it a proud place in world literature. He made a significant contribution to the development of modern poetry.
- The poetry of Yeats is deeply influenced by myth, symbolism, folklore and the occult. We see the effects of these on his poetry and drama, where he weaves mythological figures and archetypes into his narratives to create complex and layered works. Inspired by the Symbolist movement, his poetry is full of symbolic and mystic imagery.
- His involvement with the Irish Nationalistic movement was reflected in his writings that explored themes related to Irish identity, history and struggle for independence.
- His later poetry reflects his interest in the occult. He was a part of many mystical and esoteric societies and their influence was seen in the plays and poems of his later days.
- His poetry reflects certain personal experiences, such as his unrequited love for Maud Gonne. In several famous poems by the poet, like 'Easter 1916' and 'A Prayer for my Daughter', we hear echoes of his bitterness of being rejected by her.

- Although Yeats is known primarily as a poet, he wrote several plays with the aim of creating a distinctly Irish theatre. He wrote poetic dramas that were steeped in Irish folklore, mythology and the occult. His plays were performed in the Abbey Theatre and played a major role in the promotion of the Irish Literary Movement.
- Yeats's plays are full of rich symbolism and lyrical and poetic language. However, the characters are one-dimensional and are mere mouthpieces to express his ideas. He was inspired by the traditional form of Japanese theatre that was a combination of dance, music and drama, known as **Noh Theatre** or **No Theatre**.

W.H. Davies (1871–1940)

The Soul's Destroyer and other Poems (1905)
New Poems (1907)
The Autobiography of a Super-Tramp (1908)
Nature Poems and Others (1908)
Foliage (1913)
The Bird of Paradise and other Poems (1914)
Collected Poems (1916, 1928, 1934)
A Poet's Pilgrimage (1918)
Later Days (1925)
Love Poems (1935)
Poems in the Georgian Poetry series

Life

William Henry Davies was a Welsh poet born in Newport, in Monmouthshire. After discontinuing from school, he worked for a while as an apprentice to a maker of picture frames. He left this too and went to America and led the life of a tramp. He lost his leg while attempting to jump from a train with a fellow tramp. After he lost his leg, he lost his wildness. He returned to England and suffered many hardships spending his time in the shelters in London and a Salvation Army hostel.

He had begun writing poems even while at school and he continued to do so as an adult. His poetry came to the notice of George Bernard Shaw, who helped to get him published. Davies began to make more friends among the literary circle of London and slowly began to settle down to a decent life.

Works

His first major collection of poems is *The Soul's Destroyer* that was well-received and established his reputation as a poet. His love for nature can be discerned in his next collection *Nature Poems and Others*. It contains several short lyrical pieces extolling nature and the connection he felt with it.

The Autobiography of a Super-Tramp is a notable book by Davies in which he gives an account of his experiences as a tramp. Davies explores the themes of freedom and self-discovery and highlights the hardships of the life of a tramp. The book serves as a social commentary on the inequalities and challenges faced by the working class and the struggles of the poor.

His most famous poem 'Leisure' is from the collection *Songs of Joy and Others*. The opening lines, 'What is this life if, full of care, / We have no time to stand and stare?' are often quoted. Davies rues the fact that modern life has deprived one's sensibilities and has caused our rift from nature.

Davies continued to publish several collections of poems throughout his life. His reputation rests on his short poems that celebrate nature. His poems, however, do not delve deeper to reveal a profound meaning. He was content in just capturing nature in its various hues and moods.

Features

- He was a nature poet, whose poems are lyrical tributes to the beauty of nature.
- His first-hand knowledge of the struggles of the working class enabled him to authentically portray them in his poems.
- Davies is a typical Georgian poet who wrote light poems about nature.
- Davies was known for his contemplative and introspective style.

Walter de la Mare (1873–1956)

Poetry

Songs of Childhood (1902)
The Listeners and other Poems (1912)
Peacock Pie (1913)
The Fleeting and other Poems (1933)
Bells and Grass (1941)
Collected Poems (1942)
The Burning Glass and other Poems (1945)
The Traveller (1946)

Fiction

Henry Brocken (1904)
The Three Mulla-Mulgars (1910)
The Return (1910)
The Memories of a Midget (1921)
The Riddle and other Stories (1923)
The Lord Fish and other Stories (1933)
Collected Stories for Children (1947)

Life

Walter de la Mare was born in Kent and educated at St Paul's Choir School. His father was French and his mother was Scottish. In 1892, he joined an amateur dramatics club, where he met his future wife with whom he had four children. He worked in the statistics department of Standard Oil for eighteen years, but always found time to write. De la Mare is remembered as a lyrical poet who was a prominent member of the Georgian group of poets, a short-story writer and a children's writer.

Works

POETRY

De la Mare began his literary career by contributing to magazines. His first published work was *Songs of Childhood*. This is a collection of forty-seven poems about subjects and incidents that appeal to children. The poems are about gnomes, dancing fairies and dwarfs. These poems capture the magic and wonder of childhood in an endearing manner. *The Listeners and Other Poems* is an important work that includes his famous poem 'The Listeners'. This is an oft-anthologised poem and is very familiar to students of poetry. It describes the incident of a traveller knocking at the door of an uninhabited house. The poet hints at the possibility of the house being haunted and thus succeeds in creating an eerie atmosphere.

But only a host of phantom listeners
That dwelt in the lone house then
Stood listening in the quiet of the moonlight
To that voice from the world of men:

His next collection of poems, *Motley and Other Poems,* reflects de la Mare's experimentation with different forms and styles of poetry. These poems deal with themes such as love, loss and the transience of life. In *The Veil and Other Poems,* he delves into the realm of dreams. He tries to penetrate the subconscious and create vivid and evocative images.

FICTION

In addition to poetry, de la Mare wrote a number of novels and short stories. His fiction, too, reveals his fascination for the supernatural and the mysterious. Some of his notable works in this genre include *Memoirs of a Midget, The Return* and *The Three Mulla-Mulgars. Memoirs of a Midget* narrates the tale of a midget woman who has a keen sense of observation. The novel focuses on the themes of identity and loneliness. *The Return* is a collection of supernatural stories that are a blend of horror, fantasy and psychological suspense. The last book is a fantasy novel for children about three animals living in a magical world.

Features

- De la Mare's poetry and stories continue to fascinate readers even today with their rich imagery, lyrical style and sense of mystery.
- His work is written in a simple and straightforward style, typical of the Georgian poets.
- One can see his love for nature, which he imbues with a touch of magic, in his works.

John Masefield (1878–1967)

Poetry
Salt-Water Ballads (1902)
Ballads (1903)
Ballads and Poems (1910)
The Everlasting Mercy (1911)
The Widow in the Bye-street (1912)
Reynard the Fox (1919)
Collected Poems (1923)

Autobiography
So Long to Learn (1952)
Fiction
Sard Harker (1924)
Odtaa (1926)
The Bird of Dawning (1933)
The Midnight Folk (1927)
Dead Ned (1938)
Live and Kicking Ned (1939)

Life

John Edward Masefield, the son of a solicitor, was born in Herefordshire. His mother died in childbirth when Masefield was just six years old. He was brought up by relatives and was educated for a few years at a school in Warwick. He joined the merchant navy when he was thirteen and began his training. While sailing to Chile, he became violently seasick and was sent home. He went sailing again at the age of seventeen but abandoned the ship and became a vagrant in America and started doing odd jobs.

After returning to England, he began his writing career which consisted of nearly fifty volumes of poetry, twenty novels and eight plays. He was made poet laureate in 1930 and remained in the post till his death. He was invited by the United States to deliver lectures and was honoured in both England and the USA. He died after a brief period of illness at the age of eighty-nine.

Works

POETRY

Masefield used his experiences as a sailor to write poetry. His poems have a beautiful blend of adventure and romance, evoking in the readers a love for the sea. *Salt-Water Ballads* was the harbinger of a series of sea-poems for which Masefield is famous. It contains the well-loved poem 'Sea-Fever'.

> I must go down to the sea again, to the lonely sea and sky,
> And all I ask is a tall ship and a star to steer her by;
> And the wheel's kick and the wind's song and the white sail's shaking,
> And a grey mist on the sea's face, and a grey dawn breaking.

The simple style and the easy rhymes had an immediate appeal for people. The poem echoed his yearning for adventure and his love for the sea—features that can be seen in most of his poems.

His second volume of poems *Ballads and Poems* shows a development in his poetic techniques. In 'Cargoes', he talks about different types of ships like the Roman galley ship, the Spanish galleon and the contemporary British ships. *Reynard the Fox* is a collection of narrative poems that revolve around a character called Reynard the Fox. The stories reveal the cunning and trickery of the fox and show him as a complex and morally ambiguous character. This collection reveals Masefield's skill as a narrative poet and his ability to bring characters and settings to life through the medium of poetry.

FICTION

Masefield was an adept storyteller and wrote a number of novels and short stories that reveal this talent. Some of his novels are *Captain Margaret*, *Sard Harker*, *ODTAA* (The letters stand for 'One Damn Thing After Another') and *The Bird of Drawing*. *Captain Margaret* is the story of a woman who disguises herself as a man and becomes the captain of a ship. Masefield highlights the theme of gender roles in this story. *Sard Harker* is a novel set in the world of theatre and focuses on the title character who is an aspiring actor. He also wrote several collections of short stories like *Multitude and Solitude*, *Lost Endeavour* and *The Locked Chest*. These stories deal with several subjects ranging from the supernatural to the historical.

Features

- Masefield's poems are noted for their vivid imagery and lyrical language. His love for nature is evident in all his poems.
- His great love for the sea is another distinguishing feature of his work. Having spent his youth as a seaman, his experiences of the sea greatly influenced his writing. The sea, for him, was symbolic of the freedom and vastness of life.
- He was a skilled storyteller and was able to capture his reader's imagination through his captivating storytelling.

Siegfried Sassoon (1886–1967)

Poetry
The Old Huntsman (1917)
Counter-Attack (1918)
War Poems (1919)
Satirical Poems (1926)
The Heart's Journey (1928)
Vigils (1935)
Collected Poems (1947)
Sequences (1956)

Prose
Memoirs of A Fox-Hunting Man (1928)
Memoirs of an Infantry Officer (1930)
Sherston's Progress (1936)
The Complete Memoirs of George Sherston (1937)
The Old Century and Seven More Years (1938)
The Weald of Youth (1942)
Siegfried's Journey (1945)

Life

Siegfried Sassoon was born into a wealthy family and grew up in a privileged environment. He attended Marlborough College and later Clare College. When the First World War broke out, he volunteered for military service and served as a cavalry officer. As a patriot and an idealist, he enlisted in the army and was even awarded a medal for bravery under fire. But, within two years his attitude towards war underwent a drastic change. He experienced the horrors of trench warfare on the Western Front and witnessed the gruesome deaths of his colleagues. These experiences affected him profoundly and led to his disillusionment with war.

He wrote poems denouncing war and his anti-war sentiments grew stronger and, subsequently, he refused to return to duty. He was dispatched to hospital for being 'shell-shocked', which is now known as post-traumatic stress disorder. After leaving the hospital, he continued to write poetry but also organised protests against war. Sassoon is remembered today for his moving and realistic war poems.

Works

POETRY

In 1917, Sassoon published his first collection of poems *The Old Huntsman* in which he highlighted the loss of innocence and disillusionment caused by war. In the title poem, Sassoon used a hunting scene to symbolise war. He successfully contrasted the peaceful life of the huntsman in the pre-war years with the horrors of war. This collection combines war poems with poems on nature, love and some personal reflections.

In his next collection *Counter-Attack and Other Poems*, Sassoon continued to vividly portray the horrors and grim realities of war. He also touched on the psychological scars that war caused and expressed his strong anti-war sentiments. Disgust complemented by irony are a mark of Sassoon's poetry. He shocks his readers by giving a close-up view of what actually happened at the warfront in poems like 'The Rear-Guard'. In this poem, a soldier is seen groping his way through a tunnel when he comes across a man lying on the way and asks him for directions to the headquarters. Receiving no reply, he kicks him and when he still does not get an answer, flashes his torch on him. He sees a dead soldier's body with his face bearing the evidence of the gruesome death he had suffered ten days earlier.

The War Poems is a collection completely dedicated to his poems on war. It contains some of the poems that had been published in his earlier books and established his reputation as a poet. *Satirical Poems* reflects Sassoon's skill as a satirical poet. The poem 'The Hero' in this collection is a hard-hitting example of his bitter satire. This poem is about the news brought by a soldier to a mother about her son's death. Sassoon's ironic portrayal of the actual circumstances of the death and the embellished version given to the mother strikes a poignant note.

Sassoon used satire, irony and sharp wit to comment on the futility of war and the insensitivity of human beings.

PROSE

Sassoon wrote a lot of prose which includes his autobiography and several fictional narratives that reflect his perspectives and thoughts. His prose works offer a different lens through which to explore his experiences, thoughts and views on war and other themes. His first work in this genre is *Memoirs of a Fox-Hunting Officer* which is in the form of an autobiographical novel. The original names are changed and Sassoon himself appears as 'George Sherston'. His *Memoirs of an Infantry Officer* continues to give an account of his own experiences as a soldier. He portrayed in great detail the toll the war had taken on those who were directly involved in it.

Sassoon was able to convey eloquently a complex range of emotions. *Sherston's Progress* narrates the life of George Sherston, who was a lonely boy fond of hunting and cricket. He was a carefree youth who eventually lands up in the trenches and has to face a totally different world than the one he had known so far. These three books were later published as *The Complete Memoirs of George Sherston* in 1937.

The next year Sassoon published *The Old Century and Seven More Years*, which is a recollection of his childhood and youth. The next two books *The Weald of Youth* and *Siegfried's Journey* brought his narration of his life up to the year 1920.

Features

- Sassoon drew heavily from his own personal experiences for his poetry and prose. He was deeply affected by the horrors of the First World War and the impact of this can be seen in all his works.
- His poetry is marked by his penchant for evocative and vivid imagery. He could paint powerful pictures in the reader's mind by his exemplary use of sensory language.
- Sassoon's poetry exhibits a lyrical quality, with rhythm, rhymes and other aesthetic poetic techniques.
- He was a strong critic of war. Almost all his works display his anti-war sentiments. He tried to reveal the senselessness and futility of war and the emotional and physical damage it caused. He challenged the glorification of war and tried to make society realise that there was nothing honourable about it.

Rupert Brooke (1887–1915)

Poetry

Poems (1911)

Nineteen Fourteen (1915)

Collected Poems (1918)

Prose

John Webster and the Elizabethan Drama (1916)

Drama

Lithuania (1912)

Life

Rupert Brooke was born in Rugby, Warwickshire and educated at the famous public school there. After Rugby, he studied at King's College, Cambridge, where he began to write poetry.

After graduating from Cambridge, he spent his time travelling and writing. He contributed several poems to *Georgian Poetry* and shared the characteristics common to the poets of that period. He lived at Grantchester, a village near Cambridge, for a while after 1909. He immortalised this place through his poem 'The Old Vicarage, Grantchester'.

He suffered a nervous breakdown in 1912 and, after he recovered, spent the next three years travelling in America and the South Seas. He joined the army in 1914 and took part in the expedition to Antwerp. He died of blood poisoning on his way to the Dardanelles and was buried in Scyros.

Works

Rupert Brooke was the first of Britain's 'war poets'. Although he wrote very few poems in his short life, he found a lasting place in modern British poetry. He is remembered in the oft-anthologised sonnet 'The Soldier', in which his patriotism is evident. The famous lines 'If I should die, think only this of me: / That there's some corner of a foreign field / That is for ever England' are from this poem.

His first volume of poems published in 1911 contains about thirty poems written between 1908–1911. They are about various topics such as love, mythology, emotions and nature. These are typical poems that were written by a young, romantic man of leisure and found a place in *Georgian Poetry*. The poems, though lacking in depth, display remarkable metrical skill.

The next collection of poems entitled *Nineteen Fourteen* contains five sonnets that are ranked among his best. These are 'Peace', 'Safety', two sonnets entitled 'The Dead' and his famous poem, 'The Soldier'. The five war sonnets inspired Englishmen and filled them with a patriotic zeal. Brooke's death just three weeks after these poems were written struck a poignant note in the readers' hearts.

Features

- Rupert Brooke was a typical Georgian poet, in that his poetry was lyrical, sentimental and used simple rhyme schemes and metrical patterns.
- He is remembered for his patriotic poems that eulogised war. These sentiments were well received by readers until they became disillusioned with the war later.

Wilfred Owen (1893–1918)

'Anthem for Doomed Youth' 'Futility'
'Dulce et Decorum Est' 'The Sentry'

Life

Wilfred Owen was born in Shropshire where his father was a railway worker. Owen was educated in Liverpool and at Shrewsbury Technical College. After a brief stint of serving as a tutor in France, he enlisted in the British army. The horrors he experienced in the trenches aroused his fury and disillusionment with the war. In 1917, he was injured and sent home. He was awarded the Military Cross and was killed just a week before Armistice Day.

Works

Owen began writing poetry even while he was a student. His early poems were evocative of the Romantics and one could discern in them the influence of Tennyson and the French poets, too. After his meeting with Sassoon in a hospital in Edinburgh, he realised that both of them shared a similar disgust for war. One can discern a marked change in his poetry after his experience in the trenches. However, his poetry did not have the harsh bitterness of Sassoon's. Sassoon, himself, noted this aspect of Owen's poetry when he commented: 'My trench-sketches were like rockets, sent up to illuminate the darkness…It was Owen who revealed how, out of the realistic horror and scorn, poetry might be made.'

Owen wrote most of his poems between the summer of 1917 and the autumn of the following year. He was a gifted poet who experimented with verse forms. He used a technique called para-rhyme which influenced later poets. **Para-rhyme**, also known as half-rhyme or near-rhyme, involves the use of words with similar sounds but not exact rhymes. We can see an illustration of this technique in the poem 'Strange Meeting'.

> Too fast in thought or death to be **bestirred**.
> Then, as I probed them, one sprang up, and **stared**
> With piteous recognition in fixed **eyes**,
> Lifting distressful hands, as if to **bless**.

'Anthem for Doomed Youth' is another famous poem by Owen which is often anthologised. The haunting lines quoted below are from this poem.

> What passing-bells for those who die as cattle?
> —Only the monstrous anger of the guns.

Just five of his poems were published during his lifetime. The rest were published in 1931 after he died with the excellent memoir by Edmund Blunden.

Features

- Owen was known as a war poet who presented the reality of war. His main focus was on the piteous nature of war. To quote Owen himself on this subject, 'I am not concerned with Poetry. My subject is War, and the pity of War. The Poetry is in the pity.'
- Owen used graphic imagery to portray both the physical as well as the psychological trauma experienced by young soldiers in the war.
- He employed several poetic techniques like alliteration and onomatopoeia to enhance his poetry. He was famous for his use of the para-rhyme.
- He was an inspiration to the poets of the post-war period. Dylan Thomas referred to Owen as 'one of the four most profound influences upon the poets who came after him'—the others being Hopkins, Yeats and Eliot.

Robert Graves (1895–1985)

Poetry
Over the Brazier (1916)
Fairies and Fusiliers (1917)
Collected Poems (1955, 1975)
More Poems (1961)
New Poems (1962)
Historical Fiction
I, Claudius (1934)
Claudius the God (1934)
Count Belisarlus (1938)
Sergeant Lamb's America (1940)
Wife to Mr. Milton (1943)
The Golden Fleece (1944)
King Jesus (1946)
Non-Fiction
The White Goddess (1948)
The Greek Myths (1963)
Autobiography
Goodbye to All That (1929)

Life

Robert von Ranke Graves was born in London and educated in Charterhouse. He joined the army in 1914 and fought in the trenches along with Sassoon. He was disturbed mentally by his horrific experiences in the trenches. He also had a troubled marriage that finally ended in divorce.

He met an American poet, Laura Riding, with whom he spent nearly thirteen years in Majorca. During the Second World War, he returned to England and went back to Majorca with his second wife in 1946.

During his life time, he received many honours. He served as professor of poetry at Oxford from 1961 to 1966. Gradually, his memory began to fade in the 1970s and he needed constant care and support. He died at the age of ninety and was buried in Majorca, where he had spent several years of his life.

Works

Graves was a prolific writer, who wrote verse, essays, historical fiction and books for children. He is remembered primarily as a poet today. He began writing poems while he was in school and his early poetry is typically Georgian.

POETRY

After his experiences in the trenches, like Sassoon, he grew disillusioned with war. He published two volumes of poems: *Over the Brazier* and *Fairies and Fusiliers*. These two volumes of poetry established Graves as a war poet and reflect his experiences as a soldier. The title, *Fairies and Fusiliers,* highlights the contrast between the magical world of fairies and the harsh realities of soldiers. These two volumes contain poems dealing with various themes such as loss of innocence, complexities of love and mythology apart from war. Graves combines traditional forms with modernist experimentation.

His *Collected Poems* brings together poems written throughout his career. One is able to get an overview of his poetry and see his development as a serious poet from his earlier style. His poems are vigorous and straightforward.

HISTORICAL FICTION

Graves was deeply interested in history and his novels of ancient Rome *I, Claudius* and *Claudius the God* are two examples of this interest. These two novels form a duology that portray the life of the Roman Emperor Claudius. The novels offer a fascinating perspective of intrigue and corruption in the Roman Empire. *Count Belisarius* is set in the sixth-century Byzantine Empire and explores the conflicts and conspiracies of that time. He explored the world of mythology in *Hercules, My Shipmate.* Graves combined history and mythology to create a fascinating narrative.

His novel *King Jesus* explores the life of Jesus Christ, blending historical research with imagination. It delved into the political and social intricacies of the period and through his imagination Graves was able to recreate a bygone period.

NON-FICTION

Graves was considered a respected scholar and critic, but his work *The White Goddess* aroused a lot of controversy. It explores the role of mythology and the dominance of a mythic female muse. Drawing from various mythologies and folktales, he examined the archetype of the goddess across cultures and identified her as the source of poetic power and inspiration.

Features

- His experiences in the war deeply influenced his poetry. He wrote about the trauma, loss and the fragility of human existence in his war poems.
- Graves wrote about other themes such as love and human relationships too.
- In his poetry, he combined traditional forms with modernist experimentation.
- He excelled in historical fiction. He was able to take his readers to a bygone age through his meticulous eye for detail.
- As an essayist, he revealed his thorough research. He was able to delve deep into mythology, history and literature and present his arguments in an erudite manner.

Edmund Blunden (1896–1974)

Poetry

Pastorals (1916)

The Waggoner and other Poems (1920)

The Shepherd (1922)

English Poems (1925)

Undertones of War (1928)

Collected Poems (1930)

The Face of England (1932)

Choice or Chance (1934)

Poems 1930–40 (1941)

English Villages (1941)

Cricket Country (1944)

Shells by a Stream (1944)

After the Bombing (1949)

The Midnight Skaters (1968)

Biographies

Leigh Hunt (1930)

Thomas Hardy (1942)

Shelley (1946)

Life

Edmund Charles Blunden was born in London and educated at Christ's Hospital and Oxford. In 1914, he joined service and fought in the trenches for almost two years, without being injured. This fact burdened him with a sense of guilt which he carried all his life.

After leaving the army, he went back to Oxford and joined the English department along with Robert Graves. He left college without graduating and worked as an assistant editor in London.

He also taught in Japan, Hong Kong and Oxford. He continued to write and publish throughout his teaching career. After his retirement, he settled in Suffolk where he breathed his last.

Works

Blunden is primarily a pastoral poet whose poems continue the traditional style of English poetry. In his poetry, we get to experience the sights and sounds of the English countryside of which he was very fond. His poems were first published in *Georgian Poetry* and were well received. Some of the works that belonged to this period are *The Waggoner*, *The Shepherd* and *English Poems*. These were largely poems about rural life.

In *Undertones of War*, he wrote about the destruction of nature and humans in Flanders. In it, he captured the traumatic realities of war and gave an account of his own experiences. One can discern in these poems, a keen sense of empathy for his fellow soldiers. His first published volume *Collected Poems* and the biography, *Leigh Hunt*, were published in 1930. He continued to publish more of his poems entitled *Poems 1930–1940*. In *After the Bombing*, the poems are more meditative and serious in tone.

Features

- Blunden's poetry is known for its vivid and evocative imagery.
- Blunden was deeply interested in nature and in the British countryside. He was chiefly a pastoral poet.
- Another important feature of his poetry is his preoccupation with war. He was deeply affected by war and, like Sassoon, was against it. He is ranked among the important war poets of England.
- Although Blunden is counted among the Georgian poets, he had his own style of writing. His poetry is characterised by a poignancy and reflexive nature that was his own.

T.S. Eliot (1888–1965)

Poetry
Prufrock and other Observations (1917)
Poems (1919)
'The Waste Land' (1922)
'The Hollow Men' (1925)
'The Journey of the Magi' (1927)
'Ash-Wednesday' (1930)
Four Quartets (1935–42)
Old Possum's Book of Practical Cats (1939)

Drama
Sweeney Agonistes (1932)
The Rock (1934)
Murder in the Cathedral (1935)
The Family Reunion (1939)
The Cocktail Party (1950)
The Confidential Clerk (1954)
The Elder Statesman (1959)

Literary Criticism
The Sacred Wood: Essays on Poetry and Criticism (1920)
For Lancelot Andrews: Essays on Style and Order (1928)
Selected Essays (1932)
The Use of Poetry and the Use of Criticism (1933)
After Strange Gods (1934)
Elizabethan Essays (1934)
The Idea of a Christian Society (1940)
Notes Towards a Definition of Culture (1948)
Poetry and Drama (1951)
On Poets and Poetry (1957)

Life

Thomas Stearns Eliot was born in St Louis, Missouri, USA. He was a descendent of the first Puritan settlers who had emigrated from East Coker in Somerset, England. He studied at Harvard, the Sorbonne and at Oxford. Encouraged by Pound who was impressed by his poem 'The Love Song of J. Alfred Prufrock', he moved to England.

After a brief stint of teaching, he began to work for Lloyds Bank and later as editor of *The Egoist*. He also founded the quarterly journal *The Criterion* and left Lloyds Bank to become a director of 'Faber and Faber'. In 1927, he became a British citizen and a member of the Anglican Church. He married Vivienne Haigh-Wood in 1915, who later suffered terribly from nervousness and finally had to be institutionalised in1938. Eliot transcribed his one-sided 'dialogues' with his wife in 'A Game of Chess' in 'The Waste Land'. 'My nerves are very bad to-night. Yes, bad. Stay with me. / Speak to me. Why do you never speak? Speak.' He was formally separated from his wife in 1933 and she died in 1947.

Ten years after his first wife died, he married Valerie Fletcher and enjoyed a fulfilling marriage till the end of his life. His last years saw him receiving a lot of public accolades and he was a much sought-after speaker. He was awarded the Nobel Prize for literature in 1948. Eliot expressed his wish to be buried in his ancestors' parish church at East Coker, thus completing the circle of his life.

Works

POETRY

Eliot's influence on international literature has been tremendous since the 1920s. He left his mark on poetry, drama and literary criticism and was the acknowledged leader of the modernist movement along with his friend Ezra Pound. To quote the poet Karl Shapiro, 'Eliot is untouchable; he is Modern Literature incarnate and an institution unto himself.' Such was his greatness that on his death *Life* magazine declared in the obituary: 'Our age beyond any doubt has been, and will continue to be, the Age of Eliot.'

With his very first poem 'The Love Song of J. Alfred Prufrock', he shook the literary world with his unconventional and highly developed style. Although it has certain traits of nineteenth-century French poets, it follows a style of its own with abrupt jumps from a rhetorical style to cliches and indirect cross references to other texts and a unique combination of humour and gloom. It was Pound who first recognised the dazzling brilliance of the poem and introduced Eliot to the British. The poem is full of startling images:

> Let us go then, you and I,
> When the evening is spread out against the sky
> Like a patient etherised upon a table...
> The yellow fog that rubs its back upon the window-panes,
> The yellow smoke that rubs its muzzle on the window-panes,
> Licked its tongue into the corners of the evening,
> Lingered upon the pools that stand in drains,
> Let fall upon its back the soot that falls from chimneys...

Some of his other early poems are 'Portrait of a Lady', 'Preludes' and 'Rhapsody on a Windy Night'. These poems too, like Prufrock, reflect the desolation, alienation and the dehumanising features of a growing metropolis.

If 'Prufrock' made a splash in the literary circles, his next poem 'The Waste Land' created a terrific storm. Published in 1922, the same year as Joyce's *Ulysses*, it is a long and complex poem full of obscure references, sometimes in different languages. This poem more than any other work of literature holds up a mirror to the spiritual bankruptcy of Europe and reflects the emotional numbness caused by the First World War. By quoting texts from the past and other cultures, Eliot makes this bankruptcy even more poignant. 'The Waste Land' consists of five sections: 'The Burial of the Dead', 'A Game of Chess', 'The Fire Sermon', 'Death by Water' and 'What the Thunder Said'.

> Unreal City,
> Under the brown fog of a winter dawn
> A crowd flowed over London Bridge, so many,
> I had not thought death had undone so many.

Eliot was able to weave together the desolate present with an idyllic past to create a disturbing effect:

> By the waters of Leman I sat down and wept…
> Sweet Thames, run softly till I end my song,
> Sweet Thames, run softly, for I speak not loud or long,
> But at my back in the cold blast I hear
> The rattle of the bones, and the chuckle spread from ear to ear.

'The Waste Land' is full of echoes and references to other texts. One could call this style of writing a collage for it puts together, in a haphazard manner, several pieces of texts from different parts of the world. Pound, referring to this poem, said that it was 'about enough…to make the rest of us shut shop.'

After Eliot became an Anglican in 1927, his poetry underwent a change. One sees a greater interest in religion as against his earlier slant towards humanism. In 'The Hollow Men', the refrain 'For Thine is the Kingdom…' is proof of this change. Evoking the theme of despair and the emptiness of life, the poem is written in five sections, each with its own distinct voice and style. The fragmented and disjointed language of the poem reflects the bewildered state of the hollow men who are described as 'Shape without form, shade without colour, / Paralysed force, gesture without motion.' They are described as being trapped in a world that is devoid of meaning: 'This is the dead land / This is cactus land'. Eliot weaves several religious images and reference into the poem which reveals his search for salvation or redemption. The poem however ends on a very pessimistic note:

> This is the way the world ends
> This is the way the world ends
> This is the way the world ends
> Not with a bang but with a whimper.

'Ash Wednesday' reflects Eliot's deep spiritual and religious quest and his personal journey towards faith and redemption. The title refers to the Christian holy day that marks the beginning of Lent—a period of penance and reflection. The poem successfully takes us through the different stages of the speaker's faith.

His next major work is *Four Quartets*, a work in four parts representing the four seasons and the four elements. They comprise four interconnected poems written between 1936 and 1942. This work reveals Eliot's profound engagement with the Christian faith and his struggle to discover meaning in a tumultuous world. Each poem deals with different aspects of human existence. 'Burnt Norton' examines the concept of time and its effect on human consciousness. In 'East Coker', he focuses on the cycle of birth and death and the quest for spiritual rejuvenation. In 'The Dry Salvages', Eliot uses the metaphor of water as a symbol of both destruction and salvation. 'Little Gidding' reflects the connection between the earthly and the eternal and emphasises the importance of redemption.

DRAMA

After the 1930s, Eliot turned his attention to drama and literary criticism. He was interested in reviving poetic drama, which was popular in the Elizabethan age. He wrote seven plays which are all tragedies, including the fragment *Sweeney Agonistes*. In *Sweeney Agonistes*, he highlights the sterile lifestyle of the common people of Europe. His next play *The Rock* is a verse drama that is written using elements of the morality play and religious allegory. It was written as a pageant play to help raise money for building new churches in London.

Murder in the Cathedral is a historical play about the assassination of Archbishop Thomas Becket in Canterbury by Henry II. It combines the features of the miracle play and the Greek tragedies and is written in verse. It portrays the internal conflict in Becket for opposing Henry II. The chorus which consists of some poor women, representing the common people, plays an important role in the progression of the play. It provides a suitable background and plays the vital function of building up tension. Through their mental growth, from their initial fear and panic to an understanding of and reconciliation with the martyrdom of Becket, Eliot wishes to convey the message that mankind has to accept their share of the burden of sin and the glory of redemption.

The Family Reunion is a secular play that is about the hero's journey from guilt to redemption. This play, like his earlier ones, is also written in verse. Eliot introduces a few elements from classical Greek drama like the chorus represented by the detached speeches of the protagonist's uncles and aunts and his pursuit by the Eumenides (the avenging Furies), seen only by him and one or two other characters in the play.

In *The Cocktail Party*, Eliot presents the isolation and meaninglessness of human relationships in a poignant manner:

> They do not repine;
> Are contented with the morning that separates
> And the evening that brings together
> For casual talk before the fire
> Two people who know they do not understand each other,
> Breeding children whom they do not understand
> And who will never understand them.

The last two plays, *The Confidential Clerk* and *The Elder Statesman*, both reflect Eliot's interest in exploring the moral and spiritual dimensions of human existence.

LITERARY CRITICISM

Eliot's literary criticism, like his poetry and drama, had a great impact upon twentieth century literature. His critical essays and reviews played a major role in the shaping of literary criticism. In his first collection of essays *The Sacred Wood*, he examines the works of great poets like Dante, Shakespeare, Blake and Tennyson and highlights the various aspects of poetry. His famous essay 'Tradition and the Individual Talent' is one of the corner stones of modern criticism. In it, he points out the necessity for poets to have an 'historical sense'. **Historical sense**, according to Eliot, is 'a perception, not only of the pastness of the past, but of its presence; the historical sense compels a man to write not merely with his own generation in his bones, but with a feeling that the whole of literature of Europe from Homer, and within it the whole of the literature of his own country, has simultaneous existence and composes a simultaneous order....' As far as the individuality of the poet is concerned, Eliot believed that the artist should detach himself from his personal emotions and become just a medium through which universal truths and emotions find expression. He held the view that the mind that experiences should be detached from the poet who creates.

His next book on criticism *Homage to John Dryden: Three Essays* established Eliot as an important critic of the age. Apart from a biography of Dryden, the book contains essays on the Metaphysical poets and Andrew Marvell. Eliot's evaluation of the Metaphysical poets renewed interest in the seventeenth century poets. In 'The Metaphysical Poets', he points out, 'A thought to Donne was an experience; it modified his sensibility.' Eliot said there was a dissociation of thought and feeling in later poets as they were not able to 'amalgamate disparate experiences' like the Metaphysical poets. He called this lapse on the part of the later poets as **disassociation of sensibility**.

His preface to *For Lancelot Andrews* is famous for his declaration that he was a 'classicist in literature, royalist in politics and Anglo-Catholic in religion'. This book consists of seven essays that deal with a study of rhetorical devices through a close study of Lancelot Andrews' sermons. This statement serves as a key to understanding Eliot's approach to literary criticism.

In his essay 'Hamlet and His Problems', Eliot talks about another concept known as **objective correlative**, by which he means that a poet cannot directly transmit his emotions to the reader. He should use a medium such as a set of objects or a chain of ideas to do so. Through this, what the poet has to say gets objectified and the reader is able to understand the poet via the medium. Eliot firmly believed in the **impersonality** of the poet. He believed that a poet should strive for a detachment from his work and avoid expressing personal emotions directly.

Eliot's criticism has been highly influential and has helped shape the course of twentieth-century critical thinking.

Features

- T. S. Eliot has made a significant contribution as a poet, dramatist and critic. His essays and poems paved the way for new approaches and interpretations of literature.
- Eliot's poetry played an important role in ushering in the era of modernism through the innovative use of language, form and subject matter.
- The major themes of his poetry were disillusionment, fragmentation and the meaninglessness of life.
- He was adept at using techniques such as imagery, intertextuality and symbolism.
- He played an important role in the revival of poetic drama.
- His plays rekindled an interest in religion and faith and reveal Eliot as a devout Christian.
- He revolutionised the way literature was studied through his emphasis on the importance of tradition, objective correlative and the concept of impersonality in poetry.
- He played an important part in the revival of interest in the Metaphysical poets.

Cecil Day Lewis (1904–72)

Poetry
Beechen Vigil (1925)
Transitional Poem (1929)
From Feathers to Iron (1931)
The Magnetic Mountain (1933)
A Time to Dance (1935)
Overtures to Death (1938)
Poems in Wartime (1940)
An Italian Visit (1953)

Novel
A Question of Proof (1935)
The Friendly Tree (1936)

Autobiography
Noah and the Waters (1936)

Life

Cecil Day-Lewis was born in Ireland. His father was a minister in the Church of Ireland and the family moved to England when Day-Lewis was still a baby. He was educated at Sherborne and at Oxford. At Oxford, he came under the influence of a group of left-wing poets which included Auden.

He worked as a schoolmaster for a few years and later became a full-time writer. He was politically active and joined the communist party. He was also involved in writing for the *Left Review* and editing socialist articles. He served as professor of poetry at Oxford between 1951–56 and was appointed poet laureate in 1968. He died of pancreatic cancer when he was 68 and, as per his wish, was buried near Thomas Hardy's grave.

Works

POETRY

Day-Lewis was a prolific writer who published several volumes of poetry and novels. His early poetry reflects his discontentment with society and he believed that communism was the panacea for all of society's shortcomings. These preoccupations can be discerned in his works such as *Transitional Poem*, *From Feathers to Iron* and *The Magnetic Mountain*. These poems are radical in nature and reflect the poet's hope for a new dawn. He strikes a personal note in *From Feathers to Iron*, where we can also see his love for nature. The poems display his lyrical style of writing.

The Magnetic Mountain reflects the influence of Auden. This collection deals with his interest in social and political issues. Like the other poets of the group, he too was disturbed by the impact of industrialisation. 'Here where the looming factory stands, / Its windows blind as the brimstone snake's, / Its brick-hives pulsing with murmurous hands, / I would fix a vision.'

A Time to Dance, a lyric sequence, was written as an elegy on the death of his school friend. In this work, Day-Lewis combines his grief over his friend's death with his anger at the world in which children starve and men are unemployed.

FICTION

Day-Lewis embarked under the name of 'Nicholas Blake' to write detective fiction. His first work in this genre was *A Question of Proof* in which he introduced the detective Nigel Strangeways. This novel was followed by almost twenty more. These novels are known for their intricate plots, well-drawn characters and psychological depth.

Day-Lewis wrote a few historical novels like *The Otterbury Incident* set against the backdrop of the Second World War and *The Golden Echo,* which is about a seventeenth-century painter. He also wrote autobiographical novels, the first of which is *The Friendly Tree.*

Features

- His poems expressed his deep discontentment with society. He wrote about love, loss and social issues and was associated with the New Apocalyptics who reacted against the Georgian poets.
- He had a fondness for imagery drawn from machinery and other features of modern life.

Wystan Hugh Auden (1907–73)

Poetry
Poems (1930)
The Orators (1932)
Look Stranger! (1936)
Letters from Iceland (1937, with MacNeice)
Journey to a War (1939, with Isherwood)
Another Time (1940)
The Double Man (1941)
For the Time Being: A Christmas Oratorio (1944)
The Sea and the Mirror (1944)
The Age of Anxiety: A Baroque Eclogue (1948)
Nones (1951)
The Shield of Achilles (1955)
Homage to Clio (1960)
Collected Shorter Poems 1927–57 (1966)

Drama
The Dance of Death (1933)
The Dog Beneath the Skin (1935, with Isherwood)
The Ascent of F6 (1936)
On the Frontier (1938)

Prose
The Enchanted Flood (1950)
The Dyer's Hand (1962)
Secondary Worlds (1968)

Life

Wystan Hugh Auden was born in York and had an affluent childhood. He was the youngest son of a doctor and was educated at Gresham's School and Christ Church, Oxford. His contemporaries were MacNeice, Day-Lewis and Spender, with whom he is always linked as one of the **poets of the thirties**.

After leaving Oxford, he lived for some time in Berlin and returned to England and worked as a schoolteacher. He travelled to Iceland, Spain and China and wrote poems about his visits. He left England for the United States in 1939 and taught in a number of universities there. He became an American citizen in 1946. He lived mostly in New York City and later bought a house in Austria, where he spent his summers. He spent a major part of his last years in Oxford and died suddenly in Vienna.

Works

POETRY

Auden is considered the most important of this group: 'the poets of the thirties'. He is seen as a chronicler of the contemporary events and a sensitive mind attuned to the events and ideas of his time. It is difficult to classify his poetry as it displays a wide variety of styles ranging from the colloquial idiom of the streets to the ancient measures of Beowulf. In his poetry, we can see the musical cadences of the ballad and the formal mourning of the elegy. Auden wished to reach out to a wider audience by making his poetry less 'highbrow' and chose as his themes the sordid realities of everyday life.

He won recognition with his very first volume of poems which was simply titled *Poems*. This was quickly followed by *The Orators* which is a long poem, partly in prose and partly verse. It is a very complex work in which Auden made use of double perspectives, a variety of tones and styles and several concepts by thinkers like Freud and D.H. Lawrence. It has three sections sandwiched between a prologue and an epilogue.

Look Stranger! was the title that Auden had given his next work when it was published in the UK. He changed the title to *On This Island* when it was later published in the US. This is a collection of thirty-one poems which were mostly composed during the time he was working as a schoolteacher.

A visit to Iceland with MacNeice resulted in a book in prose and verse called *Letters from Iceland*, while another trip to China with Isherwood lead to the book *Journey to a War*. The latter, too, was written in both prose and verse and remains an example of travel chronicles of the inter-war years. *Another Time* contains several of his famous poems like 'September 1, 1939' and 'Lullaby'. His famous poem 'The Unknown Citizen' is also from this collection. It is cynical poem that is in the form of an epitaph of a man whose identity is just a combination of letters and numbers.

In *The Double Man,* Auden describes the 'baffling crime' of 'two decades of hypocrisy'. This lengthy verse epistle highlights man's solitude and concludes with a prayer for sanctuary and enlightenment for the 'muddled heart'.

Auden abandoned communism in 1939 after the signing of the German-Soviet pact. Soon after this, he moved to the US just before the outbreak of the Second World War. His poetry after this period reflects a religious slant as he became increasingly disillusioned with Marxist materialism and discovered a renewed commitment to Christianity. During this period, he published *For the Time Being: A Christmas Oratorio*, *Another Time*, *The Sea and the Mirror* and *The Age of Anxiety*.

The title of the last work sums up the reigning theme of Auden's poetic writing. Anxiety was the main feature of his life, which was a result of his serious approach to the political situation of the world. One notes the edgy, tense and worried nature of his verse. He had witnessed the effects of the Great Depression, the rise of Nazism, the Second World War and the Holocaust. His later poetry is less obscure and there is a change in his views, too, with his moving away from Marx and Freud.

DRAMA

Although Auden is primarily known as a poet, his contribution to drama is significant. His plays combined poetic language with social preoccupation and philosophical musings. He wrote several plays like *The Dog Beneath the Skin*, *The Ascent of F6* and

On the Frontier in collaboration with the British-American writer Christopher Isherwood. These plays reflect their shared political and social concerns and their experiments with form and content.

Auden challenged traditional theatrical conventions and experimented with innovative stage techniques in plays like *The Dance of Death*. He wrote his next play *The Dog Beneath the Skin* in collaboration with Isherwood. This is a satirical poetic drama in three acts in which the protagonist embarks on a quest to find a missing heir. The quest takes him across Europe accompanied by a dog, who turns out to be the object of his search. *The Ascent of F6*, again in collaboration with Isherwood, holds up a mirror to the drawbacks of a capitalistic and imperialistic society. One is able to discern Auden's reasons for wishing to be a political poet.

PROSE

Auden's prose comprises of several essays, lectures and critical writings composed throughout his career. *The Enchanted Flood* is a collection of essays about the Romantic movement and the impact it had on his work. *The Dyer's Hand* is considered one of Auden's most important prose works as it contains an array of essays on poetry, literature, art, religion and politics. In *Secondary Worlds*, Auden reflects on various art forms like music, literature and painting and examines the connection between art and society. Auden is considered a great intellect of his age and his prose is ample proof of this fact.

Features

- Auden is seen as an influential figure of twentieth century literature along with giants like T.S. Eliot and Yeats. He is chiefly famous as a poet although he made a mark both as a dramatist and a critic.
- He was influenced by the poetry of Eliot and was keenly aware of the shallowness of a crumbling civilisation. This awareness led him to communism, in which he saw a panacea for contemporary problems.
- His later poetry reflects his disillusionment with communism and his embracing of Christian values.

- Auden experimented with various poetical techniques and drew heavily from ancient forms like Anglo-Saxon alliterative verse forms and Norse 'kennings'. 'Day-wishing flowers' and 'cloud-soft hand' from his poem 'The Wanderer' remind us of the ancient kennings.
- He was influenced by Freud and Marx in his earlier work.
- In his later poetry, he turned more towards religion and his poetry became more experimental.
- Auden was known for his vivid use of imagery. The following example from the poem 'As I Walked Out One Evening' is proof of this skill: The glacier knocks in the cupboard, The desert sighs in the bed'

Louis MacNeice (1907–63)

Poetry
Blind Fireworks (1929)
Poems (1935)
Letters from Iceland (with Auden, 1937)
The Earth Compels (1938)
Autumn Journal (1938)
Plant and Phantom (1941)
Springboard (1944)
Holes in the Sky (1948)
Autumn Sequel (1954)
The Burning Perch (1963)

Drama
The Dark Tower (1947)

Autobiography
The Strings are False (1965)

Life

Frederick Louis MacNeice was born in Belfast and his father was a bishop. His mother died when he was hardly seven years old and his father remarried a few years later. MacNeice was educated at Sherborne preparatory school and later at Merton College, in Marlborough, England. He then continued his education at Oxford where he made his acquaintance with Auden and Spender. Although he was removed from his native Irish background and lost his Irish accent, he never lost sight of his Irish roots.

In 1930, much against his father's wishes, he married Mary Ezra who was a Jew. They lived in Birmingham, where he became lecturer of classics at Birmingham University and Bedford College. He was shattered when his wife left him and his one-year-old son in 1935. He plunged himself in work and produced some of his best poetry after this incident. In 1941, he joined BBC as a writer–producer and travelled widely. He died of pneumonia when he was just fifty-five.

Works

MacNeice's first volume of poetry *Blind Fireworks* appeared while he was still at Oxford. This established him as a poet and his name was linked to the popular group of the poets of the thirties.

He made a few unsuccessful attempts at writing drama and turned to poetry once again. Although he was a member of the Auden group, he did not believe that any political doctrine could change the world. His early work reveals his fondness for images and he had a painter's eye for details. He went back to the classic verse forms and he was noted for his use of assonance, and internal and half-rhymes and ballad-like refrains. He was also known for his humourous and unconventional rhymes. For example, in his poem 'Bagpipe Music', the following lines give us an illustration of his use of slant rhymes in which the ending sounds of the words 'rickshaw' and 'peepshow' are similar, but not perfect rhymes:

> It's no go the merry-go-round, it's no go the rickshaw,
> All we want is a limousine and a ticket for the peepshow.

A visit to Iceland resulted in the book *Letters from Iceland* written in collaboration with Auden. It is one of the most interesting travel books written in a unique style. The book reveals more about the thoughts and life of the authors than it does about the place they visited.

Autumn Journal is a long autobiographical poem documenting the poet's thoughts before the Second World War. It gives a vivid description of the life of the thirties and the pre-war political tension. These poems were based on the rise of fascism in Europe and its threat to England.

His other important works include *The Earth Compels*, *Plant and Phantom*, *Spring-Board*, *Holes in the Sky*, *Autumn Sequel* and *The Burning Perch*. His poetry is restrained and precise with overtones of melancholy. He was at his best in short lyrics as he was conscious of the musical and rhythmical qualities of language.

MacNeice made his mark as a pioneer in writing poetic drama for the radio. Some of his works in this genre are *Christopher Columbus* (1944) and *The Dark Tower* (1947).

Features

- MacNeice had a painter's eye for imagery. An example of his use of striking visuals can be seen in his poem 'Snow':
- He did not believe in any rigid system, either political or philosophical. He tried to find and present some pattern from the uncertain turmoil of life.
- He was influenced by the modernist movement and his use of fragmented narratives and experiment with form and structure bear testimony to this.
- He was interested in the social and political issues of his time and this had an impact on his writing.

Stephen Spender (1909–95)

Poetry
Twenty Poems (1930)
Poems (1933)
Vienna (1934)
The Still Centre (1939)
Poems of Dedication (1947)
Collected Poems 1928–1953 (1955)

Autobiography
World within World (1951)

Drama
Trial of a Judge (1938)

Prose
The Destructive Element (1935)
The God that Failed (with Arthur Koestler, 1949)
The Creative Element (1953)
The Struggle of the Modern (1963)

Life

Stephen Spender was born in London and his father was a distinguished political journalist. His mother was partly of German-Jewish descent. He was educated at University College School, London and University College, Oxford, where he became a friend of Auden, MacNeice and Isherwood. He moved to Germany in the early thirties where his political consciousness was awakened.

He became a political activist and travelled to Spain to promote anti-fascist propaganda during the Spanish Civil War. He was a constant visitor to the US where he held teaching positions. He served as professor of English at University College, London, from 1970 to 1977 and was knighted in 1983.

Works

Stephen Spender's poems offer us a detailed picture of the time between the two wars. Through his poems, we get to see the world slipping from the Great Depression to fascism and finally to war. He referred to the thirties as a 'low dishonest decade'. This did not, however, make him pessimistic. His poems celebrate technology while, at the same time, expressing concern at the repercussions of industrialisation.

His best-known poems are a combination of traditional romanticism and modern subject matters. His early volume of poetry called *Poems* is a collection of both political and personal poems. It contains his famous poems 'The Truly Great' and 'Pylons'. In 'The Truly Great', Spender, pays a rich tribute to the people whom he considered truly great, such as military heroes, poets or artists. 'The Pylons' is a poem about industrialisation and it was responsible for the nickname **Pylon Poets** which was given to him and his like-minded friends.

Spender was preoccupied with political and social issues. He was totally against fascism and these views are echoed in his series of poems *The Still Centre*. After the Second World War, Spender changed his approach to poetry. He had earlier believed that literature should discuss politico-moral themes but later was of the opinion that the artist should focus more on creative power. This shift in his views is seen more clearly by comparing his prose works *The Destructive Element* with *The Creative Element*. The former essay focuses on the destructive nature of human beings as seen in history and *The Creative Element* draws our attention to the creative aspects of human beings and the role of art in shaping culture and society.

His later poetry, as seen in *Poems of Dedication* and *Collected Poems*, reflects his lyrical craftsmanship and blends personal introspection and his preoccupation with society and politics.

Features

- Spender's work is known for its introspective nature. He delves into the complexities of human emotions and identity.
- He used his writings as a tool to spread his views on politics and society. His works reflect a strong sense of social conscience and a desire for a brighter future. He was like a political conscience of his generation.
- He was able to successfully blend the form of the Romantics with a modern theme, for example the poem 'The Express'.

Dylan Thomas (1914–53)

Prose
The Map of Love (1939)
Portrait of the Artist as a Young Dog (1955)
Adventures in the Skin Trade (1955)
Prospect of the Sea (1955)

Poetry
18 Poems (1934)
Deaths and Entrances (1946)
Collected Poems (1952)

Life

Dylan Marlais Thomas was born in Swansea, Wales, and was the son of the English master at Swansea Grammar School. He worked as a newspaper reporter, radio broadcaster and film scriptwriter. He moved to London in 1934, where he published his first volume of poems.

While in London, his lifestyle changed. He became more flamboyant and spent his afternoons in drinking clubs. He married an Irish girl, Caitlin Macnamara, and had three children. After he got married, he went to Wales and settled down there after wandering to several places. Although his marriage was stormy, it did not break and his wife was by his side when he died due to complications arising from his alcoholism. He died in the US while on a lecture-tour there.

Works

Dylan Thomas was a prodigy who wrote some of his best poems before he turned twenty. His poetry was free of the political themes and overtones found in the works of his contemporaries, like Auden and Spender. He wrote poems that were romantic, melodic and effusive. The readers were attracted to the rich and glowing magic of his language and enjoyed his poems in spite of the complex imagery and ambiguity. He was the most well-known of the group of poets who went under the name the New Apocalyptics.

His earliest volume *18 Poems* appeared when Thomas was twenty years old. It consists of poems based on the cycle of life—birth, childhood and death—and was set in Swansea. This book shot Thomas to immediate fame through his magical use of language and the personal element.

Deaths and Entrances contains some of his most famous poems like 'Fern Hill' and 'A Refusal to Mourn the Death by Fire of a Child in London'. His next book *Collected Poems 1934–1952* was also very well received. This volume included poems from his earlier collections apart from many new ones. Some of the frequently anthologised poems from this book are 'And Death Shall Have No Dominion' and 'Do Not Go Gentle into That Good Night'. He was a meticulous craftsman who reworked many of the earlier poems of his youth.

Thomas wrote a substantial quantity of prose. He had an ability to give detailed descriptions through his rich and vivid use of language. Many of his prose works blur the boundaries between reality and fantasy. *Map of Love* is a collection of prose and verse, while *Portrait of the Artist as a Young Dog* is a collection of short stories with an autobiographical slant. His other important works are *A Prospect of the Sea* and the radio drama, *Under Milk Wood.* The latter has been praised for its ability to capture the essence of Welsh life.

Features

- Thomas's themes were mostly related to the cycles of life and to nature and childhood.
- His prose and verse were known for their musicality. His works were written to be heard as much as to be read.

- Thomas's use of language attracted readers. Stephen Spender called Thomas 'a linguistic genius'. Another critic Louis Untermeyer said that his lines 'leap and shout and all but leave the printed page….'

Ted Hughes (1930–1998)

Poetry
The Hawk in the Rain (1957)
Lupercal (1960)
Wodwo (1967) (prose and verse)
Crow (1970)
Cave Birds (1975)
Season Songs (1976)
Moortown (1979)
Birthday Letters (1998)

Prose
Shakespeare and the Goddess of Complete Being (1992)

Life

Edward James Hughes was born in West Yorkshire and educated at Mexborough Grammar School and Cambridge University. While at Cambridge, he met the American poet Sylvia Plath and they got married in 1956. The marriage did not last long, although they had two children, and they separated in 1962. Six months later, Sylvia Plath committed suicide.

He married Carol Orchard in 1970 and they remained together till his death. He was appointed poet laureate in 1984 and was bestowed with the Order of Merit by Queen Elizabeth II just before he died.

Works

Ted Hughes has left a mark in the history of English poetry as a nature poet, which is not to be interpreted as being similar to Wordsworth and other Romantics. Extremely critical of the rapid strides being made by science and technology in the twentieth century and dissatisfied with the lack of spirituality, he turned to nature. He found in nature, a fierce will to survive against all odds. He chose animals as his subject matter in many of his poems as he found in them an unsevered relationship with nature. His fascination with nature could be traced to his childhood in Yorkshire, when he spent time going shooting and fishing with his brother. He was exposed to different types of animals and birds and this early exposure to the animal kingdom and nature led to his university studies in archaeology and anthropology.

His first volume of poems *The Hawk in the Rain* reflects his obsession with animals and the beauty and brutality that he saw in nature. It is a collection of forty poems and was very well received in England and America. The volume consists of poems on the hawk, the jaguar, the fox and horses apart from other subjects dealing with people and the First World War. He used the animals and birds to reflect the violence and meaninglessness of human existence. The poem, 'The Thought Fox' is from this collection. It explores the creative process using the fox as a metaphor.

His reputation rose even higher with the publication of his next volume of poetry *Lupercal*. His famous poem 'Hawk Roosting' is from this collection. In this poem, Hughes uses the hawk to reveal human emotions such as ruthlessness and ambition. *Wodwo,* his next book, contains a series of poems which explore the themes of human identity and the relationship between civilisation and nature.

Crow is a collection of poems that uses the crow as a symbolic and mythical creature. Through the character of the crow, Hughes delves into the darker side of human nature and the struggle for survival. The crow is portrayed as a trickster figure challenging conventional ideas and questioning the present state of affairs.

In *Cave Birds,* an illustrated collection of poems, Hughes highlights the crime of modern humanity against nature. His last collection of poems *Birthday Letters,* published just before his death, discusses his life with Sylvia Plath. After the suicide of his wife, there was a lot of speculation on Hughes's role in it. In his last work, he offered a deeply personal insight into their relationship. It provides his perspective on their marriage, Plath's mental health issues and the aftermath of her death.

Features

- Hughes had a deep connection with nature and animals and his poetry is closely connected with them.

- He was also interested in myth and folklore which can be seen in his frequent use of archetypal themes and symbolic language.
- His poetry often reflects the violent and brutal aspects of life and nature.

Seamus Heaney (1939–2013)

Poetry
Eleven Poems (1965)
Death of a Naturalist (1966)
Door into the Dark (1969)
Wintering Out (1972)
North (1975)
Field Work (1979)
Selected Poems 1965–1975 (1980)
Station Island (1984)
The Haw Lantern (1987)
Selected Poems, 1966–1987 (1990)
Seeing Things (1991)
The Spirit Level (1996)
Electric Light (2001)
District and Circle (2006)
Human Chain (2010)
Selected Poems (1988–2013)

Prose
Preoccupations (1980)
The Government of the Tongue (1988)
The Redress of Poetry (1995)
Finders Keepers: Selected Prose, 1971–2001 (2002)

Translation
Sweeney Astray: A Version from the Irish (1984)

Life

Justin Seamus Heaney was born in Northern Ireland and belonged to the Catholic minority in the largely Protestant Ulster. He, therefore, had a mixed upbringing which was the result of an Irish Catholic family living in a land governed by British Protestants. He was, therefore, divided both politically and religiously. He was educated at St Columb's College, Derry and Queen's University, Belfast.

While in Belfast, he was drawn to a new poetic movement in the 1960s. He worked as a lecturer of poetry at Queen's University for six years before moving to the Republic of Ireland. He lived in Dublin from 1972 till his death.

He turned down the offer of poet laureateship for political reasons. In his poem, 'An Open Letter', he wrote: 'No glass of ours was ever raised / To toast The Queen.'

He was awarded the Nobel Prize for Literature in 1995.

Works

Seamus Heaney published his first collection of poems, *Eleven Poems,* as a modest sixteen-page pamphlet. Some of these poems had already been published in some journals. His second collection of poems *Death of a Naturalist* consists of thirty-four short poems. Most of these poems describe his childhood experiences and rural life. His well-known poem 'Digging' is from this collection. In this poem, Heaney draws parallels between the physical digging of a field by his father and grandfather and his own mental 'digging' as a poet.

His next book *Door into the Dark* explores his native landscape. It depicts the poet's rural past in a sensuous and traditional style. The poems deal with rural subjects like a blacksmith working in a forge, threshing and thatching.

In his next two collections of poems *Wintering Out* and *North,* Heaney began to write about the contemporary political scene in Ireland and the violence that subsequently followed. Both these books reflect Heaney's remarkable skill in blending the personal with the wider cultural and political themes. 'Tollund Man', a poem from the collection *Wintering Out*, draws a parallel between ritual killings in ancient days and the senseless political violence in Derry. In *North*, Heaney uses a historical and mythological framework to comment on the political strife in Ulster.

After spending a year in California, Heaney did not go back to Belfast. Instead, he moved to the south to Glanmore and did not write for the next four years. *Field Work* was the result of these four years of internalisation. These poems are written in a richer language and imagery than Heaney was known for in his earlier poetry. The book could be divided into three sections. The first section of poems deals with political and elegiac poems, the second consists of the ten 'Glanmore Sonnets', and the third is dominated by poems of love and family.

Selected Poems 1965–1975 is a collection of nearly all his poems from his first four collections. In most of his poems, he connects the history and strife of Northern Ireland to the northern European experience.

In *Seeing Things*, Heaney used the visions of afterlife in Virgil and Dante to help him cope with the death of his father. The themes revolve around death, the transience of life and imaginary conversations with his father. The collection *Spirit Level* examines the balance between the spiritual and the political and between the past and the present.

In his later poetry *Electric Light* and *District and Circle*, he once again returns to the Ireland of his childhood. His last collection of poems was *Human Chain* which shows his preoccupation with connections between the past and the present and human relationships. It contains an outstanding sequence of poems called 'Route 101' which uses Aeneid's descent into the underworld to trace the arc of his own life from the 1950s up to the time of his becoming a grandfather.

Apart from poetry, Heaney wrote a few volumes of prose consisting of critical essays that display his gift as a critic and teacher.

Features

- Seamus Heaney is a very important Irish poet, who is regarded as one the most influential poets of the twentieth century.
- Heaney, who was exposed to both England and Ireland, blended English Romanticism with the natural assonance of the Irish language. The following lines from the poem, 'Death of a Naturalist' are an illustration of this fact: 'There were dragon-flies, spotted butterflies, / But best of all was the warm thick slobber / Of frogspawn that grew like clotted water / In the shade of the banks.'
- His work gives us a detailed and sensory description of northern Ireland.
- He was deeply interested in rural life and his poems give us an insight into the daily life of the common people.
- His work is infused with a strong sense of Irish identity. He was very interested in Irish myths, legends and history.
- His work was impacted by the contemporary political unrest in Ireland.

Donald Davie (1922–95)

Poetry
Brides of Reason (1955)
A Winter Talent (1957)
Essex Poems (1969)
Collected Poems 1950–70 (1972)
The Shires (1974)
In the Stopping Train (1977)
Collected Poems 1972–83 (1983)
To Scorch or Freeze (1988)

Memoir
These the Companions (1982)

Prose
Purity of Diction in English Verse (1952)
Articulate Energy: An Enquiry Into the Syntax of English Poetry (1955)

Life

Donald Alfred Davie was born in Yorkshire and is remembered as an important figure of the Movement, which was a popular group in the 1950s. He was educated in Yorkshire and later at Cambridge, where he was deeply influenced by the critic F.R. Leavis. He had to take a break from his studies when the war broke out and he was sent to Russia for a year.

He returned to Cambridge after the war and continued his education. He took up several teaching assignments in Caius College, Cambridge, University of Essex, Stanford University and Vanderbilt University. He died of cancer at the age of 73.

Works

Donald Davie is one of the leading figures of the Movement. As a follower of F.R. Leavis, he believed in the moral tradition of literature and denounced 'the tawdry amoralism which had destroyed Dylan Thomas'. Davie's work is known for its preoccupation with the ethical impact of poetry. He shared the Movement's rejection of imagism and leaning towards traditional and conventional forms. He believed that the content of poetry should be rational and logical and the language should be clear.

Brides of Reason is a collection of twenty-seven poems and reflects the impact that eighteenth-century poetry had on him. In the poem 'Remembering the Thirties', he points out how his generation is unable to fully understand the stories of the previous generation. 'What for them were agonies, for us / Are high-brow thrillers.' His next collection *A Winter's Talent* contains thirty-seven poems. This was followed by other works like *Essex Poems* and *In the Stopping Train*. His poems reflect the influence that the 'industrially ravaged landscape' had on him. They are written in a scholarly and philosophical style and reflect a mind that, to quote the poet himself, 'moves most easily and happily among abstractions'.

Davie's poetry is often characterised by its formal technique and precise language. His poems often touch on themes of nature, identity, history and the challenges of modern life. We get vivid pictures of the different places of the world that he had visited. For example, in *A Winter's Talent* there are different groups of poems dedicated to different places like England, Ireland and Italy.

Apart from poetry, Davie is also known for his critical works. He wrote extensively on the craft of poetry and the importance of moral and traditional subject matters. His prose works clearly map out the agenda of the Movement poets who were anti-Romantic and anti-Bohemian. In his critical writings, he upheld the rational and intellectual poets of the seventeenth and eighteenth centuries. He argued for the restoration of the traditional forms or genres of the eighteenth century and severely objected to the modernist experimentation with forms. He stressed on maintaining a logical syntax and points out that disregarding syntax 'is to throw away a tradition central to human thought'.

Features

- Davie's poetry is marked by his devotion to formal craftsmanship. He used traditional poetic forms such as sonnets and rhymed quatrains and focused on metre and rhyme.
- His poetry and prose are known for their intellectual depth and for the exploration of complex ideas.
- In his poetry, he studied the impact that industrialisation had on the individual and society.
- He used simple and clear language to express complex ideas. He avoided ornamentation and obscure language.
- As a critic, Davie advocated the value of tradition in poetry. He believed that contemporary poets should not disregard

the achievements of the past but should learn to incorporate it into their own poetry.

Philip Larkin (1922–85)

Fiction
Jill (1946)
A Girl in Winter (1947)
Prose
All What Jazz: A Record Diary 1961–1968 (1970)
Required Writing: Miscellaneous Pieces 1955–1982 (1984)
Poetry
The Less Deceived (1955)
Whitsun Weddings (1964)
High Windows (1974)

Life

Philip Larkin was born in Coventry and after completing his schooling in Coventry, went to Oxford, where he completed his BA and MA. At Oxford, he met Kingsley Amis who became a good friend. After he completed his education, Larkin worked as a librarian at the University of Hull till his death.

Larkin was a very private person who rarely left Hull. He declined all invitations to read his poetry both in England and abroad. He never married and largely kept to himself. He died of cancer while in his early sixties.

Works

Philip Larkin's production of poems was quite small, but he was the most widely admired poet of his generation. His work came to public attention at the time when the famous 'angry young men' were popular. Larkin, unlike the passionate angry young men, approached the shortcomings of the age in a more low key manner. In his handling of his themes, he strikes a balance between disgust and despair. Larkin claimed that he was influenced by Thomas Hardy, whose work he greatly admired.

His disapproval of the cerebral experimentation of the modernist poets and his traditional approach to poetry made him a part of the Movement poets. Larkin used a traditional style to treat subjects that were exclusively drawn from modern life.

The Less Deceived was an immediate success and was selected as the book of the year by *Times Literary Supplement*. The title was inspired by the words of Ophelia in *Hamlet* when she said she was 'more deceived' by Hamlet. In his usage of the term 'less deceived', Larkin wanted his readers to avoid Ophelia's state of ignorance. His poems focus on the 'sad-eyed realism' of contemporary society. This collection contains his famous poem 'Church Going' in which Larkin uses a relaxed tone and meanders from point to point to disguise the fact that it is a deeply religious poem. He holds up a mirror to an age in which science and rationality had made serious inroads into religion and faith. The pain in his voice is clear in the following words from the poem: '…wondering, too / When churches fall completely out of use / What we shall tun them into…', '…for whom was built this special shell?'

His next book, *The Whitsun Weddings* a collection of thirty-two poems, was a great success. It contains many of Larkin's best-known poems like 'The Whitsun Weddings', 'Toads Revisited' and 'An Arundel Tomb'. These poems delve into various aspects of life like love, disillusionment and the passage of time. The title poem describes a train journey from Hull to London on a Whitsun weekend, a time associated with spring and weddings. Throughout the poem, Larkin takes a cynical attitude towards marriage and looks at weddings as a 'farcical' ceremony that focuses on dresses.

High Windows, his next collection of poems, shows a preoccupation with death and the transience of life. It was his last major work and Larkin focused on ageing and the realisation of the proximity of death.

Apart from poetry, Larkin tried his hand at writing fiction. His fiction received a mixed reception from critics and readers who felt that it was lacking in emotional depth.

Features

- Larkin's poetry focused on mundane, everyday aspects of life. He highlighted the commonplace and this helped people to relate to his work.
- He wrote in a simple and straightforward style and avoided obscurity and ornamentation.

- He was interested in the inevitability of death, ageing and the passage of time.
- His poetry reflects the changing landscape of England—physically, emotionally and spiritually.
- His poems are often wry, self-critical and understated.

Thom Gunn (1929–2004)

Poetry
Fighting Terms (1954)
The Sense of Movement (1959)
My Sad Captain (1961)
Moly (1971)
Jack Straw's Castle (1976)
Selected Poems 1950–1975 (1979)
The Passages of Joy (1982)
The Man with Night Sweats (1992)
Boss Cupid (2000)

Essay
The Occasions of Poetry (1992)
Shelf Life (1993)

Life

Thom Gun, the son of a journalist, was born in Gravesend. His parents divorced when he was ten and, later, when he was fifteen, his mother committed suicide. After his schooling, he studied at Trinity College, Cambridge, where he was a contemporary of Ted Hughes. Soon after he left Cambridge, Gunn moved to California to study poetry with Yvor Winters. He settled down permanently in San Francisco until his death.

Works

Thom Gunn's work was influenced by his exposure to both British and American culture. His poetry which celebrates men of action such as soldiers, bikers and rough boys and his fascination with violence could be attributed to his time in America. He was very interested in popular culture and was a great admirer of Elvis Presley and rock music. He owed his subdued and informal manner to his British roots and refused to abandon rhyme and metre.

In his first collection of poems *Fighting Terms,* Gunn uses the image of the soldier who is struggling to interpret his life. His second volume of poems *The Sense of Movement* continues his delineation of the existential hero who is striving to strike a balance between a life of action and one of contemplation. This book contains his famous poem 'On the Move' which describes the motorcyclists riding through different towns and villages. Gunn represents them as figures of existentialism who do not know where they are headed—'They strap in doubt...And almost hear a meaning in their noise.'

In his next book *My Sad Captain*, Gunn combined his earlier use of heroic couplets with free verse. The books that followed *My Sad Captain* reflect a fusion of modern and traditional style of writing poetry.

In the 1980s when AIDS was rampant, Gunn lost many friends to the disease. His sorrow found expression in the collection *The Man with the Night Sweats*. The loss of his friends taught him to cope with mortality.

Elizabeth Jennings (1926–2001)

Poems (1953)
A Way of Looking (1955)
A Sense of the World (1958)
Song for a Birth or a Death (1961)
The Mind has Mountains (1966)
Collected Poems (1967)
Lucidities (1970)
Growing-Points (1975)
Moments of Grace (1979)

Life

Elizabeth Jennings was born in Lincolnshire and belonged to a Roman Catholic family. Her family moved to Oxford when she was six, where she attended school and college. Later, she worked at a publishing house in London. She returned to Oxford once again and worked as a library assistant for eight years.

Throughout her life Jennings struggled with mental health issues like depression. She never married and led a lonely life. She lived in various rented houses and finally died in a care home in Brampton, Oxfordshire.

Works

Elizabeth Jennings holds a special place among the poets who belonged to the Movement for two major reasons: she was the only woman in the group and, secondly, she was the only devout

Catholic, unlike the others. Her poetry was highly personal and almost confessional in nature and quite different from that of the other Movement poets who wrote in a cynical and detached manner. She was contemplative and secluded and excelled in writing introspective and contemplative verse.

Her early poems were published in several journals like *The Spectator* and *Poetry Review* and came out as a collection, *Poems* a few years later. Her next collection *A Way of Looking* reveals her mastery as a lyric poet and her preference for traditional forms rather than experimental verse. There is a clear reflection of her Roman Catholic belief in her poems.

Jennings struggled with issues of mental health throughout her life. After experiencing a mental breakdown in 1962, she produced two more collections of poems *Recoveries* and *The Mind Has Mountains.* The poems in these collections are highly personal and confessional and describe her mental condition. Her poetic style underwent a change after her breakdown and became more experimental.

This was followed by three small collections of poems: *Collected Poems*, *Lucidities* and *Growing-Points.* In these books, she explores the themes of love and spirituality and delves into the complexities of human relationships. Some of the poems in *Lucidities* are melancholy and introspective in nature. 'In A Garden', 'A Chorus', 'Answers', 'Delay' and 'In Memory of Anyone Unknown to Me' are some of her best poems.

Features

- Jennings's poetry is personal and almost confessional in nature. She used her personal experiences and thoughts as themes for her poems.
- She was a devout Catholic and this aspect is amply reflected in her work.
- She chose the ordinary things of life to expound profound thoughts. For example, in the poem 'In Praise of Creation' she sees the presence of God in the rhythmic lives of birds, stars and tigers. The poem explores the concept that one should have faith in God although one cannot see Him.

- Her poems also dealt with the complexities of relationships and the inner self. 'Winter Love' is a poem about the vulnerability of a relationship in difficult times. 'Friendship' and 'The Anniversary' are also poems that deal with relationships.

C.S. Lewis (1898–1963)

Children's Fiction
The Chronicles of Narnia (1950–56, seven novels)

Science Fiction
The Space Trilogy
I *Out of the Silent Planet* (1938)
II *Perelandra* (1943)
III *That Hideous Strength* (1945)
The Four Loves (1960)

Non-Fiction
The Allegory of Love (1936)
English Literature in the Sixteenth Century (1954)
The Discarded Image: An Introduction to Medieval and Renaissance Literature (1964)
The Problem of Pain (1940)
The Screwtape Letters (1940)

Life

Clive Staples Lewis was born in Belfast, Ireland. After receiving his early education at home, he was sent to a boarding school. After that he studied classics at Oxford University. He became a fellow and tutor there and worked for about twenty-five years. For the next ten years, he was a professor of medieval and Renaissance English at Cambridge University.

Lewis had become an atheist in his twenties but later became religious under the influence of J.R.R. Tolkien. He got married quite late in life to an American woman who had been impacted by his books. She died of cancer just a few years after their wedding.

Three years later, Lewis fell ill with kidney failure and died at the age of sixty-five.

Works

Lewis wrote several books that included children's fiction, science fiction, literary criticism and theology. It was as a writer of children's fiction that Lewis became most famous. *The Chronicles of Narnia* is a series of seven books about four siblings belonging to the Pevensie family and their adventures in the fantasy world of Narnia. They meet talking animals and mythical creature there and get involved in battles between good and evil. The first book in the series *The Lion, the Witch and the Wardrobe* narrates the discovery of the wardrobe that leads to the magical world of Narnia. Throughout the series, Lewis explores the themes of morality, faith and the triumph of good over evil. These stories have been immensely popular with children and have been made into films and television series.

Lewis is noted for his science fiction as well. *Out of the Silent Planet, Perelandra* and *That Hideous Strength* form his famous *Space Trilogy* series in this genre. These books offer a unique blend of science fiction, philosophy and theology.

The Allegory of Love is an influential work about courtly love in medieval literature. In *The Discarded Image*, he upholds the medieval understanding of human nature and the environment and projects it as a valuable alternative to the contemporary scientific approach. In his next work *An Experiment in Criticism*, he points out the fact that the merit of a literary work lies not in its objective qualities but in the reader's response to it.

His contribution to the *Oxford History of English Literature* is an invaluable addition to human knowledge. In it, Lewis gives a survey of the history of English literature of the sixteenth century, excluding drama. His works on theology are equally significant for their strong moral base. These include *The Problem of Pain, The Screwtape Letters* and *The Four Loves*.

Features

- Lewis is best remembered for his vivid imagination and creativity. Through his books, he created an entire world of fantasy called Narnia which has appealed to readers of all ages.
- His strong academic background paved the way for his books on literary criticism. These works have been consulted by scholars of English literature down the decades. His assessment of Shakespeare, Milton and the Romantic poets needs special mention.

- He was a devout Christian and his works were influenced by his beliefs. He wrote extensively on the impact of Christianity on literature and culture. His essays like in '*The Problem of Pain*' have had a great influence on Christian thought and theology.

J.R.R. Tolkien (1892–1973)

Fiction
The Hobbit (1937)
The Lord of the Rings Series
I *The Fellowship of the Ring* (1954)
II *The Two Towers* (1954)
III *The Return of the King* (1955)
The Silmarillion (1977)
Unfinished Tales (1980)

Non-Fiction
Beowulf: A Translation and Commentary (2014)

Life

John Ronald Reuel Tolkien was born to British parents in South Africa. He was a professor of English language and literature at Oxford. He married his childhood sweetheart in 1916 and remained with her till her death in 1971. He served briefly during the First World War and was exempted from active service due to poor health.

On his return, he began teaching at the University of Leeds and worked on translations and co-authored an edition of *Sir Gawain and the Green Knights*. After retirement, he settled down in a seaside resort with his wife. He died less than two years after the demise of his wife.

Works

Tolkien was an influential writer who is well known as a writer of children's fiction. He loved to make up stories for his four children and is famous for his epic fantasy novels. His Hobbit books include *The Hobbit* and *The Lord of the Rings* trilogy. He created imaginary people called hobbits who had short and hairy feet. The hobbits are portrayed as being hard-working and good-natured people living in a world called Middle-earth. In *The Hobbit,* Bilbo Baggins, a hobbit, sets out on a mission with some dwarfs and a wizard to reclaim the dwarfs' home and treasure from the dragon. It is one of the most loved children's classics.

The Lord of the Rings is a trilogy which has a complex plot and narrates the tale of Frodo Baggins, who has the task of destroying the evil Ring of Power, in order to save Middle-earth from doom. Tolkien creates a vast fantasy world with minute details. The characters are portrayed in great detail and the books focus on the conflict between good and evil. Friendship and sacrifice, too, are highlighted in these works.

The Silmarillion is a prequal that Tolkien began but left incomplete. His son completed it and published it after his father died.

Features

- Tolkien's work is known for the richness of detail, both of characters and setting. He had a rich and vivid imagination which helped him create a fantasy world. His books have maps, genealogies and timelines to give an air of authenticity to his stories.
- He was a great scholar of mythology and language and was interested in Old English and other ancient languages. He had studied Norse and Celtic mythology and this knowledge influenced his writings.
- He had a great love for nature and we find descriptions of forests and mountains abounding in his works.
- Being a devout Catholic, he believed in the traditional values of honour, duty and sacrifice.
- His aversion towards industrialisation is evident in his works.

Enid Blyton (1897–1968)

Adventures of the Wishing-Chair (1937)
The Enchanted Wood (1939)
Noddy (1949–1963)
The Famous Five (1942–1962)
Secret Seven (1949–1963)
The Five Find-Outers (1943–1961)
Malory Towers (1946–1951)
St Clare's (1941–1945)
The Naughtiest Girl (1940s–1950s)
The Faraway Tree (1939–1951)

*This list is not exhaustive.

Life

Enid Blyton was born in London and spent most of her childhood in Kent. She gave up pursuing a career in music to attend a teacher-training course. After teaching in a boys' school for some time, she became a governess to four children in Surrey.

She married an editor of a publishing house and lived in London before moving to Beckenham. Her husband encouraged her writing. They had two daughters before they were divorced in 1942. Her second husband was a surgeon with whom she settled in Dorset. Her health began to fail in the 1950s and she died in 1968.

Works

Enid Blyton is one author who has charmed her way into the hearts of children across the globe. Children in the second-half of the twentieth century have all grown up reading her books. She was a prolific writer who wrote about seven hundred books for children. She is very well-known for her series of books such as *Malory Towers*, *St Clare's*, *The Famous Five* and *The Five Find-Outers*. Through her simple style and her great gift as a story teller, she succeeded in keeping her young readers glued to her books.

Her school series taught values even while the stories kept the readers captivated. Through her tales, she conveyed the message that honesty, goodness, kindness and hard work were to be adopted by one always.

Her mystery stories are fast-paced and have a lot of action and excitement. They show us clever children who are detectives in the making. These stories have inspired several children who fancied themselves to be detectives.

Through her adventure stories, Blyton transported her readers to far-away mountains, islands and seas. Her rich descriptions of these places helped to create a great love for nature in young minds.

Enid Blyton had a special place for animals and birds in her fiction. Timmy is a much-loved dog in *The Famous Five* series. Kiki, the parrot in the *Adventure* series, is absolutely enthralling.

Noddy, the wooden toy, has several animal friends such as Bumpy Dog and Tessie Bear. There are several talking animals in *The Enchanted Wood*, which is inhabited with talking trees, animals and fairies.

However, her work has come under a lot of criticism for being sexist, with a reinforcement of gender stereotypes. Her portrayal of characters from outside England has also come under fire. In her Noddy series, the character Gollywog has become a controversial figure as he is a black doll with exaggerated features such as thick lips and frizzy hair. This is seen by many as a reinforcement of negative, racial stereotypes.

Features

- Enid Blyton was a born storyteller. She could hold the attention of children through her engaging tales.
- Her stories contain strong moral values that helped mould the characters of her young readers.
- Her books reveal a concern for ecology. Many of her books featured descriptions of nature and she encouraged children to appreciate and explore the outdoors.
- Her books encouraged children to use their imagination and creativity.

Roald Dahl (1916–1990)

The Gremlins (1943)
James and the Giant Peach (1961)
Charlie and the Chocolate Factory (1964)
Fantastic Mr Fox (1970)
Matilda (1988)
Kiss Kiss (1960)
Tales of the Unexpected (1979)
Uncle Oswald (1979)
*This list is not exhaustive

Life

Roald Dahl was born in Cardiff, Wales. He married the actress Patricia Neal and had five children. Apart from books for children, Dahl also wrote short stories for adults. He died at the age of seventy-four.

Works

CHILDREN'S LITERATURE

The Gremlins, inspired by his experiences as a fighter pilot, is about mischievous creatures that were part of RAF folklore. His *Charlie and the Chocolate Factory* is considered one of the most popular books for children. Combining fantasy, humour and a moral, it narrates the adventures of Charlie Bucket and his quest for the Golden Ticket, with which he visits Willy Wonka's chocolate factory. *Matilda* is about a brilliant young girl who uses her intelligence and supernatural powers to bring justice and kindness to the world.

SHORT STORIES

Dahl wrote several short stories for adults. These stories are marked by dark humour, cruelty and unexpected twists. They chiefly deal with revenge, greed, deception, marital conflict and moral hypocrisy and the macabre side of human nature.

J.K. Rowling (1965–)

Harry Potter series (1997–2007)
The Tales of Beedle the Bard (2008)
The Casual Vacancy (2012)
The Cormoran Strike novels (2013–2025)
The Ickabog (2020)
The Christmas Pig (2021)

Life

Joanne Kathleen Rowling was born in Yate, Gloucestershire, and graduated from the University of Exter. Her early life was marked by personal difficulties and financial struggles. With the publication of her *Harry Potter* series, she became famous internationally and received several awards.

Works

Rowling is best known for her contribution to children's and young adult literature through the *Harry Potter* series. It consists of seven books that follow the life of Harry Potter from his eleventh birthday to young adulthood, in which she combines fantasy, adventure and mystery with traditional school fiction.

The narrative creates a world of magic, skilfully weaving humour with pathos and highlighting moral principles.

Rowling has produced a significant body of adult fiction that is known for its realism, psychological depth and social commentary. She wrote a series of crime and detective stories known as *The Cormoron Strike* series under the pen name Robert Galbraith where she combined the features of traditional detective fiction with remarkable psychological insight.

Multicultural British Writing

In the twentieth century, the phenomenon of writers belonging to diverse cultural backgrounds settling down in the United Kingdom and writing in English became an integral part of the history of English literature. These writers often explore issues related to identity, ethnicity, race and culture in their works. Their writings often present a new perspective to dominant narratives.

Some of the important writers belonging to this category are Doris Lessing, V.S. Naipaul, Kazuo Ishiguro, Hanif Kureishi, Salman Rushdie and Vikram Seth, to mention just a few.

Doris Lessing (1919–2013), a Nobel Prize winner, was born to British parents in Persia, now Iran. She was brought up in Rhodesia and moved to England when she was about thirty years old. Her contribution to British literature is significant for its intellectual complexity, psychological perception and social observation. Some of her works are *The Grass is Singing* (1950), *Children of Violence* (a series of five novels written between 1852 and 1969), *Landlocked* (1965) and *A Ripple from the Storm* (1958). Her best-known novel is *The Golden Notebook* (1962). This novel explores messages deploring wars, communism and the breakdown of society. It also examines sexual revolutions and women's liberation movements. Lessing is seen as a feminist writer and her *The Golden Notebook* is hailed as an important milestone in the feminist movement. It consists of four notebooks of a writer called Anna Wulf, who is trying to balance her domestic and political life. Each of the books reflects her different approaches to experience—fiction, parody, political documentation and realistic recording of daily life. This multi-thronged approach of the character reveals her sense of fragmentation.

Lessing has written several other books which reflect her concern with politics and her distrust for technical advancement. *Briefing for a Descent into Hell* and *Memoirs of a Survivor* are in the genre of science fiction. *Canopus in Argos* is a series of five books about a number of societies at different stages of development. This series of science fiction marks a complete break with traditional realism and describes a fictional universe.

V. S. Naipaul (1932–2018) was of Indian origin, born in Trinidad and educated in Spain and England after which he settled down in England. His first three books *The Mystic Masseur* (1957) *The Suffrage of Elvira* (1958) and *Miguel Street* (1959) are all comedies of manners and are set in Trinidad. *A House for Mr Biswas* (1961), also set in Trinidad, is about a hero who bears a resemblance to the author's father. The novel traces the life of the protagonist from birth to death. His only novel set in London is *Mr Stone and the Knight's Companion* (1963). *The Mimic Men* is a story narrated by a failed politician and is set in a fictitious Caribbean Island. *In a Free State* (1971) won Naipaul the Booker Prize. It explores issues of nationality and identity through three interlinked narratives about displaced characters. Another novel set in the Caribbean Island, *Guerrillas* (1975), describes the political and sexual violence in the place. *A Bend in the River* (1979), portrays a horrifying picture of Africa.

Naipaul wrote a number of travel books and works on politics, besides fiction. All his works have the common thread of political violence, innate homelessness of the diaspora and alienation.

Kazuo Ishiguro (1954–) is a British writer of Japanese origin who won the Nobel Prize for Literature. His first novel *A Pale View of Hills* (1982), is the story of a Japanese woman dealing with the suicide of her daughter. In *An Artist of the Floating World* (1986), the protagonist is an elderly man who was an artist in imperial Japan and explores his memories. He won the Booker Prize for *The Remains of the Day* (1989). It is a first-person narrative of an elderly English butler who reviews his life. *The Unconsoled* (1995) marks a radical departure from his earlier style of writing that could be called conventional. Ishiguro attempted science fiction in his next novel *When We Were Orphans* (2000). Set against the backdrop of the Sino-Japanese War, it recounts the story of a British man in search of his parents who had disappeared in his childhood. Ishiguro strikes a warning note against the practices of genetic engineering in the novel *Never Let Me Go* (2005). *The Buried Giant* (2015) is set in an imaginary post-Arthurian England. The story is about an elderly couple living in a place where no one is able to retain long-term memories. *Klara and the Sun* (2021) is another dystopian science fiction novel. Set in an unspecified future in the US, the story is told from the point of view of a solar-powered artificial friend of a sickly child. Ishiguro's writings are marked by their subtlety, depth and emotional tone. His characters often have to grapple with a sense of personal or historical loss or regret.

Hanif Kureishi (1954–) is a British writer born to a Pakistani father and an English mother. He is famous as a screenplay writer, essayist, dramatist and novelist. His novels include *The Buddha of Suburbia* (1990), *The Black Album* (1995), *Intimacy* (1998), *Something to Tell You* (2008) and *The Last Word* (2014). *The Buddha of Suburbia* focuses on class, culture, sexuality and ethnicity from the point of view of the protagonist Karim Amir. Kureishi drew upon his own experiences to depict the London of the late-twentieth century. In *The Black Album,* he focuses on Islamic fundamentalism and freedom of speech.

His work is marked for its frankness of approach, humour and his deep understanding of the complexities of identity and culture in modern Britain. His main themes were multiculturalism, identity and immigrant experiences.

Salman Rushdie (1947–) was born in Bombay and raised in Pakistan after the Partition of India. He moved to England for his higher studies and settled there. He also became a citizen of the United States in 2016. He shot up to fame with the publication of his novel, *Midnight's Children* in 1981. The book was awarded the Booker Prize in 1981and the Best of Bookers in 2008 for being the best novel in the first twenty-five years of the prize's history. *Midnight's Children* is a story that combines history, fantasy, fable and magic realism. His next novel *Shame* (1983) is about the political turmoil in Pakistan and features characters modelled after Zulfikar Ali Bhutto and Muhammad Zia-ul-Haq. This book, too, weaves magic realism into its narrative, artistically combining the realistic with the unexpected and the incredible. The elements of dream and myth combine with the everyday to create kaleidoscopic patterns.

The Satanic Verses (1988) is his most controversial work. The novel was judged to be an affront to Islam and the late Iranian leader Ayatollah Khomeini issued a fatwa (a death sentence) and a reward for carrying it out. This novel is an amalgam of philosophy and an Arabian Nights-like entertainment. *Haroun and the Sea of Stories* (1990), often mistakenly seen as juvenile fiction, is in fact an allegory of the power of language. Rushdie did begin the story to entertain his son, but the furore over *The Satanic Verses* turned it into a parable demonstrating the responsibility of the artist to speak from his heart without being reined in by political consequences.

The Moor's Last Sigh (1995) is a family epic spanning over a hundred years. His other works include *The Ground Beneath Her Feet* (1999), *Fury* (2001), *Shalimar the Clown* (2005) and some collections of short stories and non-fiction works. His most recent novels are *Two Years Eight Months and Twenty-Eight Nights* (2015), *The Golden House* (2017) and *Victory City* (2023).

Kamala Markandaya (1924–2004) was born in Mysore, India, and graduated from the University of Madras. She began her literary career by publishing short stories in magazines and newspapers. She moved to England after India got her independence and is considered to be the first woman novelist from the Indian subcontinent.

She was keenly interested in the sharp divide between the urban and rural societies of India. Her first novel *Nectar in the Sieve* (1954) established her as a recognised novelist in England. This was followed by a series of novels like *Some Inner Fury* (1955), *A Silence of Desire* (1960), *Possession* (1963), *A Handful of Rice* (1966), *The Coffer Dams* (1969), *The Nowhere Man* (1972), *Two Virgins* (1973), *The Golden Honeycomb* (1977) and *Pleasure City* (1982).

Nectar in the Sieve is a powerful novel that describes the struggles of a small family living in a rural area. Apart from struggling with natural calamities like famine and failed crops, they have to deal with the establishment of a tannery which totally disrupts their village. The central theme of the novel is the clash between traditional agrarian life and the modern industrial world. *Possession* is the story of an English woman who takes a shepherd boy, who is an artist, with her to England. The novel explores the complex relationship between the East and the West. Markandaya highlights the tendency of the West to exploit the East, both physically and psychologically.

Her most ambitious novel is *The Golden Honeycomb,* which is a historical novel set around the time of India's independence.

In most of her novels, she focuses on the plight of the marginalised people and the complexities of Indian society. She is a gifted storyteller who features strong female protagonists. Her contribution to English literature is significant in that her work gives expression to the voices of the other.

Nirad C. Chaudhuri (1897–1999) was a Bengali writer who chose to live in England. He was a great admirer of western culture and strongly opposed the ending of colonial rule in India. He believed that the British rule was very good for the subcontinent, a sentiment that was totally against the popular feeling of independent India. As a result, he was ostracised by the Indian intellectuals.

His *Autobiography of an Unknown Indian* (1951) established him as a writer of repute. In it, Chaudhuri looks back on his life and experiences while India was still under British rule. The book was criticised for the author's critique of Indian society as it was seen as an attack on the moral hypocrisy of the Bengali middle class. Further, his dedication of the book to 'the memory of the British Empire in India…' did not go down well with Indians. Chaudhuri decided to relocate to England in the 1970s, but discovered that he was an outsider there too. His disillusionment found expression in the final volume of his autobiography *Thy Hand, Great Anarch* (1987). His last work was a book of essays called *Three Horsemen of the New Apocalypse* (1997) that was published just before his hundredth birthday. In it, he wrote about the decline of the western civilisation. It was only in the last few years of his life that he was accepted in India.

British Poets Laureate and Nobel Laureates

British Poets Laureate

1668–89 John Dryden
1689–92 Thomas Shadwell
1692–1715 Nahum Tate
1715–18 Nicholas Rowe
1718–30 Laurence Eusden
1730–57 Colley Cibber
1757–85 William Whitehead
1785–90 Thomas Warton
1790–1813 Henry James Pye
1813–43 Robert Southey
1843–50 William Wordsworth
1850–92 Alfred Tennyson
1892–1913 Alfred Austin
1913–30 Robert Bridges
1930–67 John Masefield
1968–72 Cecil Day-Lewis
1972–84 Sir John Betjeman
1984–98 Ted Hughes
1999–2009 Andrew Motion
2009–19 Carol Ann Duffy
2019– Simon Armitage

British Nobel Laureates

1907 Rudyard Kipling
1925 G.B. Shaw
1932 John Galsworthy
1948 T.S. Eliot
1950 Bertrand Russell
1953 Winston Churchill
1969 Samuel Beckett
1983 William Golding
2001 V.S. Naipaul
2005 Harold Pinter
2007 Doris Lessing
2017 Kazuo Ishiguro
2021 Abdulrazak Gurnah

Glossary

alliteration	repetition of initial consonant and vowel sounds
allegory	narrative form in which characters and events symbolise an underlying meaning
antithesis	opposing or contrasting idea emphasised by a parallel in grammatical structure
aphorism	generally accepted principal or truth expressed in a short, pithy manner
blank verse	unrhymed iambic pentameter lines
closet drama	play intended to be read, not staged
dactyl	one long syllable followed by two short syllables
decasyllabic	line containing ten syllables
epic	long narrative poem in elevated style, that describes the exploits of superhuman heroes
heroic couplet	rhyming pairs of iambic pentameter lines
heroic hexameter	six dactylic feet
iamb	metrical foot with one unstressed syllable followed by one stressed syllable
iambic heptameter	line consisting of fourteen iambic syllables
lyric	short, tightly structured poems in which the speaker conveys his or her personal feelings, discussing subjects like nature and love

masque	extravagant dramatic entertainment popular in Europe during the late-sixteenth and early-seventeenth century and chiefly performed in the court or in the houses of rich aristocrats; the characters wore masks and were usually played by the lords and ladies themselves with elaborate costumes and sets. It combined poetic drama, music, song, and dance with a slight plot usually taken from mythology.
ottava rima	eight lines with the rhyme scheme *abababcc*
Pindaric ode	poem written to commemorate the winners of the Olympics and other game and meant to be performed by a chorus, and using its threefold structure—strophe, antistrophe and epode
poulter's measure	iambic couplet of alternating twelve and fourteen syllables, popular in Elizabethan Age
rhyme royal	seven iambic pentameter lines as *ababbcc*
terza rima	tercets with interlinking rhyme as *aba bcb cdc* …

Timeline

The timeline maps historical events alongside literary works produced at the same time period in England, India and across the world.

Prehistoric Age

5000 BCE
Egyptian Civilisation begins.

3400 BCE
Mesopotamian Civilisation begins.

2600 BCE
Great Pyramid of Giza built.

2500 BCE
Indus Valley Civilisation begins.

1894 BCE
Babylonian Civilisation begins.

1500 BCE–1200 BCE
Vedas are composed.

1250 BCE
Hebrew exodus from Egypt.

961 BCE
King Solomon's reign begins.

800 BCE–500 BCE
Upanishads are composed.

700 BCE
Homer composes *Iliad*.

458 BCE
Orestia, Aeschylus.

431 BCE
Medea, Euripides.

429 BCE
Oedipus Rex, Sophocles.

423 BCE
The Clouds, Aristophanes.

399 BCE
Socrates is executed.

375 BCE
The Republic, Plato.

335 BCE
Poetics, Aristotle.

316 BCE
The Dyskolos, Menander.

300 BCE–300 CE
Ramayana and *Mahabharata* composed.

200 BCE
Panchatantra composed. Attributed to Vishnu Sharma.

55 BCE
Julius Caesar's first invasion of Britain.

29 CE
Crucifixion of Jesus.

47–50 CE
Romans settle in London and call it Londinium.

122
Hadrian's Wall built on Scottish border.

400–500
Abhijananasakuntalam, *Meghduta*, Kalidasa.

427
Nalanda University founded by Kumaragupta in Bihar.

449
Anglo-Saxon invasion of Britain.

Anglo-Saxon Age

597
St Augustine arrives in Kent. Converts Anglo-Saxons to Christianity.

658–80
Caedmon composes 'Hymn' in Old English.

731
Bede writes account of Anglo-Saxon invasion.

750
Beowulf composed.

793
Viking invasion of Britain.

871
Alfred the Great becomes king of Wessex; responsible for the translation of several Latin works into English.

886
Establishment of Danelaw by Vikings.

892
Anglo-Saxon Chronicles commissioned.

Middle Ages

1066
Norman Conquest.

1095–1291
Holy Crusades.

1321
Divine Comedy, Dante.

1327–1368
Il Canzoniere, Petrach.

1334–84
Wycliffe translates the Bible.

1337
Beginning of Hundred Years' War.

1362
English replaced French in the Parliament.

1381
Peasants' Revolt.

1362–1400
Piers the Plowman, Langland.

1386–90
Confessio Amantis, Gower.

1387–1400
The Canterbury Tales, Chaucer.

1445
Invention of movable metal type by Johann Gutenberg.

1453
End of Hundred Years' War. Fall of Constantinople, ending the Byzantine Empire.

1455
Wars of the Roses begins between houses of York and Lancaster.

1476
William Caxton creates the printing press.

1485
End of the Wars of the Roses. Tudors come to power.

Tudor Age

EARLY TUDOR PERIOD

1492
Christopher Columbus lands in America.

1499
Michelangelo completes *Pieta*, epitomising the Renaissance.

1503–1517
Leonardo da Vinci paints the *Mona Lisa*.

1513
The Prince, Machiavelli.

1516
Utopia, More.

1517
Ninety-Five Theses, Martin Luther ushering in the Reformation.

1517–47
Henry Howard, Earl of Surrey, introduces the sonnet to England with Thomas Wyatt.

1525
Tyndale translates the Bible into English.

1529–36
English Parliament reduces authority of the Pope in England.

1537
The Court of Venus, Wyatt.

1544
The Four P's, Heywood.

1552
Ralph Roister Doister, first English comedy, Udall.

1557
Tottel's Miscellany, first printed anthology of English poems.

1561
Gorboduc, first English tragedy, Sackville and Norton.

1575
Gammer Gurton's Needle, Stevenson.

ELIZABETHAN AGE

1559
Queen Elizabeth's Anglican Settlement.

1577–1580
Sir Francis Drake circumnavigates the world.

1578
Euphues: The Anatomy of Wit, Lyly.

1579
The Shepheardes Calender, Spenser.

1580
North translates Plutarch's *Lives*.

1581–83
Astrophel and Stella, Sidney.
An Apology for Poetry, Sidney.

1587
Mary, Queen of Scots executed.

1587
The Spanish Tragedy, Kyd.
Tamburlaine the Great, Marlowe.

1588
England defeats the Spanish Armada.

1588–92
Shakespeare writes his early comedies and histories.

1590–96
Faerie Queen, Spenser.

1590s
Satires and *Elegies*, Donne.

1594
Lord Chamberlain's Men established, later known as the King's Men.

1594–1600
Shakespeare writes his mature comedies and early tragedies.

1597
Essays, Bacon.

1598
Every Man in his Humour, Jonson.

1599
Opening of Globe Theatre.

1600
Establishment of East India Company.

1601–09
Shakespeare writes his great tragedies.

Seventeenth Century

EARLY STUARTS, THE COMMONWEALTH AND PROTECTORATE

1603
James VI of Scotland becomes James I of England, uniting Scotland and England.

1605
Failure of the Gunpowder Plot.

1611
King James's *Bible* published.

1616
Chapman translates Homer.
Death of Shakespeare.

1620
Pilgrims land in America aboard the Mayflower.

1623
The Duchess of Malfi, Webster.

1627
New Atlantis, Bacon.

1632–1653
Taj Mahal built in Agra.

1636
Harvard University founded in Massachusetts.

1637
'Lycidas', Milton.

1642–51
Civil War in England.

1649
Execution of Charles I.
Beginning of Cromwell's Protectorate

RESTORATION

1660
Monarchy restored with arrival of Charles II.
Royal Society of London founded.

1665
Great Plague of London.

1666
Great Fire of London.

1667
Paradise Lost, Milton.

1668
An Essay of Dramatic Poesie, Dryden.

1674
Maratha Empire founded by Chhatrapati Shivaji.

1678
All for Love, Dryden.

1684
The Pilgrim's Progress, Volume Two, Bunyan.

1685
Death of Charles II.
Succession of James II.

1687
Newton publishes laws of motion.

1688–89
Glorious Revolution.
William III and Mary II succeed to the throne.

1689
Bill of Rights passed, limits royal power and establishes parliamentary rights.

1692
Salem witch trials in Massachusetts.

1694
Bank of England established.

1700
The Way of the World, Congreve.

Eighteenth Century

AGE OF SWIFT AND POPE

1701
War of Spanish Succession begins.

1702
Queen Anne succeeds to the throne of England.

1703
St Petersburg founded by Peter the Great.

1704
Death of Queen Anne.
Succession of George I.

1707
Union of England and Scotland by the Acts of Union.
Death of Aurangzeb.

1712
The Rape of the Lock, Pope.

1719
Robinson Crusoe, Defoe.

1721
Robert Walpole becomes first prime minister of England.

1726
Gulliver's Travels, Swift.

1727
Death of George I.
Succession of George II.

1728–42
The Dunciad, Pope.

AGE OF JOHNSON

1740
Pamela, or Virtue Rewarded, Richardson.

1749
Tom Jones, Fielding.

1751
'Elegy Written in a Country Churchyard', Gray.

1752
British Empire adopts the Gregorian calendar.

1755
A Dictionary of the English Language, Johnson.

1756–63
Seven Years' War between England and France.

1757
British conquest of Bengal.

1759–67
Tristram Shandy, Sterne.

1760
Death of George II.
Succession of George III.

1761
British defeat the Marathas at the Battle of Buxar.

1762–1796
Catherine the Great reigns in Russia.

1766
The Vicar of Wakefield, Goldsmith.

1775–83
American War of Independence.

PRE-ROMANTICS AND THE ROMANTIC REVIVAL

1779–81
Lives of the Most Eminent English Poets, Johnson.

1784
James Watt improves the steam engine, essential to the Industrial Revolution.

1785
Invention of the power loom by Cartwright.

1789–99
French Revolution.

1789
George Washington elected the first president USA.
Songs of Innocence, Blake.

1791
The Life of Samuel Johnson, Boswell.
Rights of Man, Paine.

1792
A Vindication of the Rights of Woman, Wollstonecraft.

1794
Songs of Experience, Blake.

1798
Lyrical Ballads, Wordsworth and Coleridge.

1804
Napoleon Bonaparte becomes emperor of France.

1805
Battle of Trafalgar.

1808
John Dalton formulates atomic theory.

1812
Childe Harold's Pilgrimage, Byron.

1813
Pride and Prejudice, Austen.

1814
Waverley, Scott.

1815
Battle of Waterloo.

1817
Biographia Literaria, Coleridge.

1819
Keats writes his famous odes.
Don Juan, Byron.

1820
Death of George III and succession of George IV.
Ivanhoe, Scott.
'Ode to the West Wind', *Prometheus Unbound*, Shelley.

1821
Death of Napoleon Bonaparte.

1823
Essays of Elia, Lamb.

1830
Death of George IV and succession of William IV.

1831
Michael Faraday discovers electromagnetic principle, leading to creation of electric generator and electric motor.

1832
First Reform Bill expands suffrage.

1833
'Ulysses', Tennyson.

Victorian Age

1837
The Pickwick Papers, Dickens.
Death of William IV.
Succession of Victoria.

1839
First Opium War.
On Heroes and Hero Worship, Carlyle.

1842
End of First Opium War.
The British defeat the Chinese.
Dramatic Lyrics, Browning.

1846
Corn Laws repealed.

1846–47
Famine in Ireland.

1847
Jane Eyre, Charlotte Brontë.
Wuthering Heights, Emily Brontë.
Agnes Grey, Anne Brontë.

1848
Vanity Fair, Thackeray.

1850
David Copperfield, Dickens.

1857
First War of Independence, or Sepoy Mutiny, in India.

1858
East India Company transfers India's administration to the British Crown.
Death of Lakshmibai, Rani of Jhansi.

1859
The Origin of Species, Darwin.
'On Liberty', Mill.
Adam Bede, Eliot.

1861
American Civil War begins.
Great Expectations, Dickens.
Louis Pasteur develops germ theory, precursor to vaccines.

1863
Birth of Swami Vivekananda.

1865
Essays in Criticism, Arnold.
Alice in Wonderland, Carroll.
American Civil War ends.

1869
Opening of the Suez Canal.
Birth of Mahatma Gandhi.

1871
Unification of Italy.
Unification of Germany.

1877
Queen Victoria declared Empress of India.

1881
The Portrait of a Lady, James.
Tsar Alexander II assassinated.

1884
The Third Reform Bill grants suffrage to English men who hold property.

1887
Heinrich Hertz discovers electromagnetic waves, leading to the invention of radio, television and radar.

1889
Birth of Jawaharlal Nehru.

1890
The Picture of Dorian Gray, Wilde.
William James coins the term 'stream of consciousness' in *The Principles of Psychology*.

1891
Tess of the d'Urbervilles, Hardy.

1892
Lady Windermere's Fan, Wilde.

1895
The Time Machine, Wells.
The Importance of Being Earnest, Wilde.
Wilhelm Conrad Röntgen discovers the x-ray.

1899
Beginning of the Boer War.
Heart of Darkness, Conrad.

1900
Sister Carrie, Dreiser.

Twentieth Century

1901
Death of Queen Victoria.
Accession of Edward VII.

1902
End of Boer War. Britain defeats the Afrikaners.

1903
Man and Superman, Shaw.

1904
Riders to the Sea, Synge.

1905
Albert Einstein formulates 'theory of relativity'.

1907
The Playboy of the Western World, Synge.

1909
Strife, Galsworthy.

1910
Death of Edward VII.
Accession of George V.
Howards End, Forster.
Gitanjali, Tagore.

1912
Titanic sinks, killing 1503 people.

1913
Sons and Lovers, Lawrence.

1914
First World War begins.

1915
Of Human Bondage, Maugham.

1916
Easter Rising in Ireland.
A Portrait of the Artist as a Young Man, Joyce.

1917
October revolution in Russia.
Tsarist regime overthrown.
Bolsheviks, led by Lenin, seize power.

1918
End of First World War.
Assassination of Tsar Nicholas II and his family.
Poems, Hopkins.

1920
The Emperor Jones, O'Neill.

1921
Republic of Ireland granted independence.

1922
Stalin becomes general secretary of the Communist Party.
The Waste Land, Eliot.
Ulysses, Joyce.
The Hairy Ape, O'Neill.

1924
Death of Lenin.
A Passage to India, Forster.
USSR established.

1925
The Great Gatsby, Fitzgerald.
Mrs Dalloway, Woolf.

1927
To the Lighthouse, Woolf.

1928
Women above 21 years given voting rights in England.
Lady Chatterley's Lover, Lawrence.
Alexander Fleming discovers penicillin.
West-Running Brook, Frost.

1929
The Sound and the Fury, Faulkner.

1930
As I Lay Dying, Faulkner.

1934
Murder on the Orient Express, Christie.

1935
Untouchable, Anand.
Swami and Friends, Narayan.
Murder in the Cathedral, Eliot.

1936
Death of George V.
Succession of Edward VIII.
Abdication of Edward VIII.
Succession of his brother George VI.

1938
Kanthapura, Rao.
Coolie, Anand.

1939
Second World War begins.

1939
The Grapes of Wrath, Steinbeck.

1939
Gone with the Wind, Mitchell.

1940
For Whom the Bells Tolls, Hemingway.

1942
Quit India Movement.

1943
Malgudi Days, Narayan.

1944
The Glass Menagerie, Williams.

1945
Animal Farm, Orwell.
United Nations established.
USA drops atomic bombs on Hiroshima and Nagasaki.
End of Second World War.

1947
Beginning of Cold War.
India's Independence and Partition.
A Streetcar Named Desire, Williams.

1948
The Heart of the Matter, Greene.
Mahatma Gandhi assassinated.

1949
1984, Orwell.

1951
The Old Man and the Sea, Hemingway.

1952
Death of George VI.
Succession of Elizabeth II.

1953
Death of Stalin.
Waiting for Godot, Beckett.

1954
Lord of the Flies, Golding.

1956
Look Back in Anger, Osborne.

1957
Sputnik launched, beginning the space race.

1958
The Bell, Murdoch.
The Birthday Party, Pinter.

1960
To Kill a Mockingbird, Lee.
The Serpent and the Rope, Rao.

1961
Berlin Wall built.
A House for Mr Biswas, Naipaul.

1962
The Golden Notebook, Lessing.

1964
Death of Jawaharlal Nehru.
Krushchev ousted; Brezhnev and Kosygin installed as leaders of USSR.

1966
Rosencrantz and Guildenstern Are Dead, Stoppard.

1969
The French Lieutenant's Woman, Fowles.

1970
The Bluest Eye, Morrison.

1971
Decimalised currency replaces pounds, shillings and pence.

1973
Britain joins European Economic Community, now known as European Union.

1975
Wife, Mukherjee.

1976
Roots, Haley.
The Color Purple, Walker.

1978
And Still I Rise, Angelou.
World's first test-tube baby born in Oldham, England.

1979
Margaret Thatcher becomes Britain's first woman prime minister.
USSR invades Afghanistan.

1981
Midnight's Children, Rushdie.

1982
Death of Brezhnev.
Falklands War.

1984
Assassination of Indira Gandhi.

1985
Gorbachev becomes leader of USSR.

1986
The Golden Gate, Seth.

1988
The Satanic Verses, Rushdie.
USSR withdraws from Afghanistan.

1989
The Joy Luck Club, Tan.
The Great Indian Novel, Tharoor.

1990
The Buddha of Suburbia, Kureishi.

1991
USSR dissolved.
Assassination of Rajiv Gandhi.

1992
Our Trees Still Grow in Dehra, Bond.

1993
A Suitable Boy, Seth.

1994
Britain returns Hong Kong to China.

1995
Arranged Marriage: Stories, Divakaruni.
The Unconsoled, Ishiguro.

1997
The God of Small Things, Roy.
The Mistress of Spices, Divakaruni.
Princess Diana dies in a car crash in Paris.

1999
Interpreter of Maladies, Lahiri.

2001
Ladies Coupe, Nair.
9/11 terror attack on USA.

2003
Second Gulf War.

2006
The Inheritance of Loss, Desai.

2008
The White Tiger, Adiga.
The Palace of Illusions, Divakaruni

2022
Death of Elizabeth II.
Succession of Charles II.

Index of Authors

Also by Padmaja Ashok